ROUTLEDGE LIBRARY EDITIONS: LIBRARY AND INFORMATION SCIENCE

Volume 91

SERIALS LIBRARIANSHIP IN TRANSITION

SERIALS LIBRARIANSHIP IN TRANSITION
Issues and Developments

Edited by
PETER GELLATLY

LONDON AND NEW YORK

First published in 1986 by The Haworth Press, Inc.

This edition first published in 2020
by Routledge
2 Park Square, Milton Park, Abingdon, Oxon OX14 4RN

and by Routledge
52 Vanderbilt Avenue, New York, NY 10017

Routledge is an imprint of the Taylor & Francis Group, an informa business

© 1986 The Haworth Press, Inc.

All rights reserved. No part of this book may be reprinted or reproduced or utilised in any form or by any electronic, mechanical, or other means, now known or hereafter invented, including photocopying and recording, or in any information storage or retrieval system, without permission in writing from the publishers.

Trademark notice: Product or corporate names may be trademarks or registered trademarks, and are used only for identification and explanation without intent to infringe.

British Library Cataloguing in Publication Data
A catalogue record for this book is available from the British Library

ISBN: 978-0-367-34616-4 (Set)
ISBN: 978-0-429-34352-0 (Set) (ebk)
ISBN: 978-0-367-41865-6 (Volume 91) (hbk)
ISBN: 978-0-367-41871-7 (Volume 91) (pbk)
ISBN: 978-0-367-81667-4 (Volume 91) (ebk)

Publisher's Note
The publisher has gone to great lengths to ensure the quality of this reprint but points out that some imperfections in the original copies may be apparent.

Disclaimer
The publisher has made every effort to trace copyright holders and would welcome correspondence from those they have been unable to trace.

Serials Librarianship in Transition: Issues and Developments

Peter Gellatly
Editor

The Haworth Press
New York • London

Serials Librarianship in Transition: Issues and Developments has also been published as *The Serials Librarian*, Volume 10, Numbers 1/2, Fall 1985/Winter 1985-86.

© 1986 by The Haworth Press, Inc. All rights reserved. No part of this book may be reproduced or utilized in any form or by any means, electronic or mechanical, including photocopying, microfilm and recording, or by any information storage and retrieval system, without permission in writing from the publisher. Printed in the United States of America.

The Haworth Press, Inc., 28 East 22 Street, New York, NY 10010-6194
EUROSPAN/Haworth, 3 Henrietta Street, London WC2E 8LU England

Library of Congress Cataloging in Publication Data
Main entry under title:

Serials librarianship in transition.

"Has also been published as the Serials librarian, volume 10, numbers 1/2, fall 1985/winter 1985/1986"—T.p. verso.
   Includes bibliographies and index.
   1. Serials control systems—Addresses, essays, lectures. 2. Serial publications—Addresses, essays, lectures. 3. Libraries—Special collections—Periodicals—Addresses, essays, lectures. 4. Newspaper and periodical libraries—Addresses, essays, lectures. 5. Library science—Technological innovations—Addresses, essays, lectures.
Z692.S5S46   1986   025.3'432   85-16439
ISBN 0-86656-497-7

Dedication

Sandy A. O. Gellatly
1925-1985

Serials Librarianship in Transition: Issues and Developments

The Serials Librarian
Volume 10, Numbers 1/2

CONTENTS

EDITORIAL: A Decennary Message	1

The Serials Department, 1975-1985
    Don Lanier
    Norman Vogt
	5

Dealing With Serials: A Sketch of Contextual/Organizational Response *Michael Gorman*	13
Serials Organization: A Time for Reappraisal *Sue Anne Harrington*	19

Serials Automation: An Annotated Bibliography and Review 1976-1984
    Janis D. Fleischmann, MLS
    Jean Houghton, MLS, MA
	29

What Has Technology Done for Us Lately? *Lenore S. Maruyama, MALS*	65
Serials and Automation: Yesterday, Today and Tomorrow *Huibert Paul*	91
Networking and Serials Control, 1975-1985 *Gloria A. Kelley, MLS*	97

A Decade of Serials Cataloging
    Jim E. Cole, MA
    Olivia M. A. Madison, MA
	103

The AACRs and Serials Cataloging *Carole R. McIver, MSLS*	117

Serials Cataloging in Transition *Lynn Mealer Cummins, BA, MSLS*	129
Serials Cataloging Developments, 1975-1985: A Personal View of Some Highlights *Frank E. Sadowski, Jr.*	133
And in Hindsight . . . The Past Ten Years of Union Listing *Marjorie E. Bloss*	141
Accessibility of Serials *Ruth B. McBride*	149
Out of the Shoebox and Into the Computer: Serials Indexing 1975-1985 *Martha Cornog*	161
Article Access—Too Easy? *Martin Gordon, MLS*	169
Budgeting and Planning: A Tandem Approach *Bertha R. Almagro*	173
A Lesson Learned the Hard Way, or, the Cost of Relinquishing Acquisitions Control *Donna M. Goehner, PhD*	181
Serials Claiming *Mary J. Bostic, BA, MLS, MS, CAS*	185
The Use of Microforms in Libraries: Concerns of the Last Ten Years *Jean Walter Farrington*	195
Store It, But Don't Ignore It *Valerie Jackson Feinman*	201
Introducing Serials Education *Thomas W. Leonhardt*	211
Access to U.S. Government Periodicals in Health Sciences Libraries: An Overview *Valerie Florance*	215

1975-1985: Formulative Years for the Subscription Agency
    Rebecca T. Lenzini
    Judith Horn
	225

Serials at the British Library Lending Division
    Stella Pilling
    David Wood
	239

A Decade of Serials Librarianship in Australia: An Overview *Jean A. Conochie*	253

Serials Librarianship in India
    K. C. Garg, BSc, MA, Associateship in Information Science
    S. P. Gupta, BSc, MA, MLib, ISc
	263

Serials Librarianship in Nigeria, 1975-1985 *Briggs C. Nzotta, PhD*	269
Ten Years of Living With Magazines *W. A. Katz, PhD*	281

The Journal, Scholarly Communication, and the Future
    Kathy G. Tomajko
    Miriam A. Drake
	289

Index	299

EDITORIAL

A Decennary Message

The Serials Librarian begins its tenth year, and this is enough to make us want to look back to see what the past ten years have held for serials people and the craft they practice. There may not have been any moon shots—the closest to one was the instituting in some lucky places of online check in and claiming—but it is nevertheless clear that serials librarianship has been changed in ways not foreseen at the start of the decade. Serials librarianship, if not transmuted, will not be the same again.

It is equally clear that during the past ten years serials librarianship has been challenged, defended, belittled, praised, disassembled, reassembled and examined endlessly by friendly and not-so-friendly eyes. As a man who suffered reverses in 1984 said of that year—"Thank goodness it is over"—so serials librarians might heave a sigh of relief to have emerged from the past decade reasonably whole. They unquestionably feel battered, but are busily, and it is to be hoped with grace, organizing their gains and preparing for whatever lies ahead.

Nothing is more certain than that we are now living in a computerized, mathematicized society. Twenty or more years ago, Rod Serling, in a segment of *The Twilight Zone,* spoke of a self-operating typewriter; and while such a machine might have appeared unusual then, it seems lumpish and ordinary now. It may not be true, as Wozniak says, that operating a computer is as easy as putting on one's coat, but it is certainly expected that everybody in this day and age, even children in elementary school, know something about the computer. If Serling's machine no longer merits a second glance, others are coming along that are bound to make heads turn and eyebrows rise. Kurzweil has invented a computer that takes dictation and can actually read from a page out loud (presumably in tones more pleasing than those of the voice that instructs one to close the car door and buckle up). At the same time, Toshiba has perfected a machine that translates Japanese into English, and does it one-third more quickly than a human translator can. The self-operating typewriter is nothing really. Not long ago a Warner Communications' computer wrote a novel all by itself. As the title of this work was *The Policeman's Beard is Half-Constructed,* the suspicion is that the computer's facility with the English language is still not what it ought to be, but no doubt this will change. It is not certain, incidentally, that a novel written in thirty hours on a minicomputer by a Texan living in Toronto is more meritorious than this other.

According to Berry, librarianship is undergoing massive change and at a rate much faster than normal. He says also that librarians are readier to accept change now than at any time in the past. Change is of course the element in which we live. If librarians were ever in fact of the conservative bent that Berry postulates, that condition, as he makes clear, is itself of the past. No librarian nowadays, for instance, would think of trying to run a library without some acquaintance with statistical theory and more than a dollop of computer know-how. A distinguished professor of English literature, small in physical size but with a fine fierceness of eye and bearing, on entering the lecture hall on the first day of classes one year long ago, declared that there would be silence when he entered the hall. And he would have it, he promised, even if this meant that he had to throw the talkers out bodily. "I'm little," he said, looking meaningfully at a six-foot-ten football type, "But I have science." Librarians have never wanted for science; and it is no surprise that they should have brought their inventiveness to bear with vigor and sometimes brilliance in dealing with obstreperous problems. We are convinced that some of the changes that have appeared in libraries over the past ten years' time will be accounted among the great achievements of library history. If twenty or thirty years ago catalog revision were being contemplated uneasily, who would have thought then that the three-by-five card catalog would itself be replaced before long? The rules obviously needed changing, but the catalog was immutable, fixed forever in its card format. Over the past few years, however, not only have the rules been drastically revised—if not to the point at which UBC is a reality, at least to that at which interlibrary operation is not the harried and uncertain thing it was— but the online catalog has also become a reality. Cost and other factors are delaying its implementation, but the delay will end.

Another occurrence of the past decade has been remarkable growth in the number of extant library publications. There has always been a plenitude of small newsletters and bulletins, and of course ALA, SLA and the like and some library schools publish full-scale and important journals. In addition, the profession has been blessed with a handful of first-rate commercial magazines, which, as Katz might put it, drift on year after year from excellence to excellence. As for anything else, this has until recently been lacking. Within the past few years, however, a number of small and medium-sized publishing houses have turned their attention to the needs of the library profession. Among these, apart from Haworth, are Mountainside, Pierian, JAI, Meckler, Oryx, Knowledge Industries and Pergamon. The result is what has been termed a proliferation of library publications. The fact is that while their number is still not huge, it is far from the paucity and skimpiness of ten years ago. It can be said without exaggeration that library activities are now being reported upon more thoroughly and to greater effect than ever before. The new journals not only report the news, but they also support and even initiate some of the research now being undertaken. Moreover, the opportunity is greater now than at any time in the past for an author to have his or her work appear in print. The editor of a large organization-sponsored journal once admitted that his journal rejected about ninety papers a year; and although one can hardly suppose that this condition still holds, it is apparent that some at least of the papers rejected then must have been worthy of publication. The conclusion is that there are fewer disappointed authors now than there once were. And by extension it can be said that the profession is being better served than heretofore by the increased size and openness of the library press.

Proliferation is not really a worry. It is doubtful that the number of library publications with a national or larger audience is much more than a hundred. If it is wanted to consider proliferation in its true sense, one need only look at what is taking place in the computer science area. Shirinian says that there are over 1,000 computer journals in existence (almost too many to keep track of by computer?) and that new ones keep coming along at the rate of one a week. The attrition rate, however, is high. As someone else puts it, computer magazines rate only slightly below the bald eagle as an endangered species, and in support of this offers the fact that twelve fold every month. If this is so, one can assume that as deaths are outnumbering births, the proliferation here, which is real, will eventually disappear. Another instance of course in which the final word is unknown.

So far as libraries are concerned, the record of the past ten years has been both meticulous and crabbed. Many good and worthwhile things have been accomplished, but much remains to be done before the millenium is reached, if this is in fact reachable. The world is of course an imperfect place—Walden Pond is (or was until recently) littered with candy wrappers and pop bottles, and Delius's Paradise Gardens, despite their name and the roses in them, have always been dismal. Nevertheless, if libraries are not yet beyond the point at which necessity and expedience dictate compromises that nobody is happy about, hope exists that past achievements will encourage even greater effort and productivity in the future.

As for *SL* itself, it is nothing short of an astonishment to those of us responsible for putting it out to realize that we have come so far along the road. In the beginning the editor at least had qualms about the deadlines stretching endlessly ahead, but as things turned out these did not prove the problem he expected them to be. Future problems are of course the most serious kind, and deadlines, no matter what, are always a worry. Still, ten years have gone by, and any calamities in these years have been counterbalanced by the satisfactions of equal or greater size.

From the start, outstanding help has been available to *SL*. Gary Pitkin, *SL*'s news editor, Joe Morehead, its government publications columnist, and Jean Farrington, its microserials columnist, have all been unfailingly industrious, punctual and solicitous of the journal's wellbeing. Others, too, have been helpful: Bill Cohen and his fine staff at Haworth; the members of our board of editorial advisers, who have kept us on course and topical; our authors, of whom there have been several hundred; and our readers, a good few of whom have sent letters of encouragement and sometimes of criticism—brickbats and bouquets, as occasion warranted. When all is said and done, *SL* has been lucky in many ways, and we are grateful for this.

Rukyser, in an anniversary telecast of *Wall Street Week*, remarked that his program had come a long way from its beginnings, and added, after listing some of the program's milestones, "Well, that is where we have been. Now what are we going to do about it?" For its part, *SL*, as it enters its tenth year of life, offers its readers this collection of essays in which the biggest and most important happenings of the past ten years in serials librarianship are examined. It does this believing that if we know where we have been, a sense is attained of where we are going.

PG

The Serials Department, 1975-1985

Don Lanier
Norman Vogt

ABSTRACT. The increase in the number of serial publications, the growth of holdings in libraries, and the maturation of librarianship are seen as largely responsible for the development of a specialty in serials librarianship by the time of the American Library Association's centennial celebration in 1976. This development often resulted in the organization of a separate serials department. In the decade following the ALA centennial several trends (e.g., economic stringency and automation) have converged to cause a re-evaluation of organizational patterns. In particular, the form versus function debate regarding serials organization is examined by reviewing professional activities and the published literature.

INTRODUCTION

Organizationally speaking, technical services and serials began their identity in libraries approximately fifty years ago. In 1935 J. Harris Gable gave birth to "The New Serials Department,"[1] and in 1938 Donald Coney provided the foundation for the technical services unit.[2] The growth of libraries and the maturation of librarianship during this last half century have been accompanied by corresponding developments in technical services generally and serials specifically. These developments have resulted in a substantial body of literature and professional activity devoted to these specialties. Maurice Tauber's classic work on technical services served as an imprimatur for the literature that focused on these library activities.[3] Andrew Osborn's *Serial Publications* (now in its 3rd edition) served the same purpose for the literature of serials work.[4] Now, however, organizational approaches to accomplishing most library work are being re-evaluated.

In 1976 *College and Research Libraries* celebrated the ALA centennial by publishing a monumental series of articles that provided an historical overview of developments in a number of highly visible areas of librari-

---

Don Lanier is Head of the Acquisitions and Serials Department, University Libraries, and Lecturer in the Department of Library Science, Northern Illinois University, DeKalb, IL 60115-2868. Norman Vogt is Serials Librarian, University Libraries, Northern Illinois University.

anship. The September, 1976, issue of *College and Research Libraries* contains two excellent articles reviewing organization patterns and developments in American libraries during the period 1876-1976. Connie Dunlap dealt with "Organizational Patterns in Academic Libraries,"[5] and Helen Welch Tuttle wrote of "Technical Services Developments in Academic and Research Libraries."[6]

It is no exaggeration to suggest that, since the events chronicled by Dunlap and Tuttle, developmental activity has taken place more rapidly than ever. The societal/technological influences on library operations are widely discussed and accepted. Likewise, the phenomenal publishing output and growth in expenditures for serials is well documented. (Faxon's serials database, for example, has grown from 62,211 records in 1974 to 222,328 in 1984). This review of salient events in the last decade focuses primarily on professional activities related to serials, library literature devoted to serials work, and particularly developments concerned with organization.

ORGANIZATION FOR SERIALS WORK—
THE VIEW FROM ALA/RTSD/SS

Tuttle's article (*College and Research Libraries,* September, 1976) suggests an early beginning to ALA's interest in serials as such. And, a survey of the records of the Serials Section of RTSD during the period 1975-1985 presents a phenomenal variety of activity that can be matched by few, if any other, ALA units. The published reports of groups specifically interested in serials shows that concern about organization of serials departments is limited—at least as it has been reported in the literature. The Serials Section of ALA's Resources and Technical Services Division reports limited activity of interest between 1975 and 1984. Though it is one of the goals of this section to provide a forum for the discussion of all topics relating to serials and serials management, the subject of the philosophy and organization of separate serials departments per se has not been widely addressed. Reports reflect limited concern for organization except for 1980-81 when staffing patterns were considered.[7] At ALA in Philadelphia (1982) the Technical Services Administrators of Medium-Sized Research Libraries Discussion Group presented a program on the organization of serials work in technical services in which the pros and cons of separated vs. integrated serials departments were discussed. At this meeting Michael Gorman propounded his philosophy that all libraries should be reorganized frequently. The effect of this philosophy on libraries, which are rather bureaucratic organizations, cannot be overestimated.

In a broader sense, and not restricted to any one organized serials group, some activity regarding the organization of serials has taken place. Of interest to serials librarians in the mid and late seventies were developments in bibliographic control, standards and automation, new cooperative programs and trends in microform publications. Discussions relative to organization centered around the phenomena of inflation and its impact on all aspects of budget and personnel. Because of rising costs that resulted in cuts in subscriptions and in personnel, libraries began to look more closely at ways in which they could both control their serials and organize their serials departments. This long, hard look at the costs of serials activity may have been responsible for planting the seed that resulted in questioning traditional patterns of serials organization. Dorothy Glasby notes in her 1980 serials report that the pendulum began to swing away from the concept of the separate serials department. Budget restraints certainly had an impact here, and the effects of the computer were becoming more pronounced.[8]

In addition to comments in the LRTS annual serials reviews and the RTSD Serials Section annual reports, other vehicles addressed the issue of the trend toward reorganizing serials in nontraditional ways. Nancy Melin noted in her wrap-up speech at the First Annual Serials Conference that she opposed the notion that serials departments are no longer necessary and expressed concern that, because of serials integration, serials decisions would be made by non-experts.[9] At the Second Annual Serials Conference, the matter of serials organization was broached in a panel entitled "Format Librarian: Fact or Fiction." Irene Wernstedt and Valerie Kleinman spoke of firsthand experience with functionally merged departments. Wernstedt appealed for a sympathetic approach toward personnel management during functional reorganization, but did not offer a definitive solution to the problem.[10]

In the literature, topics concerning bibliographic matters greatly outnumber those addressing developments in and philosophy of organization. The sheer number of bibliographic topics (e.g., CONSER, union listing, cataloging trends) that have affected serials in the last ten years may explain this unbalanced treatment. What can be deduced from the fact that organization of serials work virtually takes a back seat to bibliographic matters in professional forums? Librarians may feel that they have less control over this controversial administrative problem and simply zero in on those bibliographic complexities that affect their daily routines. Ideas regarding the form and function debate might be tempered by our general misconception about what really comprises a serials unit. Local tradition may be the greatest influence in how departments are now organized.

Administrators play a large role in determining organizational fate. They are the "futurists" who thrive on change to develop a record of accomplishment and perhaps to support their egos. Some can't sit still long enough to let the dust settle. Hanson aptly calls this syndrome "the ever present desire for novelty."[11] Other library leaders feel it is important to be in the forefront of current library administrative issues in order to exert influence in the profession. Still others must satisfy demands to prove that good things are being accomplished. John Gardner, former Secretary of Health, Education and Welfare, has spoken bluntly about the need to bring about necessary change for people:

> People need periodic change in the nature of their duties . . . Rotate them. Promote them. Reassign them. Give them added duties. Anything to prevent the boredom, the staleness that afflicts most people in most organizations most of the time.[12]

WHAT THE LITERATURE SAYS

Dunlap's article (*College and Research Libraries,* September, 1976) pointed to several trends affecting library organization, including the replacement of bureaucratic organization with collegial systems, a growth in complexity accompanying similar patterns in society and higher education, and the increased application of automation that would result in the reassignment of staff from technical to user services. Evidently, the trend toward a blurring of the distinctions between technical and public services was not anticipated. This result of automation has enabled the profession to be more open and creative regarding which jobs actually require professional competencies and where these competencies are to be practiced. Recently, reputable institutions like the University of Illinois and Pennsylvania State University have implemented organizational patterns which call for generic librarians—i.e., librarians whose competencies are at the same time technical and service oriented.

Irene Godden's recent text, *Library Technical Services: Operation and Management* (Orlando, Florida: Academic Press, 1984), provides a valuable overview of current technical services operations and management. It is the most substantial work on technical services since the appearance of Maurice Tauber's classic, *Technical Services in Libraries* (New York: Columbia University Press, 1954). The organizational identity that Tauber gave to technical services has undergone significant rethinking and change in the work edited by Godden. Nevertheless, both emphasize a functional organization of technical services operations as opposed to organization determined by the form of material.

Donald Coney indicated that size was the decisive factor in determining whether or not a division head should be interposed between the chief librarian and others. Size has also been the chief factor in determining when it is appropriate to organize operations around a specific form of material (e.g., serials, microforms, documents). More recently it has been suggested that automation contributes not only to the obsolescence of manual activities but also points to the inadequacy of previous organizational patterns. Back in 1967 Barbara Westby quoted a paper in which it was suggested that a computer-oriented system may be more efficient if organized around form.[13]

In the last decade the organization of serials work in libraries has received considerable attention in library literature in spite of the little attention in professional circles previously mentioned. In most of this literature there is a stated or assumed preference for organizing a separate operational unit around this form. The theoretical base to most of this literature consisted of the size of the operation, the special nature of the format (serials), and the need for an integration of all functions related to serials, including cataloging and user services. A recent article on "The Integrated Serials Department" by Sue Ann Harrington and Deborah J. Karpuls provides an excellent review of the literature and a case study of the University of Oklahoma Library's serials organization, which supports organization by form.[14]

Between 1980 and 1984 a number of articles appeared dealing directly with the organization of serials operations. A review of this literature, which specifically addresses the controversy over separate vs. integrated serials functions, reveals that certain trends and concerns appear repeatedly. Most often cited are technological (automation) and economic factors, the need for communication, careful planning, and the importance of cataloging as an integral part of the serials unit.[15]

Collver advocates the principle of reciprocal interdependence as a basis for organizing the work in serials departments, stressing the need for maximum coordination between many diverse functions. She concludes that automation, often thought to be the bugbear of separate serials departments, actually strengthens the need for them. McKinley addresses the importance of communication channels and mutual support structures when serials functions are dispersed. She contends that, whether planned by administrators or not, natural communication patterns that aid work performance will develop. Unlike Collver, who champions the computer as a force to justify separate serials departments, McKinley makes us aware, with equally sensible judgment, that automated centralized records can be maintained from any area within the library.

When the form vs. function debate arose in the early 1980s, Stine conducted a survey of ARL libraries to determine how serials were processed and how departments were organized, particularly emphasizing staffing. She found that serials staff responsibility differed greatly among libraries polled and concluded that this was attributable to the fact that not enough attention has been given to the levels and kinds of staffs needed for serials work. Harrington and Karpuls support Collver's feeling that serials cataloging should be a centralized force in an integrated serials department.[16] It is a real puzzlement that, in the organization of serials, the cataloging function is so vital, yet it appears that many serials units do not incorporate it into their work.

Potter set the serials world to thinking once again about organization with his controversial analysis of the form and function debate. His obvious leaning toward organization by function reflects his experience at the trend-setting University of Illinois Library, where traditional technical and public services structures are being demolished. However, preliminary findings of a 1985 ARL survey found no examples of libraries where public and technical services were completely integrated. Nevertheless, the organizational changes at Illinois are not so much based on form vs. function considerations as they are on an overall administrative philosophy and strategy related to meeting user needs with available resources. Hepfer takes a comprehensive approach in viewing the pros and cons of the form and function issues, and his work represents one of the least biased approaches in the literature.

Organization of serials operations by form has not been without its detractors. To some extent it appears that there has been a "backlash" phenomenon in response to the position of some serials librarians who have promoted their responsibilities as unique and extraordinarily special. In any case, the depth of feeling about the issue is highlighted by a rather emotional column by Tom Leonhardt which recently appeared in the *RTSD Newsletter*.[17] Leonhardt, newly appointed editor of the *Newsletter*, takes issue with much of what serials department advocates have written. While provocative, his comments add little to the theoretical discussion about the merits of form or function organization. In fact, Leonhardt's letter to the editor in *The Serials Librarian* (Fall, 1984) may indicate that the entire column is more of a response to a personal, local situation than it is an attempt to professionally address the form vs. function debate.

Local conditions, the impact of the economy, and forward thinking administrators will continue to shape the organizational future. New ideas about an old issue do not come easily, though differing viewpoints abound. It is healthy discussion that keeps philosophies and realities in balance. As job responsibilities become more specialized, there will be new developments and, one hopes, new perspectives. Electronic publishing will have an as yet unpredictable effect. Technology will unleash new challenges and perhaps even lead us to some solutions.

The debate will, no doubt, be carried on for several more years. It is not too far afield to suggest that the impetus for functional organization comes not so much from a theoretical approach as from a pragmatic one. Organizational and budgeting strategies in library management (as elsewhere) are aimed at reducing complexity in library operations, including staffing. Simplification is one benchmark of scientific management and functional organization. A trend toward more functional organization is visible. A Consultation Panel of the Center for Research Libraries recently recommended that the Center should organize its acquisitions department along functional lines. What such a trend portends for the future of the serials department is yet to be seen. However, if job ads for "Heads of Serials Departments" are any indication, the situation will not change dramatically.

REFERENCES

1. J. Harris Gable, "The New Serials Department," *Library Journal* 60:869-87 (November 15, 1935).
2. Donald Coney, "The Administration of Technical Processes," in Carleton B. Joeckel, ed., *Current Issues in Library Administration: Papers Presented Before the Library Institute at the University of Chicago, August 1-12, 1938*. Chicago: University of Chicago Press, 1939.
3. Maurice F. Tauber and Associates, *Technical Services in Libraries*. New York: Columbia University Press, 1954.
4. Andrew Osborn, *Serials Publications*. Chicago: American Library Association, 1955.
5. Connie R. Dunlap, "Organizational Patterns in Academic Libraries, 1876-1976," *College & Research Libraries* 37:395-407 (September, 1976).
6. Helen W. Tuttle, "From Cutter to Computer: Technical Services in Academic and Research Libraries, 1876-1976," *College & Research Libraries* 37:421-451 (September, 1976).
7. Annual reports of the Serials Section of ALA's Resources and Technical Services Division have appeared regularly in issues of *Library Resources and Technical Services*, 1975-1984.
8. Dorothy J. Glasby, "The Year's Work in Serials: 1980," *Library Resources and Technical Services* 25:317 (July/September, 1981).
9. *Serials Management in an Automated Age: Proceedings of the First Annual Serials Conference, October 30-31, 1981, Arlington, VA*. Edited by Nancy J. Melin. Westport, CT: Meckler, 1983.
10. Alan Schaplowsky, "Second Annual Serials Conference, October 22-23, 1982: the LAPT Report," *Library Acquisitions Practice and Theory* 7:154-157 (1983).
11. Jo Ann Hanson, "Trends in Serials Management," *The Serials Librarian* 8:7 (Summer, 1984).
12. John W. Gardner, *Personal and Organizational Renewal*. Austin, TX: Hogg Foundation, University of Texas, 1984, p. 4.
13. Barbara M. Westby, "Mind Over Morter, or, Advanced Planning for Technical Services," *Library Resources and Technical Services* 11:479-487 (Fall, 1967).
14. Sue Ann Harrington and Deborah Karpuls, "The Integrated Serials Department: Its Value Today and in the Future," *The Serials Librarian* 9:55-64 (Winter, 1984).
15. Mitsuko Collver, "Organization of Serials Work for Manual and Automated Systems," *Library Resources and Technical Services* 24:307-16 (Fall, 1980); Margaret M. McKinley, "Serials Departments: Doomed to Extinction?" *The Serials Librarian* 5:15-24 (Winter, 1980); Diane Stine, "Serials Department Staffing Patterns in Medium-Sized Research Libraries," *Serials Review* 7:83-7 (July/September, 1981); William Gray Potter, "Form or Function? An Analysis of the Serials Department in the Modern Academic Library," *The Serials Librarian* 6:85-94 (Fall, 1981); William Hepfer, "Serials Organization in Academic Libraries: Is There a Best Way?" in *The Serials Collection: Organization and Administration*, (Ann Arbor, Pierian Press, 1982), p. 1-8.
16. Harrington and Karpuls, 1984, p. 55-64.
17. Thomas Leonhardt, "The Place of Serials in Technical Services," *RTSD Newsletter* 9: 84-85 (1984).

Dealing With Serials:
A Sketch
of Contextual/Organizational Response

Michael Gorman

ABSTRACT. Discusses the environment in which academic libraries operate. The constraints are economic and societal. Automation is a major factor. These general factors are applied to a discussion of the place of the serial in academic libraries and the ways in which serial processing might be organized. Mention is made of the future of the serial and the role that librarians can play in effecting change.

There are, it seems to me, certain ineluctable practicalities that color the nature of administration in academic libraries. In truth, they color that process in all kinds of libraries and in all facets of public and corporate life. Many of these facts of life are in opposition, if not actually in conflict. Most are obvious, but they can be, and are, ignored—to the peril of our institutions and the library users that they serve. Before I focus upon the topic of dealing with serials from an administrative and organizational point of view, I would like to discuss the general pressures upon libraries and the responses that these pressures evoke.

The first and most obvious is that of money. Libraries are chronically underfunded. With this underfunding and with increasing demands on library services, it is now more important than ever that we devise ways of making the best of this bad job and extract the maximum value from each dollar. Libraries are not underfunded because money is short in this country (or, indeed, relatively speaking, in any of the "developed" countries), but because they, and the group of cultural and social activities to which they belong, are undervalued constantly by those who control the pursestrings at the local, state, regional, and national level. The reasons for this latter are very complex and deep-rooted. They have to do with the nature of "Western" society and the materialistic and hedonistic values upon which that society is based. High culture is the pursuit of the few. Mass-culture is more a matter of manipulation than it is of com-

---

Michael Gorman is Director, General Services Department, 246A Main Library, University of Illinois at Urbana-Champaign, 1408 West Gregory Drive, Urbana, IL 61801.

© 1986 by The Haworth Press, Inc. All rights reserved.

munal expression. It is imposed from above rather than arising from the people themselves. All of this brings me to my second major fact, that we (librarians and library users) swim in a new kind of pond in these days. Prior to the destruction of cultural homogeneity in the last couple of decades, there existed a process of transmission between high-culture and mass-culture. No matter how much they differed one from the other, the two cultures shared certain common assumptions. Each, to a certain extent, vitalized the other. Libraries could reconcile the two and could accommodate the two without friction. This is no longer true. Libraries have to recognize that they are, on the cultural level, dealing with two societies.

The next major circumstance to which attention must be paid is that of the inexorable march of automation. I once met a librarian who said that, on the whole, she was in favor of library automation. I was reminded of Carlyle's observation upon hearing that Margaret Fuller had said that she accepted the universe—"Gad, she'd better!" Automation is, for a variety of reasons, noble and ignoble, a mainstay of modern library operations. No strategy that ignores that patent fact can succeed. No strategy that comprehends and takes automation fully into account can fail absolutely. The key point is that library automation must be understood truly, not on the superficial whiz-bang level but based on a clear appraisal of its potential and actual contribution and upon its economics and logistics.

The last major pressure that must be taken into account is that of the changing nature of work and the expectations of the work force at all levels. No one knows what happens to a society that shifts from a reliance on heavy industry to a reliance on white-collar and "service" industries. We shall all find out before the end of this century. In the wider world, this shift is often dramatised as being from, say, steelwork to, say, slinging plastic hash in a burger joint. (No business mogul has been observed to weep upon learning that such a shift is also from unionized reasonably-paid hourly work to unprotected minimum-wage hourly work.) In the library world (as in many other mini-worlds) that shift is more complex than the cartoon of the shift from Big Steel to Ronald Wilson McDonald. Two eddies of the current can easily be seen. Sweated labor is vanishing from our libraries—the monotonous task of filing cards is merely the most obvious example. In addition, a large number of professional (loosely defined) jobs are vanishing. Machines and support staff are carrying out many tasks that used to be considered the exclusive right of professional librarians. Other such tasks have been seen to be unnecessary and have simply vanished. It all boils down to a smaller work-force in which fewer jobs will be available to professional librarians, fewer jobs will require unskilled labor, and, crucially, a trained non-professional white-collar group with higher expectations than in the past will need to be accommodated. Outside the library work force, wider forces will be at work and different patterns of library use and expectations will become apparent. This last does not imply any endorsement of the blather about the "Coming Information Age," the "Paperless Society," or similar passé tosh, but the simple observation that, as society changes, the institutions serving that society will also change.

What has all this to do with serial departments in academic libraries? A lot more than one might think. After all, serials are the product of one aspect of modern culture. If that culture differs radically from that of the past, its products and the use to which they are put also will differ from those of the past. The people who acquire, process, and maintain those new products live in the new society, as do the people who use those products for education, research, and leisure. Modern culture is like a modern city. It has great diversity and enormous advantages unknown to the inhabitants of the past. It also has modern scourges that were unknown to those inhabitants—alienation, violence, and pollution. Only some of these attributes can be dealt with. All must be understood.

It may be pertinent to ask why one is taking this general view of what is, after all, a rather specialist process devoted to a particular subset of the materials of one profession. The answer is that many administrative errors and misjudgements in libraries arise from a blinkered view, a tendency to react to particular circumstances rather than to understand the wider context. Instead, we should place processes and techniques in the context of the whole library world, of learning and society. Allied to the blinkered view has been the tendency to believe that libraries are passive organisms that have to float with the cultural currents; bound on a journey that leads to who knows where. I do not believe that such a view is correct or necessary.

The first cultural phenomenon with which we have to deal is the nature and place of the serial in modern society. It can safely be asserted that the modern serial is radically different in content, type, purpose, and distribution/use patterns from the eighteenth century journal from which it is distantly descended. Indeed, it is radically different from its predecessors in the first half of this century. The differences affecting the library directly are number, price, complexity of publication patterns, and specialization. These obvious characteristics also have a strong influence on the use of serials that, at the microthought level (to use Ranganathan's term), is extremely low. As serials become more numerous and more expensive, more complex bibliographically, and more specialized, the rate of use per article must and does decline. Librarians are faced with spending more money and time to achieve ever-diminishing returns. Abstracting and indexing services struggle to provide access to the intellectual units that are the main reason for the existence of the serial. Library budgets creak as they attempt to accommodate continuously growing serial expenditures, expenditures that are so voracious they gobble up whole sections of monograph budgets. Organizationally, a typical response to this difficult and, at times, overwhelming set of problems has been to develop an elite corps of "serialists"—guerrilla fighters in the steamy serials jungle. I believe that this response, though understandable, has been a counsel of despair and one that tends towards professional fragmentation and alienation. The invention of the sub-profession of "serialism" has led to an inadequate use of human resources and, in some instances, to the perpetuation of the problems to which "serialism" was thought to be the solution. No one will dispute that serial publications present difficult and, sometimes, unique problems for technical processing, nor that there is a need for expertise in dealing with those problems. However, I do not believe that those problems and the expertise they need are of a magnitude that calls for a separatist organizational response. In my organizational scheme, therefore, serials would be dealt with, insofar as it is possible, together with all other materials. In short, I do not believe we need *as separate entities* serial acquisition departments, serial cataloguing departments, or serial binding/marking operations. Moreover, serial control (which has always been viewed as uniquely "serialist") can be seen as one, or even the main, manifestation of a particular phenomenon—the arrival in the library of physically discrete objects (books, journal issues, maps, etc.) that are not accompanied by specific invoices and that were not ordered separately. Other examples of this phenomenon are subsequently-published volumes of a multi-volume monograph, gifts, material received on blanket order and approval plans, depository documents, and exchange materials. Rather than setting up a separate and different routine for these depending upon their type or form, it seems to me that the library should evolve an organizational response based on the nature of the problem posed. Thus, a check-in/control section of Acquisitions can be established to deal with all the manifestations of this (as yet unnamed) phenomenon and, subsequently, to feed the results of their work into the mainstream of cataloguing and other processing. Similarly, a unit of cataloging can deal with the future control of serial and multi-volume monographic materials by establishing open ended records that can deal with closely related items yet to be acquired—most easily understood as "extended serial records."

Given that technical processing of serials should and can be carried out within a non-discriminatory and function-oriented organizational framework, there still remains the question of the number and the level of staff that should deal with serials and other related materials. If my heretical views on "serialism" have not yet caused enough offence, I daresay that my next observation will add fuel to the flames. I believe an enormous percentage of serials processing (and, indeed, of all processing) to be of a clerical or, at best, a quasi-professional nature. If this is true, it happens, conveniently, to meet an earlier concern—that of finding a role for the emerging semi-professional and clerical class. That class, freed by automation from much of the worst drudgery of library work, is seeking rewarding occupation within the library and, by and large, failing to find it. The "serialists" (some with a banshee howl) will have vanished from the scene and I offer, in their place, a set of technicians dealing with the ordering, claiming, receipt, copy cataloguing of, and payment for, library materials of all kinds. Those clerical and quasi-professional technicians will work within frameworks devised by librarians and, in many cases, under the direction of librarians. They also will be allowed a measure of decision-making, which will enable their worklife to be rewarding and responsible. A stripped-down materials control operation thus staffed will meet the requirements of efficiency and, also, of societal pressures calling for job-fulfillment.

All of these changes and improvements, however, skirt the central "serials problem." That problem is inherent in the nature of the modern serial. It, and its many defects, have been accepted and, in a covert way, encouraged by libraries and librarians. I strongly believe that the many inconsistencies and inefficiencies of modern serial publications need not be accepted in a passive way by librarians and libraries. Why should we accept the constant and irrational changes of title, format, subject, etc., to which the serial is heir? Why should we accept the ludicrous cost of these little used materials? Why should we accept the expenditure of public and private funds on macro-assemblages of loosely related short pieces whose very randomness would be a fatal defect in any other type of publication? The answers to all of these questions are both simple—only passivity can explain our acceptance—and complex—cultural prejudice dictates acceptance of what is and militates against what might be. Libraries, in not questioning this form of disseminating knowledge and information, have, in one sense, betrayed their trust. I believe that librarians should use their accumulated experience with serial publications to propose and carry out, as equal partners with the publishing and serials distribution trades, a radical revision of the way in which "microthought" (short and specific assemblage of knowledge and information) is disseminated and preserved. Space does not permit me to detail the numerous possible methods by which this might be accomplished, but they do exist conceptually and they can be achieved.

Last, before that change can be accomplished, libraries have to deal with the serial publications that they gather currently. The distinction between the two cultures that I mentioned earlier is a prerequisite to understanding the handling and use of those serials. It is common for libraries to treat all materials as if they were of equal importance and value, and as if the paths to their use were all the same. In fact, high culture serials are as different from mass culture serials as the classics of literature are from "How-to-earn-a-billion-dollars-selling-insurance" books. That is not to say that it is always a qualitative difference but simply that the processing, accessibility needs, life span, and value to an institution of these two classes of publication are very different.

All of the preceding consists merely of sketches of the context of the modern serial and plans for its present and future in libraries. To sum up, we need to understand the culture in which we live and its products before we can deal effectively with them as librarians; we need to base our organization on modern realities and exigencies; and we need to work to revise radically the form itself. Oh, incidentally, the future is what happens to you if you don't get out of the way!

Serials Organization: A Time for Reappraisal

Sue Anne Harrington

ABSTRACT. A revolution in serials work has occurred during the last decade as libraries have moved from manual operations to the age of automation. For economic and technological reasons, a renewed interest in the organization of serials activities has developed, and there is debate between those who favor continuing the separate serials department (organization by form) and those who favor merging serials activities into other departments (organization by function). In this study, the views of each school of thought are considered. The conclusion is reached that serials specialists must organize, anticipate and plan for further organizational changes.

Change occurs constantly throughout our lives. We cannot escape it. Those who work with serial publications are certainly well-equipped to deal with change because serials, sometimes referred to as the biggest problem in librarianship, are continually changing.[1] Nothing stays the same for long in serials work. Titles change, merge, split into parts, suspend publication, cease and then start up again. Changes in frequency, numbering, publisher and place of publication, occur all too often. Although some people might think that serials work is frustrating, most of us love the challenge and learn to cope decently enough with the myriad problems that arise in it. Nevertheless, a revolution in serials work during the last ten to fifteen years has severely tested our abilities.

Reflect back, for a moment, to the days when library budgets were increasing, serials collections were growing, staffing was adequate, salaries were rising, and automation was something we read about in the literature. Ordering, check-in, claiming, and cataloging of serials were all carried out manually, and catalog cards were typed or ordered from the Library of Congress. Serialists spent their time worrying about such things as: whether to establish a central serials record; how to eliminate backlogs of unrecorded materials; what to do with duplicate issues; and how to spend generous budgets. In the late 1960s the University of Mas-

---

Sue Anne Harrington is Acting Director, Library Technical Services and Head, Serials Department at The University of Oklahoma Libraries, Norman, Oklahoma 73019.

© 1986 by The Haworth Press, Inc. All rights reserved.

sachusetts Serials Department was actually ordering over 300 new serial subscriptions per month. Librarians were mainly concerned with acquiring more and more.[2]

THE REVOLUTION

Consider now, the multitude of changes that have taken place since the '60s. Significant events during this time have included: the development of the machine-readable (MARC) serials format; the rise of on-line cataloging systems like those of OCLC, RLIN and WLN; the establishment of CONSER; the organization of the National Serials Data Program (NSDP); the increasing interest in standards and standardization at both the national and international level; the publication of the second edition of the *Anglo-American Cataloging Rules* (AACR2); and the *International Standard Bibliographic Description for Serials (ISBD(S))*; as well as, the movement to freeze the card catalog; the development of automated on-line serials control systems; and the increasing use of microcomputers.

> The fact is that in little more than 10 years' time libraries have proceeded from the point of manual operation to that in which the computer has been called into play in every major area of library activity. If at the beginning of the '70s librarians could scarcely imagine what it would be like to use the computer, they found themselves at the end of that decade wondering how on earth they had previously managed without it.[3]

Rapidly increasing serial prices, the proliferation of journals being published, shrinking budgets and rising personnel costs also have had their effect. Greater emphasis is now being placed on more efficient and cost effective serials management, on the preservation and maintenance of the serials collection, on the sharing of resources, and on improving access and delivery of materials to the user. "The push is on to 'cope' to do the work with 10-25-40 percent less staff, to use nonprofessionals or para-professionals for tasks done by librarians in the flush years, to simplify."[4]

A TIME FOR REAPPRAISAL

The computer revolution, which has had so strong an impact on serials operations, has brought about a renewed interest in the organization of serials activities. In 1979, Michael Gorman shook us all with his call for the abolishment of technical services departments. He visualized "a central automated processing system for the ordering, receipt, rapid cataloging and routing of library materials with little or no professional involvement." He advocated the abandonment of the "sweatshop" cataloging department and the redeployment of professional librarians around subject or service categories. As he saw it, these librarians would perform all professional functions connected with their subject or service, including selection of materials, original cataloging, reference services and bibliographic instruction.[5]

Although Gorman's theories may have startled us in 1979, numerous writers have espoused similar ideas since then. The first issue of *Technical Services Quarterly* is devoted entirely to a discussion of the future of technical services. The prediction is made that technical services of the future will be decentralized and that the distinctions between public and technical work will disappear.[6] Serialists can no longer avoid this possibility. We must quit hiding our heads in the sand, like the ostrich, and thoughtfully examine the issues.

At a 1980 serials automation conference in Milwaukee, Gorman again spoke out. He recommended organizing technical processing by function rather than by form. He advocated the abolishment of serials departments and the establishing of departments that would deal with ordering, claiming, receiving, cataloging, binding, etc. Organization by form, according to Gorman, leads to pointless differences in the treatment of materials. Organizing by function, on the other hand, leads to a more consistent treatment of materials. This results in improved service to the user.[7] It may well be that Gorman's remarks set off the heated "form or function" debate that has ensued.

FORM OR FUNCTION DEBATE

Serials departments have been organized in a variety of ways throughout the years. Little thought, however, was given to the subject until the 1930s, and serials units consequently evolved to suit the occasion. They first became established as part of acquisitions or catalog departments and, in some cases, serials responsibilities were actually dealt with by reference or circulation departments. Attention was suddenly focused on the organization of serials when libraries were called upon to contribute information and holdings to the *Union List of Serials*.

In 1935, Gable started a trend with his landmark article advocating the separate serials department.[8] Although little progress was made for a number of years, most libraries followed the trend and gradually moved toward the establishment of separate serials departments. A survey, conducted in 1975, revealed that 74 percent of the responding libraries had separate serials departments.[9] Little uniformity of duties existed in these departments, however. Two recent studies showed numerous organizational variations. The one common feature among the libraries surveyed by Dyal was the central serials record, and Johnson determined that check-in and claiming were the only duties universally performed by all departments in the libraries that she surveyed.[10]

The history of serials organization has come to show a cyclical pattern, according to Hanson. After a push toward the establishment of unified serials departments, the trend is now toward the reintegration of serials functions into those of other library departments. Changes in technological and economic factors as well as the ever present desire for novelty may account for this, she feels.[11]

Cargill also sees a clear trend in the direction of eliminating separate serials departments and relocating personnel and duties in other departments. She says that the movement to organize work by function rather than by form is behind the abolition of separate serials departments. Since few new subscriptions are being added to serials collections and cancellation of titles has become commonplace, the feeling has arisen that serials operations can be effectively merged with those of other departments, she says. Serials, as opposed to monographs, change titles, format and frequency on an all too regular basis, and these changes must be correctly identified and recorded. These differences, Cargill feels, account for the unique quality of serials work more than does any other single factor. Claiming of serials is a problem also. Nevertheless, the approach to problem-solving is much the same for both serials librarians and monograph librarians, she says, and the same staff should be able to deal with whatever problems there are.[12]

In this excellent article, Cargill indicates that the following advantages are found in merging serials activities with those of other departments: elimination of the stereotype of technical services librarians as persons who feel that their work is highly complex and unique and requires librarians with special talents; better comprehension of the importance of other people's jobs; and elimination of the mystique of generally misunderstood operations. The best justification for the change, she says, is the improved performance of the resulting organization.[13]

Staff attitudes will cause the most problems in merging departments, according to Cargill. Entrenched serials or acquisitions librarians may not want to give up the prestige of separate departmental status. They may claim no knowledge of the other area and resist taking on any additional duties. Monograph units may have a negative attitude toward serials that will also have to be overcome. The attitude of people involved in the merger is extremely important, she feels. A positive attitude is absolutely essential.[14]

Another enthusiastic advocate of organizing serials activities by function rather than by form is William Potter. In a recent somewhat controversial article, he maintains that the selection, ordering, cataloging, updating of holdings, and circulation of serials do not require special treatment. He does admit, however, that separate procedures and units for claiming and check-in of serials are necessary. At the same time, he goes on to say that these procedures are largely clerical and can be supervised by professional librarians who are responsible for broader functions involving all types of materials.[15]

Mary Monson argues well for the placing of serials catalogers in catalog departments. She maintains that the adoption of AACR2 has narrowed the gap between serials and monographic cataloging since there is no longer a separate rule for choice of main entry for serials. She sees the benefits to be derived from such an arrangement as: improved lines of communication; increased understanding; a better arrangement for serials catalogers whose serials department supervisor may have little cataloging experience; and increased sharing of tools and resources.[16] Her strongest argument is perhaps that catalogers in a serials department may not receive enough of their supervisor's time and attention especially if the supervisor is not particularly interested in or knowledgeable about cataloging. This is a valid argument that deserves further consideration.

"The shift toward automated library systems and the adoption of a cataloging code that has narrowed the gap between serials cataloging and monographic cataloging have combined to create a climate favorable to the placement of serials catalogers in a catalog department where interaction with other catalogers encourages high quality cataloging, thereby providing the framework for high quality service," according to Monson.[17] Although this article advocates the placing of serials catalogers in the catalog department, it fails to discuss the organizational arrangement of other serials operations.

Hanson suggests that it is difficult to justify continuing to divide monograph and serial materials since the present trend is to integrate materials into one collection. She further suggests that we look at the business world where functional division is usually favored. Nevertheless, she concludes her article by saying that each library must make its own decision about its organizational structure and that it is unwise for us to be rigid in support of either traditional or innovative forms of serials management for all libraries.[18]

Despite the arguments of these and other writers who support the organization of serials activities by function rather than by form, library literature is filled with articles supporting the continuation of the separate serials department.

Pamela Bluh worries that the abolition or merger of serials departments is often carried out without the benefit of preliminary studies or without determining the need for the change. "One hesitates to suggest that changes may be introduced as a result of trends or because it is 'fashionable,' but often the arguments presented in favor of decentralization seem weak and arbitrary,'' she says. A small serials collection may be easily handled as part of a functional arrangement but according to Bluh it is absolutely essential for a large serials collection to be handled in an integrated, centralized serials department. She further states that we need to recognize that as technical services activities become more complex, the need for experts and specialists becomes more important.[19]

Stine is also disturbed about the trend toward decentralization of serials processing. She says that serials and monographs are not the same, and so cannot be treated in the same way. "Serials present special problems due to their nature. Because of these problems, library personnel handling serials need a special expertise which can only come after a great deal of exposure to the materials and proper training by other serials experts," Stine contends. She further worries that serials will be neglected in a decentralized organization and not receive the attention they need.[20]

Weber, another serialist who expresses concern that serials will be neglected in a decentralized organization, says, "There is unfortunately a tendency for those who work only with monographs to shunt serials aside, perhaps in the hope they will go away if ignored, since they can frequently be imbued with more problems and changes than one might reasonably expect." Although he admits that small libraries may not have the staff to handle serials in a separate department, he takes a strong stand for the separate serials department in larger libraries. He feels that it is imperative for an institution with 5,000 or more serial subscriptions to consolidate certain functions by form for optimum efficiency.[21]

Mitsuko Collver also is a leading spokesman for the separate serials department. According to her theory, serials activities are reciprocally interdependent. The major activities of ordering, receiving, cataloging and processing of serials are repeated over and over again during the lifetime of a publication, and serials workers must interact with one another in order to carry out these functions. Collver contends that all serials activities should be located in one unit for their effective coordination. She further finds that the grouping of serials activities and personnel together into a serials department results in improved technical operations and more effective public service. While those who favor a functional arrangement argue that automation eliminates the need for the separate serials department, Collver, to the contrary, says that automation reinforces the advantages of the separate serials department and weakens the argument for other structures.[22]

Harrington and Karpuk express their preference for the separate serials department also. They maintain that this type of arrangement is as viable today as it was in Gable's time, and impute the success of the integrated serials department to three considerations: greatly improved bibliographic control, with the serials cataloger at the center of the department; more effective service to the public; and better avenues of communication. They conclude: "Through the integrated serials arrangement, all staff have the opportunity to develop the expertise and flexibility needed to assist in either the public or technical work of the department. These serials specialists take pride in their ability to deal with complicated serials problems, and work hard to provide better service to the user."[23]

On the other hand, Margaret McKinley admits that function may, indeed, triumph over form in some libraries. She maintains, nevertheless, that some kind of organizational structure will continue to be necessary to handle the processing of serials. When serials departments are abolished, informal communication networks will develop among serials specialists, she says. "There is reason to believe that wherever serials departments have been abolished, serials specialists and the communications networks they have created are alive and well and flourishing in the organizational underground," according to McKinley. She closes her thoughtful article by saying, "Motivated and experienced specialists are necessary to the efficient operation of a serials processing network and . . . will work best if they can do so within the established organizational structure. If this support is denied, library planners should anticipate the development of an unpredictable communication system outside the organizational framework and should hope that it will meet their stated objectives."[24]

From the preceding comments, it is obvious that the form or function debate must not be taken lightly. Both sides present strong arguments for their organizational preference.

Those who favor the elimination of the separate serials department and the merging of this department into other departments (organization by function) present the following arguments:

1. Automation eliminates the need for a separate serials department.
2. Organization by function is more economical.
3. Static serials budgets and title cancellations make this arrangement more feasible.
4. The arrangement allows for better utilization of staff and more flexibility in training.
5. It promotes a more consistent treatment of materials.
6. Adoption of AACR2 has narrowed the gap between serials cataloging and monographic cataloging.
7. The arrangement relieves librarians of clerical work and allows them to assume other more appropriate responsibilities.

Those who favor the separate serials department (organization by form) advocate the following:

1. Serials present special problems and need specialists to deal with them.
2. These materials would be neglected in a decentralized organization.

3. Serials activities should be located in one unit for optimum efficiency and coordination.
4. This arrangement provides greatly improved bibliographic control, with the serials cataloger at the center of the department.
5. It provides more effective service to the public and better avenues of communication.
6. Staff develop expertise, flexibility through cross-training, and pride in their work.
7. Automation reinforces the need for separate serials departments.

SUMMARY

Although serialists are used to dealing with change, the revolution in serials work during the last ten to fifteen years has severely tested our abilities. A multitude of changes have taken place since the '60s as libraries have moved from manual operations to the age of automation. Increasing prices, proliferation of journals, shrinking budgets and rising personnel costs have also had their effect. Greater emphasis is now being placed on more efficient and cost effective serials management.

Because of economic and technological changes in libraries, a renewed interest in the organization of serials activities has developed. It is predicted that technical services of the future will be decentralized and that the distinctions between public and technical work will disappear.

Although serials departments have been organized in a number of ways, Gable started a clear trend toward the establishment of separate serials departments in 1935. Now some librarians are calling for the reintegration of serials functions into those of other library departments. This has set off a debate between those who favor continuing the separate serials department (organization by form) and those who favor merging serials activities into other departments (organization by function). Those who favor organization by function maintain that this method is more cost efficient and say that automation eliminates the need for separate serials departments. Those who advocate organization by form argue that automation reinforces the need for the separate serials department. They maintain that serials activities should be located in one unit for optimum efficiency and coordination.

Whether we agree with those who favor the elimination of the separate serials department or with those who want to retain it, we must be willing to admit that automation is making enormous changes in the library world, especially in technical services. Those who favor the separate serials department have reason for concern in the demise of serials departments in such institutions as the University of Illinois, Kent State University, the University of California at San Diego, the University of

California at Riverside and elsewhere. But this is not to say that the battle is lost.

As serials librarians, we must stop and consider what we will do if such organizational changes come about in our own libraries. "Are we then to concede defeat and retire whimpering to our offices in meek anticipation of the inevitable collapse . . ." of the familiar serials organization we work in?[25] Surely that will not be the case. It is surely preferable to believe that we will rise to the occasion and face any new challenges that the future brings. We who deal with materials that are constantly changing, are certainly well-equipped to cope with any changes that occur. "Serials specialists must then recognize that the only sensible solution is to organize for change, to anticipate it and to plan for it."[26] Rather than conceding defeat, we must be prepared for the future, be flexible, be adaptable, and remain confident that we are capable of dealing with any crises that may occur in the coming months.

REFERENCES

1. Michael Gorman, "The Current State of Standardization in the Cataloging of Serials," *Library Resources & Technical Services* 19, no.4 (Fall 1975):301-313.
2. Nancy J. Melin, "Serials in the '80s: A Report From the Field," *Serials Review* 7 (July/Sept. 1981):79-82.
3. Peter Gellatly, "The Eighties," *The Serials Librarian* 5, no.1 (Fall 1980):3-5.
4. Mary W. Ghikas, "Technical Services in the '80s: Challenge and Change," *Illinois Libraries* 62 (Sept. 1980):588-590.
5. Michael Gorman, "On Doing Away with Technical Services Departments," *American Libraries* 10, no. 7 (July/Aug. 1979):435-437.
6. Peter Gellatly, "What is Ahead in Technical Services," *Technical Services Quarterly* 1, no.1/2 (Fall/Winter 1983):3-10.
7. Michael Gorman, "The Future of Serials Control and Its Administrative Implications for Libraries," in *Serials Automation for Acquisition and Inventory Control,* ed. William G. Potter and Arlene F. Sirkin (Chicago: American Library Association, 1981), p.126-127.
8. J. Harris Gable, "The New Serials Department," *Library Journal* 60 (Nov. 15, 1935): 867-871.
9. Donald H. Dyal, "A Survey of Serials Management in Texas," *Texas Libraries* 38 (Winter 1976):164-172.
10. Dyal, "A Survey of Serials Management in Texas," p.167; Victoria A. Johnson, "Organization of Serials Departments in University Libraries" (Master's thesis, Univ. of Chicago, 1973), p.2-3.
11. Jo Ann Hanson, "Trends in Serials Management," *The Serials Librarian* 8, no.4 (Summer 1984):7-12.
12. Jennifer Cargill, "Serials: Separate or Merged?," in *The Serials Collection: Organization and Administration,* ed. Nancy J. Melin (Ann Arbor, Mich.: Pierian Press, 1982), p.15-22.
13. Ibid., p.18-19.
14. Ibid., p.19.
15. William G. Potter, "Form or Function? An Analysis of the Serials Department in the Modern Academic Library," *The Serials Librarian* 6, no.1 (Fall 1981):85-94.
16. Mary H. Monson, "Serials Catalogers: Isolation or Integration?," *Serials Review* 9, no.3 (Fall 1983):65-67.
17. Ibid., p.67.
18. Hanson, "Trends in Serials Management," p.11-12.

19. Pamela Bluh, "Serials Control: Is There a Need for Change?," *The Serials Librarian* 6, no.1 (Fall 1981):17-23.

20. Diane Stine, "Centralized Serials Processing in an Automated Environment," *Serials Review* 9, no.3 (Fall 1983):69-75.

21. Hans H. Weber, "Serials Administration," *The Serials Librarian* 4, no.2 (Winter 1979): 143-165.

22. Mitsuko Collver, "Organization of Serials Work for Manual and Automated Systems," *Library Resources & Technical Services* 24, no.4 (Fall 1980):307-316.

23. Sue A. Harrington and Deborah J. Karpuk, "The Integrated Serials Department: Its Value Today and in the Future," *The Serials Librarian* 9, no.2 (Winter 1984):55-64.

24. Margaret M. McKinley, "Serials Departments: Doomed to Extinction?," *The Serials Librarian* 5, no.2 (Winter 1980):15-24.

25. Margaret M. McKinley, "Serials Staffing Guidelines for the '80s," in *The Serials Collection: Organization and Administration,* ed. Nancy J. Melin (Ann Arbor, Mich.:Pierian Press, 1982) p.35-52.

26. Ibid., p.36.

Serials Automation:
An Annotated Bibliography and Review 1976-1984

Janis D. Fleischmann, MLS
Jean Houghton, MLS, MA

ABSTRACT. This is a review of the literature and a selective, annotated bibliography on serials automation from 1976 to 1984 with an emphasis on recent English language publications. The bibliography is subdivided by topic: bibliographies; reviews and collections; bibliographic control, including ISBD(S), ISDS, ISSN, NSDP, CONSER, and AACR2; serials control, including check-in, claiming, binding and routing; systems and vendors; standards; union catalogs; fiscal control, and the organization of serials work. The selection of 150 citations highlights important events and trends and describes some lesser known developments. This review is written from the point of view of the working technical services librarian. Subjects for further research are suggested.

INTRODUCTION

We will spare the reader any more definitions of the term "serial."

It was our intention to produce a workable and informative bibliography with annotations for those who wish to trace the development of an idea or who need information on a serials automation-related subject. Our own institution has been engaged in an exhaustive search for the perfect integrated system; and as we have had numerous occasions to comb the literature for something (ANYTHING) on a subject or a system, appreciate the difficulty of the task, even in these days of LISA and the OCLC ILL subsystem. For this reason, we have divided the bibliography by subject and have been somewhat selective, emphasizing more recent publications that are not covered elsewhere.

SCOPE/ARRANGEMENT

The years covered are 1976-1984. Topics included are: Bibliographies, Collections and reviews, Bibliographic control, Serials control

---

Ms. Fleischmann is Technical Services Unit Coordinator, Wayne State University Libraries, Detroit, MI 48202. Ms. Houghton is Acting Assistant Director for Technical Services, Wayne State University Libraries, Detroit, MI 48202. Both are former serials librarians.

© 1986 by The Haworth Press, Inc. All rights reserved.

(check-in, routing, claiming, binding), Systems/vendors, Union catalogs (union lists, catalogs), Standards, Fiscal control and Organization of serials work. Publications on applications using microcomputers and minicomputers have been included in the appropriate category above. Each topic is subarranged in alphabetical order.

Although all of the subjects dealt with are international concerns, and many reflect international cooperative efforts, the bibliography is directed toward an English language readership, and consists primarily of English language titles with Canadian and U.S. imprints.

Included also are other references, either because they are very interesting or important, because the subject is truly international in scope or origin, or occasionally because it is desired to show the similarity of problems being worked on in very different corners of the globe.

Excluded are general automation developments, system or vendor supplied documentation, short newsletter and announcement-type citations. We did not review the growing literature on electronic publishing and alternative forms of text storage, such as optical disk vs. digital storage. We excluded literature on indexes and abstracts, both manual and online, as well as the technical aspects of electronic document delivery.

We made every attempt to actually read and review all cited articles and books. This was not always possible, of course, and in some cases we had to depend upon secondary sources for the annotation.

Bibliographies

Pitkin should be viewed as the base of all subsequent bibliographies on serials automation. He covers *Library Literature* through 1974 in his first work, and then published an amendment extending coverage through 1980. Allison covers the decade 1970-1979. The American Library Association Resources and Technical Services Division attempted to produce an annual bibliography starting in 1980 (Linkins). Unfortunately, we have not seen follow-ups announced after April 1981.

Collections and Reviews

The summer issue of *Library Resources and Technical Services* contained a review of serials events and publications throughout this period ending with the review for the year 1982. In 1983, the serials review was combined in an overall technical services article written by Joe A. Hewitt, who does not have much to say about serials. None of the 18 references are unique to serials. The 1984 review had not appeared at the time of our writing in early 1985.

Conferences are covered in this section, beginning with the Canadian

Association of College and University Libraries Serials Dynamics conference in 1976. Proceedings of the annual meetings of the International Federation of Library Associations are represented. There was an important LITA serials conference in 1980. The Meckler Communications-sponsored annual serials conferences began in 1981. No conference in this series was held in 1984. However, beginning that year, there was increased attendance at the annual UK Serials Group Conference; and many guests from outside the UK were welcomed at the 7th annual Serials Group Conference, Guildford, England, March 1984. Also in 1984, a pre-conference on serials was held in conjunction with the American Library Association annual conference.

Several important collections, especially Gellatly's *Management of Serials Automation* and Melin's *The Serials Collection,* were published in the early 1980s. A new series, *Current Issues in Serials Management,* was introduced in 1982. And the James E. Rush Associates' *Serials Control* was a welcome addition to the literature.

Because of the number of articles in our area of interest and overall subject matter, we have cited some publications covering the field of serials automation by title: *The Serials Librarian, Serials Review, Title Varies, Voice of Z39.* All of these are alive and well (with titles unchanged) in 1985, except *Title Varies,* which issued its penultimate issue in December 1980 and presumably the final issue in January 1981.

Bibliographic Control

Nineteen seventy-six to nineteen eighty-five has been an action-packed decade for serials cataloging, including but not limited to: OCLC acceptance of serials records; anticipating and accommodating the second edition of the Anglo-American Cataloging Rules (AACR2); the growth of the CONversion of SERials (CONSER) concept and database; the International Serials Data System and its various national implementation agencies; the development and use of the International Standard Serial Number (ISSN); the use of machine-readable cataloging records as the base for other systems and products; Title IIC projects; and much, much more.

At the heart of all these developments is concern for international standards and machine-readable information exchange. We have attempted to reflect this in our choice of citations. Articles are included on subjects on which no great body of literature exists, either because of this fact or because of the stature of the author (Gorman) or simply because they are interesting (Lupton).

This high activity level obviously produced a lot more print than is represented in this bibliography, much of it outdated a few months after publication as communications attempted to keep up with changing rules and events. We have tried to assemble salient articles and representative samples, not to cover the universe on AACR2, CONSER, and all the rest.

Serials Control

This section covers ways and means of "nailing jello" (Allison), except when confined to implementation experience with a single system. These are treated under Systems/Vendors.

First, we have included articles illustrating the debate: is automation better than the existing manual system? The Kardex is easy to grasp, has all pertinent information in one handy place and suffers no down-time. This point of view is adamantly expressed by Huibert Paul. Dan Tonkery replies to Paul's defense of manual systems, while Riddick objectively compares cost and check-in time between OCLC and the Iowa State University manual system.

Most serialists, however, have stopped fighting the do or don't battle, and are instead thinking when/how much/which system. System comparisons exist but are not as numerous or recent as most of us would like (Schmidt, Saxe).

Internal histories of serials automation at a single site covering several types or generations of systems are also interesting and informative. We are including those of Lister Hill (Forsman) and the British Library Lending Division (Harley).

Although it is assumed to be best when check-in, claiming, routing and binding are all integrated in a single system, no system to date incorporates all four. Independent, although still automated, components, such as binder-produced control slips (*Preservation of Library Materials,* Columbia) or homegrown stand-alone binding control systems (Kim) are parallel developments we have tried to cover, including the increased use of microcomputers for task control.

Systems/Vendors

In the early 1980s integrated systems that included functional or planned online cataloging capability, OPAC, circulation, acquisitions and serials control, were advertised as available (and in some cases, actually were available). At the same time, more and more stand-alone serials control systems were developed including the successful subscription agent systems, which neatly link some fiscal information, but provide no link to the catalog (Lowell).

In-house systems, which had proliferated in the '60s, showed remarkable resilience (Fallon), and some went commercial, notably PHILSOM (Pletzke) and NOTIS (Willmering). Most recent entries are turnkey vendor systems. Very few institutions now have the resources to program serials control from scratch, although they may be cooperating on a pilot project or alphasite installation of a system, such as the Geac International system at the University of Waterloo, Ontario, where serials control has been tested.

The literature is replete with articles describing implementation of a particular system in a particular place at a particular time. These "how we did it" articles can be invaluable to those attempting the same or a similar implementation. The more established serials control systems are very well covered, e.g.: NOTIS, OCLC, PHILSOM. Even systems developed in the early 1980s have been around long enough to be found in the literature, e.g.: CHECKMATE, EBSCONET, LINX, PERLINE. Other systems such as Geac or INNOVACQ have not been written about at all to our knowledge.

Union Catalogs/Union Lists

Title IIC money provided an opportunity for many libraries to convert bibliographic records to machine readable format as well as to complete union listing projects.

Union listing literature is dominated by the reports of or descriptions of individual projects. We have chosen a selection ranging from British Columbia (Komorous) to Grenoble (Barral), and from large (Upham) to small (Kimzey), usually preferring the latest article on a system when several were available. Likewise, we have cited the most recent in the case of general surveys or histories, since the later tend to recap the earlier, unless especially unusual (Zhogoleva).

Articles about technical concerns such as summary holdings statements (Bales) have been included in this section when they were not primarily about standards, which is treated as a separate topic.

Increasingly, bibliographic records have been linked to or formed the basis of, other systems/products, especially union lists. As Reid, at the beginning of the decade said: "The serial concerned has to be defined and described; if it is not defined in such a way as to be compatible with the definitions of other libraries, then it is, to all intents and purposes, a different serial. The holdings statements will not mesh with other statements and a union list or union catalogue environment will not be possible." Writings on cataloging implications (Carter, Bloss) are therefore included in this section.

Standards

Throughout this period the International Organization for Standards (ISO) and its member agents had an impact on library operations. The

U.S. agent, American National Standards Institute (ANSI) Z39 Committee issued publications under the name of American National Standards Committee (Z39) until 1984 when it changed its name to National Information Standards Organization (Z39), generally known as NISO.

Five standards were drafted, revised or issued during this period. This section includes citations for the latest version of the serials standard itself, guidelines for use, and works discussing implementation of the standards.

On the international level, guidelines for union listing, edited by Whiffen, were published by the Haworth Press, Inc., and by the International Federation of Library Associations (IFLA).

Fiscal Control

Payment and fund accounting are not unique to serials. Accounting systems must work for all purchases on the materials budget. It is, therefore, not surprising that there is little written on fiscal control for serials alone (Myers). It is surprising that there is so little written about fiscal control of acquisitions in general, especially considering that this is a major concern of library administrators. Serials payment control and fund accounting are subjects on which we think more writing is needed.

On the other hand, many articles appear in the literature on shrinking library budgets and the use of automation to control serials holdings. For example, cancellation lists using automated means are frequent, and these are included in this section (Carter, Fuller).

Organization of Serials Work

Are separate serials departments better for the patron and/or more efficient in an automated environment? There are regular appearances in the literature of an ongoing debate between the form defenders and the function advocates, with more representation from the serialist-separatist side (Collver, Melin) than the function folks (Cargill). A selection of these are included in this final section.

CONCLUSION

Our search of the literature revealed some gaps, especially research or writings on fiscal control of serials, binding and other follow-up serial functions, and the place of serials systems within integrated systems. Is it significant that our search of the literature using LISA, ERIC, and *Library Literature,* as well as the more old-fashioned methods of tracking down citations in other works and wading through all issues of important titles, could turn up only one method of serials fiscal control and that using punched cards? Similarly, we found only one treatment of binder-produced control slips, although we know many libraries are using this feature. Is there no writing on why CODEN fell from favor? We would like to suggest these as areas of further research or reporting of experiences.

BIBLIOGRAPHIES

Allison, Anne Marie. "Automated Serials Control: A Bibliographic Survey." In *The Management of Serials Automation. Current Technology and Strategies for Future Planning,* edited with an introduction by Peter Gellatly. New York: The Haworth Press, 1982.
 A review and selective bibliography spanning the 1970s, with special emphasis on the latter half of the decade.

Allison, Anne Marie, and Donahue, Janice E. "Automated Serials Control: A Selected Bibliography." In *The Management of Serials Automation. Current Technology and Strategies for Future Planning,* edited with an introduction by Peter Gellatly. New York: The Haworth Press, 1982.
 Companion-piece to the bibliographic survey above. Arranged chronologically. Intended to complement Pitkin; does not duplicate citations.

Hensley, Charlotta C. "Serials Standards: A Bibliography." in *Library Serials Standards: Development, Implementation, Impact. Proceedings of the Third Annual Serials Conference,* edited by Nancy Jean Melin. 149-161. Westport, CT: Meckler Publishing, 1984.
 Comprehensive, includes about 85 entries.

Linkins, Germaine C. "Bibliography of Articles and Monographs on Serials." *Serials Review* 7, no. 3 (July/September 1981):105-109.
 A continuation and update to the First Annual Bibliography of Articles and Monographs on Serials published in August of 1980 by the American Library Association, Resources and Technical Services Division. Like the first it was compiled by the Library School Education Committee of the Serials Section, RTSD/ALA.
 Covers May 1980-April 1981.

Pitkin, Gary M. *Serials Automation in the United States: A Bibliographic History.* Metuchen, NJ: Scarecrow Press, 1976.
 Covers the literature from 1951 to 1974, including some citations that go back to 1949. Approximately 100 entries are arranged in chronological order (which may not appeal to some), with annotations relying heavily on quoted matter. Perhaps restricting the review to *Library Literature*

alone is the only criticism of this classic work. A comprehensive index by serials control function, indicating type of library and name of the institution, appears as an appendix.

Pitkin, Gary M. "Serials Automation: A Selected and Annotated Bibliography," in *Serials Automation for Acquisition and Inventory Control,* edited by William Gray Potter and Arlene Farber Sirkin, 160-177. Chicago: American Library Association, 1981.

Contains 35 references to post-1974 material relating to computerized periodicals control. Intended as a supplement to his 1954-1974 bibliography.

COLLECTIONS AND REVIEWS

Glasby, Dorothy J. "Serials in 1978." *Library Resources and Technical Services* 23, no. 3 (Summer 1979): 203-212.

Responsibility for CONSER is taken over by OCLC, which also announces a limit of 150 libraries on its serials control subsystem until claims can be added and other problems resolved. The effect of the new cataloging rules is an important concern and price increases continue, spawning in-house systems for evaluation and cancellation of serials.

Glasby, Dorothy J. "Serials in 1979." *Library Resources and Technical Services* 24, no. 3 (Summer 1980): 274-82.

CONSER continues to be a major topic; and an increased interest in union listing, holdings and location information is noted. The author is, significantly, the CONSER Operations Coordinator at the Library of Congress. Prices go on rising.

Glasby, Dorothy J. "Serials in 1980." *Library Resources and Technical Services* 25, no. 3 (July/September 1981): 310-318.

The cost of serials and ways and means of acquiring and controlling subscriptions, explorations in resource sharing, especially union listing, and worries about AACR2 are important issues. The reorganization of serials work by function in response to the computer environment is increasingly evident and hotly debated.

Hewitt, Joe A. "Technical Services in 1983." *Library Resources and Technical Services* 28, no. 3 (July-September 1984): 205-218.

The year's work in serials has been abandoned in favor of an overall treatment of technical services issues, perhaps paralleling the organizational move from separate serials departments to a functional approach. Automation is a part of every issue discussed, but serials are hardly mentioned as a separate concern.

International Federation of Library Associations. Collections and Services Division. Serials Publications Section. *Papers Presented at the 48th Annual Meeting of the International Federation of Library Associations.* The Hague: IFLA, 1982. Microfiche. ED227872 IR050193

Papers presented at the IFLA 48th Annual Meeting, Montreal, August 22-28, 1982. Includes papers on CONSER; ISDS; NOSP (Nordisk Samkatalog over Periodica) and other Scandinavian developments; and periodicals agents.

International Federation of Library Associations. Collections and Services Division. Serials Publications Section. *Papers Presented at the 49th Annual Meeting of the International Federation of Library Associations.* The Hague: IFLA, 1983. Microfiche. ED239632 IR050598

Papers presented at the IFLA 49th Annual Meeting, Munich, August 21-27, 1983. Includes papers on ISDS; automated check-in at a university in Florence; evaluation of serials control systems.

James E. Rush Associates, Inc. *Serials Control. Library Systems Evaluation Guide,* vol. 1. Powell, OH: James E. Rush Associates, 1983.

Includes description of functional requirements for automated serials control systems; methodology for systems evaluation; data element definitions; inventory of available serials control systems; and more.

The Mitsuko Collver review in *Serials Review,* Spring 1984, states that the work "admirably fulfills the author's intention to present in concise, easily usable format basic information on the requirements for and techniques of evaluation of automated library applications" and that it is "well organized and not overly technical." Discusses serials control in isolation from the library's overall information network, but its shortcomings are greatly outweighed by its strengths.

James, John R. "Serials in 1976." *Library Resources and Technical Services* 21, no. 3 (Summer 1977): 216-231.

Inflation was the major preoccupation of 1976, followed by the CONSER project, revision of the cataloging code, ISBD(S), National Serials Data Program (NSDP), and the development of standards. New publications are reviewed, including *The Serials Librarian.*

James, John R. "Serials in 1977." *Library Resources and Technical Services* 22, no. 3 (Summer 1978): 294-309.

Nineteen seventy-seven is described in this review as a "watershed year" in that many ongoing projects reached a significant stage of development, including the printing of the second edition of AACR (Anglo-American Cataloging Rules) and the first standard edition of ISBD(S). OCLC check-in and catalog card production are hailed, as is completion of the first stage of CONSER. Increasing costs continue to be a major issue.

Library Serials Standards: Development, Implementation, Impact. Proceedings of the Third Annual Serials Conference, edited by Nancy Jean Melin. Westport, CT: Meckler Publishing, 1984.

Contains 18 papers—more than you ever wanted to know about standards. Not confined to bibliographic and union listing standards. Performance measures for staff are included, for instance. Claiming standards are included, but serials control standards are otherwise not covered.

The Management of Serials Automation. Current Technology and Strategies for Future Planning, edited with an introduction by Peter Gellatly. New York: The Haworth Press, 1982.

Monographic supplement to *The Serials Librarian,* Volume 6, 1981/82. There are 26 articles, all of which fall within the scope of this bibliography and could be separately cited. Includes reviews of several serials control systems (University of California at San Diego, NOTIS, University of Illinois, OCLC and Brigham Young); conversion experiences from the University of Illinois and Ohio State, updates on OCLC, ISSN and NSDP; Neal Edgar on computerized serials cataloging; union listing; serials treatment on WLN and RLIN and the viewpoint of the subscription agent.

In the Minna Saxe review (*Serials Review,* Fall 1983), it is "highly recommended, well organized, well indexed" although there was a considerable delay in publication, as most articles seem to have been written in 1979.

Pitkin, Gary M. "Serials News." *The Serials Librarian.*

Pitkin, as news editor, writes the Serials News section in each issue of *The Serials Librarian.* Covers the ground in serials librarianship in these four categories: (1) Networks/Consortia and Library-Oriented Organizations; (2) Library Schools; (3) Vendor/Publisher Services; (4) Libraries. Includes automation issues.

Serials and Microforms: Patron-Oriented Management. Proceedings of the Second Annual Serials Conference and Eighth Annual Microforms Conference, edited by Nancy Jean Melin. Westport, CT: Meckler Publishing, 1983.

Conference held October 22-23, 1982, Columbus, Ohio. Includes 15 papers, 6 of which are included below as separate citations.

Serials Automation for Acquisition and Inventory Control, edited by William Gray Potter and Arlene Farber Sirkin. Chicago: American Library Association, 1981.

Papers from the Institute, Milwaukee, September 4-5, 1980, Library and Information Technology Association, American Library Association.

The actual emphasis of the published papers is on inventory control and receiving functions, rather than acquisitions functions. Phillips in a *Library Acquisitions: Practice & Theory* (7, no. 2, 1983) review, states that "Serials acquisitions is a specialized segment of the overall problem of serials automation and is difficult to discuss without treating the entire subject."

The Serials Collection: Organization and Administration, edited by Nancy Jean Melin. *Current Issues in Serials Management,* no. 1. Ann Arbor, MI: Pierian Press, 1982.

Contains an introduction and 14 articles, some of which deal with serials automation, for example, the impact of AACR2 and automated check-in.

Serials Dynamics: Proceedings of a Workshop, edited by Jean Whiffin, Workshop Convenor. *The Serials Librarian* 3, no. 3, Spring 1979: 219-314.

Sponsored by the Canadian Association of College and University Libraries, Halifax, Nova Scotia, June 11-12, 1976. Five of the 6 papers presented at a continuing education workshop for serials librarians and a summary of the 6th paper, plus an introduction and concluding statement by the convenor. The workshop attempted to provide a state of the art review of bibliographic and holdings control, with particular reference to present and future uses of the MARC-S formats.

Outdated but still interesting. Canadian emphasis.

The Serials Librarian. New York: The Haworth Press, v.1, no.1 (Fall 1976)-

Quarterly. Edited by Peter Gellatly. Definitely a "must" on the reading list of all serials librarians.

Serials Management in an Automated Age: Proceedings of the First Annual Serials Conference, edited by Nancy Jean Melin. Westport, CT: Meckler Publishing, 1982.

Conference was held October 30-31, 1981, Arlington, Virginia. Eight papers of which 3 are cited below.

Serials Review. Ann Arbor, MI: Pierian Press. v. 1, no. 1, (January/June 1975)-

Quarterly. Began by 1980 to cover serials automation topics in earnest. Nancy Jean Melin was the editor from 1978 to 1983. Volume 10, no. 1, announced new editors: Will Hepfer and Carolyn Mueller.

Taylor, David C. *Managing the Serials Explosion. The Issues for Publishers and Libraries.* White Plains, NY: Knowledge Industry, 1982.

A practical look at serials work and serials budgets in the 1980s. Serials automation is covered in Chapter 8. Analyzes what can and can't be automated and gives cost data. Has an excellent bibliography.

Unfavorably reviewed by Margaret McKinley (*Serials Review,* Summer 1983). "Taylor's summarization of well-known efforts to develop computer-assisted processing systems for serials is an inadequate description of the current state of the art."

Title Varies. East Lansing, MI, etc.: D. C. Taylor. v.1, no.1-v.6, no.6 (December 1973-January 1981).

The brainchild of David Taylor and Henry Yaple. Taylor was also editor from 1973 to 1977 and again in 1980-81 (July/November 1977 with Marcia Tuttle). Edited in 1979 by Lynn S. Smith. Newsletter format. Primarily for exchange of title/organization name changes between serials practitioners, but frequently included serious articles on AACR2, CONSER and other serials automation issues.

Union Lists: Issues and Answers, edited by Dianne Ellsworth. *Current Issues in Serials Management,* no. 2. Ann Arbor, MI.: Pierian Press, 1982.

Proceedings of a workshop on union lists of serials held in San Francisco, December 8, 1979, sponsored by the Technical Services Chapter of the California Library Association. Includes numerous short papers including reports on the California Library Authority for Systems and Services (CLASS), various California union lists, Blackwell North America (B/NA), OCLC, Inc., Research Libraries Group, University of Toronto Library Automation Systems (UTLAS), Washington Library Network (WLN), Title IIC, AACR2, union listing on microcomputers, and more. Must be viewed as a report on the state of affairs in 1979; a great deal has happened since then.

Voice of Z39. Washington, DC: National Information Standards Organization (Z39). v.1, no.1- (January 1979)-

A quarterly publications with "news about library, information science, and publishing standards," reports of recent activity on standards in development or in draft, as well as price and availability of published standards.

Weber, Benita M. "The Year's Work in Serials: 1981." *Library Resources and Technical Services* 26, no. 3 (July/September 1982): 277-293.

Day One of AACR2 is described as the "first step on the road to AACR2 1/2 or AACR3," not much comfort for traditionalists. The first

Annual Serials Conference is held, union listing is hot and dialog on the best organizational pattern for serials work goes on.

Weber, Benita M. "The Year's Work in Serials: 1982." *Library Resources and Technical Services* 27, no. 3 (July/September 1983): 243-258.

Nineteen eighty-two is characterized by the author as a year of reflection on past events rather than one of great advances. The author predicts, from the literature, that collections will take a back seat to access to resources. The cost of subscriptions, bibliographic control, automated systems, and the future of serials departments are covered.

BIBLIOGRAPHIC CONTROL

Anderson, D. "Compatibility of ISDS and ISBD(S) Records in International Exchange." *International Cataloguing* 12 (April 1983): 14-17.

International Serials Data System and International Standard for Bibliographic Description (Serials) update.

Bartley, L. K. "ISSN and NSDP (National Serials Data Program): A Guide For the Initiated," in *The Management of Serials Automation. Current Technology and Strategies for Future Planning,* edited with an introduction by Peter Gellatly, 171-177. New York, The Haworth Press, 1982.

Bartley, L. K. "International Standard Serial Number (ISSN) and Its Use by the United States Postal Service." *Unesco Journal of Information Science, Librarianship and Archives Administration* 2 (October-December 1980): 245-251.

Blixrud, Julia C. "CONSER A & I Project Update." *CONSER* 9 (December 1984): 3-5.

The latest word on progress on the addition of abstracting and indexing coverage to CONSER records, including information on the number of titles, analysis by type, methodology and a list of titles covered.

Bloss, Alexander. "AACR2 North and South: Serials Cataloging from the Library of Congress and the National Library of Canada." *Serials Review* 9, no. 4 (Winter 1983):84-90.

Discusses differing interpretations of AACR2 by LC and the NLC. "These may include such data elements as parallel edition statements, other title information and linking entries in AACR1, choice of entry." Illustrates concern for potential "continental drift" in response to institutional or national need.

Bourne, Ross. "Building A Serials File." *Program; Automated Library and Information Systems* 12, no. 2 (April 1978): 78-86.

This is a straightforward summary of international standards, such as ISDS and ISBD(S). The author describes CONSER, the authentication process and the role of CONSER participants. He discusses implications and recommendations for BLAISE, the British Library Automated Information Service, which was introduced in 1977.

Bradley, Isabel. "International Standard Serial Numbers and the International Serials Data System." *The Serials Librarian* 3, no.3 (Spring 1979): 243-253.

Traces history of ISSN and ISDS from 1967, with more detail about ISDS Canada, uses and sources of ISSNs, key titles, etc.

Braithwaite, R. J. et al. "The UTLAS CATSS System." *VINE* 39 (August 1981): 46-49.

Describes the University of Toronto Library Automation Systems, a total approach to library automation for French and English libraries. Comprised of three distinct yet compatible systems: the Acquisitions and Serials Control System (ASC); the Catalogue Support System (CATSS); and the Library Collection Management System (LCMS). Describes CATSS, which is at the heart of all UTLAS services.

Carter, Ruth C. "Playing by the Rules—AACR2 and Serials," in *Serials Management in an Automated Age: Proceedings of the First Annual Serials Conference,* edited by Nancy Jean Melin, 11-29. Westport, CT: Meckler Publishing, 1982.

Cole, Jim E. "AACR2 and ISBD(S): Correspondence or Divergence." *Serials Review* 8, no.3 (Fall 1982):67-69.

Shows differences in a clearly outlined summary.

Corey, James F. "OCLC and Serials Processing: A State of Transition at the University of Illinois." *The Serials Librarian* 3, no. 1 (Fall 1978): 57-67.

Describes the University of Illinois experience with serials cataloging on OCLC and the reasons for the decision *not* to use OCLC for serials check-in (proprietary nature of files, lack of cost data, response time, etc.). Includes suggestions for further research.

Davis, Carol C. "OCLC's Role in the CONSER Project." *Serials Review* 6, no.4 (October/December 1980):75-77.

The CONSER Project was established under the administration of the Council on Library Resources, Inc., to develop a high-quality database of serials cataloging information. When grant funds for the Project expired, the administration of the Project was assumed by OCLC. The Library of Congress now assumes the financial responsibility for the staff necessary to authenticate the serial records, while OCLC hosts the bibliographic database and is responsible for the day-to-day administration of the project. Describes the maintenance of the database; processing of duplicate record reports; administrative support of CONSER project; etc.

Durance, Cynthia J. "International Serials Cataloging." *The Serials Librarian* 3, no.3 (Spring 1979):299-309.

Idealistically outlines the benefits of UAI (Universal Access to Information) and UBC (Universal Bibliographic Control.)

The second part of the article describes the need for revising AACR and the mechanisms for national or interest groups to suggest rule revisions, followed by an overview of how serials cataloging would probably be affected (a long way from settled at the time this paper was delivered in 1976).

Edgar, Neal. "ISBD(S): A Descriptive Evaluation." *Title Varies* 4, no. 4-6 (July-November 1977): 33-34.

Describes the concept, function and purposes of the International Standard Bibliographic Description (Serials), calling it "logical, well-constructed and reasonable" and stressing its importance to serials. Edgar urges serials librarians to study the standard and prepare for its application.

Gorman, Michael and Robert H. Burger. "Serial Control in a Developed Machine System." *The Serials Librarian* 5, no. 1 (Fall 1980):13-26.

Vintage Gorman. The system of the future is constructed so that the end user knows the structure of a complex serial/series publication, how the individual piece fits in and its relationship to all the other parts.

Graham, Crystal. "Serials Cataloging on RLIN: A User's Viewpoint." *Serials Review* 9, no. 3 (Fall 1983):87-91.

The Research Libraries Information Network is described as "a top-quality bibliographic network. Sophisticated search keys, the content of the database, and the availability of local data online are only some of its valuable features."

Griffin, David E. "Serials Review in the Washington Library Network." *Serials Review* 10, no.1 (Spring 1984):61-73.

Since its inception in 1976, WLN has remained committed to the concept of a single bibliographic file for all participants and a single record per bibliographic item. A "review" process was instituted, and this is described by the author, who admits that it is "always labor-intensive, usually systematic, sometimes frustrating and misunderstood."

Hartman, Matt. "Serials Cataloging: UTLAS and the Machine Environment at the University of British Columbia." *Serials Review* 7, no.1 (January/March 1981):93-95.
   Written in 1981 after the decision to abandon UTLAS in favor of the National Library of Canada version of DOBIS. Transition will take two years if there is government funding. This is one serials cataloger's view of automation and its impact on daily work.

Jacobs, Mary Ellen, et al. *"Online Resource Sharing II. A Comparison of: OCLC, Incorporated, Research Libraries Information Network, and Washington Library Network.* San Jose: California Library Authority for Systems and Services, 1979.
   Compares three major online bibliographic systems in these areas: services and access, searchability, process and products associated with online cataloging, acquisitions and serials control, applications to other library functions, financial and administrative considerations, and system administration.

Kilton, Tom D. "OCLC and the Pre-Order Verification of New Serials." *The Serials Librarian* 4, no. 1 (Fall 1979):61-64.
   Describes the University of Illinois experience on a small sample of pre-order verification work.

Lupton, David Walker. "Tracking the ISSN." *The Serials Librarian* 4, no. 2 (Winter 1979): 187-198.
   Colorado State University completed a study of International Standard Serial Numbers and their occurrence on the serial piece. Nearly 13,000 serials were examined. Approximately 25% of the titles contained an ISSN in one or more of seven dominant locations.

Neubauer, K. W. "The National Serial Data System in the Federal Republic of Germany." *Serials Review* 7, no.1 (January/March 1981):73-81.
   Describes and traces the history of the organizational structures of the three large West German serial systems. Although they were developed separately, it is planned that they will either link to or be supervised by the national serials data system. Includes a list of products with holdings and prices.

Reuland, Beth. "Successive Entry: Another Look." *Serials Review* 9, no. 3 (Fall 1983):92-3.

A short article on the virtues of successive entry cataloging. Also points out some weaknesses, such as keeping ordering and payment information together, the increase in the number of cards in the catalog, and problems with unstable titles, and explores implications for the online catalog.

Rice, Patricia. "ISBD(S): A Review." *Title Varies* 4, no. 4-6 (July-November 1977): 32.
  A short article reviewing major provisions of the 1977 version of the International Standard Bibliographic Description (Serials) and a companion piece to Edgar. "The main purpose of the ISBD program is to aid in the international exchange of bibliographic information across language barriers and among various types of national bibliographic agencies." "One can only hope that these developments will make serials cataloging more rational, more satisfying, and more helpful to the user."

Szilvassy, Judith. "ISDS: Worldwide Serials Control." *IFLA Journal/International Federation of Library Associations* 8 (November 1982): 371-378.

SERIALS CONTROL

Cargill, Jennifer. "The Vendor Services Supermarket: The New Consumerism," in *Serials and Microforms: Patron-Oriented Management. Proceedings of the Second Annual Serials Conference and Eighth Annual Microforms Conference,* edited by Nancy Jean Melin, 98-109. Westport, CT: Meckler Publishing, 1983.
  Looks at products available from subscription agents and other vendors and suggests ways to assist the librarian in serials work. For example, machine-readable invoices are available from Faxon and EBSCO. Both of these vendors also provide adhesive-backed labels to use for posting payments in the library's check-in file, informational aids such as claim reports, listings of titles sorted in various ways such as by frequency and off-site check-in. Librarians should also consider electronic ordering, binder-supplied pre-printed slips, and USBE online.

Clasquin, Frank F. "Library and Subscription Agent Electronics." *The Serials Librarian* 7, no. 3 (Spring 1983): 7-16.
  Discusses the future and the changing role of subscription agents as we move toward electronic information transfer systems. Publishing, billing processes, and library records will all change, but the agent will still be needed.

Cole, Susie and Cindy Hill. "Automating Library Systems with PFS." *Access; Microcomputers in Libraries* 2 (Oct. 1982): 11-14.

Describes how the library of the U.S. company Acurex Corporation has automated its serials acquisitions and circulation procedures using an Apple microcomputer and the database management system, PFS (Personal Filing System).

De Gennaro, Richard. "Wanted: A Minicomputer Serials Control System." *Library Journal* 102 (15 April 1977): 878-879.

An early view of serials control and viability of interface with bibliographic databases. Maintains that separate online catalogs, circulation systems and serials control will give libraries flexibility and eventual interface if MARC and CONSER records are used by all.

Forsman, Rick B. "EBSCONET Serials Control System: A Case History and Analysis." *Serials Review* 8, no.4 (Winter 1982):83-85.

The Lister Hill Library of the Health Sciences, University of Alabama, has about 5,000 active and inactive serials controlled by EBSCONET. In the late '60s Lister Hill experimented with a local batch process modeled on the PHILSOM system. In 1975 they began, through grant funding, converting records to the format used by the UCLA system. Owing to hardware differences, several major changes were made to the software obtained from UCLA, resulting in a system unique to the environment and needs of Lister Hill. In December 1976 it was considered successful enough to discontinue the Kardex. Enhancements were impossible because, after the funding was lifted, Lister Hill had no programming staff. By 1981 a new system was needed, and a switch made to EBSCO in May 1981.

Franz, Ted. "Automated Standing Order System, Blackwell North America." *Serials Review* 7, no.1 (January/March 1981):63-66.

Describes the B/NA standing order system in response to a "Tools of the Trade" column on manual standing order control. Gives the history from 1975 (the system was developed by Richard Abel & Co.) including conversion, entry description, operation, interface with approval programs and future plans.

Grosch, Audrey N. "Serial Arrival Prediction Coding: A Serial Predictive Model for Use by System Designers." *Information Processing and Management* 12, no. 2 (1976): 141-146.

Useful information for library systems staff writing specifications.

Harley, A. J. "Automated Serials Control at the British Library Lending Division." *Program; Automated Library and Information Systems* 15, no. 4 (October 1981):200-208.

Describes serials automation at BLLD from the early 1960s to 1981. Serials work at the BLLD is shared by four sections: Serials Acquisitions, Serials Records (Cataloging/Bibliographic), Serials Accessions (check-in), and Stores (interloans). This article reviews development of serials acquisitions automation (subscription and payment records) and of the handling of interloan requests (350,000 per year) using minicomputer equipment. Microfiche keyword indexes are produced from the Serials Master File.

Hines, Theodore C., Lois Winkel, and Rosann Collins. "Microcomputers and the Serials Librarian." *The Serials Librarian* 4, no.3 (Spring 1980): 275-279.

Reports on ways to use a micro in serials work: creation of a periodicals list with indexing; word processing; Index to Criminal Justice periodicals. As seen at the University of North Carolina.

Kim, David U. "Computer-Assisted Binding Preparation at a University Library." *The Serials Librarian* 9, no. 2 (Winter 1984):35-42.

Describes a system for control of approximately 3,000 titles. This is an in-house system, involving a master file (Binding Information File with a 138-character record) and a Bindery Shipment File. Bindery slips and packing/binding lists are printed. This system is used at Houston State University Library, which reports that a great deal of time is saved in bindery record keeping.

Koenig, Michael E. "Serials Processing and Scale Economies." *Journal of Library Administration* 3, no.1 (Spring 1982): 59-66.

History of automated serials processing, and cost analysis.

Lupton, David Walker. "Magazines, Supermarkets, and the Universal Product Code." *The Serials Librarian* 1, no. 4 (Summer 1977):373-383.

Describes utilization of bar-codes by publishers of popular cross-over magazines. Interesting and unusual topic not often seen in library literature (the bibliography is almost entirely of marketing specialty titles). Bar-coded titles are possible future check-in access point.

Marcum, Deanna and Richard Boss. "Information Technology." *Wilson Library Bulletin* 57, no. 2 (October 1982):154-155.

This is a very short article without very many details, but it is still useful since it compares OCLC's Serials Control Subsystem, Faxon's LINX, Ebsco's EBSCONET, and CLASS' CHECKMATE.

Morton, Donald J. "The Use of a Subscription Agent's Computer Facilities in Creating and Maintaining a Library's Subscription Profile." *Library Resources and Technical Services* 22, no. 4 (Fall 1978): 386-389.

The ability to meet title and cost targets in a given discipline in deselecting and maintaining a subscription core collection can be greatly enhanced through use of the agent's computer services.

Paul, Huibert. "Automation of Serials Check-in: Like Growing Bananas in Greenland? Part 1." *The Serials Librarian* 6, no.2 (Winter 1981): 3-16.

Staunch and emotional defense of the Kardex. Manual systems are efficient and cheap; they are updated every 30 seconds. Among automated systems, only NOTIS is recommended, but it has not been proven cost-effective. An ideal automated system should do everything including writing checks. Check-in is the most important serials function—the rest of serials work can be compared to planets revolving around a sun.

Paul, Huibert. "Automation of Serials Check-In: Like Growing Bananas in Greenland? Part 2." *The Serials Librarian* 6, no. 4 (Summer 1982): 39-62.

Like Part 1, this article serves to draw attention to serials issues and complexities. Paul is very concerned about costs. He refers to printed union catalogs and printouts of check-in information as "information inflation" and "bibliographic overkill." He admits Kardex sweeps are tedious and that using bindery ticklers and slips are time-consuming. He states again that NOTIS is perhaps to be recommended, but suggests that there is no sense in automating if a library has fewer than 8,000-10,000 serials.

Pitkin, Gary. "Automated Serials Systems: Putting the Patron First," in *Serials and Microforms: Patron-Oriented Management. Proceedings of the Second Annual Serials Conference and Eighth Annual Microforms Conference,* edited by Nancy Jean Melin, 27-43. Westport, CT: Meckler Publishing, 1983.

Describes task analysis at Appalachian State University, comparing a manual method of check-in and claiming using Faxon's LINX. Discusses cost effectiveness, and makes a case for automation. The methodology of the study is well described. As a result, the Kardex was discontinued after five months on LINX. Tells of plans to bring system up for patrons using "display only" mode, due Summer 1984.

Potter, William Gray. "Available Automated Check-In Systems: A Panel Discussion," in *Serials Automation for Acquisition and Inventory Control,* edited by William Gray Potter and Arlene Farber Sirkin, 77-99. Chicago, American Library Association, 1981.

A panel discussion from the LITA Institute moderated by Potter, with dialog between Jim Stephens of EBSCO, Jerry Lowell of Faxon, Ronald

Gardner of OCLC, and Millard F. Johnson representing PHILSOM. A 1980 comparison of the four systems.

Preservation of Library Materials: A CUL Handbook: Guidelines and Procedures. New York: Columbia University. The Libraries, 1980. Microfiche. ED212258 IR009964

Contains a detailed review of the procedures involved in sending materials for treatment, including the preparation of a standard binding slip and a description of the General Bookbinding Company's Automated Binding Control System.

Reeve, Phyllis and Geraldine F. Dobbin. "An Automated Processing System for Government Serials: Its Merger with the General Serials System in an Academic Library." *The Serials Librarian* 7, no.2 (Winter 1982): 41-49.

Experiences in the Government Publications Division of the University of British Columbia Library.

Regenstreif, Herbert. "Automated Serials Management Systems in Law Libraries: The Acquisitions Component." *The Serials Librarian* 9, no.2 (Winter 1984): 133-141.

Highlights special needs of law libraries for sophisticated serials control, not only for check-in and claiming, but also for searching, verification, and ordering. Currently available bibliographic utilities and serials control vendors are briefly described.

Riddick, John. "Manual vs. Automated Check-in: A Comparative Study of Two Academic Libraries." *Serials Review* 6, no.4 (October/December 1980):49-51.

The manual system is used at Iowa State University Library and the automated is OCLC at Central Michigan University Library. A careful, structured cost study comparing activity level and average processing time per issue.

Riddick, John. "OCLC's Claims Component: Implementation at CMU." *Serials Review* 9, no. 4 (Winter 1983):75-79.

The claims component of the OCLC Serials Control Subsystem is being used at Central Michigan University. The author gives specifics about the OCLC capability and describes concerns, problems and the need for training, as well as the "eventual success" of the program.

Saxe, Minna C. "Going Online With Serials." in *Serials in an Automated Age: Proceedings of the First Annual Serials Conference,* edited by Nancy Jean Melin, 31-41. Westport, CT: Meckler Publishing, 1982.

Compares 10 systems: Faxon's LINX, EBSCONET, OCLC, RLIN, UTLAS, WLN, CLASS CHECKMATE, PHILSOM, UCLA, and NOTIS for both bibliographic control and serials control.

Schmidt, Nancy P. "Choosing an Automated Serials Control System." *The Serials Librarian* 9, no. 1 (Fall 1984): 65-86.
This paper examines several of the major existing automated serials control systems in light of the purposes and objectives of serials automation. It offers some criteria by which the different systems can be compared. The systems reviewed are: CLASS:CHECKMATE, EBSCONET, Faxon:LINX SC-10, OCLC:Serials Control Subsystem, and NOTIS.

Steiner, Phyllis A. "On-Line Journal Subscription Records." *The Serials Librarian* 6, no.4 (Summer 1982):25-38.
Describes an on-line system at the Amoco Research Center Information Center designed to keep track of journal subscriptions and journal inventory. Original batch system also described. A tailored subscription management system based on 24 data files controlling 1500 records. There is full control of acquisitions functions such as ordering, renewals, payments (but not fund accounting); check-in, routing, location/retention patterns. A great deal of field manipulation and management reporting. Uses SCRIPT, an IBM Installed User Program (IUP); the operating system is CMS (Conversational Monitor System).

Tonkery, Dan. "The Necessity of Serials Automation." *The Serials Librarian* 7, no.4 (Summer 1983): 57-60.
A rebuttal to Huibert Paul's "Greenland" articles, describing Paul as out of date. Tonkery outlines costs (using UCLA ORION) at 12.5 cents/month per title to do check-in (this in a day the cost of putting a book on the shelf is $45.00. Favorably compares ORION to manual system at UCLA, where no claiming was done and check-in was weeks behind schedule.

Tuttle, Marcia. "Serials Files: What, Where, Why?" in *Serials and Microforms: Patron-Oriented Management. Proceedings of the Second Annual Serials Conference and Eighth Annual Microforms Conference,* edited by Nancy Jean Melin, 9-18. Westport, CT: Meckler Publishing, 1983.
The author discusses the "Central Serial Record" and various serials control functions, primarily from a manual point of view. Characteristics and interrelationships of serials files and the impact of AACR2, as well as comments on automation in a large academic library.

SYSTEMS/VENDORS

Allcock, David. "The Development of LIDAS." *UK Serials Group Newsletter* 7 (December 1981):7-10.

LIDAS is Library Information on the Distribution of All Serials. Describes online serials control system developed for the Central Management Library of the UK Civil Service Dept.

Bailey, Dorothy C. and Helen R. Citron. "Automated Serial Control: One Library's Perspective." *The Serials Librarian* 8, no. 3 (Spring 1984): 43-53.

Outlines procedures for implementing Faxon LINX for online check-in at the Georgia Institute of Technology. Over 6,000 titles were converted (the first 4,300 in 7 weeks). Kardex check-in was eliminated immediately, and no double check-in was maintained. The authors disagree with Riddick that online check-in takes longer than manual. Claiming and other benefits are discussed. Drawbacks include downtime and the lack of a binding component. Overall online serials control is seen as cost-effective.

Begg, Karin E. and Linda D. Miller. "Faxon's LINX: Test Library Reports." *Serials Review* 8, no. 2 (Summer 1982):57-62.

A brief overview of LINX, an on-line, remote access serials management system, and DATALINX, which is comprised of 18 online reference files. Test libraries were surveyed regarding their use of LINX, and results are reported.

Brown, David J. "The Use of INFOSERV: An Online Interactive Buying System to Enhance Collection Development Within the Library." *Library Hi Tech* 6 (1984): 33-36.

An interesting new development for serials acquisitions and collection development, INFOSERV contains new (up to three years old) serial titles on all subjects with brief bibliographic description and availability information. "Many entries include more in-depth descriptive information such as forthcoming articles." Available through Telenet and accessible by 50 types of ASCII terminals. Not restricted to Faxon customers.

Buckeye, Nancy Melin. "The OCLC Serials Subsystem: Implementation/Implications at Central Michigan University." *The Serials Librarian* 3, no. 1 (Fall 1978): 31-42.

CMU was the first user of OCLC check-in in Michigan (1976). At that time successive rather than latest records were common; there were search key problems; no ISSNs on otherwise good records, many dead-end searches and many duplicate records. Describes the conversion process. The conversion timetable was short, and all work done on-line (without producing catalog cards). Double check-in was still being done at the time of writing.

Card, Sandra E. "Serials Automation at UCLA: Planning, Conversion, Impact." *Serials Review* 10, no. 2 (Summer 1984):83-96.
 Card describes the UCLA Library system, which consists of 19 libraries with more than 60,000 current titles. Includes discussion of planning for automation, and includes screens, flowcharts, and coding forms. Conversion was begun in April 1980; half of the titles had been converted at the time of writing.

De Bardeleben, Marian Z. et al. "Off-Site Journal Check-in: An Alternative to Internal Control of Serials." *Serials Review* 9, no. 4 (Winter 1983):56-62.
 Describes check-in of a small library's subscriptions (750) by EBSCO. It is considered to be less expensive than hiring staff and satisfactory for the situation. Light on text, heavy on illustrations.

Fallon, Marcia. "Planning and Implementing an On-Line Periodicals System." *The Serials Librarian* 9, no. 1 (Fall 1984): 87-98.
 The four libraries of Miami-Dade Community College are using an on-line periodical system designed by the College to replace a batch processing system.

Garten, Edward D. and Georganne Rummel. "AMOS: The Tennessee Tech University Library Acquisitions System." *Library Acquisitions: Practice & Theory* 7, no. 1 (1983):41-45.
 The home-grown AMOS (Automated Materials Ordering System) was developed by TTUL acquisitions staff and the University Computer Center. Stand-alone, and does not interface with other current or projected automated systems. Books, serials and media materials are processed on the system.

Graham, Frank and Eric Holt. "PERLINE at Risley: Blackwell's Serials System." *Serials Review* 9, no. 3 (Fall 1983): 77-85.
 Describes getting started with PERLINE, including: file creation, staffing and training, operation, features, performance, assessment, viability, and conclusions. Includes statistical data. The library has 1800 subscriptions. Risley is the headquarters of the UK Atomic Energy Authority.

Holmes, P. "Blackwells: PERLINE." *VINE* 40 (Oct. 1981): 10-14.
 Description of PERLINE online serials service as announced in 1981.

Three central functions are: user access, access to publication information and a claims facility. The PEARL (Periodicals Enquiry Acquisition and Registration Locally) software package will operate the local functions of the online serials control system. PEARL includes: check-in, claiming, routing/circulation, fund accounting, ordering and subscription renewals.

Holmes, Phil, Angela Pacey and Taube Marks. "Blackwells Beaver Away: FIBER, PERLINE and BOOKLINE." *VINE* 54 (June 1984): 22-28.

Summarizes the automated services and systems provided by Blackwell Technical Services. FIBER is the hub of the network, acting as the front-end processor for all inquiries of the user. BOOKLINE and PERLINE share some files, such as supplier, patron, and fund accounting files, and together form an acquisitions system. Recent enhancement of PERLINE serials control include: binding control, circulation history, public inquiry, supplementary holdings, and issue details maintenance.

Kamens, Harry H. "OCLC's Serials Control Subsystem: A Case Study." *The Serials Librarian* 3, no. 1 (Fall 1978): 43-55.

Describes implementation at Kent State University, which was a test library in 1975-76. OCLC was chosen because of its public service components. The project required cataloging several thousand records. The OCLC title was accepted if there were a conflict. Cards were not produced. Describes the practical aspects of check-in, which was found to be slower than manual check-in. Manual claiming and binding files were retained.

Lowell, Gerald R. "LINX; the Integrator." *The Serials Librarian* 7, no. 3 (Spring 1983): 17-27.

Vendor's description of the F. W. Faxon Company's acquisitions and serials control services available through the LINX network: DataLinx and SC-10. Technical and pricing information is included.

Mullane, Ruth. "The ILS—The Pentagon Library's Experience." *Information Technology and Libraries* 3, no. 2 (June 1984): 149-162.

Paper presented at the Midwinter Meeting of the American Library Association, Washington, D.C., January 7-12, 1984. Describes the implementation of the Integrated Library System (ILS) and its five subsystems, which include bibliographic and serials control.

Pletzke, Chet. "PHILSOM and the Uniformed Services University of the Health Sciences Learning Resources Center." *Serials Review* 10, no.2 (Summer 1984):77-82.

The Washington University School of Medicine Library in St. Louis developed PHILSOM in 1962. PHILSOM II was developed in 1969, to accommodate a group of libraries rather than only one, still operating by batch mode. PHILSOM III was developed in 1978/79—a redesign to further utilize emerging minicomputer and telecommunications technology. PHILSOM III is a system designed for medical libraries. It is not based on traditional serials cataloging records. This article describes the first installation of PHILSOM III. Cost information is included.

Roughton, Karen. "Thinking of OCLC Serials Control? Read This." *The Serials Librarian* 7, no. 1 (Fall 1982): 23-30.
Presents hidden problems in the system. The author describes flaws encountered by the Iowa State University Library during a test of the system.

Schrader, David and Dan Houlne. "Serials Automation at 3M—An Unusual Telecommunications Implementation." *Information Technology and Libraries* 3, no. 4 (December 1984): 398-404.
This is a network of nine libraries in St. Paul with 3,000 total subscriptions. Describes ordering of library journals using Faxon LINX, and all other serials activities related to 3M's 12,000 corporate subscriptions.

Steele, Peggy. "Automated Serials Control Using NOTIS." *Serials Review* 9, no.4 (Winter 1983):64-73.
Written by the Information Services Librarian at NOTIS. She describes file relationships between LUIS (Public Access) and the serials operations, showing screens, and describing ordering, check-in, claiming, payments, cataloging, and holdings records. NOTIS is viewed as very versatile, a system that handles difficult publications and has relieved staff of tedious jobs.

Van Houten, Stephen. "The PHILSOM Automated Serials Control System: An Introduction." *Serials Review* 7, no.3 (July/September 1981): 93-99.
Describes the PHILSOM automated serials control system developed at the Washington University School of Medicine Library in St. Louis. Includes a full range of services. Used for a network of 16 libraries with 15,000 total titles.

Vogel, J. Thomas. "Serials Management by Microcomputer: The Potential of DBMS." *Online* 8, no.3 (May 1984): 68-70.
Describes serials management at Philadelphia College of Textiles and Science Library, using microcomputers. A file manager, PFS, and a relational database management system, dBASE II, are used. Includes check-in, claiming and more.

Willmering, William J. "On-Line Centralized Serials Control." *The Serials Librarian* 1, no. 3 (Spring 1977): 243-249.

Describes Northwestern University's conversion to the NOTIS system, when first developed. Thirty-eight thousand records were converted to brief machine-readable form (a minimum of 4 fields). The system is used to order, search, check-in and claim. The article is specific without being detailed, and does not mention any shortcomings (payment controls, binding) or look to future developments (except for throwing away the card catalog).

UNION CATALOGS/CATALOGS

Adams, Marjorie E. "On-Line Public Access to Serial Holdings: Ohio State University," in *Serials and Microforms: Patron-Oriented Management. Proceedings of the Second Annual Serials Conference and Eighth Annual Microforms Conference,* edited by Nancy Jean Melin, 63-77. Westport, CT: Meckler Publishing, 1983.

Access to serial holdings at the volume-specific level through LCS (Library Control System), the on-line catalog. Describes online fields and their relationship; provides details of the holdings statement content.

Bales, Kathleen. "The ANSI Standard for Summary Holdings Statements for Serials: The RLIN Interpretation." *Serials Review* 6, no.4 (October/December 1980):71-73.

A short article outlining conventions of the Research Libraries Information Network, using the American National Standard for summary holdings statements.

Barral, Sabine, and Andre Nivet. "The CPI System at Grenoble. Automated Union List of Serials." *Bulletin des Bibliothèques de France* 25, no. 11 (November 1980):533-538.

This articles describes the Catalogue Collectif de Périodiques Informatise (CPI), developed in 1971 as bibliographic and holdings databases at Grenoble University, Grenoble, France. Products include union lists and subject catalogs. In French.

Bloss, Marjorie E. "The Dregs in the Union List Bottle: Titles Not in the Database." *Serials Review* 10, no. 2 (Summer 1984):49-53.

A review of the Rochester (New York) Union List of Serials experience. The author describes options in dealing with titles not yet in existence on OCLC, including working from surrogates.

Bowen, Johanna, Anne-Marie Hartman, and Marjorie Bloss. "Quality Control: Centralized and Decentralized Union Lists." *Serials Review* 8, no. 3 (Fall 1982):87-96.

Three papers from SUNY/OCLC sessions on the interaction of union listing and interlibrary loan subsystems, April 1982. Management, bibliographic, fiscal, staff training, and other concerns are discussed from general and from local New York experiences.

Carter, Ruth C. "Cataloging Decisions on Pre-AACR2 Serial Records from a Union List Viewpoint." *Serials Review* 7, no.2 (April/June 1981): 77-78.
Cataloging decisions affect union list access. Describes problems with pre-AACR2 serial records in PaULS (Pennsylvania Union List of Serials) and in general.

Carter, Ruth C. and Scott Bruntjen. "The Pennsylvania Union List of Serials: From Development to Maintenance." *The Serials Librarian* 8, no. 4 (Summer 1984): 55-67.
Describes the development of PaULS, an OCLC-based union list of over 60,000 records, with approximately 250 participants. A core list of titles was produced on COM fiche during the third year of the project (1981-82).

Ellsworth, Dianne. "Union List Access Using Online Reference Retrieval Software." *Serials Review* 8, no. 4 (Winter 1982):87-89.
Describes access to the California Union List of Periodicals (CULP) via Bibliographic Retrieval Services (BRS) as an improvement over use of a microfiche product. Online access became available in October 1981.

Grosch, Audrey N. "Theory and Design of Serial Holdings Statements in Computer-Based Serials Systems." *The Serials Librarian* 1, no. 4 (Summer 1977): 341-352.
Describes holdings statements options, machine manipulation and updating and output in natural language. Based on the author's work at the University of Minnesota. An excellent article, both theoretical and practical.

Kimzey, Ann C. and Roland Smith. "An Automated Book Catalog for a Learning Resources Center Periodicals Collection." *The Serials Librarian* 2, no.4 (Summer 1978): 405-410.
Describes the experience of a small college library (400 titles). A book "catalog" (really more like a union list without the union) was created for previously uncataloged periodicals by listing title, dates and subject. Subjects are restricted to 49. The programs are locally-produced; the catalog is issued 3 times a year.

Komorous, Hana. "Union Catalogue of Newspapers in British Columbia Libraries." *The Serials Librarian* 3, no.3 (Spring 1979):255-288.

Describes the British Columbia Newspaper Project begun in 1973. Careful, detailed and extensively illustrated with worksheets, etc. Probably good reading for any group putting together a newspaper project.

Meinardi, Michel. "AGAPE Online: A New Look For Automated Union Lists of Serials." *Bulletin des Bibliothèques de France* 25, no. 11 (November 1980): 519-532.
Describes the University of Nice's online system AGAPE (Application de la Gestion Automatisée aux Périodiques), which has been operational since 1970. Although not yet a union catalog at the time of writing, the database included bibliographic information (incorporating ISSNs) and holdings/location information. In French.

Moen, Michael, et al. "Bibliographic Utilities and Networks," in *Union Lists: Issues and Answers,* edited by Dianne Ellsworth, 37-52. Ann Arbor, MI: Pierian Press, 1982.
Presentations by representatives of Blackwell North America, OCLC, Inc., Research Libraries Group, University of Toronto Library Automation Systems, and Washington Library Network, outlining union listing capabilities and products.

Moules, Mary L. "Producing a Local Union List of Serials with Word Processing Equipment." *The Serials Librarian* 7, no.2 (Winter 1982): 27-34.
The Illinois Valley Library System (IVLS) produces the *Heart of Illinois Library Consortium Union List of Serials* on an IBM Office System 6 word processor. Arrangement is by latest title. Contains the combined holdings of 72 libraries. Design and production of the union list are described.

Preston, Jenny. "Missouri Union List of Serial Publications." *The Serials Librarian* 5, no.1 (Fall 1980):65-77.
Straightforward article on how it is done in Missouri (well, it seems).

Radke, Barbara and Theresa Montgomery. "CALLS ISSN Project." *Serials Review* 8, no. 2 (Summer 1982): 65-67.
The California Academic Libraries List of Serials (CALLS) tested ISSNs as matching devices for the consolidation of serials records. Outlines problems encountered.

Reid, J. E. Trent. "CANUC Serials Reporting and the Canadian Mini-MARC Serials Holdings Format." *The Serials Librarian* 3, no.3 (Spring 1979): 231-242.
Covers relationships to cataloging, an important area which has to be

considered in thinking about holdings statements. Gives current status of standards committees and explains Mini-MARC solution, which allows use of fill characters for fields, subfields, etc., when non-standard data is used. Details 5 alternatives for holdings field, allowing for everything from a nonformatted volume statement to issue by issue check-in.

Spalding, Helen H. "A Computer-Produced Serials Book Catalog With Automatically Generated Indexes." *Library Resources and Technical Services* 24, no. 4 (Fall 1980): 352-360.

Iowa State University Library's serials book catalog provides access to 33,000 serial records by title, corporate body, and subject headings. The catalog is widely distributed for maximum access to holdings. Describes a locally controlled program, with the intention of developing serials control at a later date.

Upham, Lois. "Minnesota Union List of Serials." *The Serials Librarian* 3,no.3 (Spring 1979):289-297.

A brief history and background of MULS from 1971. Solid funding from the Minnesota State Legislature and easy reporting mechanisms for participants drew wide range of support. MULS was used as the "grass roots" base for CONSER.

Wecker, Charlene D. and Susan Fayad. "OCLC Union List Product: Michigan's Recommendations on Design Options." *Serials Review* 10, no. 4 (Winter 1984): in press.

The Michigan Library Consortium Union List Peer Council has assumed a prominent role in examining the offline product design and options for the purpose of making recommendations for the Michigan group. Recommendations on record selection criteria, arrangement of entries, field selection (for bibliographic information), cross references, and indexes (for example, holding library indexes, CLNO indexes) are given.

Zhogoleva, L. N. "Union Lists of Periodicals in the USA." *Bibliotekovedenie i Bibliografiva za Rubezhom* 71 (1979):14-26.

Written in Russian about union listing in the United States, including discussion and criticism of the National Serials Data Program and the CONversion of SERials Project, from a Russian point of view.

STANDARDS

American National Standards Committee on Library and Information Sciences and Related Publishing Practices, Z39. *American National Standard for Library and Information Sciences and Related Publishing Prac-*

tices—*American National Standard for Serial Holdings Statements.* Washington, D.C.: American National Standards Institute. ANSI Z39.44-draft 1983.

This draft is now in final form and has circulated for vote to ANSC Z39 members. The 1980 standard: *Serials Holdings Statements at the Summary Level* (Z39.42) has been incorporated into Z39.44.

American National Standards Committee on Library and Information Sciences and Related Publishing Practices, Z39. *American National Standard for Library and Information Sciences and Related Publishing Practices—International Standard Serial Numbering.* Washington, D.C.: American National Standards Institute. ANSI Z39.9-1979.

American National Standards Committee on Library and Information Sciences and Related Publishing Practices, Z39. *American National Standard for Library and Information Sciences and Related Publishing Practices—Periodicals, Format and Arrangement.* Washington, D.C.: American National Standards Institute. ANSI Z39.1-1977.

This standard was first published in 1935, with revisions in 1943, 1967, and 1977. It underwent revision again in 1983-1984, and the results will soon be issued.

American National Standards Committee on Library and Information Sciences and Related Publishing Practices, Z39. *American National Standard for Library and Information Sciences and Related Publishing Practices—Serial Holdings Statements at the Summary Level.* Washington, D.C.: American National Standards Institute. ANSI Z39.42-1980.

This standard may be withdrawn after publication of Z39.44, which is intended to merge standards for both summary level and detailed level holdings statements.

American National Standards Committee on Library and Information Sciences and Related Publishing Practices, Z39. *American National Standard for Library and Information Sciences and Related Publishing Practices—Serials—Claims for Missing Issues.* Washington, D.C.: American National Standards Institute. ANSI Z39.45-1983.

This recent publication identifies and describes the data elements to be included in a serial claim; indicates whether data elements should be considered required or optional for a claim. The standard does not specify the physical format of a claim but includes a recommended preprinted claim form in an appendix.

Bloss, Marjorie E., and others. *Guidelines for Union Lists of Serials.* Chicago: Serials Section, Resources and Technical Services Division, American Library Association, 1982.

Bloss, Marjorie E. "The Standard Unfurled: ANSI Z39 SC42: Holdings Statements at the Summary Level." *Serials Review* 9, no. 1 (Spring 1983): 79-83.

Summarizes the Standard; discusses implementation at Rochester (NY) Regional Research Library Council, a non-CONSER library. Gives many examples of holdings statements pointing out problem areas. "There are still sections with the Standard which require further interpretation."

Hensley, Charlotta C. "Serials Standards (and Guidelines): Who Cares?" in *Library Serials Standards: Development, Implementation, Impact. Proceedings of the Third Annual Serials Conference,* edited by Nancy Jean Melin, 85-97. Westport, CT: Meckler Publishing, 1984.

Defines and lists international and national standards.

Tannehill, Robert S. "Technical Bibliographic Standards Development in the United States," in *Library Serials Standards: Development, Implementation, Impact. Proceedings of the Third Annual Serials Conference,* edited by Nancy Jean Melin, 55-59. Westport, CT: Meckler Publishing, 1984.

Summarizes the four types of ANSI standards: official, technical, voluntary, and consensus. Outlines the draft and approval process.

Whiffin, Jean. *Union Catalogues of Serials. Guidelines for Creation and Maintenance, with Recommended Standards for Bibliographic and Holdings Control. The Serials Librarian,* vol. 8, no. 1, Fall 1983. New York: The Haworth Press, 1983.

"The IFLA Section on Serial Publications, recognizing a strong need to establish international guidelines for the compilation of union catalogues/lists of serials, sponsored, with the financial assistance of UNESCO, a project to survey and analyze the existing bibliographic tools, and subsequently to formulate a code of good practice. The complete text of the first draft of the proposed new international standard is presented, preceded by a brief history of the project and its background."

Wittorf, Robert. "ANSI Z39.42 and OCLC: OCLC's Implementation of the American National Standard Institute's Serial Holdings Statements at the Summary Level." *Serials Review* 6, no.2 (April/June 1980):87-94.

The ANSI standard reflecting the complexity of serials allows for three levels of detail. Reviews the holdings statement data elements, selection of bibliographic records, and retrieving and displaying of union listing information.

FISCAL CONTROL

Carter, Ruth C. and Scott Bruntjen. "Pittsburgh Regional Library Center Serials Cancellation Project." *Library Resources and Technical Services* 28, no. 4 (October/December 1984): 299-307.

The PRLC project involved developing an online system (via OCLC) of communicating cancellation of serial subscriptions (during the period August 1981 to December 1982). Stresses collection development decisions as opposed to the reporting of holdings statements.

Feller, Siegfried. "Library Serials Cancellectomies at the University of Massachusetts, Amherst." *The Serials Librarian* 1, no. 2 (Winter 1976-77): 140-152.

Describes the review and online record-keeping process of a cancellation project. Over 16,000 serials were reviewed and evaluated. Data were added to an existing automated system; records were coded at six priority levels. Printouts were produced for the review process and also sorted by vendor, serving as cancellation notices.

Myers, Judy. "A Subject Fund Accounting System for Serials." *The Serials Librarian* 3, no. 4 (Summer 1979): 373-380.

A University of Houston Library local system using punched cards supplied by Faxon or produced by library staff. The card contains the library fund code (in four digits) and the dollar amount. The library sorts the cards and runs them on the university computer. A printout and summary punch card for each fund is produced. They are used as the basis of the next run.

ORGANIZATION OF SERIALS WORK

Cargill, Jennifer. "Serials: Separate or Merged?" in *The Serials Collection: Organization and Administration,* edited by Nancy Jean Melin, 15-22. Ann Arbor, MI: Pierian Press, 1982.

Discusses advantages of organization by function.

Collver, Mitsuko, "Organization of Serials Work for Manual and Automated Systems." *Library Resources and Technical Services* 24, no. 4 (Fall 1980): 307-16.

Recommends organization by form so that all serials functions are unified; appraises the expected organizational impact of automation on centralized serials departments.

Feinman, Valerie J. "Factors and Flexibility: The Form Vs. Function Dilemma," in *Serials and Microforms: Patron-Oriented Management.*

Proceedings of the Second Annual Serials Conference and Eighth Annual Microforms Conference, edited by Nancy Jean Melin, 149-158. Westport, CT: Meckler Publishing, 1983.

Gives a history of serials organization, lists factors influencing form vs. function, and describes the situation at Adelphi University.

Gellatly, Peter. "Deserialization." *The Serials Librarian* 4, no. 4 (Summer 1980):367-369.

An editorial on the impact of The Machine on organizational patterns in libraries. While accepting the benefits and inevitability of the automation of serials work and probably the breakup of the serials department, Gellatly obviously does not prefer the latter.

Gorman, Michael. "The Future of Serials Control and Its Administrative Implications for Libraries," in *Serials Automation for Acquisition and Inventory Control,* edited by William Gray Potter and Arlene Farber Sirkin, 120-133. Ann Arbor, MI: Pierian Press, 1981.

Perspectives on the place of serials, serials records and serials work in the library.

Hepfer, William. "Serials Organization in Academic Libraries: Is There a Best Way?" in *The Serials Collection: Organization and Administration,* edited by Nancy Jean Melin, 1-8. Ann Arbor, MI: Pierian Press, 1982.

Concludes that there is no single scheme for organizing serials and other technical services work that is ideal for all libraries.

McKinley, Margaret. "Victims, Villains or Victors: The Impact of Serials Automation on a Library Organization." *Serials Review* 10, no. 2 (Summer 1984):43-48.

A thought-provoking article for managers and supervisors planning for or in the midst of change. The author sees a general tendency toward a reduction in the number of divisions within an organization.

Melin, Nancy Jean. "Automating the Serials Manager: New Directions, New Opportunities," in *Serials in an Automated Age: Proceedings of the First Annual Serials Conference,* edited by Nancy Jean Melin, 81-88. Westport, CT: Meckler Publishing, 1982.

Alludes to presentations of other speakers at the First Annual Serials Conference and looks ahead to the future role of the serials departments: a serial manager must act as Informer and Clearinghouse, as Coordinator, and as Preparer.

Wernstedt, Irene J. "Serials' Greener Pastures," in *Serials and Microforms: Patron-Oriented Management. Proceedings of the Second Annual*

Serials Conference and Eighth Annual Microforms Conference, edited by Nancy Jean Melin, 142-147. Westport, CT: Meckler Publishing, 1983.

Maintains that there is a tendency to follow the leader in organization patterns. In 1979 the trend was pro-form; in 1982 the trend was pro-function. The trend will probably reverse after a period of time.

What Has Technology Done for Us Lately?

Lenore S. Maruyama, MALS

ABSTRACT. Up to 1976, serials automation had progressed to a point where the activities of the bibliographic networks was increasingly important, and the CONSER project had been launched. However, most union lists of serials were still being compiled manually, and the computers used for library applications consisted primarily of (expensive) mainframe computers. Several events took place in 1976: the Library of Congress received a grant for CONSER II; OCLC's serials check-in system became available; NCLIS established a Task Force on a National Periodicals System; and the first major revision of the copyright law was passed. This article discusses the progress made or the changes that have occurred since 1976 in: CONSER, the bibliographic networks, union lists of serials, stand-alone systems, electronic mail, full text services, copyright, and organizations providing services involving serials.

INTRODUCTION

The first issue of *The Serials Librarian* appeared in the fall of 1976. In retrospect, library automation in the mid-1970s seemed to be shifting from decentralized **development** in individual institutions to centralized development, primarily by the nationwide bibliographic networks, the organizations that operate computer facilities to maintain large machine-readable bibliographic files for their members to use for different library and information services. At the same time, decentralized **activity** such as input of retrospective records was increasing.

Lenore S. Maruyama is President of Maruyama Associates, Inc., a firm specializing in technical writing and documentation (mailing address: 1611 North Kent Street, Suite 805, Arlington, VA 22209).

The author wishes to thank George A. Parsons, formerly of the Council on Library Resources, for his assistance in providing many helpful ideas, obtaining a number of historical documents, and reviewing this article.

How Had Automation Affected the Work of Serials Librarians Up to 1976?

The activities of the bibliographic networks became a critical factor in library automation, although their serials control systems were largely undeveloped. OCLC, or Online Computer Library Center, Inc., still stood for the Ohio College Library Center, but its members were already spread throughout the United States. In 1975, its acquisitions and serials cataloging subsystems became operational, the latter through the stimulus of the CONSER (Conversion of Serials) project. The Research Libraries Group (RLG) consisted of the New York Public Library and the libraries of Columbia, Harvard, and Yale Universities, and did not have its own network computer facilities. The entity that became RLG's Research Libraries Information Network (RLIN) was still under the control of Stanford University (which was not an RLG member at the time) as Bibliographic Automation of Large Library Operations Using a Time-Sharing System or BALLOTS. BALLOTS, however, had been opened to other libraries for shared cataloging and searching functions; it did not have serials control capabilities at that time. The Washington Library Network (WLN) was still a year away from full implementation of its on-line system. Finally, the University of Toronto Library Automation Systems (UTLAS) was operating only in Canada.

The CONSER (Conversion of Serials) project to build and maintain a high-quality data base of serials cataloging records was begun in 1974 with partial funding and management from the Council on Library Resources. By 1976, the portion of the project referred to as CONSER I had thirteen participants, including the Library of Congress, providing input and updating of serial records through OCLC's online facilities. CONSER was viewed as a natural progression of efforts begun at the Library of Congress, namely the publication of a MARC (Machine-Readable-Cataloging) format for serials, the inclusion of serials in the Library's MARC Distribution Service, and the National Serials Data Program, through which International Standard Serial Numbers and key titles were assigned.

Most union lists of serials were still being compiled manually. The few that were in machine-readable form were produced through cumbersome batch systems. One of the biggest problems facing union list compilers at that time was that no large data bases existed from which bibliographic data in a standard format could be drawn for the union list. It was significant, therefore, that the 75,000 records comprising the Minnesota Union List of Serials (MULS) were included in the initial CONSER data base.

Computers used for library applications consisted primarily of mainframe computers. The online searching and cataloging functions provided by the bibliographic networks for their member libraries were handled through telecommunications links between terminals and mainframe. The systems developed by the University of Chicago, Northwestern University, or the University of California, Los Angeles, also operated on mainframe computers. A few institutions had developed systems for stand-alone serials functions like check-in, claiming, or binding on minicomputers, and commercial vendors had started to use minicomputers in conjunction with bar-code readers for stand-alone circulation systems. But costs were still prohibitive for the great majority of libraries. William Saffady in an article on automated text editing noted, "For libraries, a considerable disadvantage of currently available CRT systems is their relatively high price. The Vydec Editor, developed by Vydec, Inc. (and one of the most advanced word processing devices on the market at the time, is) priced at around twenty thousand dollars . . ."[1]

Several Significant Events Related to Serials Took Place During 1976

In early 1976, the Library of Congress received a grant from the Council on Library Resources to support the systems design and programming needed for the Library to assume responsibility for the management and permanent maintenance of the CONSER data base. LC takeover, or what was called CONSER II, was scheduled for November 1977.

OCLC's serials check-in capability was made available to its member libraries.

The National Commission on Libraries and Information Science established a Task Force on a National Periodicals System to develop plans for a national system to provide periodical materials. Much of this work was based on an earlier study issued by the Association of Research Libraries in 1974.

On October 19, 1976, the President signed into law the first major revision of the copyright law since 1909. The Copyright Act of 1976, which went into effect in January 1978, contained sections on photocopying, an issue of great concern to librarians and archivists.

What has happened since 1976? Has automation helped the serials librarian? Serials control, as everyone knows, is labor-intensive and dynamic. It has a heavy transaction load although most of the transactions are relatively short and uncomplicated compared to the more complex operations needed, for example, to perform Boolean searching. Also, every serial seems to be an exception to the rule. How could computers requiring unambiguous instructions cope with the ambiguities inherent in serials?

The following section highlights the progress made since 1976. In this context, "technology" is not limited to computer technology. At the same time, this article does not attempt to discuss the entire range of technology used by librarians or serials librarians.

PROGRESS SINCE 1976

"Change is not progress." H. L. Mencken

The late 1970s and early 1980s were characterized by enormous changes in the computer industry, brought about in large part by the widescale availability of microcomputers. Although we are still a long way from having a personal computer in every home, there is no doubt that large numbers of the population became aware of the capabilities of computers, which were now affordable by an individual and could be operated in an interactive mode without the intervention of computer professionals.

Libraries had already recognized the advantages of computers for their behind-the-scenes file creation and maintenance (i.e., cataloging) through the online facilities of the bibliographic networks or their own online systems, but now the use of computers in many libraries became much more visible to their users with the arrival of stand-alone circulation systems or terminals for using the large data bases of the commercial vendors like Dialog, System Development Corporation, or Bibliographic Retrieval Service, or special systems like MEDLINE or online public access catalogs. This section discusses the progress made or the changes that have occurred in the following areas: CONSER, the bibliographic networks, union lists of serials, stand-alone systems, electronic mail, full text services, copyright, and organizations providing services involving serials.

CONSER

CONSER (Conversion of Serials) would not have been able to meet its objectives without online, interactive file creation and maintenance capabilities. And by and large, it has met its objectives, which are to provide a reliable and authoritative serials data base to meet the needs of library users and the developing national and international bibliographic networks; assist the national libraries of Canada and the United States to establish and maintain a machine-readable serials data base; support local, regional, and union list serial activities; ensure the use of national and international standards; and identify deficiencies in the data base such as subject, language, and retrospective coverage and implement appropriate remedies.

The methods by which CONSER achieved these objectives, however, changed from original plans. As noted earlier, CONSER began its operations by using OCLC's online facilities with the expectation that the Library of Congress would assume the responsibility for the management and maintenance of the data base in November 1977 as CONSER II. Because the Library was not permitted to allow users outside its internal constituencies (i.e., LC and Congressional staff) to access its data base and because of higher priorities that precluded the expansion of its internal system at that time to provide online input and maintenance of serials, the management and maintenance of CONSER has remained with OCLC.

Other changes occurred because the original procedures were restrictive and self-defeating. The CONSER authentication process, for example, has been expanded recently beyond the original four authenticating agencies: the National Library of Canada, the Library of Congress, the (U.S.) National Serials Data Program, and the International Serials Data System/Canada. Authentication involves certifying that the data content and content designation of a serials bibliographic record have been reviewed and that the record meets the standards and practices agreed upon by CONSER participants. Records input or updated by participants other than the four agencies mentioned above had to be authenticated by the National Library of Canada (for Canadian serials) or the Library of Congress (for all other serials). Once authenticated, these records were "locked"; only the authenticating agencies were allowed to make changes. This meant that vital information such as title changes or cessations could not be updated on a timely basis because the Library of Congress or the National Library of Canada had to be notified first.

In addition to correcting this defect, the change in the authentication process reflected an expansion of other cooperative efforts. A number of CONSER participants were also part of the LC Name Authority Cooperative Project (NACO). After extensive training in LC practices and procedures, NACO participants provided name authority data that became part of the LC name authority data base. Since a large part of the CONSER authentication process involved name authority work, it was more efficient to let the CONSER participant handle the remaining authentication tasks and updates. In addition, OCLC's Online Data Quality Control Section can now modify authenticated records from documentation submitted by its other member libraries.

Although the advantages of building a large data base cooperatively have outweighed the disadvantages, CONSER has experienced growing pains. First, the existence of a(ny) large data base means that changes to reflect new cataloging rules become increasingly difficult to implement. *AACR2* involved, among other things, changes in the formulation of corporate name headings (which affected the vast majority of name headings used in serial records) as well as changes in the rules as to when a serial is entered under title rather than "author" or when a new record must be made (i.e., the serial changed its title). Then, CONSER as a cooperative effort meant that certain files were added to the CONSER data base, thus increasing to some degree the number of unique titles but also increasing the number of duplicate records. Finally, CONSER has shown that cooperation and high-quality records can be a mixed blessing. Few libraries can afford, for example, to recatalog all of their serial entries to place them under successive entries rather than latest entry, but if this is not done cooperative efforts like union list projects will produce a confusing array of titles. Also, the different cooperative projects existing under the CONSER umbrella do not have the same goals and objectives, which is natural but can also lead to "tinkering" to accommodate certain requirements.

Nonetheless, CONSER has built a data base of over 240,000 authenticated records and even more unauthenticated ones.[2] With the file creation and maintenance functions under better control, CONSER has turned its attention to other aspects of serials, such as the Abstracting and Indexing Coverage Project.[3] Co-sponsored by the Association of Research Libraries and the National Federation of Abstracting and Information Services, the project will: (1) Ensure that the CONSER data base contains records for all serial titles covered by a core group of the most widely used abstracting and indexing (A&I) services in the U.S. and Canada; (2) add to those records the information as to where each serial is indexed or abstracted; (3) provide the participating A&I services with standardized bibliographic data (e.g., International Standard Serial Number, key titles, library entries) for each serial title they cover, enabling them to cite the serials they index in standardized library form; (4) develop the capability to produce machine-readable serial lists for use by participating A&I services; and (5) keep the A&I information in the CONSER data base up-to-date.

By the end of 1984, seventy-six A&I services had identified 96,000 titles appearing in 118 indexes or abstracts for the project, which is scheduled to be completed in April 1985. The project constitutes the first step in forging a link between the A&I services that provide virtually all the access to the vast amount of literature appearing in periodicals and the libraries that house the periodicals themselves. It also constitutes the first step in transforming a bibliographic data base into a management information tool.

CONSER, it should be noted, began its operations at a time when the only nationwide online bibliographic facility available was OCLC. Most CONSER participants were already OCLC members; the ones that were not (e.g., the national libraries) joined OCLC to participate in the project. Since then, several CONSER participants have left OCLC to join RLG/RLIN, and their new records or their holdings are no longer being added to the CONSER data base. In the case of the University of Washington, which is a member of the Washington Library Network, records are input twice: first, into OCLC for CONSER; then, into WLN.[4] With OCLC's participation in the Linked Systems Project (which will provide computer-to-computer links among RLIN, WLN, and the Library of Congress to transmit data), there is a possibility of resolving the problem in the long term. For the short term, however, the Linked Systems Project will transmit only name authority data. The problem of access to a "national" serials data base is still unresolved.

Bibliographic Networks

As noted in the previous section, OCLC has housed the CONSER data base since the inception of the CONSER effort. By the mid-1970s, its serials cataloging and acquisitions subsystems were operational. Serials check-in was added in 1976, followed by the interlibrary loan and union list components, and finally in 1984 a claiming component, all operating on the mainframe. Developments to include serials control in OCLC's local systems have occurred much more rapidly. In early 1985, it introduced a complete system (Serials Control 350) to run on a microcomputer with links to and from the central data base at OCLC. Later in 1985, serials control functions will be added to the minicomputer-based LS/2000 system.

The other major bibliographic networks, the Research Libraries Information Network, the University of Toronto Library Automation Systems, and the Washington Library Network, have taken a different approach to implementing serials control. Although all of them have serials cataloging components, other aspects of serials control such as check-in or binding have not been introduced except through links with stand-alone local systems, e.g., INNOVACQ or Geac (see the discussion on Stand-Alone Systems in a subsequent section of this article). This state of affairs occurred because potential serials control applications were probably overtaken by developments in the technology rather than through deliberate planning.

Because their files are structured differently, RLIN, UTLAS, and WLN handle other functions like interlibrary loan, acquisitions, or union catalogs/lists in ways different from those used at OCLC. UTLAS and WLN are the only networks that provide automated and interactive authority control for the records claimed by their members. The WLN system is worth noting because it is tied to an automated and centralized review process that is similar to CONSER authentication. WLN review includes the following: (1) validation of name and subject headings input by member libraries; (2) review of individual fields for newly input records or for existing records requiring changes or revisions; (3) review of duplicate records when attempting to merge LC MARC/CONSER records with WLN records; and (4) the means to communicate via the network system between the central reviewing agency and the cataloger at his/her terminal. Within tasks #2 and #3 are the complex cataloging problems associated with serials, such as successive entry vs. latest entry or other changes associated with *AACR2*.

The WLN review process is unique in that it provides most of the procedures and techniques needed for these tasks through its network system. Although other enhancements to the system would make the process more efficient, it is more likely that future changes in the review process will reflect changes in policy, such as a shift to decentralize the process. A WLN user says: "There are many factors other than human review that determine the quality of a database. The sophistication of a network's software, its ability to correct malfunctions and develop enhancements, the importance it places to quality in management decisions—all are important factors in the overall quality and usefulness of any database. But perhaps the most important ingredient of all is a commitment to quality by the participants themselves."[5]

CONSER has definitely not lacked a commitment to quality. What it has lacked is sophisticated software that would allow the central agency or the participants to carry out the authentication process and to modify the process over the years as CONSER requirements change. But it is probably too late to introduce a WLN-like review process now because the two biggest systems associated with CONSER, OCLC and the Library of Congress, have taken different approaches to the authority/bibliographic record review process. It is still intriguing, however, to imagine what the CONSER data base would be like if such a capability had been available from the beginning.

The bibliographic networks' greatest contribution to serials control has been to provide the online creation and maintenance facilities that have accelerated the availability of a large number of serial bibliographic records. In the case of OCLC, the availability of the large data base became the foundation for other systems, such as interlibrary loan or union lists, that would not have been successful otherwise. On the other hand, its serials check-in component, while popular, was cumbersome to use. This deficiency was corrected with recent system enhancements, but access to local data records is still governed by the hours during which the OCLC system is available and by the searching techniques used by OCLC.

Union Lists

Two of the biggest problems faced by union list compilers ten years ago are, if not completely solved, under control: the availability of a large number of high-quality, machine-readable bibliographic records for serials and maintenance of the union list. Union lists can be created and maintained on a variety of systems, such as those of the bibliographic networks (e.g., OCLC), commercial vendors (e.g., Faxon), or other automated systems (e.g., the National Library of Canada's DOBIS). These are described briefly as examples of the capabilities available at present.

OCLC has two systems directly related to union list creation and maintenance: its serials cataloging and union list components. The serials data base contains over 600,000 records, including CONSER authenticated and unauthenticated records, but even this seemingly large data base does not result in a 100% match between the records required for a particular union list and the records already available in machine-readable form. (For example, a union list project containing about 50,000 titles and 90,000 holdings statements had an 87% "hit" average against the OCLC data base.)[6] There is no doubt, however, of the invaluable assistance obtained from the serials data base used in conjunction with the machine-readable name authority file in doing original cataloging. Once the bibliographic data are available, users can add summary holdings to the union list component, which can provide a group display for a single serial title showing the names of each institution holding that title and its summary holdings or an institution display showing one institution's summary holdings for a serial title.

The Faxon Company offers union list capabilities through its LINX system as well as other serials control functions (described under Stand-Alone Systems in a subsequent section of this article). Faxon's union list system operates in a similar fashion to the OCLC system in that serials bibliographic data, if already available, can be transferred to the union list system or can be created online. Although arranged differently and more legibly, the Faxon online displays also distinguish between a group display and an institution display. The principal drawback to the system at present is that records created by the user are not in a MARC format, although they contain the necessary links to a MARC serials record, e.g., International Standard Serial Number, LC card number, etc.

The National Library of Canada uses its DOBIS data base to produce two union lists: *Union List of Serials in the Social Sciences and Humanities Held by Canadian Libraries* (a computer-output-microfiche product published by the National Library) and *Union List of Scientific Serials in Canadian Libraries* (a printed product, soon to be issued in microfiche, published by the Canadian Institute for Scientific and Technical Information). Reports to these lists can be submitted in printed form (i.e., printed cards) or in machine-readable form on tape in the Mini-MARC format, which specifies a level of content designation sufficient for NLC to process the record to add it to the DOBIS data base but which is less detailed than the MARC serials format.[7] Following a matching process, holdings are added to existing records. If the title is unique, a new record is input in the full MARC format (for the reports received in printed form), or the incoming machine-readable record is added to the file, a process involving links to the NLC bilingual name and subject authority files and possibly some enhancement of content designation in certain fields. (It should also be noted that NLC uses the DOBIS data base to produce an annual microfiche listing of all authenticated CONSER records with several indexes to access the entries.)

Although union lists of serials can now be created and maintained online, whether through the bibliographic networks, commercial vendors, or locally-developed stand-alone systems, virtually all of them must provide the list in printed form or as a microform from a computer-output-microform (COM) process. All of their users do not have access to the same online facilities. And some union lists are compiled through a batch system (similar to DOBIS) because several large contributors create their records (online) through different systems.

A brief word about *New Serial Titles,* which has been produced from MARC serial records through the CONSER project since 1981. Automation affected this publication in a number of ways. Prior to 1981, *NST* had limitations on the type of serials included and the beginning date of publication because it continued the *Union List of Serials,* which covered serials through 1949. These restrictions were removed, and the publication became a mirror of the CONSER data base. But more far-reaching changes occurred because of the relationship between the Library of Congress and OCLC for CONSER. Although authenticated CONSER records can be accessed through LC's own online system, all record creation and maintenance must be handled through OCLC, which in turn sends LC a weekly tape of all authenticated records processed during the week. With at least four units in the Library of Congress providing transactions to these serial records (serials cataloging for new titles, CONSER authentication for records input by other CONSER participants, the National Serials Data Program for key titles or International Standard Serial Numbers, or New Serials Titles staff), in addition to transactions input by other CONSER members, the OCLC Online Data Quality Control Section, or special projects like the CONSER A&I Project, the number of replacement records being generated is very high.

Since 1981, *NST* reflects the activity in the CONSER data base, and its entries resemble the cataloging records in the CONSER file. These changes would have been beneficial if *NST* had adopted a new publication format at the same time. A cumulative microform product, while not the total solution, would have been superior to the present printed format, which includes monthly issues and quarterly and annual cumulations. *NST* has changed, but is it better now than it had been? Is there still a need for a "national" union list of serials, or will the increasing number of statewide, regional, or local union lists be able to meet individual library requirements? Similar questions have been raised concerning the *Na-*

tional Union Catalog and the *Register of Additional Locations,* and it will be interesting to review this issue ten years hence to see if any progress has been made in resolving these problems.

An additional problem with union lists has been the lack of a standard format for (serial) holdings in machine-readable form. Although the National Information Standards Organization (Z39) had issued *Serial Holdings Statements at the Summary Level (ANSI Z39.42-1980),* conflicts arose when NISO attempted to draft a standard for holdings statements at the detailed level. At this writing, NISO has issued a draft revision of the existing standard to incorporate specifications for detailed holdings statements, but the proposed standard has not been officially accepted yet.

Stand-Alone Systems

The term "stand-alone system" is used here only to differentiate between the systems operated by or under the control of the bibliographic networks and those that are not. The ideal system does not stand alone: its serials control functions should be integrated with other automated library functions, and it should be linked with other external systems.

The number of systems that provide automated serials control is surprisingly large. In a survey conducted at the end of 1983, nineteen out of the forty-seven bibliographic networks, serials subscription agencies, automated library system vendors, and library software developers contacted had operational automated serials control systems, with another twelve planning to implement such systems during 1984.[8] This diversity, however, does not simplify the selection process. As the authors of the survey note: "Current options for the automation of serials management range from a $75 program for an Apple microcomputer, through a $93,750 package of hardware and software for a stand-alone system capable of managing a collection of . . . 50,000 subscriptions, to multifunction turnkey systems costing hundreds of thousands of dollars and capable of automating numerous functions in a large library consortium."

Commercial vendors have been particularly active in introducing serials control functions to their existing product line of stand-alone library systems. (It should also be noted that OCLC, a not-for-profit organization, has enhanced or will be enhancing its stand-alone local systems to include serials control.) An even more interesting development is the increasing number of links between these systems: Blackwell and INNOVACQ; Blackwell and CL Systems; Geac and Faxon; INNOVACQ and Faxon; EBSCO and INNOVACQ. Three of these systems (INNOVACQ, Faxon, and Geac) are described briefly to indicate the different approaches used in solving the problems of serials control.

Innovative Interfaces, the developer of INNOVACQ, got its start by developing an interface between the bibliographic networks and a stand-alone circulation system that allowed the individual library's records in the network's file to be downloaded to the local system. This interface became the foundation for its own online system providing acquisitions and serials control functions and, more recently, online public access catalogs. The system operates on a multiple-processor computer system. INNOVACQ's serials module provides check-in, claiming, routing, and binding, with acquisitions functions provided by the acquisitions module. Full bibliographic records can also be input directly into the system if they are not available from the networks.

Faxon developed LINX, its online information management system, as an adjunct to its library subscription business. The LINX subsystems include: LINX Courier, an electronic mail service to place orders, claims, or other communications; DataLinx, access to a variety of Faxon's data bases and files, including authenticated CONSER records; SC-10, an interactive serials check-in and claiming service; Route, the online creation, updating, and printing of routing slips; and Union List, the online creation and maintenance of union lists. Full fund accounting and binding control subsystems are being planned. Access to LINX is available through a dedicated line network or dial-up. Users of the OCLC M300, an IBM Personal Computer modified for use with the OCLC network, can access LINX with a modem and an asynchronous communication (software) package.

Geac has recently added serials check-in and claiming functions to its acquisitions subsystem. (Binding functions had already been available through the circulation subsystem.) In addition to acquisitions, the Geac Library Information System consists of the following subsystems: circulation (including materials booking and reserve room functions); and online catalog (including public access catalog and authority control). Records can be downloaded from a bibliographic network and added to the file by batch processing (for tapes), or created locally on the system. A useful adjunct to the Library Information System is the Geac Office Automation System, which provides word processing, spreadsheet, or electronic mail capabilities. The Geac system also operates in a multi-processor environment, allowing a library flexibility in selecting a configuration based on the size of its collection, the volume of its activity, and its projected growth.

These systems are run on different kinds of hardware: INNOVACQ, microcomputer; Geac, minicomputer; and Faxon, mainframe. They are similar in that all three are closely tied to an acquisitions system (in the case of Faxon, a subscription service), and they have links or plan to have links with other systems.

Not-for-profit organizations are also marketing software to handle serials control functions. NOTIS (Northwestern Online Total Integrated System) was created by and for the Northwestern University Libraries and supports acquisitions, serials control, cataloging, authorities, circulation, and online user access functions. The first version of the system was in operation in the early 1970s, but it was only after major revisions were completed in the early 1980s that Northwestern began marketing the NOTIS software, which is designed to run on IBM 4300 series mainframe or compatible computers. The specific serials processing functions handled by NOTIS include check-in and claiming; acquisition and cataloging of serials are part of the NOTIS acquisitions and cataloging subsystems.

On the other end of the spectrum is the software for Checkmate, which runs on the IBM Personal Computer (PC) and PC/XT. The software was developed by CLASS (Cooperative Library Agency for Systems and Services, formerly California Library Authority for Systems and Services), and is marketed by several commercial vendors as well as by CLASS. Checkmate provides support for check-in, claiming, routing, and acquisitions in addition to data base building.

The stand-alone systems provide solutions for serials control for all types of libraries, but they do not provide all solutions for serials control or all solutions for library automation. When viewed with the services offered by the bibliographic networks (including the stand-alone local systems marketed by OCLC), these systems handle most of the routine aspects of serials control efficiently, allowing the serials librarian to concentrate on the not-so-routine aspects and the exceptions. In addition, the management reports generated by these systems help administrators and managers by providing data needed for budget preparation, long-term planning, collection development, and other library functions.

Electronic Mail

Electronic mail is not, strictly speaking, a serials control function, but it provides the means by which a number of library and information services related to serials can be carried out. For example, periodical orders and claim notices can be transmitted online to a subscription agency or a publisher; interlibrary loan requests for a serial can be transmitted to another library; photocopy orders for a particular article in a periodical can be transmitted to a commercial document delivery service, A&I service, or library; cataloging questions related to serials can be transmitted to a central agency with answers sent back to the library making the query.

The number of services geared to the library and information service market has increased tremendously in recent years. The four bibliographic networks discussed earlier in this article (OCLC, RLG/RLIN, UTLAS, and WLN) provide electronic mail capabilities for interlibrary loan, direct ordering to a document supplier, and "mail" (e.g., messages, queries, notices). Most library book jobbers and subscription agencies have electronic mail for orders, claims, and other communications. Commercial data base vendors like Dialog, SDC, or BRS have online document ordering services to document delivery services of all types. Two library organizations, Cooperative Library Agency for Systems and Services (CLASS) and the American Library Association, are respectively brokers for the electronic mail services of Tymshare's OnTyme and ITT Dialcom, Inc., (ALA's service is called ALANET). And, then, there are a large number of services like MCI Mail that have no "library" connection.

The availability of so many systems, however, means that a library must subscribe to several because no interconnections exist among them at present. Although an OCLC member library has access to the largest bibliographic data base with the largest number of contributing libraries, it cannot send an interlibrary loan request to a non-OCLC library without using a different terminal (the OCLC 100 series terminals can only access the OCLC system) and logging on to a different (electronic mail) service.

Full Text

When talking about "serials control," serials librarians are generally referring to bibliographic control for a title and inventory control for a bound volume or individual issue. Users, on the other hand, are concerned about getting a particular article in a journal. What do they do if neither the journal nor the specific issue is available?

The information industry has introduced a number of products recently to meet these needs. Full text services are not in themselves a new or even recent development. Legal materials, e.g., laws, statutes, decisions, opinions, etc., have been available in machine-readable, full text form for over ten years, followed by newspapers like the *New York Times* or the *Wall Street Journal.* In the early 1980s, the data base producers began offering full text services for magazines as well as an increasing number of non-bibliographic data bases. (A brief note about non-bibliographic data bases. Perhaps the terms "secondary source" and "primary source" would be more accurate to describe citations (and their access points) to a work and the work itself. Primary sources encompass a wide range of data from the price of securities to census data to what is found in the *Official Airlines Guide.*)

Although many vendors of full text services exist, the ones most familiar to librarians are those offered by Mead Data Central for its LEXIS/ NEXIS data bases and Information Access Corporation (IAC) for its Magazine ASAP and Trade & Industry ASAP (accessed via Dialog). Retrieval of the information is handled through keyword searching on the text itself, a controlled indexing vocabulary, or a combination of the two. Dialog can be accessed through a number of different terminals and microcomputers. Access to LEXIS/NEXIS had been limited to dedicated and leased equipment but has been expanded recently to the IBM Personal Computer and other microcomputers. The price of the service(s) includes royalty fees to the publishers of the original articles. At IAC, the articles are rekeyed from the published issues rather than attempting to merge the machine-readable tapes generated by the publisher.

IAC and OCLC had planned a joint development project to establish an overnight electronic document delivery service using IAC's full text data base and the OCLC interlibrary loan subsystem and telecommunications structure. OCLC ILL users would be able to transmit an online request for an article to IAC, which in turn would process the request and transmit the article overnight to the requesting library via the OCLC telecommunications network. As originally planned, the OCLC terminals at the user's site would be set up for "auto-receive" and be equipped with printers to produce legible article text. The project appears to be in abeyance, since nothing more has been heard since the original announcement was made in the summer of 1983.

In actuality, only a very few of the full text services, with the exception of those associated with newspapers, can be called electronic publishing because the text is usually rekeyed. Another drawback is that high-quality illustrations cannot be included. In 1982, a consortium of international publishers (Academic Press, Blackwell Scientific Publications, Elsevier Science Publishers, Pergamon Press, Springer Verlag, and John Wiley & Sons) began planning a project that would eliminate these deficiencies. The ADONIS (Article Delivery Over Network Information Service) project attempted to develop a system using optical disks to store digitized text for articles in about 1,500 scientific, technical, and medical journals. Upon demand from the user, the article (including text and illustrations) could be transmitted directly to a user for printing or sent by mail in hardcopy form. Charges for the service would include fees for royalty payments.

By early 1983, three members of the consortium (Pergamon Press, Academic Press, and John Wiley & Sons) had dropped out of the project, and the remaining publishers (Elsevier, Blackwell, and Springer Verlag) were reconsidering their plans. It is assumed that since nothing more has been heard about ADONIS since 1983, the project, at least in the United States, has been shelved. An interesting experiment that was planned with ADONIS implementation was a special program for the British Library Lending Division, which supplies over two million journal photocopies a year.

The Library of Congress Optical Disk Pilot Program was not planned as an electronic publishing effort but as an experiment for preservation of fragile or rare materials and rapid public access for high-use materials. Analog optical disks or videodisks have been produced for photographs, photonegatives, glass and regular transparencies, color slides, posters, architectural drawings, motion picture publicity stills, color films, films on paper print, and television newscasts. These disks can be viewed on a disk player and a video monitor, both off-the-shelf equipment. Special viewer terminals and printers are required, however, to view the digital optical disks containing print materials. For the pilot, the following materials were included: high-use items provided by the Congressional Research Service for its Selective Dissemination of Information service (e.g., articles and government documents on public affairs topics); journals in science, technology, and business; periodicals in German, Portuguese (from Brazil), Japanese, Thai, French, and Hebrew; and a selection of government documents like the Budget of the United States, the Congressional Record, United States Agriculture Decisions, or Social Security Rulings.

Although copyright, royalty, and distribution concerns affect both methods, the videodisks are less likely to cause a problem because they contain images of items that either could not be viewed at all because the original was too fragile or could not be viewed because the original was at a distant location. In contrast, the digital optical disks do not appear to offer substantially greater capabilities than the (computerized) full text services currently available. In its present configuration, the digital optical disk system requires a special terminal and printer, and the system is not capable of (re)producing illustrations of the quality contemplated for ADONIS.

In the final analysis, however, the device that has played the most influential role in changing and facilitating the research process is the photocopying machine. Used in combination with digital facsimile transmission, photocopying is another means of providing full text rapidly and efficiently. Like computerized full text retrieval, facsimile transmission is independent of most distance or location constraints. (A recent article described two projects involving transmission among users in New York City, the other between libraries in Seattle and the state of Alaska.[9] The distance between sending and receiving sites was obviously not a problem for the New York City users; speed and convenience mattered, as did the fact that many of the receiving sites already owned some type of telefacsimile equipment. The Seattle/Alaska link involved not only distance but two different time zones. The project started by using the (Washington) state WATSYSTEM, which was relatively inexpensive but caused innumerable disconnects for out-of-state calls; then direct dial, at greater cost but with fewer disconnects; and finally long distance communications via satellite, at less cost than direct dial.

Since facsimile transmission requires photocopying to produce single sheets, the problem of reproducing illustrations remains. The Institute for Scientific Information offers another alternative, a document delivery service called The Genuine Article, which provides original pages torn directly from the journals or high-quality photocopies if the supply of tear sheets of an article is exhausted. (The service was originally named OATS for Original Article Tear Sheets, later Original Article Text Service.) The Genuine Article covers over 7,000 journals published from 1981 to the present in the sciences, social sciences, and arts and humanities, i.e., the journals covered by ISI's abstracting and indexing products. Prices for The Genuine Article include royalty payments and in some cases a royalty surcharge to cover unusually high royalties set by some publishers.

If the user is willing to pay the cost, computerized full text services or services like The Genuine Article offer advantages even if the library subscribes to the periodical. For example, the desired issue may have been sent to the bindery, and certainly librarians do not want to encourage users to tear pages from the library's copy. But the real benefits for computerized full text or facsimile transmission are obtained when any one or a combination of the following factors are present: the user wants to get an article as soon as possible, but his/her library/business/organization does not hold that journal in its collection; the user is located in an area that has limited library resources; the user is located in a metropolitan area with a wealth of library resources but does not have the time to obtain the periodical or to depend on a courier service to have the item delivered. Obviously, someone must be willing to pay the costs, whether it is the library, the business, or the patron.

Full text availability (in the context of this article, computerized full text, facsimile transmission, or optical disk) has become an increasingly important option to traditional methods of document delivery. Although it is unlikely that the work of most serials librarians will be affected by the electronic services or by electronic publishing in the very near future because their cost is still relatively high, it is also true that the growth in the number of primary data bases (including full text) and the corresponding growth in users of these data bases outside a library setting indicate potential changes in the provision of library and information services. The question is not when these changes will occur but how soon.

Copyright

Copyright is not, strictly speaking, a serials control issue either, but it is included in this discussion because it is definitely an area that has been affected by (photocopying) technology. The majority of photocopy requests are for journal articles, and there is disagreement as to whether resource sharing and photocopying have decreased the number of subscriptions held by a library. Implemented in January 1978, the Copyright Act of 1976 constituted the first major revision of the copyright law since

1909. The provisions that have caused the most controversy and disagreement are in Subsection 108(g)(2) dealing with, among other things, limits on interlibrary (or interactive) photocopying arrangements.

In 1977, the Copyright Clearance Center was established to provide a central agency to which libraries and other photocopying organizations can pay for the right to make photocopies from serials in quantities that exceed the fair use provisions and library/archive exemptions in the new copyright law. The fees, if any, are set by the participating serial publishers, with a small handling and service charge from the center. Users of the service pay for the copies, usually on a monthly basis, after they have been made. In late 1984, two major corporations, Warner-Lambert and General Electric, signed photocopy license agreements allowing their employees to make copies from copyrighted publications at all company sites throughout the United States. The agreements are effective for one year and renewable for a second year. Instead of a monthly fee, a yearly fee is charged based on data derived from a three-month copying survey at various company sites. The projected volume of copying is calculated for each publication copied during the survey, and the fees charged by each publisher are included. It should be noted that most libraries do not register or report to the CCC, since most library photocopying falls within the limits of Section 108.

Two recent developments in the copyright arena, also not directly related to serials control, have occurred because of developments in technology. Intel Corporation registered a chip design to secure legal protection from piracy under the provisions of the Semiconductor Chip Protection Act of 1984, signed into law on November 4, 1984. Intel was followed by Motorola and the Harris Corporation, which registered the topographical designs for integrated circuits called "mask works." Although administered by the U.S. Copyright Office, the statutory protection is neither patent nor copyright. The law makes it illegal to reproduce any registered semiconductor pattern for ten years after it is registered or first introduced, whichever occurs first.

The other development has caused considerable controversy. Two organizations, OCLC and the Cleveland Public Library, have copyrighted their respective data bases. OCLC's action, of course, is the more critical because its data base is not only the largest of its kind but also because it has the largest number of member libraries. It should be noted that the issue of ownership and distribution of bibliographic data surfaced earlier in 1979 and 1980, but had been dormant after OCLC issued guidelines for third-party use in mid-1980. By late 1982, when OCLC announced its decision to register its data base for copyright, the pendulum had swung to use of legal protection "to assure that OCLC members' rights to use of the database are protected and that unauthorized use does not increase the cost or decrease system performance for authorized users."[10] After nearly two years of negotiations between OCLC and the regional networks on contract language, it appears that contractual protection rather than copyright, except in the case of third-party infringers, will prevail, but an official announcement has not been made as of this writing.

Organizations Providing Serials Services

The United States does not have a comparable document delivery service such as that provided by the British Library Lending Division. Attempts to merge the bibliographic control aspects (e.g., cataloging or location reporting) with actual delivery of the item using available technology have had a mixed record. The organizations described below are examples of the successes and failures.

The need for a National Periodicals Center was first outlined in a study prepared by the Association of Research Libraries in 1974. In 1976, the National Commission on Libraries and Information Science established a Task Force on a National Periodicals System to carry this work further, resulting in a report *Effective Access to Periodical Literature* in 1977. The report, in addition to reiterating the need for a National Periodicals Center, recommended that the Library of Congress assume responsibility for developing, managing, and operating the center. The Library of Congress in turn requested that the Council on Library Resources prepare a technical development plan (*A National Periodicals Center: Technical Development Plan*), which was completed in 1978.

The technical development plan proposed, among other things, that the NPC contain a centralized collection beginning with about 36,000 serial titles and growing to about 60,000 current titles. Requests for items not in the NPC collection would be forwarded to referral libraries. In addition, the plan, at the request of the Library of Congress, addressed implementation of the NPC independent of any relationship to the Library. The concept of a National Periodicals Center as described in the technical development plan was opposed by several segments of the library and information service community, such as the information industry, many publishers, some scholarly societies, and library organizations like the American Association of Law Libraries or the Pacific Northwest Bibliographic Center. The National Commission on Libraries and Information Science offered the community several opportunities to debate this issue, including a public forum in April 1979 and an all-day session in February 1980 held in conjunction with the midwinter meeting of the American Library Association.

In July 1979, NCLIS commissioned Arthur D. Little, Inc. to prepare a technical/economic evaluation of alternative systems to provide effective access to periodical literature. This report, *A Comparative Evaluation of Alternative Systems for the Provision of Effective Access to Periodical Lit-*

erature, was submitted to NCLIS in September 1979 and provided data to support both the opponents of and advocates for the NPC.

Concurrently and somewhat unexpectedly, legislation to establish a not-for-profit corporation, the National Periodical Center Corporation, to provide reliable and timely national document delivery from a comprehensive collection of periodical literature was introduced and passed by the U.S. House of Representatives in the summer of 1979 as part of Title II-D of the Higher Education Act reauthorization bill. Title II-D encountered considerable opposition in the Senate until a revised Part D was proposed and passed in the spring of 1980: The National Periodicals System Corporation would be established with a three-year authorization of $750,000 for a fourteen-member board that would assess the feasibility and, if viable, design a system to provide reliable and timely document delivery from a comprehensive collection of periodical literature. Both houses passed the final legislation in September 1980, but Title II-D was not funded for fiscal year 1981. Since it appeared unlikely that Federal funding would be available for this effort, two advocates of the NPC, the Association of Research Libraries and the Center for Research Libraries, decided to explore the means by which CRL's journal collections could be accessed by researchers in institutions that were not CRL members.

Ironically, one of the library groups opposing the NPC, the Pacific Northwest Bibliographic Center, officially ceased to exist after March 23, 1983. Established in 1940 to act as a clearinghouse for matters related to library cooperation in the Pacific Northwest, PNBC formed a regional union catalog as the basis for its interlibrary loan and referral services and was housed in and, in large part, subsidized by the University of Washington Libraries. By 1970, PNBC began supplying photocopies of journal articles from the University of Washington's collections rather than forwarding requests to holding libraries. Although PNBC played an active role in resource sharing and networking in the area, two things occurred in the late 1970s and early 1980s that threatened its existence: (1) The poor economic condition of the Pacific Northwest with state and local government budget cuts and business and industry retrenchment coupled with decreasing amounts of federal funding affected the center, which received fewer interlibrary requests and experienced higher per unit costs (support for the center was based entirely on the number of interlibrary requests received); and (2) access to the data bases of the Washington Library Network, UTLAS, or OCLC meant that more libraries had direct access to location and verification information and no longer needed to go through PNBC. In July 1981, the PNBC board decided to close the union catalog, whose maintenance could no longer be justified since the majority of member libraries were entering their holdings into WLN, UTLAS, or OCLC. A year later, PNBC ceased to provide all services and terminated all staff. As of July 1, 1982, the University of Washington Libraries established a Resource Sharing Program as a self-sustaining unit to continue some of the services that had been provided by PNBC, such as interlibrary loan, document delivery (of photocopies) including a telefacsimile project, location reporting, bibliographic verification, and management of the CLASS OnTyme service in the region.

Another regional service, the New England Serials Service, existed from 1976 to 1978 as a pilot project to offer a periodical reprint service for libraries not having a network of interlibrary loan resources. Like PNBC, the New England service found that increasing fees to cover costs resulted in a dramatic decline in requests. Interestingly enough, after the service was phased out in 1978, its parent body, the New England Library Board, began studying the feasibility of creating a New England Bibliographic Resource Service in conjunction with a regional repository. It was anticipated that the new service would have access to the substantial collections of an academic library as its primary resource, the lack of which was noted in the pilot project. Since nothing has been heard about this service since 1978 and since the New England Library Board no longer exists, it appears that regional resource sharing in New England exists only on an informal basis.

Two other regional networks, the Pittsburgh Regional Library Center (PRLC) and the Minnesota Interlibrary Telecommunications Exchange (MINITEX), produce two union lists, the *Pennsylvania Union List of Serials* and the *Minnesota Union List of Serials,* respectively, as part of a range of services offered. Both union lists have been produced from the OCLC data base since the two organizations have had their records added to the CONSER data base. As regional organizations, however, MINITEX is the one that resembles PNBC in that it is heavily dependent on the facilities and collections of a large academic research library, in this case, the University of Minnesota Libraries. On the other hand, MINITEX began as a Minnesota effort, and the libraries within the state are still its primary users and sources of support. The success of *MULS* led to expansion of the listing to neighboring states. PRLC is also undertaking cooperative collection development efforts, such as a serials cancellation project, that would not have been possible without the union list in machine-readable form.

Another regional effort, the Southeastern ARL Libraries Cooperative Project, is designed to facilitate regional resource sharing for current serial publications. Funded with grants from Title II-C of the Higher Education Act, the project began in 1981/82 with the research libraries of the following institutions: University of Florida, University of Miami, Florida State University, University of Georgia, Emory University, University of Tennessee, University of Kentucky, and Virginia Polytechnic and State University. The original grant focused on the following objectives: creation of a data base of current serial titles held by the participating institutions; preparation of a draft of computer-readable notations for detailed serials holdings; preparation of a cooperative collection development plan encompassing both acquisitions and deselection; preparation of a rapid cooperative interlibrary loan plan; and extending participation among all southeastern ARL institutions.

Objectives for the second-year grant included plans to: permit two additional research libraries to add their current serial titles to the data base begun by the original members; allow the original eight libraries to add to the data base those serial titles that are needed for the cooperative serials collection development program; provide support for OCLC to add the new MARC format for holdings and locations to its system; permit the libraries to perform an in-depth test of the new MARC format; and allow the libraries to begin implementation of a cooperative serials acquisition and de-selection program. Although many of these objectives (including the earlier ones) have been met, there is a question as to whether the momentum of the project can be sustained without federal funding.

In general, then, the record of not-for-profit organizations in providing serials document delivery services has been mixed. The effort to develop a national, comprehensive system failed. Organizations like the Center for Research Libraries and the Universal Serials and Book Exchange provide services throughout the nation but on a much more limited basis than envisioned for the NPC. Similarly, the record of regional organizations has been mixed, and it is difficult to learn from the failures because the conditions and the environment in which they operated are diverse and hard to compare.

CONCLUSIONS

"What we call progress is the exchange of one nuisance for another."
Havelock Ellis

What has technology done for the serials librarian? The large data bases of the bibliographic networks and the abstracting and indexing services would not have been built without the developments in computer technology. Affordable telecommunications made it possible for large numbers of users to access these data bases. Powerful but affordable micro- and minicomputers have allowed users to acquire stand-alone local systems to meet their particular requirements as well as to have links with the large bibliographic and A&I networks. Computerized full text services and more rapid and efficient photocopying/telefacsimile equipment provide alternatives for document delivery, with optical disk and videodisk applications as possible alternatives for the future.

The real progress has taken place in the bibliographic aspects of serials control, such as the input and maintenance of bibliographic data. The inventory aspects, e.g., check-in, binding, routing, have been developed at a much slower pace although these particular functions (as well as acquisitions) were probably among the first library applications to be automated in the 1960s by individual libraries using batch systems. With the increased use of micro- and minicomputers for library applications in the 1980s, library system designers began to include these inventory functions of serials control in their systems.

In 1976, Audrey Grosch commented: "Even though the profession is entering a new era of research, it is clear that the research and development involving large online integrated MARC-based applications may increasingly be restricted to those institutions that have considerable expertise, specialized staffs, and can attract the necessary fiscal support to permit such work. However, more and more smaller institutions will be able to acquire minicomputers and intelligent terminals which will permit them to undertake research that would previously have required vastly more expensive computer systems"[11] Of course, she did not foresee the introduction of microcomputers in the industry or the role that the commercial vendors would play in the development of local systems, but by and large, her forecast was correct.

The negative side of the widespread availability of local systems is the possibility of uncoordinated decentralization and fragmentation of automation activities. We are unlikely to have a national data base or a national network, but the requirements of a national system are still valid: adherence to standards, firm commitment of financial resources from parent institutions, marketing surveys to determine users' needs, and a clear understanding of the "political" ramifications of the system. The latter is clearly the most important, particularly in this period when institutions will be competing for decreasing amounts of outside funding. Cooperation and coordination are part of every librarian's vocabulary, but now they entail new or different responsibilities, such as ensuring the utility of a project beyond the needs of its immediate participants. This is not an easy task when the participants are dissimilar in function; it is much easier to implement a cooperative project when the participants have similar missions, e.g., projects among academic research libraries, art libraries, or public libraries within a county. Nonetheless, cooperative projects must take the larger view and at the minimum, for example, provide products that can be used beyond their immediate constituencies.

The questions serials librarians must ponder are no longer "Where can I get cataloging information for a particular title?" "Has the library received this issue?" or "Is this volume back from the bindery?" The questions are "What data do we need to carry out collection development, preservation, or document delivery functions?" "What data do we need from other serials control functions?" "Can these data be obtained from existing machine-readable records?" "If not, how can we input them?" and "How can these data be presented in meaningful form for managers, administrators, or elected officials?" It was noted in the previous section that the CONSER A&I Project was the first step in bringing together the operations of the A&I services with those of libraries. What additional steps must be taken to form a permanent link that will aid users as well as the A&I services and libraries?

Technology is making it possible for the library of the future with its integrated automated library system to operate with the office of the future with integrated spreadsheet, graphics, word processing, and decision support capabilities using integrated voice and data communications. Like the office of the future, libraries must look for vendors that provide upward compatibility in their equipment, new or improved capabilities that take advantage of new hardware/software and linkages among internal and external systems. And serials librarians must remember that the goal we have is not only an integrated automated serials control system for serials information but an integrated automated library system for management information.

NOTES

1. William Saffady, "Automated Text Editing: The State of the Art and Its Implication for Libraries," *Journal of Library Automation* 9 (June 1976), p. 106.

2. The total number of authenticated and unauthenticated CONSER records is not known. By early 1985, the Library of Congress had distributed approximately 240,000 authenticated records for serials, including records created for the U.S. Newspaper Project. It also distributes a file called the Second CONSER Snapshot, containing 339,000 authenticated and unauthenticated records input by CONSER participants through Aug. 1, 1981, and a monthly service of unauthenticated CONSER records issued after Aug. 1, 1981. (Although approximately 261,000 records had been distributed through March 31, 1984, the number of unique titles is not known either.) In an OCLC brochure, "Serials Control—Union List Component," the figure of "over 600,000 serial bibliographic records, including the CONSER database" is given. Therefore, it is assumed that the CONSER file contains more than 240,000 records but less than 600,000.

3. Julia C. Blixrud, "CONSER Abstracting and Indexing (A&I) Coverage Project," *OCLC Newsletter*, no. 155 (Nov. 1984), p. 13. "OCLC Gives In-Kind Grant for A&I Project," *OCLC Newsletter*, no. 155 (Nov. 1984), p. 15-16.

4. The University of Washington "inputs interim records (brief, temporary cataloging records) into WLN for what they are contributing to the CONSER data base; the CONSER record is added to WLN through the MARC tapes and replaces the interim record." David E. Griffin, "Serials Review in the Washington Library Network," *Serials Review* 10 (spring 1984), p. 64.

5. David E. Griffin, "Serials Review in the Washington Library Network," *Serials Review* 10 (spring 1984), p. 70.

6. Marjorie E. Bloss, "The Dregs in the Union List Bottle: Titles not in the Database," *Serials Review* 10 (summer 1984), p. 50.

7. The Canadian Mini-MARC format handles both monographs and serials and was designed to allow libraries that did not create full MARC records to contribute their data to a national file. If these records are in the full MARC format, they can be processed as well.

8. Judy McQueen and Richard W. Boss, "Serials Control in Libraries: Automated Options," *Library Technology Reports* 20 (March/April 1984), p. 91

9. Janet Tracy and William DeJohn, "Digital Facsimile: Columbia Law Library and Pacific Northwest Library Facsimile Network," *Library Hi Tech* (winter 1983): 9-14.

10. David P. Lighthill, "Why OCLC Is Implementing a Copyright Protection Program for the Database," *OCLC Newsletter,* no. 144 (Dec. 1982), p. 3.

11. Audrey N. Grosch, "Library Automation," *Annual Review of Information Science and Technology* 11 (1976), p. 249.

Serials and Automation: Yesterday, Today and Tomorrow

Huibert Paul

ABSTRACT. An attempt is made to demonstrate that the frustrations and difficulties created for serials departments by the introduction of automation are coming to an end that the principal benefit automation provides—the making of serials information immediately available to users—is making itself felt. It is indicated also that irony resides in the fact that the computer, which in its early uses proved refractory, now makes the work of the serials person as simple and effective as in the days of the manual check in arrangement. Some predictions are made as to the look of serials and serials departments in coming years.

The tenth anniversary of the debut of *The Serials Librarian* is approaching rapidly. In these ten years the periodical has become the indisputable leading magazine for serials work. It actually has been the leader in this still so specialized work almost from the day Volume 1 Number 1 was published. The occasion calls for a look at the past, the present, and the future.

The predominant theme in *The Serials Librarian* (*SL* for short) in these first ten years of its existence has been computerization, its promises, its feasibility. and even its threats. In this climate my two-part article: *Automation of Serials Check-in: Like Growing Bananas in Greenland?* (Winter 1981, Summer 1982) saw the light of publication and generated scorn as well as praise. The article was conceived and born in an environment of rather chaotic development of automation in general. It was the product of many years of frustration with subscription agents and publishers who were sailing into the then uncharted waters of the computer world, with all the consequences, good and bad, that this entailed. The early days of the computer and the library world were days of struggle. It was a time when even the simplest request seemed to cause insurmountable problems: Library A wants a second subscription to the *Journal of XYZ,* Library B wants to drop a second subscription, and Library C wants a billing adjustment so that both subscriptions will henceforth expire at the same time. How on earth can our computer take care of that?

Huibert Paul, Cataloging Department—Serials, University of Oregon Libraries, Eugene, OR 97403-1299.

This kind of thing is rapidly fading into history. Gone is the high-flying salesperson of yesteryear. He or she no longer deals with awe-struck librarians who have no experience at all with automation. In the ever increasing sophistication of library automation, even serials no longer form an exception. Hence the danger of total disaster has become less and less likely. Some of us have met our Waterloos and Stalingrads. We are older now, and definitely wiser.

During these first ten years of *SL,* another breed has become extinct: the doomsayers who were so impatient to get on with automation, come hell or high water. We are all familiar with the pronouncements of these people. They envisioned hopelessly old fashioned librarians and libraries, totally bypassed in the information age. All information would be handled by non-librarians, and libraries would become practically extinct, crowded out by private enterprise. This has not happened and will never happen. The impatient doomsayers have become extinct themselves, while those seemingly old-fashioned librarians, including the serialists, continue to thrive. With all the networking, databases, bibliographic utilities, etc., that are now part of everyday life in the library world, librarians prove to be as necessary and progressive as anyone else.

This first decade of *SL* also saw the virtual disappearance of the pioneering librarian. In their anxiety not to be left behind, as predicted by the doomsayers, some libraries attempted to develop systems by themselves, with widely varying results. It seems to me more and more, as I look back on those years, that librarians have caused themselves a great amount of grief, among this financial hardship, by forging ahead with automation before library computer technology had developed sufficiently. And this was certainly the case with computerization of serials check-in. The work with punched cards, the expected arrival file with each expected issue in the form of such a card, has never worked well. The computer was still in a stage of development, and manual systems were still superior because of that. In any case, librarians are no longer pioneering.

At present there are quite a number of systems to choose from. Subscription agents, publishers, and others in the non-library, private enterprise world, have developed viable systems, much more in tune with library needs then used to be the case. In the years of struggle the salespeople and the few analysts who knew something about libraries, used to dictate to the librarians: You had better adapt your procedures to the mighty computer or else! It was as if they were saying: Ask not what the computer can do for you, but what you can do for the computer. These days we are getting closer and closer to the reverse: the librarians are making the specifications, and the computer had better adapt to these demands or else!

When the first issue of *SL* was in the making, way back in 1976, online systems were mostly still the ideal, the promised land of the future. Now the promised land is here; all of a sudden the future is with us. Online is now the rule rather than the exception. And lo and behold, the online computer world is rapidly giving back to us the good old versatility of the manual system, the versatility the 80-column card had taken away from us. (Does anyone remember the number of columns in the old punched card? Wasn't it 80?) Information is again instantly up to date. We no longer have to struggle with reams and reams of printouts; supplements are slowly but surely sinking into oblivion. The information in the old manual serials file was up to date the minute another issue was recorded, but there was one major flaw: the total information package was available in one location only. In the online environment, it is available in as many locations as there are computer terminals.

Another aspect that has come about is computer friendliness. Even the unsophisticated can use the computer terminal. Commands and search requests are now more and more catering to library users whose expertise and sophistication lie in quite different fields. User friendly terminals are now sprouting up everywhere, like flowers in spring. And with user friendliness, quality control has come about, or rather more of it, and it is here to stay. Computer products used to be ugly, hard to read, unwieldy, and programmers were annoyed if users said something about it. This is no longer the case, thanks to a great extent to the online environment. The technology is now sufficiently advanced that even such luxuries as products pleasing to the eye are becoming more and more in style. The computer is no longer the master of society, but rather a slave, as it should be.

These are also the days of quality control. With various systems competing with each other, such as OCLC, RLIN, WLN, etc., quality control is deemed essential. Networks can no longer afford to give it a low priority. As for catalogers, their products were once visible only locally. Nowadays, an error or omission is visible to as many libraries as are members of the bibliographic utility involved. We can no longer hide behind anonymity. Quality control and the appearance of the computer in general have led to vastly improved serial cataloging records. Serials cataloging products used to be skimpy and incomplete. Now the reverse is the case: records are as complete as can be, at least where non-minimal level cataloging is concerned. In fact, there is still danger of what I have years ago coined "information inflation." Long lists of rather obscure editors and lengthy lists of where a journal is indexed cause computers to have to resort to screen 2, 3, or even 4. Still, my recent experience as a serials cataloger makes me value overinflated records more than underinflated ones. I might as well stick my neck out again: minimal level cataloging is a disservice to mankind.

At present our immaturity where automation is concerned is changing to maturity. We are now more aware of the capabilities as well as the limitations of the computer. We are no longer content with products that are unpleasing to the eye. A more sober outlook has made us aware of vulnerability. Backup tapes are a "must," and we have even given thought to possible power failures. It used to be that computers were shown to anyone who cared to look at them. Now the security at a place such as OCLC in Dublin, Ohio, is surely as tight as that of any government outfit working on such things as advanced weaponry. Even health hazards and glare have been taken into account, largely as a result of a more mature outlook in general and in particular of concern expressed by unions.

As for the future, I am shy about predicting things. Too many futurists have made fools of themselves with their predictions. Remember the overabundance of electricity generated by atomic energy, too cheap and plentiful to be metered? There are, however, a few things we can predict with certainty. The manual serial record system will disappear, eventually even in the Third World. Whatever its virtues, the information age will not tolerate information that is not instantly accessible in various places. It simply is the spirit of the times. The well-run manual system was a mighty warhorse, but even the most noble of fiery steeds must give way to the tank and the armored vehicle.

The information age is upon us, a fact just as visible in the library world as anywhere else. The card catalog is still mostly with us as *SL* enters its second decade, but there can be no doubt that it will give way to the online catalog. Along with online information in general there will be a demand for online information about serials: what is the most recent issue received, which volumes are bound, which are at the bindery, and, if at the bindery, what is the expected date of return? Whether anyone likes it or not, this information is going to be demanded at the computer terminal just as frequently as is information about monographs, their circulation status, etc. And this means, of course, automation of check-in, claiming, and binding. Even the last of these matters has recently been written about in *SL,* even though not as definitively as might be desired.

Where personnel is concerned, the computer is now sufficiently friendly that anyone can learn to handle the terminal just as readily as anyone could learn previously how to work with a manual system. On a higher level, there is some danger that librarians will become strictly technicians and administrators. The old scholarly librarian is indeed not equipped to handle automation and networking. Indeed, the ever increasing demand for automation of the big four (Acquisition, Cataloging, Circulation, and Serials) leaves the present administrator in a position not to be envied. There are now good systems to choose from, each with its strengths and weaknesses. To choose the right system, to automate each of the big four, retrospective conversion, integration . . . , it's all very demanding. But who knows? The scholarly librarian may well return when automation has reached a high plateau. When the whole catalog is online and the big four have been automated, librarians may again have time to indulge in scholarly pursuits. To say that the scholar will never return and that books and journals will forever be regarded as mere commodities is to view history as a straight line. Such it is not. History goes round in circles or describes irregular patterns.

Finally, what will happen to serials work as *SL* enters its second decade? Will it be dispersed under the pressures of automation? Will form forever give way to function, as now seems to be happening? Not necessarily. Serials work once was dispersed, farmed out to acquisitions, cataloging, reference, etc. Then centralization was opted for as serials became ever more important. Now this process has gone into reverse because of the giant task of building an integrated system based on the computer. Once this has been built, serials work may again come to be regarded as sufficiently complex and unique to warrant a distinct subsystem as do acquisitions work and interlibrary loan. We will then have gone full circle, much like the semester system which gave way to the quarter system, the latter apparently making way again for the old semester system.

History is not a straight line. It has already been predicted that the journal in paper format will disappear, except for the most common newsstand type. Thus even *SL* may never see its third decade in paper format, but eventually become available only in bits and pieces, on demand. The electronic journal may for a time flourish until we discover that for the great majority the old paper format was not so bad and not so expensive after all. The paper format may be more pleasing aesthetically than the high speed computer printout of bits and pieces produced on demand. The electronic storing and dispersement of data is likely here to stay, although it may reach a high plateau and remain there for a long time. As for centralized serials work and the paper periodical, they may have some rough sailing ahead, but they are likely to prevail in the end.

Networking and Serials Control, 1975-1985

Gloria A. Kelley, MLS

ABSTRACT. The purpose of this paper is to review how networking has affected serials control over the past ten years in the areas of bibliographic description, acquisitions and inventory control.

INTRODUCTION

Networking has profoundly affected the area of serials control. In 1974 the networking of serials was only in the planning stage. The past ten years have included the planning, testing, evaluating, and marketing of various serials control systems.

For the purpose of this paper, networking will be defined as the act or process of a group of libraries sharing a computer-based bibliographic database system for various cooperative purposes.[1] This definition will include services provided by networks (e.g., OCLC and the Washington Library Network), turnkey vendors (CLSI) and some subscription agents (Faxon, LINX; Ebsco, EBSCONET).

Serials will be defined as a publication in any medium issued in successive parts bearing numerical or chronological designations and intended to be continued indefinitely.[2]

Glyn Evans, in a speech at the LARC Institute on Automated Serials Systems in May, 1973, stated that a library has three modes in which it applies control to serials. These are acquisitions control, bibliographic description, and inventory control. He also stated that these three modes are often blurred and overlaid, particularly in automated systems, and that they need to be re-established.[3] These will be discussed separately to obtain a better understanding of how networking has affected acquisitions control, bibliographic description, and inventory control in the area of serials over the past ten years' time.

Gloria A. Kelley is Assistant Head of Technical Services, Dacus Library, Winthrop College, 810 Oakland Avenue, Rock Hill, SC 29733.

BIBLIOGRAPHIC DESCRIPTION

The term "bibliographic description" is synonymous with "cataloging." Before networking can occur, a base file of bibliographic records must be available for use.

In 1975 nearly everyone agreed that the rules governing the cataloging of serials needed revising. The concern over these rules was, moreover, stimulated by emerging international standards for description and identification of serial publications. Beginning with 1975, the Resources and Technical Services Division Catalog Code Revision Committee (CCRC) made several requests to the editors of the revised Anglo-American Cataloging Rules (AACR) for devising of new rules of entry for serials.[4]

These requests for new cataloging rules for serials were only the beginning of an effort to give added attention to the bibliographic description of serials. During the years following, cataloging rules for serials continued to be a major topic of discussion. AACR2, was published in 1978, and provided new cataloging rules, and various works on standardization began to appear. The Library of Congress published the *National Level Bibliographic Record-Serials,* and the second edition of the *MARC Serials Editing Guide* was made available. Each publication provided standards for inputting data for future use in networking.

As a new incentive in the area of serials networking, the Council on Library Resources and OCLC signed an agreement providing the use of OCLC's computer network as the vehicle through which the cooperative effort to convert 200,000 to 300,000 serial records to machine-readable format would be carried out. In 1975, this project, known as CONSER (CONversion of SERials), moved toward its objective of building cooperatively a high-level database of serials, and it did this using OCLC facilities.[5]

Other developments in bibliographic description included making some use of ISSN as the official United States Postal Service (USPS) identification number for serials, and the defining by the American National Standards Institute (ANSI) Z39 subcommittee of data elements for recording and reporting serials holdings and its format and arrangement of periodicals.[6]

Developments of the past ten years in bibliographic description were important from the standpoint of serials networking in that uniform rules and standards were established for use by all networks.

ACQUISITIONS CONTROL

Acquisitions includes the functions of ordering, checking-in and claiming.[7] Networks supplying automated acquisitions systems for serials need access to a bibliographic file, searching capabilities to find material in the file, and a mechanism for manipulating this data for in-process control of materials by libraries.

The check-in function of serials was the first area in which networks, vendors, and subscription agents began applying automated techniques. As early as 1977, two of the major networks were promising librarians a better way of managing their serials records. The check-in module of OCLC's Serials Control Subsystem became operational as of January 20, 1977. In 1977 also subscription agents started supplying their customers with various products for in-house application.[8]

As the 1980s approached, the subscription agents Faxon and Ebsco committed resources to the research and development of serials acquisition functions. These agents started incorporating check-in, accounting and claiming into their systems. On the other hand, the OCLC Serials Control System only supported the check-in function until the OCLC Acquisitions Subsystem was started up. Through the Acquisitions Subsystem, libraries authorized to use it were able to order serials using an on-line database. There were, however, difficulties in ordering serials through one subsystem and checking in through another. The two subsystems were not linked beyond sharing the same on-line bibliographic database. Then in 1984 the claiming component of the OCLC Serials Subsystem was made available to users of the Serials Subsystem.

Standardization was also necessary in dealing with claims. An ANSI Z39 committee published a standard serials claim form.[9]

The early 1980s also witnessed a rise in the development of local systems. These local systems used bibliographic information downloaded from a national serials database to a minicomputer. Local systems were deemed highly practical by some because the considerable volume of activity involved in serial acquisitions could be dealt with by such systems at affordable cost.[10] Telecommunications costs were also important to users, and local systems eliminated this cost.

In 1985 OCLC developed its new serials control system, SC350, using the principle of having a library's local information stored on-site instead of at a remote site (in this case at Dublin, Ohio).

In ten years, networking has produced a wide variety of systems for serials acquisitions control with no system complete enough to handle all of the processes involved in the matter.

INVENTORY CONTROL

The inventory function of serials control comprises those actions that deal with a serial after it has been received. They include binding, routing, circulation control and union listing.[11]

Networks, commercial vendors and subscription agents are all developing binding and routing features for their serials systems. Binding procedures are usually part of the automated check-in function. The procedures are used by libraries to identify volumes ready for the bindery and/or to print binding slips. The routing features involve generating a slip to accompany volumes being sent to library personnel or patrons.

The major development in inventory control is in the area of union listing. In 1975 the American National Standard's Committee on Library and Information Sciences and Related Publishing Practices, Z39, set up its Subcommittee on Serial Holdings Statements at the Summary Level. The Subcommittee issued the *American National Standard for Serial Holdings Statements at the Summary Level.* This standard defined the data elements libraries should record and report to union lists. Then in 1979 a third ANSI Z39 subcommittee was appointed to design a standard for detailed holdings statements.[12] Although the statements produced by both subcommittees are still being debated, these statements constitute the beginning of standardization in automated union listing.

By 1981 union listing activities had gathered momentum. More libraries were utilizing OCLC's union listing capability. F. W. Faxon also announced their union listing capabilities.

To help libraries interested in participating in a union list project, two projects were started, one on a national level and the other international. A set of guidelines for compiling union lists of serials was drafted by the ALA RTSD Serials Section Ad Hoc Committee on Union Lists of Serials. And at about the same time the IFLA *Guidelines for Union Catalogues of Serials* were promulgated.[13]

In the area of automated circulation control, local in-house systems are appearing, and larger systems are being developed by commercial vendors. The major networks have not so far provided much help in this area.

Inventory Control is one function of serials management to which it is hoped the networks will soon commit resources for research and development, as it is one that merits serious attention.

CONCLUSION

The past decade can be described as one in which libraries, networks, and commercial vendors turned their attention to serials automation. Bibliographic databases and serials control systems appeared during those years. The systems marketed were all successful in handling some, but definitely not all, aspects of serials control. The knowledge gained in these ten years about serials automation should bring forth the ultimate serials system—one that provides for all aspects of bibliographic description, acquisitions control and inventory control.

REFERENCES

1. Sheila S. Intner, *Access to Media: A Guide to Integrating and Computerizing Catalogs* (New York: Neal-Schuman Publishers, Inc., 1984).
2. *Anglo-American Cataloging Rules,* 2nd ed., (Chicago: American Library Association, 1978).
3. Glyn T. Evans, "State of the Art Review," in *Proceedings of the LARC Institute on Automated Serials System,* edited by William H. Axford. (Arizona: LARC Association, 1973).
4. John R. James, "Serials '75—Review and Trends," *Library Resources & Technical Services* 20:259-269 (Summer 1976).
5. John R. James, "Serials in 1976," *Library Resources & Technical Services* 21:216-231 (Summer 1977).
6. Benita M. Weber, "The Year's Work in Serials: 1981," *Library Resources & Technical Services* 26:277-293 (July/September 1982).
7. Evans, "State of the Art Review," p. 8.
8. James, "Serials in 1976," p. 224-225.
9. Sally McCallum, "Standards: Three Serials Standards," *RTSD Newsletter* 9:19 (1984).
10. Dan Tonkey, "Evolution of Automated Serials Control: Technical Philosophical and Political Issues," in *Serials Automation for Acquisitions and Inventory Control,* edited by William Gary Potter and Arlene Farber Sirkin. (Chicago: American Library Association, 1981).
11. Evans, "State of the Art Review," p. 11.
12. Susan L. Miller, "Inventory and Holdings Features of Serials Control," in *Serials Automation for Acquisitions and Inventory Control,* edited by William Gray Potter and Arlene Farber Sirkin. (Chicago: American Library Association, 1981).
13. Weber, "The Years Work in Serials," pp. 285-286.

A Decade of Serials Cataloging

Jim E. Cole, MA
Olivia M. A. Madison, MA

ABSTRACT. Serials cataloging has undergone a revolution since the beginning of the 1970s. Various forces on both national and international levels have played an important role in the transformation of traditional cataloging practices. This paper summarizes the development of the International Serials Data System and the International Standard Bibliographic Description for Serials and their impact on both of the editions of the *Anglo-American Cataloging Rules*. The CONversion of SERials Project is also examined in depth.

Since the beginning of the 1970s, cataloging has undergone a revolution. The introduction of the International Standard Bibliographic Description and other efforts toward international standardization, increasing computerization, and the revision of the *Anglo-American Cataloging Rules* have dramatically transformed traditional cataloging practices. This is especially true of serials cataloging. This paper will attempt to examine the major national and international forces that have shaped serials cataloging since the early 1970s.

ISDS AND NSDP

The International Serials Data System (ISDS) is an international registry of serial publications. ISDS has its roots in resolutions passed at the 1966 and 1968 sessions of the general conference of Unesco, which authorized a feasibility study into the establishment of UNISIST, a scientific information system. A working group on bibliographic description, formed in July 1967, recommended the establishment of a registry of scientific periodicals; a further study, carried out by INSPEC at the Institution of Electrical Engineers, resulted in the publication in 1970 of a recommendation for the establishment of ISDS. With the help of funds from

---

Jim Cole is Assistant Professor and Serials Cataloger, 204 Parks Library, Iowa State University Library, Ames, IA 50011. Mr. Cole is the ALA RTSD Serials Section liaison to the Committee on Cataloging: Description and Access. Olivia Madison is Associate Professor and Head of the Monographs Department, 204 Parks Library, Iowa State University Library, Ames, IA 50011. Ms. Madison is Chair of the ALA RTSD Committee on Cataloging: Description and Access.

© 1986 by The Haworth Press, Inc. All rights reserved.

the French government, an International Centre for the Registration of Serial Publications was established in Paris.[1] A network of national or regional centers has also been established.

ISDS, through its *Guidelines*,[2] began to identify serials, assigning each a key title and its numerical counterpart, an International Standard Serial Number (ISSN). With the key title as its main access point, ISDS can operate independently of cataloging rules, since it does not use corporate headings as access points. The key title, based on the title of the serial, is unique to that serial. If the title consists solely of a generic term, the name of the issuing body is included in the key title, separated from the generic term by a space-hyphen-space. Qualifying information is added when necessary in parentheses to make the key title unique.[3] Further mandatory and optional elements are also added to complete the record.

An important provision in the ISDS *Guidelines* is the fact that when a serial title changes, a new key title and ISSN are assigned. However, to minimize the updating to the ISDS file, the *Guidelines* do include exceptions for "minor" title changes, such as the addition or deletion of prepositions or articles, minor spelling changes that do not affect the meaning of the words, etc.[4] Serials catalogers have discussed at length what constitutes a major title change, and they are finding advantages in certain aspects of the ISDS concept of a minor title change.

The National Serials Data Program (NSDP) is the national ISDS center in the United States. It began as a cooperative project between the Library of Congress, the National Library of Medicine, and the National Agricultural Library. In 1974 NSDP became part of the Processing Department of the Library of Congress, later being incorporated into the Serial Record Division.[5] As stated in the ISDS *Guidelines,* NSDP has several major responsibilities, including the systematic registration of serials published within the United States, response to user demand, communications with publishers of serials, and the active promotion of the use of the ISSN in this country.[6] An example of the great success NSDP has had in its promotional efforts is an agreement between the Library of Congress and the United States Postal Service that allowed the use of the ISSN as the official registration number for some serials qualifying for a second class mailing rate. Beginning in January 1979, all serials mailed second class have had to carry either an ISSN or a USPS identification code.[7]

ISBD(S)

ISBD(S), the International Standard Bibliographic Description for Serials, was first published in the spring of 1974.[8] Closely resembling its counterpart for monographs in layout and style, it is part of the International Federation of Library Associations and Institutions' program in universal bibliographic control. ISBD(S) brings international standardization to the descriptive cataloging of serials by assigning an order to the elements of the bibliographic description and grouping these elements into certain areas. It further specifies a system of punctuation for the resulting description. ISBD(S) concerns itself solely with the description of a serial. As stated in the first standard edition, "the description resulting from the application of ISBD(S) will not normally be used by itself, but will form part of a complete entry in a catalogue or other bibliographic list. Organizational and retrieval factors such as headings or filing titles used within or for the arrangement of entries in a catalogue or listing do not form as such part of ISBD(S) . . ."[9]

Among the distinguishing features of the 1974 edition of ISBD(S) were the lack of an edition area and a numbering area. The rules also concerned themselves with the "distinctive title" rather than the title proper as found in ISBD(M). The distinctive title resembled the key title of ISDS, although there were certain differences. Cannan points out that a distinctive title did not have to be unique, since parenthetical qualifiers were not permitted. ISBD(S) also allowed a generic common title to be qualified, with the qualifier thus coming before the section title.[10]

In October 1975 representatives of the Joint Steering Committee for the Revision of AACR met with representatives of the various IFLA ISBD committees and working groups to discuss the mechanism by which harmonization could be achieved in the ISBD program. The participants agreed upon a broad framework for a general ISBD (ISBD(G)), and that all specialized ISBDs should conform to this structure. The Joint Steering Committee was to prepare the draft of the new ISBD(G) in accordance with the decisions of the meeting.[11]

The ISBD(G) meeting and the decisions reached there had a profound effect on the further development of ISBD(S). ISBD(G) contained provisions for an edition area and also an area specific to the medium or type of publication. At an ISBD(S) revision meeting, also held in October 1975, two task forces were established to consider these new areas. Both areas were included in the first standard edition of ISBD(S), published in 1977; the latter area had become the numbering area. The same ISBD(S) revision meeting also agreed that the concept of "title proper" should be incorporated into area 1 of ISBD(S), and that the key title should be given in area 8 with the ISSN.[12] Area 6, in which a series title is recorded, was similarly affected.

INTERACTION OF ISDS AND ISBD(S)

One sees the influence of the ISDS *Guidelines* on the early development of ISBD(S) in its original concept of distinctive title. The interaction of the two documents, however, did not end with the publication of the first standard edition of ISBD(S). While ISDS is concerned with the registration and identification of a serial as a whole and ISBD(S) addresses the matter of descriptive cataloging, these two functions—registration and description—are generally performed by the same national center. Consequently, a desire has existed not only to harmonize the ISBD(S) text with those of the other ISBDs, but also to ensure the compatibility, as far as possible, between the ISDS *Guidelines* and ISBD(S). Certain ISBD(S) elements, notably the title proper and numbering of the serial, are not included in ISDS records prepared according to the *Guidelines.* Further differences exist between the two documents not only in punctuation, but also in terminology and definitions. As Anderson stated in 1983:

> there has been concern among national ISDS centres that divergences between ISDS requirements and current cataloguing rules for the preparation of the record for the national bibliography have resulted in the need to make two separate cataloguing operations . . . In the interests of economy and efficiency there would be benefits if those elements common to the two kinds of record were recorded in the same way; or if one extended serial record could contain all the elements for the description and identification required for national needs and to serve the international system.[13]

In 1981 the annual meeting of the directors of ISDS passed a resolution expressing the need to achieve the greatest possible compatibility with ISBD(S). In the same year, IFLA initiated a review process for the ISBDs published in 1977 and 1978, including ISBD(S).[14] As a result of the efforts of the groups involved, both documents have been revised. The *ISDS Manual*,[15] replacing the *Guidelines,* was published in 1983; the second edition of ISBD(S) still exists in draft form only. Changes have been incorporated into both documents. A new field for the title proper is included in the ISDS format, definitions and terminology have been standardized with ISBD(S), and references, where appropriate, have been made to ISBD(S) provisions. Among the changes to ISBD(S) are those made to the statement of responsibility in area 1 and area 6 to meet ISDS requirements for linking fields; also, notes in area 7 dealing with the bibliographic history of the serial have been harmonized with ISDS requirements, and references have been included to the *ISDS Manual* regarding minor title changes.[16]

AACR

The publication of the ISDS *Guidelines* and ISBD(S) had an early impact on the North American text of the *Anglo-American Cataloging Rules* (AACR) and its application in the United States. In April 1974 the

Library of Congress (LC) announced the deletion of rule 162B of AACR, with the result that when the name of a corporate body was included in the title of a serial, it would be transcribed as such in the body of the entry.[17] For example, a title such as *University of London Historical Studies* had formerly been recorded as merely "Historical studies"; henceforth it would be transcribed as "University of London historical studies." In May 1974, LC instituted the policy that if the title of a serial consisted solely of a generic term, the title was to be followed by the name of the issuing body, separated by a space-hyphen-space. The name was to be transcribed as found on the item cataloged, but elements in a corporate hierarchy not essential to the identification of the corporate body could be omitted.[18] Further changes were later announced, including the use of the key title and ISSN in linking entries, and the inclusion of a publisher statement in all records.[19,20]

The waning hours of AACR saw the publication of two important works. Lynn Smith's *A Practical Approach to Serials Cataloging*,[21] published in 1978, is of interest not only to students of cataloging but also to practicing serials catalogers; it covers every aspect of serials cataloging, including entry and description, and subject work. Judith Cannan's *Special Problems in Serials Cataloging*[22] was based on a course offered in the Cataloging Instruction Office of Processing Services at the Library of Congress. Cannan's work provided information regarding LC policies in the selection of a title page, choice of main entry, choice and transcription of the title, and the remainder of the description, and thus helped to standardize AACR cataloging practice in this country.

AACR2

In March 1974 the Joint Steering Committee for Revision of AACR was formed. The committee had several objectives, including the reconciliation of the North American and British texts of AACR, the incorporation of already approved amendments and changes into the code, and the consideration of other work and proposals for amendments.[23] In July of the same year, the American Library Association's Catalog Code Revision Committee held its first meeting, at which it endorsed ISBD(S) as a basis for the revision of Chapter 7 of AACR.[24] After four and a half years of international deliberations, the second edition of the *Anglo-American Cataloguing Rules* (AACR2) was published in December of 1978 and fully implemented in January of 1981.

In terms of serials cataloging, AACR2 contains three important differences from the first edition of AACR. First, there is no special rule regarding the choice of main entry for serials. Second, the format of the bibliographic description is different; in particular, serials entries may carry a statement of responsibility. Third, the bibliographic description is based on the first published issue or the earliest issue available. For serials as well as for monographs, the implementation of AACR2 meant massive changes in the way headings are constructed, signaling the end of the Library of Congress' policy of superimposition, and the way microforms would be described.

The major change in AACR2 relating to serials involved choice of entry. ISBD(S) directly affected the revision of the descriptive rules for serials and, along with the ISDS *Guidelines,* also played an important role in the discussion regarding their entry. Changes in AACR already mentioned—the deletion of rule 162B and the inclusion of a corporate name following a generic title—both added impetus to a movement toward an arbitrary title main entry for serials. As Cannan stated, "Now that catalogers can transcribe the title page as it appears on the piece in hand and must qualify titles consisting solely of a generic term with the name of an issuing body, the need for entry under corporate author to identify a title has been removed."[25] The problem was discussed at length in an article by Joseph Howard[26] and in a series of articles in the fall 1975 issue of *Library Resources & Technical Services.* The article by Carpenter proposed an interesting alternative—the elimination of a separate rule for the entry of serials.[27] Carpenter's proposal was eventually accepted. The second edition of AACR contains no special rule for the entry of serials and drastically restricts the use of corporate main entry for all publications.[28]

Shortly after its implementation AACR2 faced its first major battle over its theoretical basis for description. Questions revolved around Chapter 11 and the general AACR2 provision for describing the piece in hand; therefore, for a microform reproduction, information regarding the original work would be placed in a note. Early in 1981 the Library of Congress, the National Agricultural Library and the National Library of Medicine announced that they would continue to follow the AACR principle of describing the original when cataloging microform reproductions. However, they would still use AACR2 for choice and form of entry for access points. This decision had been recommended to the Library of Congress by the Association of Research Libraries and a variety of other U.S. libraries. Strongly worded letters and impassioned discussions took place within the library community regarding the announcement. Ultimately the Resources and Technical Services Division's Committee on Cataloging: Description and Access, on a split vote, formally endorsed the Library of Congress' proposal regarding the descriptive cataloging for microform reproductions.

Even before AACR2's implementation it was obvious to serials catalogers that the new rules did not provide a mechanism for the unique identification of serials, whether as main entries, linking entries or added entries. Rule 21.1B2 of AACR2, because it drastically limited the use of corporate main entry for all types of publications, served to magnify the need for some remedy. The Library of Congress drew up guidelines for uniform titles for serials, first appearing in *Catalog Service Bulletin* no. 5, and revised and republished as rule interpretations six times, most recently in no. 25 of the *Bulletin*.[29,30] The uniform title, based on the title proper of the serial, adds qualifiers in parentheses to make the entry unique. Originally favoring corporate name as the qualifier, the rule interpretation as now formulated favors place of publication. LC has also issued other rule interpretations covering chapters 1, 12 and 21 of AACR2 that have had a great impact on the application of AACR2 in this country.

CONSER (CONversion of SERials)

One of the most obvious success stories in the last ten years of serials cataloging is that of the CONversion of SERials Project (CONSER). CONSER evolved from specific recommendations of the Ad Hoc Discussion Group on Serials Data Bases. The precursor to the discussion group was an informal meeting, held at the American Library Association's Annual Meeting in 1973, at which a variety of individuals representing twenty institutions from the United States and Canada met to discuss primarily the "generation and maintenance of machine-readable union files of serials."[31] Discussion centered on the following topics:

1. The lack of communication among the generators of machine-readable serial files.
2. The incompatibility of format and/or bibliographic data among existing files.
3. The apparent confusion about the existing and proposed bibliographic description and format "standards."[32]

The initial membership of the discussion group was composed of representatives from the Council on Library Resources, the Association of Research Libraries, OCLC Inc., the Library of Congress, the National Library of Canada, ISDS/Canada, the National Serials Data Program, the Joint Steering Committee on the Union List of Serials, the Canadian Union Catalogue Task Group and its Subgroup on the Serials Union List, Northwestern University, the State University of New York, the University of California University-wide Library Automation Program and an observer from the British Library. This discussion group became known as the Toronto Group both because it's prime mover, Richard Anable, was from York University in Toronto and the first formal meeting was held in Toronto, Canada, in September 1973.[33] The purposes of this meeting, which was funded by the Council on Library Resources, were the following:

1. To establish a mechanism for creating a set of "agreed upon practices for converting and communicating machine-readable serials data."
2. To establish a mechanism for cooperatively converting a comprehensive retrospective bibliographic data base for serials.[34]

The Toronto Group and its various subcommittees finally reached consensus on the following major points:

1. The MARC Serials Distribution Service of the Library of Congress and the National Serials Data Program together were not building a national serials data base in machine-readable form fast enough to satisfy the requirements of developing library systems . . .
2. The MARC serials format developed at LC offered the only hope for machine format capability. Every system represented planned to use it . . .
3. There existed some difference between the LC MARC serials format and that used by the National Serials Data Program . . . We cannot continue with two serial records, both of whom claim to be national in purpose but which are incompatible with each other . . .
4. Major Canadian libraries are active in cooperative work on serials and these two national efforts should be coordinated.[35]

In addition to the above stated recommendations, the Cooperative Conversion Subcommittee also recommended: "1. a proposal for a cooperative project be prepared as soon as possible; and 2. that the conversion vehicle for such a project be the OCLC facilities."[36] The discussion group approved these recommendations as well and, on their basis, formally established the CONSER Project.

Throughout the discussion group's activities it became apparent that the project needed a legal sponsoring organization. The final choices were the Library of Congress, the Association of Research Libraries and the Council on Library Resources. In the end, the discussion group, with the agreement of the National Library of Canada, selected the Council on Library Resources (CLR) as the project's interim manager.[37]

The founding purpose of CONSER was "to establish a data base of bibliographic records on serials publications that can be used at the very least by the generators and maintainers of union lists of serials. The data base will also be usable on the local, regional, national and international levels as a base file for maintaining machine-readable serials files."[38] The original CONSER Project was planned to last two to three years, and it's purpose was the creation of a machine-readable data base of 200,000 to 300,000 serial titles through the cooperative efforts of its participating institutions.

In early 1974 CONSER faced formidable and unresolved problems. One by one they were resolved, but not without strong differing opinions voiced and compromises made.

In April 1974 CONSER decided to use the OCLC data base to input and edit its bibliographic records; after which CLR and OCLC began contract negotiations. One of the major bargaining points was the "ownership" of the resulting file. CLR was committed to the availability, at a minimal cost, of the CONSER file to the general library community, while OCLC was equally committed to its exclusive rights to its data base and concerned over possible negative financial ramifications of such easy access. On January 8, 1975, the council and OCLC announced that both organizations had signed a contract. In the end, both parties agreed that the ownership and free distribution rights to the CONSER data base would belong to the Library of Congress and the National Library of Canada.[39] The Library of Congress and the National Library of Canada later decided to make CONSER records available on their MARC tape subscription services. OCLC retained the "full use and distribution rights to the CONSER file."[40]

CONSER chose to use as its machine-readable format the LC MARC serials format, which was expanded to include data elements of the Canadian MARC serials format and the International Serials Data System.[41] The project wanted to have a base file of serials in order to limit the amount of original input into its data base. It chose the Minnesota Union List, into which were later merged the Library of Congress MARC serials file and OCLC member serial records. The MULS data base was selected by CONSER because it was compatible with the MARC serials format and was a comparatively large file, which contained around 72,000 serial records.[42]

The initial CONSER participants were the Library of Congress, the National Library of Canada, the National Library of Medicine, the National Agricultural Library, Cornell University, the State University of New York, the New York State Library, the University of California, the University of Minnesota and Yale University. The selection of any given participating institution was based on "the number of serial titles held, the quality of cataloging and the ability of an institution to absorb a portion of local costs."[43] In addition to these members, the U.S. and Canada ISDS centers were also original CONSER participants. In April of 1975 CONSER added two more participants, Boston Theological Institute and the University of Florida, along with the Florida Union List of Serials.

Because the CONSER data base was to become a composite file of records from a variety of sources, CONSER recognized at the outset that it needed to codify its input standards. This codification had to respond to a variety of national and international standards, among which were the Anglo-American Cataloging Rules, the ALA catalog code, ISSN, ISBD, U.S. MARC II, Canadian MARC, and any other local standards used by the participants.[44] The resulting document was called "Agreed Upon Practices."

As can be imagined, CONSER encountered a variety of problems, the major ones being what to do with serials records using both ALA latest entry cataloging and AACR successive entry, the Library of Congress' policy of superimposition and the general authentication policy.

Within its initial discussion on input standards CONSER had wanted all titles to be cataloged according to AACR. However, the majority of the records contained in the various files represented latest-entry cataloging.[45] To break up these latest-entry title records into separate successive records would have been an impossible task. Therefore CONSER decided to allow duplication of records in its file; some titles would be cataloged under the latest-title convention and others under the successive-title convention.[46] CONSER requested that all new cataloging input into the data base be done according to the successive entry principle.

CONSER also faced the problem of what to do with the Library of Congress' policy of superimposition vis-à-vis CONSER's desire for an AACR-based data file with only one form of heading for any given name. To resolve the problem, the Library of Congress created alternate variable fields in the MARC serials format that would permit the input of both the ALA and AACR forms of heading. Therefore, the ALA form of entry, when used by the Library of Congress, would be input in one of the new fields and the newly determined AACR form entered in the originally-designated variable field. In addition, if a CONSER participant input a non-AACR form of entry that was used in a bibliographic record, the appropriate Center of Responsibility would add the AACR form of entry. Thus the responsibility of AACR verification of name headings shifted dramatically from the participants to the Library of Congress and the National Library of Canada.

CONSER agreed to create Centers of Responsibility that would have responsibility for reviewing non-LC and non-NLC cataloging records for names and adding ISSNs and key titles. The National Library of Canada and the Library of Congress became responsible for their respective name headings, and the ISDS centers for Canada and the United States responsible for assigning ISSNs and key titles. Under CONSER's initial procedures, when a CONSER participant cataloged a new serial title it sent its surrogate to the Library of Congress or the National Library of Canada for authentication purposes. A CONSER participant could update any unauthenticated record but it then needed to send a surrogate of the publication to its appropriate Center of Responsibility. Once the Library of Congress or the National Library of Canada inputs its authentication code onto a record, the record is then distributed by the MARC Distribution Service.

The year 1977 will be remembered by serial catalogers for two reasons: OCLC began card production for serials input using its serials format and the original CONSER Project ended in November. At the end of 1977 the CONSER data base contained around 200,000 records. This data base included over 72,000 authenticated records and contained over 80,000 records input by the CONSER Project itself.[47,48] In 1978 CONSER announced that the project would continue under OCLC's management and that the Centers of Responsibility would continue to monitor bibliographic quality, verify name headings and add ISSNs with the corresponding key titles.

Over the following years CONSER has continued occasionally to add participants and by 1983 some of the previous participants, who had left CONSER because of their RLIN memberships, had rejoined and presently are adding their serials records into both OCLC's CONSER data base and the RLIN data base. There are now 22 active CONSER participants. CONSER has also extended limited membership to those institutions participating in the U.S. Newspaper Project, which is funded by the National Endowment for the Humanities. The U.S. Newspaper Project should prove to be an extremely important addition to CONSER as it systematically will add the only type of serial publication, the newspaper, that CONSER had previously given a low-priority status.[49]

In July 1984 the Library of Congress formally announced two recent CONSER developments that should have significant impact on the content of CONSER records as well as on the availability of additional CONSER records for distribution by the MARC Subscription Service.[50]

The CONSER Abstracting and Indexing Coverage Project has begun to enhance CONSER records by adding citation notes for serial titles indexed and/or abstracted in the major indexing and abstracting services. This project will also check for the presence of ISDS data elements in the records it works on. If ISDS data are missing or incomplete the project will add the information, time permitting, or send the records to the appropriate ISDS center. Everytime an authenticated record is enhanced by the project it will be redistributed by the MARC Distribution Service as a replacement record. If the record is not authenticated, it will be formally distributed only when a Center of Responsibility authenticates it.

The second announcement stated that CONSER participants may now authenticate non-Canadian serials records. The immediate impact will be that these participant-authenticated records will not have to wait for LC authentication before being distributed by the MARC Distribution Service. This new procedure will serve to reduce the authentication workload for the Library of Congress, while providing the Library of Congress' staff additional time to "concentrate on its role as a CONSER participant, authenticating records for serials held by the Library of Congress and to resolve reported problems in CONSER records."[51]

At CONSER's beginning, various members of the library community raised serious questions concerning its potential for outliving its original two to three year grant life, the availability of its file to non-OCLC participating libraries, its cataloging standards, and the overwhelming task placed on both the Library of Congress and the National Library of Canada to authenticate the CONSER bibliographic records. Despite all of these initial uncertainties, CONSER has evolved into a major ongoing cooperative cataloging project. Libraries using the CONSER data base have usually experienced substantial savings in cataloging personnel time and have access to extensive bibliographic information for their serials.

CONCLUSION

The past decade of serials cataloging has been marked by significant national and international efforts towards standardization and cooperation. Both AACR2 and ISBD(S) proved to be important and successful international standards. As future revisions are made to these standards, their areas of commonality will, no doubt, increase. CONSER evolved into the decade's major cooperative serials cataloging project and remains the driving force in keeping the costs of serials cataloging as low as possible through its cooperative efforts.

This next decade already has its bibliographic and corresponding machine-readable standards in place; however, an area still in dire need of standardization is that of serials holdings data. The U.S. MARC holdings and locations format is still in a final draft stage; it will be essential that the online library community begin implementing the finalized format in order to facilitate standardized transmission of this vital data. In addition, there will no doubt be an increased emphasis on serial retrospective conversion projects as a result of the rapid and continuing growth of local, state-wide and regional online systems and union list projects. With so many large research and academic libraries facing massive serials and monographs retrospective conversion projects, it remains imperative for libraries to continue cooperatively to convert their collections to machine-readable form.

REFERENCES

1. C. J. Koster, "International Standard Serial Numbers and the International Serials Data System," *Libri* 23, no. 1 (1973):71-72.
2. International Centre for the Registration of Serial Publications, *Guidelines for ISDS* (Paris: United Nations Educational, Scientific and Cultural Organization, 1973).

3. Ibid., p. 23-29.
4. Ibid., p. 32-35.
5. Mary Sauer, "National Serials Data Program," *Drexel Library Quarterly* 11, no. 3 (July 1975):40.
6. *Guidelines*, p. 6.
7. Mary E. Sauer, "National Serials Data Program," *The Bowker Annual of Library & Book Trade Information* 24 (1979):70-71.
8. Joint Working Group on the International Standard Bibliographic Description for Serials, *ISBD(S)* (London: IFLA Committee on Cataloguing, 1974).
9. Joint Working Group on the International Standard Bibliographic Description for Serials, *ISBD(S)*. 1st standard ed. (London: IFLA International Office for UBC, 1977), p. 2.
10. Judith Proctor Cannan, "The Impact of International Standardization on the Rules of Entry for Serials," *Library Resources & Technical Services*, 19, no. 2 (Spring 1975): 165-168.
11. "ISBD(G) Meeting, Paris, 16-17 October 1975," *International Cataloguing* 5, no. 1 (Jan./Mar. 1976):1-2.
12. "ISBD(S) Revision Meeting, Paris, 21-22 October 1975," *International Cataloguing* 5, no. 1 (Jan./Mar. 1976):3.
13. Dorothy Anderson, "Compatibility of ISDS and ISBD(S) Records in International Exchange: the Background," *International Cataloguing* 12, no. 2 (Apr./June 1983):15.
14. Judith Szilvássy, "ISDS and ISBD(S) Records in International Exchange: Compatibility Issues," *International Cataloguing* 12, no. 4 (Oct./Dec. 1983):38-39.
15. ISDS International Centre, *ISDS Manual* (Paris: ISDS International Centre, 1983).
16. Anderson, "Compatibility," p. 16.
17. *Cataloging Service* 108 (Apr. 1974):2.
18. *Cataloging Service* 109 (May 1974):9.
19. *Cataloging Service* 119 (Fall 1976):13-14.
20. *Cataloging Service* 112 (Winter 1975):12.
21. Lynn S. Smith, *A Practical Approach to Serials Cataloging* (Greenwich, Conn.: Jai Press, 1978).
22. Judith Proctor Cannan, *Special Problems in Serials Cataloging* (Washington: Processing Services, Library of Congress, 1979).
23. "Revision of AACR," *Library Resources & Technical Services* 18, no. 4 (Fall 1974): 400-401.
24. Minutes of the RTSD Catalog Code Revision Committee's July 1974 Meeting," *Library Resources & Technical Services* 19, no. 1 (Winter 1975):80-82.
25. Cannan, "The Impact of International Standardization," p. 165.
26. Joseph H. Howard, "Main Entry for Serials," *Drexel Library Quarterly* 11, no. 3 (July 1975):11-19.
27. Michael Carpenter, "No Special Rules for Entry of Serials," *Library Resources & Technical Services* 19, no. 4 (Fall 1975):327-332.
28. *Anglo-American Cataloguing Rules*. 2nd ed. (Chicago: American Library Association, 1978).
29. *Cataloging Service Bulletin* 5 (Summer 1979):5-9.
30. *Cataloging Service Bulletin* 25 (Summer 1984):70-77.
31. Richard Anable, "The Ad Hoc Discussion Group on Serials Data Bases: Its History, Current Position, and Future," *Journal of Library Automation* 6, no. 4 (Dec. 1973):207.
32. Ibid.
33. Lawrence G. Livingston, "A Composite Effort to Build an On-Line National Serials Data Base," *Library of Congress Information Bulletin* 33 (Feb. 1, 1974):A-35.
34. Anable, "The Ad Hoc Discussion Group," p. 208.
35. Livingston, "A Composite Effort," p. A-35-A-36.
36. Anable, "The Ad Hoc Discussion Group," p. 209.
37. Lois Upham, "CONSER, Cooperative Conversion of Serials Project," *Library of Congress Information Bulletin* 33 (Nov. 29, 1974):A-246.
38. Richard Anable, "CONSER: An Update," *Journal of Library Automation* 8, no. 1 (Mar. 1975):28.
39. Lawrence G. Livingston, "The Conser Project: Current Status and Plans," *Library of Congress Information Bulletin* 34 (Feb. 14, 1975):A38.
40. Ibid., p. A39.

41. Anable, "CONSER: An Update," p. 26.
42. Upham, "CONSER," p. A-246.
43. Anable, "CONSER: An Update," p. 27.
44. Paul Fasana. "Serials Data Control: Current Problems and Prospects," *Journal of Library Automation* 9, no. 1 (Mar. 1976):28.
45. Anable, "CONSER: An Update," p. 29.
46. Ibid., p. 30.
47. John R. James. "Developments in Serials: 1977," *Library Resources & Technical Services* 22, no. 3 (Summer 1978):303.
48. Ibid.
49. Upham, "CONSER," p. A-247.
50. Library of Congress. Cataloging Distribution Service, *Announcement—MARC Distribution Service—Serials.* (Washington, D.C.: Library of Congress, July 1984), p. 1.
51. Ibid., p. 2.

The AACRs and Serials Cataloging

Carole R. McIver, MSLS

ABSTRACT. A review from a serials cataloger's viewpoint of how the AACRs have affected the practice of serials cataloging for the past ten years, 1975-1984. Emphasis is on AACR2 with relevant comparisons to AACR1 in the revision, planning and implementation years. A future AACR is also discussed.

INTRODUCTION

It's getting easier! Not easier to deal with the constant changes in titles and corporate bodies that typically characterize serials. Not easier to cope with cataloging copy formulated from different sets of cataloging codes. But easier from the standpoint of actual application of the rules themselves. Each new code is more logical, more consistent and better organized than the codes before it.

Cataloging codes continually change and each new code must be dealt with in relation to past, present and future codes, and in relation to their interpretations and changes. The continuing nature of serials, in combination with the span of years over which serials are cataloged, requires serials catalogers "to learn the new but remember the old."

This article will attempt to provide a review of how the two most recent codes, the *Anglo-American Cataloging Rules* (AACR1)[1] and the *Anglo-American Cataloging Rules, 2d ed.* (AACR2)[2] have affected the practice of serials cataloging over the past ten years, from 1975-1984. Emphasis will be on AACR2 as it is the code that was planned for and came into existence during this decade. AACR1 will be discussed mainly to point out interesting differences and similarities in the revision, planning, and implementation stages between the two codes.

REVISION YEARS

Fear and hope best characterize the attitude of serials catalogers during the "revision years" of 1973-1977. Fear of the unknown, and hope for

---

Carole McIver is Head of Technical Services at Dacus Library, Winthrop College, Rock Hill, SC 29733. In addition she has been Head of Serials Cataloging for the past five years. She is co-author of *LC and AACR2: an Album of Cataloging Examples Arranged by Rule Number* (Scarecrow, 1984).

© 1986 by The Haworth Press, Inc. All rights reserved.

an end to superimposition and AACR1 Rule 6 and a chance to do away with copies of AACR1 that were "overflowing with tip-ins." Serials catalogers realized that a revised code was needed because AACR1 had been under constant revision since it was published. In many cases, it was causing more problems than it solved. James points out in his review of serials in 1975 that the "rules governing the cataloging of serials need to be revised especially in light of the emerging international standards for description and identification of serial publications."[3] *The Guidelines for ISDS*[4] and *ISBD(S): International Standard Bibliographic Description for Serials*[5] were the subject of many journal articles in 1975 and 1976. Two of the most significant problems were discrepancies between AACR1 and the key-title concept of ISDS and discrepancies between the ISBD(S) use of the first issue available and the AACR1 use of the latest issue.

A need for standardization was also an important issue in the revision of AACR1. Dewton stated that "uniformity of cataloging has not been accomplished in the United States under the existing *ALA Cataloging Rules.*"[6] This need for standardization primarily came from the publication of the *National Union Catalog*[7] in 1956 and other cooperative ventures, all of which suffered from a lack of consistent catalog entries.

Automation efforts were demanding a more standardized cataloging code. Soper noted that "automation had become even more pervasive in this and other countries since the AACR was published, and has generated increasing pressures to change the cataloging rules to conform to the new technology."[8] These changes led to changes in related areas that affected serials cataloging. In 1970, the Library of Congress (LC) published its preliminary edition of *Serials: a MARC Format,* which contained the specifications for magnetic tapes containing catalog records for serials.[9] Another edition was published in 1974.[10] Final contracts were signed for the CONSER (Conversion of Serials) Project in December, 1974, by OCLC and the Council on Library Resources, and the dream of serials catalogers for a comprehensive database of machine-readable bibliographic records of serial publications began to take shape. Serials catalogers were able to enter serials records in machine-readable form in the OCLC Online Union Catalog in 1974. They were not able, however, to receive serial cards until 1977.[11] In 1975, a conference, "The Catalog—Its Nature and Prospects," was sponsored by three ALA Divisions. Its central issue was the impact of modern technology on traditional cataloging principles and practice.[12]

The concept of corporate authorship and how it should be applied to serials led to the "entry of serials" controversy that filled the pages of literature in 1975 and 1976. Ironically, this was a topic that also caused much controversy during the revision of AACR1.

In 1973, the RTSD Cataloging and Classification Section's Descriptive Cataloging Committee (CCS/DCC), the committee through which were channeled the revisions for AACR1, opted for a new edition of AACR1.[13] Official efforts to formulate an updated catalog code began in 1974 with the formation of the Joint Steering Committee for the Revision of AACR1 (JSC).

With the establishment of these committees began the "revision years." For serials catalogers these were years of reading and hearing about the heated debates over the entry of serials, about ISBD(S) and how it would affect the new code and about how serials were going to be treated just like all other library materials. But even with a broader grass roots involvement than had been available with AACR1 and the extensive coverage in the literature, serials catalogers were still apprehensive about the new code. With so much debate and controversy they felt that nothing would be definite until the actual appearance of AACR2.

And so they waited. Still patiently trying to apply AACR1 with its Rule 6, which Edgar so aptly described as "a marvel of fuzzy language."[14] Still trying to cope with such problems as title changes, title transcription of initialisms and description of loose-leaf publications. And still trying to clean up the backlogs caused by superimposition and the change to successive entry cataloging. Library directors offered scant help in meeting catalogers' needs for positive support during this period. Most directors were in a state of panic over the costs of implementing a new code without having automation firmly in place to help, and over the impending need to justify implementation costs to non-library administrators with no firm data about the benefits of the change to support their requests.

THE PLANNING YEARS

Years of planning rather than immediate implementation followed the publication of both codes. AACR2, like AACR1, was not implemented by most libraries in the year it was published. AACR2 was published in 1978 and not implemented until 1981. AACR1 was published in 1967 and not fully implemented by LC until 1971. With AACR1, most libraries were in a quandary over whether or not to implement the rules at all, even though LC planned to adopt them. A project sponsored by the Council on Library Resources to determine the current application of AACR by large research libraries in early 1975 revealed that only 24.3 percent of the seventy-four responding libraries had fully applied the rules of AACR1 Chapter 7.[15] If research libraries were not following the rules that were "drawn up primarily to respond to the needs of general research libraries,"[16] what reason would other libraries have for adopting them? All changes cost money, and as Brown pointed out, ". . . the Anglo-American Cataloging Rules were not written to make life easier for catalogers."[17]

Unlike AACR1, AACR2 was adopted by the majority of libraries. Libraries had become more and more dependent on LC's leadership and services, and so followed LC's example and waited until 1981 to implement the rules. Also, many libraries were members of bibliographic utilities which had mandated the use of AACR2 and adherence to LC's policies.

The actual appearance of AACR2, however, did not settle the unrest over the new code. LC's decision to postpone its implementation until January 1, 1980, the date selected for the closing of their catalogs, was later followed by another postponement until January 1, 1981. This second postponement, done at the request of several large library organizations including the Association of Research Libraries (ARL), tended to increase anxieties over the code's effect on card catalogs. If the "big guys" were afraid, what was in store for serials catalogers? Dougherty, in an editorial aptly entitled "Leaping into the Void," expressed the attitude of many librarians: "As librarians assimilate the full implications of AACR2, they express dismay, anger, apprehension, resignation, or a sense of foreboding. None I have heard has expressed any eagerness."[18] He also voiced the opinion of many when he questioned whether the benefits of adopting a new code would outweigh the limitations, an opinion that had been expressed many times about AACR1.[19]

The fear of what it would be like changed to a fear of how it could be implemented. The changes in headings (now called "access points" to reflect the new technology) would require much refiling and interfiling in card catalogs. Online catalogs were still too far in the future for most libraries to receive serious consideration. Gellatly's "new crisis in cataloging"[20] had begun, and the big question now was, "Should we close our card catalogs or start new ones?" No one seemed to know the best solution, and the literature began to fill with information about the future of card catalogs. Articles appeared on interpretations and applications of AACR2, catalog closings, COM (Computer Output Microfiche) catalogs, and machine-based catalog formats. The future of the catalog was discussed in two books published in 1979, *The Future of the Catalog* by Malinconico and Fasana[21] and *Requiem for the Card Catalog,* papers presented at the AMC Conference on Management Issues in Automated Cataloging held in 1977.[22] A new publication, *The Alternate Catalog Newsletter,* was created to meet the need for "how-to-do it" information relating to the development of automated catalogs.[23] Many meetings about AACR2 were held in the years before it was implemented. The RTSD Division of ALA sponsored a pre-conference in Dallas in June, 1979, to train catalogers to teach AACR2 in workshops throughout the country. A series of institutes designed by LC for the RTSD Division and its Council of Regional Groups were held throughout the country between May of 1980 and June of 1981. Most of these meetings had sessions on serials cataloging that were helpful, but they concentrated more on rule-by-rule explanations rather than addressing specific cataloging problems in detail. Perhaps the emphasis on general information at these meetings was meant to reflect that in AACR2 all types of library materials were to be treated the same.

In trying to find the best way to integrate library materials cataloged under the new rules into catalogs containing materials cataloged under earlier rules, it became very obvious that serials could not be treated exactly like monographs. Serials were more complex in nature and, not only did they change frequently, but they continued. Serials did not receive as much attention as monographs by those studying the options on how to best integrate these new rules. An article by Decker, in 1979, is one of the few articles written specifically about catalog closings and serials.[24] Possibly this lack of attention occurred because it was taken for granted that serials would be affected by the same form of entry changes as monographs. But these changes along with the changes in how materials would be entered would cause many serious problems with serials. Not only would linking entries between serials be affected but so also would be the many other library records that had to be maintained for control of serial publications. It is very important that serials cataloging records contain a consistent form of entry as they are the basis for all other serials files.

IMPLEMENTATION YEARS

"Day One," January 1, 1981, or as Decker described it, "C-Day (C for closing or conversion)," finally arrived.[25] Many libraries did not follow LC's example. Many decided not to close their old catalogs. Very few were able to choose what Decker recommended as the best course of action for serials based on information that was available in 1979. This was a separate serials catalog with all records made compatible with AACR2.[26]

The literature during these years contained many articles with "how-we-are-doing-it" type information. An overview of this literature seems to indicate that most small and medium-sized libraries chose to maintain one catalog consisting of old and new entries interfiled. Larger libraries with large, over-burdened catalogs seemed to choose either two catalogs consisting of old entries in one, interconnected with new entries in the other, or two catalogs consisting of "frozen" old entries in the one and new entries in the other.

Changing all serials cataloging records to conform to AACR2 was an impossible dream for the majority of serials catalogers. Very few libraries could afford to hire additional personnel, and even those that could were faced with the fact that serials catalogers were "few and far between."

Also, during the years following the publication of AACR2, many standard cataloging texts such as those by Ackers,[27] Wynar,[28] and Maxwell[29] were rewritten to reflect the new code. Unfortunately, serials cataloging was not emphasized in them, and the excellent text by Smith on serials cataloging has not been updated.[30] Cannon's book, *A Comparison of AACR1 and 2*,[31] is helpful, as are the several books of examples of AACR2 cataloging that include chapters on serials such as *LC and AACR2*.[32] And for those catalogers willing to peruse LC serial cards not in rule order, *New Serial Titles,* beginning in 1981, provides a multitude of examples in cardlike format.

AACR2—ADVANTAGES AND DISADVANTAGES

Gorman, one of the editors of AACR2, described the code as "truly a second edition of the Rules and not a completely new code of rules."[33] He stated that it contained "differences in presentation and style rather than in substance or in ultimate results in the cataloging process."[34] The AACR2 rules were "written in the imperative mode (rather than in a mixture of the imperative and the passive as in AACR1),"[35] and they were "written in short sentences within short paragraphs."[36] What a relief this new style of writing was for serials catalogers who had been forced to read and re-read AACR Rule 6 in order to understand and apply it!

AACR2 contains two chapters for describing serials—Chapter 1 for general information and Chapter 12 for more specific information relating to serials. Other chapters on different formats are to be used if they are needed to supplement Chapters 1 and 12, as "seriality" has been redefined as "a condition that may apply to any type of library material."[37] Peregoy pointed out that the use of so many chapters would cause a "great deal of page flipping in AACR2" and that serials catalogers would sometimes need to add notes in the margins as reminders.[38] This has not turned out to be a problem, especially for those catalogers who had used AACR1, as it also had required them to refer to other chapters. It was much more difficult to get used to the AACR2 concept of "chief" and "prescribed" sources.

The eight basic areas of ISBD(S) are incorporated in Rules 1-8 of Chapter 12, as well as in all other chapters. They are especially visible in the new punctuation which separates and identifies the different areas. As predicted by Peregoy, learning the new punctuation has turned out to be the least troublesome aspect of the AACR2 descriptive rules.[39]

The chief source of information for serials is a complete reversal of that indicated by AACR1. Serials are to be described from the first issue published or the earliest issue available, rather than from the latest issue. This change represents a major step toward standardization, as it conforms with the *Guidelines for ISDS,* which require the use of the first issue to select the key-title. Nor has the change to first issue cataloging caused many problems in the cataloging of new titles because there has been relatively little growth in new serial titles in most libraries. It has caused some problems with title changes and in conversion projects, as most old titles were cataloged from the latest issue available.

Two other AACR2 changes that have caused relatively few problems for serials catalogers are the change in the order of the elements in the chronological, numeric, etc., designations and the replacement of AACR1 "supersedes." A title change now always "continues" a former serial, regardless of whether the numbering is continuous or starts over.

One AACR2 change that has affected serials cataloging "for the good and the bad" is the new concept of corporate authorship. The elimination of AACR1 Rule 6 and the emphasis on title main entry brought shouts of cheers from most serials catalogers, but the resulting problems for serials with nondistinctive titles brought groans of dismay. Fortunately, in 1983, LC came to the rescue and issued a rule interpretation on uniform titles to deal with the problem of generic and other nondistinctive titles.[40] While not a perfect solution, the interpretation did help tremendously. LC further refined it and issued another interpretation in 1984.[41] Now, all serials catalogers have to figure out is how to interfile these uniform titles with older forms of main entries in their many serials files. Also, with so many serials entered under title, there is the additional problem that many changes in the names of corporate bodies may not be caught by check-in personnel.

LC changed several other potential problems caused by AACR2. The inclusion of a statement of responsibility, a new concept for serials catalogers, was modified when LC defined the level of description to be used in cataloging serials.[42] The inclusion of a statement of frequency as the first note even if it appeared as part of the title proper was added.[43] And AACR2's requirement that microform serials be described as microforms was modified. LC decided to continue to follow AACR1 when cataloging microforms that reproduce previously published books and articles.[44]

Two of the more helpful AACR2 changes are the clear definition in 21.2 for changes in title proper that require a new serial record and the elimination of the abbreviation for number in the physical description area. Also, AACR2's concept of three recommended levels of description was a major step in standardizing the contents of bibliographic descriptions.

Some problems in serials cataloging were not solved by AACR2. One of these is lack of "provision for the indecisive, basically insecure serial which vacillates back and forth between its established title and a new one for a number of issues, 'trying it on,' as it were, or the 'tried and didn't like it' serial . . ."[45] AACR2 Rule 12.7B4, the variations in title note, does not help because it limits the variations in title to titles other than the title proper. Another type of "title change" problem not adequately dealt with is that concerning bilingual serials that undergo a title change in the title proper of one language but not in the other. And Soper points out a problem with "bound withs." While AACR1 had a rule for "bound withs" (AACR1, Rule 171), AACR2 Chapter 12 says nothing about two or more serials issued or bound together except in Rule 12.7B21.[46] Even if AACR2 12.7B21 is combined with AACR2 1.1G and similar rules in other chapters, it still is not as clear as the AACR1 rule.

AACR2 AND ONLINE CATALOGS

In his review of technical services in 1983, Hewitt stated that the "transition to online catalogs continued its inevitable advance. . . ."[47] This advance was looked upon favorably by serials catalogers who were trying to cope with the increased workload caused by the implementation of AACR2. Online cataloging systems, capable of manipulating and updating data seemed an ideal way to eliminate the expensive and time-consuming "add-to cards" work and to control the many name authority problems that superimposition and AACR2 had caused. Many serials catalogers had been using online records for card production for years, but until the advent of AACR2 and the controversy over closed/open catalogs, few seriously had considered online catalogs. In addition, procedures for cataloging current serial titles were fairly well established and most libraries were looking for a way to bring their retrospective serial titles into closer conformity with AACR2.

Many things falling into place made online catalogs the best choice for future control of serial records. Machine-readable serial records were available. LC had been distributing records in the MARC serials format since 1973, and the CONSER Project had produced a database of 467,588 serial records as of September, 1984.[48] The descriptive part of AACR2, based upon the ISBD(G), provided a consistent framework and made it easier to convert data to machine-readable form.

Converting to online catalogs is not without problems for serials catalogers. Extensive editing might be required to clean up serial records taken from bibliographic utilities such as OCLC before they can be added to an in-house data base. Many of the available online records have linking entries and titles in pre-AACR2 form. Unique serial identifiers and other changes in entry also slow conversion effort.

It is hoped that in the years ahead the literature will fill with information about serials conversion projects and that meetings will be held to provide serials catalogers with the opportunity to share ideas.

CONCLUSION

The question that is currently predominant in serials catalogers' minds is, "Will there be an AACR3?" Their copies of AACR2, like their old copies of AACR1, are now "overflowing with tip-ins." Martell says that "code making appears to have become a continuous process. Each completed cycle results in a published code. Almost immediately, a new cycle begins."[49] Crismond cautions "that in the future cataloging rules may change more frequently than they have in the past to accommodate and to take advantage of the capabilities of a machine-readable record."[50] Martell drew up a chart of the history of modern code revisions, and from its trend line he predicted that the next code revision is due between 1983 and 1988.[51] Maybe the question should be not will there be another new code, but when will it come, since its arrival seems inevitable.

What will the next code revision have in store for serials catalogers? Will there be another round of revision years filled with heated debates about the entry of serials? Will the main entry concept be abandoned altogether? Will the next revision process be as Lewis described that of AACR2, "the pursuit of the satisfactory on behalf of the unsatisfiable?"[52]

If the next code makers really want to take advantage of modern technology and make the next code "user friendly," they could put the entire text including subsequent revisions and interpretations into machine-readable form so that catalogers could edit and update their texts with personal computers. And, if they would also follow Gorman's suggestion of adding an additional section on the standard display of bibliographic information on terminal screens and print-outs,[53] serials could be cataloged and tagged for machine processing at the same time without having to consult several different sources.

REFERENCES

1. *Anglo-American Cataloging Rules.* North American Text. (Chicago: American Library Association, 1967).

2. *Anglo-American Cataloguing Rules,* 2d. ed., Michael Gorman and Paul Winkler, editors (Chicago: American Library Association, 1978).

3. John R. James, "Serials '75—Review and Trends," *Library Resources & Technical Services* 20, no.3 (Summer 1976):259.

4. International Centre for the Registration of Serial Publications (Paris), *Guidelines for ISDS* (Paris: United Nations Educational, Scientific, and Cultural Organization, 1973).

5. *ISBD(S): International Standard Bibliographic Description for Serials* (London: IFLA Committee on Cataloging, 1974).

6. *The National Union Catalog: a Cumulative Author List Representing Library of Congress Printed Cards and Titles Reported by Other American Libraries* (Washington: Library of Congress, 1956-).

7. Johannes L. Dewton, "The Grand Illusion," *Library Journal* 86 (May 1, 1961):1719.

8. Mary Ellen Soper, "Entry of Serials," *The Serials Librarian* 1, no.1(Fall 1976):28-29.

9. Library of Congress. Information Systems Office, *Serials: a MARC Format,* Preliminary ed. (Washington: Library of Congress, 1970).
10. Library of Congress. MARC Development Office, *Serials: a MARC Format,* 2nd ed. (Washington: Library of Congress, 1974).
11. John R. James, "Developments in Serials: 1977," *Library Resources & Technical Services* 22, no.3 (Summer 1978):302.
12. "The Catalog—Its Nature and Prospects," (Conference held October 9-10, 1975, in New York).
13. Neal L. Edgar, "What Every Librarian Should Know About Proposed Changes in Cataloging Rules: a Brief Overview," *American Libraries* 6 (November 1975):604.
14. Idem, "Serials Cataloging Up To and Including AACR2," *The Serials Librarian* 7, no.4 (Summer 1983):33.
15. John D. Byrum, Jr. and D. Whitney Coe, "AACR as Applied by Research Libraries for Serials Cataloging," *Library Resources & Technical Services* 23, no.2 (Spring 1979):142.
16. AACR1, p.1.
17. Margaret C. Brown, "New Cataloging Rules—an Open Letter to Administrators," *Pennsylvania Library Association Bulletin* 23 (November 1967):93.
18. R. M. Dougherty, "Leaping into the Void," *Journal of Academic Librarianship* 6 (July 1980):131.
19. Ibid., p.131.
20. Peter Gellatly, "The New Crisis in Cataloging," *The Serials Librarian* 5, no.4 (Summer 1981):1.
21. S. Michael Malinconico and Paul J. Fasana, *The Future of the Catalog: The Library's Choices* (White Plains, N.Y.: Knowledge Industry Publications, 1979).
22. Daniel Gore and others, ed. *Requiem for the Card Catalog: Management Issues in Automated Cataloging* (Westport, Conn.: Greenwood Press, 1979).
23. *Alternate Catalog Newsletter* (Baltimore: Milton S. Eisenhower Library, 1978-1980).
24. Jean S. Decker, "Catalog Closings and Serials," *Journal of Academic Librarianship* 5, no.5 (November 1979):261-265.
25. Ibid., p.263.
26. Ibid., p.265.
27. Susan Grey Akers, *Akers' Simple Library Cataloging,* 7th ed., completely revised and rewritten by Arthur Curley and Jana Varlejs (Metuchen, N.J.: Scarecrow Press, 1984).
28. Bohdan S. Wynar with the assistance of Arlene Taylor Dowell and Jeanne Osborn, *Introduction to Cataloging and Classification,* 6th ed. (Littleton, Colo.: Libraries Unlimited, 1980).
29. Margaret F. Maxwell, *Handbook for AACR2: Explaining and Illustrating Anglo-American Cataloging Rules, Second Edition* (Chicago: American Library Assn., 1980).
30. Lynn S. Smith, *A Practical Approach to Serials Cataloging* (Greenwich, Conn.: Jai Press, 1978).
31. Judith Proctor Cannan, *Serial Cataloging: a Comparison of AACR1 and 2.* (New York: New York Metropolitan Reference and Research Library Agency, 1980).
32. Alan M. Greenberg and Carole R. McIver, *LC and AACR2: an Album of Cataloging Examples Arranged by Rule Number* (Metuchen, N.J.: Scarecrow Press, 1984).
33. Michael Gorman, "Main Themes," in *The Making of a Code: the Issues Underlying AACR2: Papers given at the International Conference on AACR2 held March 11-14, 1979, Tallahassee, Florida,* Doris Hargrett Clark, ed. (Chicago: American Library Association, 1980):p.41.
34. Ibid., p.41.
35. Ibid., p.47.
36. Ibid., p.47.
37. Gorman, Michael, "The Anglo-American Cataloging Rules. Second Edition," *Library Resources & Technical Services* 22, no.3 (Summer 1978):214.
38. Marjorie Peregoy, "AACRII and Serials Cataloging," *The Serials Librarian* 3, no.1 (Fall 1978):22.
39. Ibid., p.24.
40. "25.5B [Rev.]. Serials/Including Series," *Cataloging Service Bulletin,* 23 (Winter 1983): 38-45.
41. "25.5B [Rev.]. Serials/Including Series," *Cataloging Service Bulletin* 25 (Summer 1984): 70-77.
42. "1.0D [Rev.]" *Cataloging Service Bulletin* 13 (Summer 1981);3-4.

43. "12.7B1. Frequency," *Cataloging Service Bulletin* 21 (Summer 1983):16.
44. "Chapter 11," *Cataloging Service Bulletin* 11 (Winter 1981):15-16.
45. Ann Turner, "The Effects of AACR2 on Serials Cataloging," *The Serials Librarian* 4, no.2 (Winter 1979):178.
46. Mary Ellen Soper, "Description and Entry of Serials," *The Serials Librarian* 4, no.2 (Winter 1979):174.
47. Joe A. Hewitt, "Technical Services in 1983," *Library Resources & Technical Services* 28, no.3 (July/Sept. 1984):205.
48. *CONSER: Conversion of Serials* 9 (December 1984):7.
49. Charles Martell, "The War of AACR2: Victors or Victims?" *Journal of Academic Librarianship* 7, no.1 (March 1981):5.
50. Linda F. Crismond. "Quality Issues in Retrospective Conversion Projects," *Library Resources & Technical Services* 25 (Jan./March 1981):48.
51. Martell, "The War of AACR2," p.5-6.
52. Peter R. Lewis, "The Politics of Catalog Code Revision and Future Considerations," in *The Making of a Code: the Issues Underlying AACR2:* Papers given at the International Conference on AACR2 held March 11-14, 1979, Tallahassee, Florida, Doris Hargrett Clark, ed. (Chicago: American Library Association, 1980):p.3.
53. Michael Gorman, "New Rules for New Systems: Should We Scrap All Bibliographic Codes and Standards and Start Anew?," *American Libraries* :13 (April 1982):242.

Serials Cataloging in Transition

Lynn Mealer Cummins, BA, MSLS

ABSTRACT. Serials cataloging is a task in transition. In 1976, it was performed in isolation at each library. In 1985, librarians are developing standardized, cooperative, automated, integrated cataloging systems.

What a time to be a Serials Cataloger! The first volume of *The Serials Librarian* contained only two articles about cataloging.[1] The *LRTS* annual review "Serials in 1976"[2] lists only a few more. Not much was written because serials cataloging in 1976 was a stable task, relatively well understood; but it was about to undergo drastic change. This paper is one librarian's view of serials cataloging then and now. It demonstrates the meaning of the ancient curse: "May you live in interesting times."

In the mid-seventies, Library of Congress proof slips were the major outside source of cataloging copy. *New Serial Titles* supplied additional information, otherwise the cataloger was on his or her own. Cards were produced locally and filed manually. Problem situations, such as isolated issues of several titles all bound together, could be described in creative ways, without setting precedents for other times and other places. Variations in cataloging of an item from one library to another were of concern only to editors of union lists of serials, who had to determine which reports were duplicate items and which represented separate titles. Local mistakes in interpreting rules or publishers' intentions could be fixed quietly or even let ride until the next title change, when the history of the publication would be summarized anew on a card entered under this latest title. The cataloger was not aware of problems in ordering, claiming, and binding, which were taken care of by someone else who, in turn, did not need to know about the mysteries of cataloging.

Today, catalogers are dealing with major transitions in rules, methods, and displays of serials cataloging. As individuals at separate institutions, they are at different stages of each transition. Some are planning future systems, others are running parallel operations, and a few have fully implemented state-of-the-art catalogs. Collectively, they are working toward standardized, cooperative, automated, integrated output.

Ms. Cummins is Serials Cataloger at California State University, Northridge, 18111 Nordhoff Street, Northridge, CA 91330.

© 1986 by The Haworth Press, Inc. All rights reserved.

The key to this future is standardized cataloging. Only if all libraries adhere to the same rules and practices can they understand and make maximum use of one another's work. Ironically, the vehicles for this are ISBD(S), with its unique use of punctuation marks, and AACR2, with its seemingly endless capacity for allowing local variation in application. The bibliographic utilities and Library of Congress have provided instructions and interpretations (not often conflicting) to help limit differences. An area of particular concern is authority control. Its importance is not in doubt, but its optimum position in workflow has not yet been established.

Although many libraries still have records to adjust to other AACR2 clean-up projects calculated to provide catalogers a measure of job security, librarians have made the adjustment to thinking in terms of the new rules. Retrospective cataloging increasingly requires referring to the serial issues, not just to their former cataloging, because the cataloger is unable to remember what something used to mean. As they learned the rules and adjusted to the AACR2 choice of main entry, catalogers were aided by the decision to create more uniform titles. The more restricted use of corporate body main entry, which was anticipated with so much concern, has not caused nearly as much recataloging as the unheralded change to successive entry cataloging, which requires the creation of a separate record for each title occurring in a serial's history. As usual, the major problem came from an unexpected direction. Editors of union lists face particular problems in interpreting records as individual libraries contribute recataloging at a pace that is unique to each.

Cooperative cataloging is perceived as the major benefit provided by the bibliographic utilities. No longer must each library duplicate the research of librarians across the country; it can let a library assistant use that work by pushing the "Produce" button on the terminal. This development, however, has caused trauma known as fear of cataloging for some librarians who now feel "everybody is depending on me," and "my mistakes will be on display for all to see." Fortunately, the libraries involved in the CONSER project have the power to revise serials format records and keep the quality up. True errors and incomplete information are not perpetuated; they are removed from the record very soon. Chances are good that a printout two weeks old no longer matches the on-line record.

Automated cataloging is just beginning for most libraries. Use of computers to produce cards for manual filing is obviously only an intermediate step to automated creation of records for an online catalog. In anticipating future needs of sophisticated catalogs, there is a problem with perceived inflexibility of the current fledgling models. Catalogers tell reference librarians, "we can't do that any more; the computer won't let us." Some of the rigidity is in fact the result of standardization that was agreed to without provision for nonstandard holdings, and some the result of reluctance to demand creative use of the few options that are available. The amount of flexibility available in future versions of online catalogs is probably being limited even now because of the image of docile acceptance projected to designers by decision makers.

Integrated library systems have been the official goal of many libraries for some time, but new developments in microcomputer technology are spawning greater interest in interfaced specialized systems instead.[3] The serials cataloger is becoming less involved with one isolated, discrete task and more involved in the entire range of automated serials activities. For instance, display of local holdings is a new interest for the librarian who previously referred to a pattern of cryptic notes written on a check-in card according to traditional ancient practices. As ordering, claiming, and binding functions are automated in systems built with MARC bibliographic records, there is necessarily a growing professional involvement and policy development by the cataloger with serials expertise.

The eventual outcome of all these changes is not clear, as new possibilities are imposed on transitions-in-progress. Many writers offered their speculations as 1984 loomed.[4] Today's state-of-the-art technology will undoubtedly be obsolete in five years. Further transitions will be necessary. Staying aware of trends in this formerly quiet corner of librarianship has become a full-time assignment. Involvement in these developments is cursedly interesting.

REFERENCES

1. Mary Ellen Soper, "Entry of Serials," *The Serials Librarian* 1, no. 1 (Fall 1976): 23-38; Neal L. Edgar, "Some Implications of Code Revision for Serials Librarians," *The Serials Librarian* 1, no. 2 (Winter 1976-77): 125-134.

2. John R. James, "Serials in 1976," *Library Resources and Technical Services* 21, no. 3 (Summer 1977): 216-231.

3. Joe A. Hewitt, "Technical Services in 1983," *Library Resources and Technical Services* 28, no. 3 (July/September 1984): 205-218.

4. See, for instance, articles in the special issue *Beyond "1984": The Future of Library Technical Services* that appeared as *Technical Services Quarterly* 1, nos. 1/2 (Fall/Winter 1983): 1-265.

Serials Cataloging Developments, 1975-1985: A Personal View of Some Highlights

Frank E. Sadowski, Jr.

ABSTRACT. Serials cataloging developments from 1975 through 1985 are discussed. Emphasis is placed on changes in cataloging rules, especially the effects of AACR2. Also discussed are uniform titles for serials and other title problems, microform problems, and CONSER.

INTRODUCTION

The decade 1975 to 1985 was a time of some turmoil for serials catalogers. The following is a personal selection of the major developments in serials cataloging that occurred during this decade. This is not meant to be an exhaustive treatise, but rather touches on some of the more important developments as seen from this author's viewpoint.

CATALOGING RULES

During the decade, proposed and actual revisions of cataloging rules dominated the attention of serials catalogers. In particular, attention was focused on the desire for a change in the rules regarding authorship and choice of entry, and second, on the need to adapt to the second edition of the Anglo-American cataloging rules and the changes caused by it. In his article on serials developments in 1975, John James[1] indicated this, stating that:

> Cataloging has been in the forefront of serials activity during the past year as the most cursory perusal of journal articles and conference themes will demonstrate. Nearly everyone seems to agree that the rules governing the cataloging of serials need to be revised, but

---

Frank E. Sadowski, Jr. was with the Serials Division, Thomas Jefferson Library, University of Missouri-St. Louis, MO. He is presently Assistant Director for Technical Services, Claude Moore Health Sciences Library, University of Virginia Medical Center, Jefferson Park Avenue and Lane Road, P.O. Box 234, Charlottesville, VA 22908.

© 1986 by The Haworth Press, Inc. All rights reserved.

just what form this revision should take has been the topic of much heated debate. (p.259)

He continues:

At the root of the differences among the various proposals is the concept of authorship and how it applies to serials and the related question of what constitutes a title and, therefore, a title change. (p.260)

The authorship question boiled down to two opposing viewpoints: adoption of title main entry for all serials vs. retention of the concept of corporate authorship in some form. The Catalog Code Revision Committee first recommended in 1975 that title main entry be required in all cases,[2] then reversed itself in 1976, recommending that entry under corporate body be limited to "publications dealing with the administrative affairs of the body and published by it or in some other way bearing its authority."[3] Lois Mai Chan entered this debate with an interesting point of view, suggesting that works of corporate authorship "should more appropriately be considered works of multiple authorship"[4] (p.65), which would essentially result in title main entry for most serials.

The revision of the *Anglo-American Cataloging Rules* was reported on and publication of the second edition anticipated by a number of instructive articles. In particular, Mary Ellen Soper's discussion of rules for entry of serials from a historical perspective,[5] Neal Edgar's preview of implications for serials librarians,[6] and Cynthia Durance's international perspectives[7] were notable introductions. The discussions of what should be and might be were, to a large extent, supplanted with the publication of AACR2 on 7 December 1978, by a spate of articles, institutes and in-house workshops designed to inform us and teach us how to use the new cataloging rules before their implementation in January 1981.

One of the major advantages, and to some extent a disadvantage for serials catalogers, of AACR2 is its consistency from chapter to chapter and its concomitant lack of distinction between formats. Thus, the choice of entry for serials is the same as the choice of entry for monographs. Corporate authorship has largely disappeared, to a large extent following the 1976 recommendation of the CCRC mentioned above. The changes brought about by AACR2 were introduced by Mary Ellen Soper[8] and Ann Turner,[9] and discussed in more detail by Ann Turner in a later article,[10] where she points out what has now become somewhat obvious: AACR2 is good in some areas and questionable in other areas. In general, AACR2 is an improvement over the earlier rules, especially in terms of corporate authorship, where a sensible compromise has been reached. Nonetheless, there are a number of areas affecting serials cataloging where AACR2 could stand some improvement. Thus begins the next round of discussions of serials cataloging rules.

UNIFORM TITLES

One of the problems anticipated in the discussions of corporate authorship was the question of how to enter generic titles. AACR2's restrictions on entry under corporate body led to the next major development of the decade: uniform titles for serials, also called unique serial identifiers. Developed by the Library of Congress and the National Library of Canada, this concept was introduced by Judith Cannan of LC at the 1981 ALA Midwinter meeting, and has undergone some major metamorphoses since that time. The LC rule interpretation (25.2B) was first published in *Cataloging Service Bulletin* no.11 in 1981,[11] and was subsequently revised in CSBs 12,14,20 and 23. The latest manifestation in CSB 25[12] differs from the CSB 11 version in a number of respects. CSB 11 gave corporate body predominance as the first choice of qualifier, whereas CSB 25 gives place of publication predominance. This major change was proposed by the Library of Congress at the 1983 ALA Midwinter meeting to the Cataloging Committee: Description and Access. CC:DA set up a Task Force on Serial Unique Identifiers, which recommended against LC's proposal at the 1983 ALA Annual meeting. Notwithstanding the Task Force's recommendation, after some discussion, CC:DA voted in support of the LC proposal. The Library of Congress originated this proposal in order to speed up the cataloging process. Unfortunately, the patron will find that qualification by place is not sufficiently distinctive to clearly identify the serial, whereas qualification by corporate body is most distinctive. It would appear that the patron's need to know is the victim of expediency.

Most of the other changes to the rule interpretation have been clarifications, although CSB 25 extends the concept to monographs and titles entered under author. The basic concept of using uniform titles to distinguish, rather than collect, otherwise identical serial titles has been generally accepted as a useful and sensible solution to an epidemic problem, although the choice of qualifier has caused serials catalogers some confusion.

OTHER TITLE PROBLEMS

Judging from the number of rule interpretations and articles concerned with choice of title proper, recording of title proper, title changes and the like, one would think that AACR2 was sadly deficient in this area. In fact, this does appear to be one of the weaker areas of AACR2. A number of problems stem from the lack of distinction between serial and monograph description. Notable rule interpretations from LC on title problems include those covering fluctuating titles and title changes (21.2A), common and section title (12.1B3), and parallel titles (12.7B5). While on the subject of rule interpretations, although not on titles, two other areas covered by most important rule interpretations are monograph vs. serial treatment (12.0A) and numeric and/or alphabetic designation (12.3).

One question that caused some confusion and frustration for serials catalogers was the problem of initialisms that abbreviate the full titles of serials. In 1979, this author discussed the problem and referred to a survey of periodical publishers, suggesting that serials should not be entered under the initialism.[13] This led to an LC interpretation of rule 12.1B1 that called for entry under the full form of the title, with the initialism given as other title information. This question, approved by the Committee to Study Serials Cataloging at the 1979 ALA Midwinter meeting, was brought up again at the 1985 ALA Midwinter meeting. The Committee once again approved the idea, and voted to recommend the LC rule interpretation as an AACR2 rule addendum. A number of related title questions still remain, notably the question of what constitutes a title page in periodicals, considering the use of the cover as a place for graphic experimentation.

Title changes continue to vex serials catalogers. In an attempt to stem the flow by public ridicule, David Taylor and his now ceased publication *Title Varies*[14] initiated the Worst Serial Title Change of the Year awards. Responsibility for continuing these awards passed to the Serials Section Worst Serial Title Change of the Year Award Committee of ALA in 1981. The Committee may have noted a glimmer of success as it attempted to come up with award candidates. The selection of "silly, unnecessary" serial title changes seemed to get harder each year as it appeared that at least the major serials publishers had gotten the word that title changes are the cause of much expensive, unnecessary and unappreciated work for libraries. The seriousness of the title change problem was clearly pointed out by Howard Robertson in his detailed description of the amount of work made necessary by title changes in a medium-sized research library.[15]

MICROFORM PROBLEMS

Serials tend to magnify problems otherwise shared with monographs. Such is the situation with the cataloging of serials reproduced in microformat. Following AACR2 strictly, while accurately describing the physical item, tends to obscure the bibliographic content of the item. This was discussed by Diane Stine as a reversal of earlier practice and a disservice to the patron, who is interested in the content of an item regardless of format.[16] The Library of Congress introduced an interim policy, awaiting final resolution of this problem, which basically followed the older principle of describing the original item, with the microform characteristics described in a note.[17] This policy, described as an alternative to provision 0.24 in AACR2, was supported by a vote of the CC:DA at the 1981 ALA Annual meeting, and has been adopted by most libraries.

The serials magnification of the problem lies in three related areas: purchase of back runs of periodicals in microform while maintaining a hard copy current subscription and binding the issues at the end of a volume; purchase of microform copies at the end of a volume in lieu of binding; and, purchase of replacement copies of missing or damaged volumes available only in microform. These situations lead to two cataloging problems: description of the serial microform as a microform that is incidentally a serial or, as a serial that is incidentally a microform; and, cataloging the two different formats on one record or two. LC has indicated in their rule interpretation that they will follow the second option for the first problem.

The second problem was addressed in a meeting of the Serials Section Research Libraries Discussion Group at the 1985 ALA Midwinter meeting. The speakers indicated that there were a number of ways to approach the problem, but the general consensus of the meeting was to favor treatment on one record with notes about the different formats. It was noted that automated catalogs as well as some manual serials files allow the distinction between formats to be made at the holdings level. Treatment on one record appears to be both economical from the point of view of the serials cataloger and effective in respect to the needs of the library patron, although no decision is immediately forthcoming on this issue.

CONSER

The CONversion of SERials project, which began in 1973 under the aegis of the Council on Library Resources, actually got off the ground in 1975 as CLR and OCLC signed an agreement for OCLC to be the vehicle through which the CONSER effort would be carried out. By November 1975, the base file of 80,000 Minnesota Union List of Serials records and existing MARC/Serials records were loaded. In 1979, CONSER development included publication of a microfiche collection containing 75,000 authenticated records. In the following year, the CONSER database was made available on tape from the Library of Congress, and included 259,000 records, both authenticated and nonauthenticated. The Government Printing Office joined the CONSER effort as a participant in 1981, and the second CONSER "snapshot" of 338,574 titles (approximately 124,000 of which were LC and NLC authenticated) was issued. CON-

SER has since grown to over 220,000 authenticated records and 21 participants, and has proven itself to be invaluable to serials catalogers as a source of quality cataloging records. The only problem presented by CONSER is what Alexander Bloss called "the evolving serial record"[18]: what a library may use as a base for its serial cataloging record today may look rather different when that library looks at the record again later. This is actually a small problem, a small price to pay for such a useful source.

OTHER DEVELOPMENTS

This discussion of the major developments in serials cataloging during the last 10 years would be incomplete without at least passing mention being made of a number of other happenings.

Successive entry was, of course, a product of the previous decade, but its effects continue to be felt up to the present day. Most library catalogs contain many older records cataloged under ALA or earlier rules, and many libraries did not begin to apply the AACR rule calling for successive entry until long after AACR was published. Union listing efforts and the development of online catalogs and their accompanying retrospective conversion projects are now facing the problem of whether or not to convert these earlier records to successive entry. Utilization of CONSER records has helped to some extent, but libraries will continue to face this problem for some time.

Minimal level cataloging (mlc) of serials has received much attention in recent years. The Committee to Study Serials Cataloging discussed the mlc concept at the 1983 ALA Midwinter meeting, and the Library of Congress has begun using it for the cataloging of serials of low priority. Candidates for mlc include: discards, microforms, items not needing full cataloging, and low use foreign language materials. Reporting on serial developments in 1982, Benita Weber[19] noted that LC conducted an experiment using mlc and found that it was four and a half times faster than full cataloging and reduced cataloging costs to $9.50 per title from an average of $75 per title for full cataloging. With some hesitancy as to the value of a minimal cataloging record, it can be said that this appears to be a development worth watching.

A few other developments deserve a brief note. The U.S. Postal Service adopted the ISSN in 1977 as the postal identification number that must appear on serials in order to qualify for the lower second class mail rate. This increased the workload for the National Serials Data Program, but has resulted in many more periodicals using the ISSN. OCLC catalog card production for serials became operational in 1977, thus making it possible for libraries to legally produce serial catalog cards. The OCLC database, however, still includes records for serials cataloged on monograph workforms up until 1977. The Committee to Study Serials Cataloging was formed as a part of ALA's Serials Section in 1978, and has been studying serials cataloging ever since, providing a much needed forum for the discussion of serials cataloging issues.

SUMMARY AND FORECAST

It can be seen from the above comments, that the decade 1975 to 1985, which was a time of much activity affecting serials, was marked primarily by discussions of serials cataloging rules. The first half of the decade was spent anticipating, and the second half coping with AACR2. The next decade will bring further discussion of cataloging rules, but the primary item of interest may well be the automation of serials functions and the development of the online public access catalog. This process has already begun in many large libraries, and will most likely spread to smaller libraries as a result of the development of statewide systems and networks. It looks like an interesting decade ahead.

Author's Postscript

As mentioned in the introduction to this paper, this has been a personal selection of both the developments discussed and the articles cited. In some cases, the omissions have been deliberate, but any others have been accidental and apologies are herewith tendered. I also wish to dedicate this paper to the memory of Neal Edgar, who, were he still with us, would probably have been the one to write it. Neal was intimately involved in the developments of this past decade, and I thank him for his efforts on behalf of us all.

REFERENCES

1. "Serials '75—Review and trends" / John R. James. *Library Resources and Technical Services* 20:259-269 (Summer 1976).
2. "Progress on code revision" *Library Resources and Technical Services* 19:416-418 (Fall 1975).
3. "Progress on code revision" *Library Resources and Technical Services* 20:287 (Summer 1976).
4. "AACR 6 and the corporate mystique" / Lois Mai Chan. *Library Resources and Technical Services* 21:58-67 (Winter 1977).
5. "Entry of serials" / Mary Ellen Soper. *The Serials Librarian* 1:23-37 (Fall 1976).
6. "Some implications of code revision for serials librarians" / Neal L. Edgar. *The Serials Librarian* 1:125-134 (Winter 1976/77).
7. "International serials cataloging" / Cynthia J. Durance. *The Serials Librarian* 3:299-309 (Spring 1979).
8. "Description and entry of serials in AACR2" / Mary Ellen Soper. *The Serials Librarian* 4: 167-176 (Winter 1979).

9. "The Effects of AACR2 on serials cataloging" / Ann Turner. *The Serials Librarian* 4:177-186 (Winter 1979).

10. "AACR2 and serials" / Ann Turner. *The Serials Librarian* 6,no.1:27-39 (Summer 1981).

11. *Cataloging Service Bulletin* 11:46-49 (Winter 1981).

12. *Cataloging Service Bulletin* 25:70-77 (Summer 1984).

13. "Initially, we need some definitions: the problems of initialisms in periodical titles" / Frank E. Sadowski, Jr. *Library Resources and Technical Services* 23:365-373 (Fall 1979).

14. *Title Varies* v.1, no.1 (1 December 1973)—v.6, no.3/5 (December 1980).

15. "What every serials publisher should know about unnecessary title changes" / Howard W. Robertson. *The Serials Librarian* 3:417-422 (Summer 1979).

16. "The Cataloging of serials in microform under AACR2 rules" / Diane Stine. *The Serials Librarian* 5,no.3:19-23 (Spring 1981).

17. *Cataloging Service Bulletin* 14:56-58 (Fall 1981).

18. "Coping with the evolving serial record" / Alexander Bloss. *Serials Review* 8,no.4:91-94 (Winter 1982).

19. "The Year's work in serials: 1982" / Benita M. Weber. *Library Resources and Technical Services* 27:243-258 (July/September 1983).

And in Hindsight . . . The Past Ten Years of Union Listing

Marjorie E. Bloss

ABSTRACT. The impact on union listing activities of growth in serials publishing and of budgetary stringency is discussed. Evidence is presented to show how advances in computer technology are making possible uniform representation of bibliographic and holdings information and so contributing to the success of union listing projects. Some important union listing publications are described, and the future of union listing is commented upon.

SETTING THE STAGE

Ten-year retrospectives on any topic can throw even the best of writers into tailspins, especially if the activities surrounding the subject have been uneventful. Fortunately for the contributors to this tenth anniversary issue of *The Serials Librarian,* Peter Gellatly and The Haworth Press in their infinite wisdom selected a very fruitful time to begin a journal dealing specifically with serials. This past decade in particular has seen great creativity and productivity in the way librarians handle serial functions.

Although often viewed as peripheral to the mainstream of serial activities, union lists of serials have greatly benefited from the advances made in serials cataloging, the standard representation of serials holdings information, and the storage of these data in machine-readable form. For the most part, these activities are internal. They are handled by the library staff and take place within the library itself.

While the uniform representation of bibliographic and holdings data and the machine storage of this information is extremely important, circumstances outside a library's walls are equally important to union list compilation. Even before the first bibliographic record is selected for a union list, even before the first holdings statement is added, the economic and political climates surrounding union list creation must be examined. Only by considering all of these conditions (internal and external) and by

---

Marjorie E. Bloss is Assistant Director for Technical Services and Automation, Illinois Institute of Technology, IIT Center, 3300 South Federal Street, Chicago, IL 60616.

© 1986 by The Haworth Press, Inc. All rights reserved.

examining how one influences the others can we come away with a total picture of union listing activities over the past ten years.

THE EXTERNAL CIRCUMSTANCES

Union lists of serials are the only library tool whose creation is predicated on a negative assumption. This assumption (that the day will come when a library lacks a particular issue of a particular title and will want to borrow it) has been reinforced during the past decade. We have watched the number of available serials proliferate and the cost of serials escalate. Granted, the same observations were made in the preceding decade as well, but during the past ten years especially library budgets have dwindled dramatically. Over the past decade these budgets have become inseparably linked to a decreasing population, be it a population based on enrollment or on general community demographics. The buying power we had in the '60s or even the early '70s no longer exists. The combination of these factors has set a political climate sympathetic to resource sharing.

The reality of the situation (that a library cannot afford subscriptions to all desired or even needed titles) has set the stage for cooperative library ventures like the compiling of union lists of serials. While union lists are initially created for the purpose of resource sharing, they may also serve their users as collection development tools. In some cases, agreements are made among participants to retain titles in specific subject areas. In other cases, participants may decide whether or not to purchase or cancel a subscription based on one another's holdings. Carrying this concept one step further, the Pittsburgh Regional Library Center uses the holdings area of its union list to indicate when a library cancels a subscription and the volume with which the cancellation became effective.[1]

The growing number of serial titles, the high cost of currently published titles, and the declining population which so strongly affects library budgets, have all set the stage for libraries to depend on one another more heavily for the serials they lack. As a result, we have seen a marked increase in the number of union lists in existence over the last decade. While new technologies have permitted us greater ease, greater speed, and greater flexibility in creating these lists, it is doubtful that librarians would be so eager to participate in union list activities if the need for resource sharing did not exist.

THE IMPACT OF LIBRARY DEVELOPMENTS
ON UNION LISTS

As libraries' abilities to share bibliographic data via computers became more commonplace, the need for standardizing these data became more apparent. Uniformity is required not only for the carriers of data for computer identification (as seen in the various MARC formats), but also for the rules governing the information contained in those carriers (e.g., *AACR2* and the Library of Congress Rule Interpretations, and the ANSI *Standard for Serial Holdings Statements at the Summary Level*). With the possible exception of the ANSI Standard these guidelines and standards were not established with union lists in mind. The differences in union list activities before and after their adoption, however, can be likened to the vast technological differences between a horse and buggy and an airplane.

The MARC formats and the rules governing the standardization of bibliographic and holdings data perform on a principle similar to the activities of Siamese twins: when one moves, the other accommodates it by moving too. Thus, when *AACR2* was adopted, modifications in the MARC formats were necessary. A change in one automatically meant a change in the other.

Throughout the past decade, we have seen refinements in both cataloging rules and the MARC formats. The increased standardization seen in cataloging and holdings rules and the MARC formats has increased our ability to share serials data. This, in turn, has permitted us considerable flexibility in our use of bibliographic and holdings data. As was just mentioned, we can now share bibliographic data but in a conceptually different way from that used when we purchased catalog cards from the Library of Congress. Bibliographic and holdings data stored in the MARC formats can be reused when necessary. These data can be updated, modified, or deleted easily. They can be formatted in different ways: either to display all stored information, or just selected portions of it. From magnetic tapes containing serials information we can generate offline products sorted on any delimited field. Furthermore, over the past decade we have seen more and more online union lists that provide continuous access to union list data. For union lists of serials previously criticized as being out-of-date even before they were produced, these achievements cannot be underestimated.

We have also seen dramatic changes in the ways union lists of serials are regarded in general, and are compiled and produced in particular. Certainly, union list data were entered into computers, and offline products were derived from magnetic tapes before the MARC-S format existed. Data entry in most cases was done in batch mode and the information was rarely available for immediate retrieval. Adding, modifying, or deleting union list information was cumbersome at best. Manually compiled union lists (those that were typed or typeset) were even more time-consuming to update. Any changes to the data could only result in having to redo the list completely.

To say these limitations discouraged participants from producing new editions of their lists is an understatement. The popularity of union list revision was second only to shelf-reading. The difficulties encountered in updating data prevented new editions of a union list from being produced in a timely fashion. Frequently, years would elapse between new editions. Once a list was produced, it was often viewed as a permanent library fixture rather than as a dynamic and constantly changing entity. Users of the list clung to it with a desperation that grew with the list's obsolescence.

The flexibility provided by the MARC-S format, its acceptance as a standard by the library community, plus the accessibility of serials stored in this format have greatly minimized our earlier concerns about union list updating and production. Libraries can independently subscribe to the MARC tapes or can access the data in them through library networks like OCLC, RLG and UTLAS. Linking libraries and networks together by computer terminal is now an everyday occurrence, with databases remaining literally at one's fingertips for many hours at a time. Union list updates can be done on a daily if not hourly basis, with the results seen instantly. This does not necessarily mean that the process of union list compilation can be done quickly or cheaply. Once the bibliographic record and holdings information are entered into a computerized database, however, there is no need to re-key the data for each new edition of the list. Union list production of offline products also can be regularly scheduled with the computer generating the products. Today, we accept these achievements almost casually. Ten years ago, we were only at the wishful thinking stage.

APPLYING THE TECHNOLOGY

Advances made in computer technology in general and library applications of that technology in particular have opened the doors for cooperative ventures in sharing bibliographic data. This in turn has necessitated the standardization of serials bibliographic and holdings data as well as the machine formats used to contain these data. To these ends, we have witnessed the adoption of *AACR2* along with MARC-S as the communications format for serials bibliographic data, and for other data the ANSI *Standard for Serial Holdings Statements at the Summary Level* with its parallel communications format *USMARC Format for Holdings and Locations*. The financial constraints on library budgets during the past ten years have been recognized. The results have led to a greater need for resource sharing, with union lists of serials receiving attention as a major vehicle for this process. This section of this paper will identify some of the activities surrounding union lists of serials that grew out of our need for resource sharing and some of the technological advances that made them possible.

The CONSER Project is probably the best known example in the

United States and Canada of the application of technology to the sharing of serials bibliographic data. Like *The Serials Librarian,* the CONSER Project began in 1975. At this writing, twenty participants are permitted to upgrade serials bibliographic data that are stored as part of the OCLC database. Online access through OCLC as well as magnetic tapes and other offline products make the CONSER file available to many users. The availability of high quality serial bibliographic records provides the first component in any vision of union list activities.

Of the bibliographic networks, OCLC in particular has taken advantage of standardization in the technologic and bibliographic advances to develop union lists of serials activities. Its Serials Control Subsystem was created to contain a Local Data Record (LDR) for institution-specific serials data such as check-in, claims, and bindery information. Two fields in the LDR were included solely for union listing purposes: one field for an institution's composite holdings, the second for its copy-specific holdings. Coupled with a serial's bibliographic data, the holdings information contained in one or both of these fields comprise the content of OCLC's Union List of Serials function.

In addition to the immediate online access of union list data, offline union list products are generated from the OCLC database in paper and COM form. (Magnetic tapes of a union list group's data should be available some time in 1985.) It is in the offline products that the flexibility inherent in the computer storage of data is seen. OCLC union list groups can select which fields of the bibliographic record they want displayed in their lists. They can easily change their minds with each new edition of the list, adding more fields when desired or deleting ones that proved superfluous. Holdings data can be similarly manipulated.

Although each OCLC union list group must designate an agent responsible for the list, once a library's holdings have been entered into an LDR, they can (with the library's consent) be used as part of any other union list. To date, 59 union list groups participate in the OCLC Union List function. This represents some 2,000 libraries and/or processing centers. This number increases to an average of 4,000 participants when identifying the actual number of libraries whose holdings are represented through processing centers. More than three million holdings statements, all formatted according to the ANSI *Standard for Serial Holdings Statements* have been entered into OCLC's Serials Control Subsystem for union listing.

By no stretch of the imagination does OCLC claim to be the only network providing computerized union list activities. California's two major union lists, CALLS and CULP, have provided their users with innovative access to union list data for a number of years. More recently, Faxon has developed union list capabilities as part of its LINX system. Unquestionably, many more union list groups of varying sizes exist. OCLC has been singled out, however, because it has been a leader in the application of the standards and the technological developments to union lists of serials. In doing so, OCLC has provided users with access to union list data in a more timely fashion and with greater flexibility than ever experienced before.

UNION LISTING ACTIVITIES AND GUIDELINES

A search on union lists of serials in the library literature prior to 1975 results in many listings of actual union lists but very little on union list compilation itself. This situation has noticeably changed in the past ten years. As more union lists have been created, more attention has been paid to the activities surrounding their creation. One apparent difference has been in the increase of articles published on this subject. Another difference has been seen in the attention given to union listing activities by professional organizations such as the American Library Association (ALA) and the International Federation of Library Associations and Institutions (IFLA). At the 1980 Midwinter Conference, the ALA Resources and Technical Services Division's Serials Section established an Ad Hoc Committee on Union Lists of Serials. Initially created to write guidelines for the compilation of union lists of serials, the Committee fulfilled its charge with the document entitled *Guidelines for Union Lists of Serials*.[2] This publication describes the steps in union list creation from the inception of the list to maintenance and user education. The Ad Hoc Committee also presented an all-day workshop on union listing at the 1981 ALA Annual Conference. As part of this program, the *Directory of Union Lists of Serials*[3] was distributed. The *Directory* identifies union list projects on a state-by-state basis as well as union list vendors. A second edition of the *Directory* is currently underway.

With the publication of the *Guidelines for Union Lists of Serials* and the fulfillment of its charge, the Ad Hoc Committee was granted standing committee status. Recently, the Committee has included as part of its meetings discussions on particular aspects of union list compilation. These discussions have focused on the different vendors used for union list creation, conversion from a manual to an automated list, the bibliographic fields appropriate to a union list record, and union list maintenance. Updating the *Directory of Union Lists of Serials* is also high on the Committee's agenda.

On the international scene, the IFLA Section on Serial Publications' Working Group on Union Catalogues of Serials has many of the same concerns as the ALA Union List of Serials Committee. In 1979, Jean Whiffin, then a personal member of the IFLA Section on Serials Publications, agreed to draft guidelines for the compilation of union catalogues of serials in partial fulfillment of a contract between IFLA and UNESCO. The resulting document entitled *Guidelines for Union Catalogues of Serials*[4] was extensively distributed in 1981 and generated a substantial number of comments.

Both guidelines and comments were analyzed in 1982 by an international panel of experts. The panel extracted those pieces of information deemed essential for the final document but did not include either a minimum bibliographic data element set or a minimum holdings data element set. The resulting document, *Guidelines for the Compilation of Union Catalogues of Serials*[5] was published in late 1982. Jean Whiffin's original work complete with minimum data element sets for both bibliographic and holdings information was later issued both as a separately published monograph and as an issue of *The Serials Librarian* with the title *Union Catalogues of Serials: Guidelines for Creation and Maintenance, with Recommended Standards for Bibliographic and Holdings Control.*[6]

Even though they cover much of the same material, each one of these three guidelines on union lists/catalogues contains a slightly different slant from that of the others. Miss Whiffin's document is the most prescriptive of the three, setting high standards for union catalogue compilation. The publications issued by the ALA Union List of Serials Committee and the IFLA international panel are considerably more descriptive and fall more into the "guidelines" rather than the "rules" category. Regardless, all three documents complement each other and offer union list compilers valuable information previously unavailable in written form.

As a result of her work, Miss Whiffin presented some 20 recommendations stemming from her research to the IFLA Section on Serial Publications' Working Group on Union Catalogues of Serials. From numerous sources, Miss Whiffin determined that there was an urgent need for a mechanism to standardize serial holdings statements at the summary level. Subsequently, a project proposal for a working paper towards the development of an international standard for serial holdings statements was accepted by the IFLA Professional Board. The working document entitled *Recommendations on Serial Holdings Statements at the Summary Level*[7] was distributed to Section members in late 1984, and should be published as an occasional paper by the IFLA International Office for Universal Bibliographic Control in 1985.

LOOKING TO THE NEXT DECADE

This article has focused on the major events and activities influencing union lists of serials over the past decade. New technologies have permitted us more speed and flexibility in the ways in which union lists are compiled. At the same time, economic conditions have been such that independent libraries have felt a greater need to engage in resource sharing activities. The result has been a marked increase in the number of union lists in existence.

Although we have witnessed many changes in union list compilation, the basic concepts of resource sharing have remained the same. As with all library services, those who create and participate in union list activities have benefited from the new technologies that permit us to respond more quickly and efficiently to our users' needs. Unquestionably library technology will continue to develop in the next decade. Serials on optical discs, and the further development of the electronic journal, to name but two, will affect not only how we pay for, access, and transmit data, but will force us to re-examine existing library network structures with regard to resource sharing. No matter how wonderful and revolutionary the technologies, our first concern must be—as it always has been—our users' needs.

REFERENCES

1. Carter, Ruth C. and Bruntjen, Scott. "Pittsburgh Regional Library Center Serials Cancellation Project." *Library Resources Technical Services.* Vol. 28, no. 4 (Oct./Dec. 1984). pp. 299-307.

2. Bloss, Marjorie E. et al. . . . *Guidelines for Union Lists of Serials.* Chicago: American Library Association, Resources and Technical Services Division, 1982.

3. Bloss, Marjorie E. *Directory of Union Lists of Serials.* Chicago: American Library Association, Resources and Technical Services Division, 1981.

4. Whiffin, Jean. *Guidelines for Union Catalogues of Serials.* First draft. Victoria, British Columbia, 1981.

5. *Guidelines for the Compilation of Union Catalogues of Serials.* Prepared by an Ad Hoc Group in consequence of a contract between UNESCO and the International Federation of Library Associations and Institutions, 1982.

6. Whiffin, Jean. *Union Catalogues of Serials: Guidelines for Creation and Maintenance, with Recommended Standards for Bibliographic and Holdings Control.* New York: The Haworth Press, 1983. (Also published as *The Serials Librarian,* Vol. 8, no. 1 (Fall 1983).)

7. Bloss, Marjorie E. *Recommendations on Serial Holdings Statements at the Summary Level.* Prepared for the IFLA Section on Serial Publications. Finalized version. Chicago, 1984.

Accessibility of Serials

Ruth B. McBride

ABSTRACT. Serials present many problems for both librarians and library patrons. For librarians, problems generally involve the management and control of serial collections. For patrons, the problems stem from efforts to access and use the collection. While some of the problems are the same for both librarians and patrons, some are different. Through analysis of the local situation, librarians can change some policies and procedures in management to reduce user frustrations. The author describes the efforts of the Library at the University of Illinois at Urbana to minimize the problems of librarians and at the same time increase serials accessibility for patrons.

Serial literature is an important source of knowledge and information for all classes of library users. This is particularly true in research libraries where serial literature reports the latest research findings to science and social science researchers. Serial literature, however, is a source of problems for librarians and frustration for users. Librarians are continually analyzing the "serial situation" in an attempt to control better this segment of the library's collection and make it more available to patrons. From SISAC to ISSN, from automated ordering to automated check-in, from CONSER to shared cataloguing, from OCLC to AACR2, from staff reorganization to automated circulation—all are efforts to process serials more quickly, more accurately and more effectively in order to provide immediate and complete serials information to library users.

The management of serials is a complex process with many inherent problems for libraries and librarians. Accessing those serials for needed information is also a complex process with many problems for users. While some of the problems are the same for both librarians and users, some are different, and some user problems are actually the result of librarians' efforts at serial control. If the ultimate goal of good serials man-

---

Ruth B. McBride, Central Circulation Librarian and Associate Professor of Library Administration at the University of Illinois at Urbana, formerly served as Serials/Analytics Coordinator in the Automated Systems Department at the University Library, University of Illinois at Urbana-Champaign, 1408 West Gregory Drive, Urbana, IL 61801.

The author wishes to thank Professor Michael Gorman, Director of General Services, and Professor Patricia Stenstrom, Head of Library and Information Science Library, at the University of Illinois at Urbana for their valuable advice and comments on this paper.

agement is equally good serials accessibility, some consideration needs to be given to the effect of library policies, procedures and problems on users.

Agreement on and understanding of what constitutes a serial may be a common problem for both librarians and patrons. The identification of a title as a serial title is very likely to determine its treatment in the library from selection to shelving, and, consequently, is very important to the patron in his or her efforts to access the title. There are several sources of definitions which can be used to identify serials. The official definition in *AACR2* of a serial reads as follows: "A publication in any medium issued in successive parts bearing numerical or chronological designations and intended to be continued indefinitely. Serials include periodicals; newspapers; annuals (reports, yearbooks, etc.); the journals, memoirs, proceedings, transactions, etc. of societies; and numbered monographic series."[1] *AACR2* further defines the term "series" as "a group of separate items related to one another by the fact that each item bears, in addition to its own title proper, a collective title applying to the group as a whole." *The ALA Glossary of Library and Information Science* defines a periodical as "a serial appearing or intending to appear indefinitely at regular or stated intervals, generally more frequently than annually, each issue of which is numbered or dated consecutively and normally contains separate articles, stories and other writings. Newspapers disseminating general news, and the proceedings, papers, or other publications of corporate bodies primarily related to their meetings are not included in this term."[2]

Such definitions, while primarily for purposes of cataloguing, may be useful in determining whether a particular title is a monograph or serial. Such library units as acquisitions, binding or circulation need further categorization in order to determine future treatment. Few libraries give periodicals, newspapers, annuals, society publications, and monographic series the same treatment. Libraries frequently develop their own criteria as to what constitutes a periodical, a monographic series, an analyzed series, etc. For example, the category to which a particular serial is assigned may depend upon its frequency (annual? biennial? monthly? weekly?); or on its format (monographic? newspaper? magazine?); or on its content (one subject with one author or editor? several subjects with several authors?); or even how it is purchased (by subscription? by invoice? through gift or exchange?); or perhaps by the idiosyncracies of a particular subject area or a special library. The designated category to which a serial title is assigned (periodical, newspaper, annual, society publication, monographic series, etc.) may determine its future with regard to whether it is classified, where it is located in the library (e.g., "current periodicals reading room"), its binding type and priority, its circulating status, its loan period, etc. The category may be assigned by acquisitions staff according to certain criteria, or by cataloguing staff according to a different set of criteria. If circulation librarians assigned serial titles to the various categories, such assignments would probably be made according to an entirely different set of criteria.

While defining and categorizing serials in the library is largely for the purpose of control, such treatment influences the way patrons must access those serials, including the use of indexes and other bibliographic sources to find citations. There is small wonder that patrons rarely have any understanding of the complexity or even the reasons for such divisions of materials. To them, a journal is a journal, a book is a book.

The locally accepted definition of the various kinds of serials is very important to librarians, however, who devote much of their time, energy and expertise to matters related to serials management or "control." Many of the professional meetings and much of the library literature are directed toward librarians' attempting to manage a serials collection from selection and ordering to cataloguing and record keeping, from binding and weeding to shelving and circulating, from fines and losses to photocopying and mutilation.

Selection, whether done by subject specialists or others, must be done with the research and teaching needs of the faculty and the present strengths of the collection carefully in mind. Keeping informed of new and important journals published all over the world in many languages and in a variety of subject areas is a monumental task. The high cost of serial subscriptions, of which we are constantly reminded, makes such careful selection especially important. Sometimes "de-selection" is necessary; the need to cancel some serials in order to add titles more in demand. Faculty must be consulted and the effect of such cancellations on the entire collection ascertained. In some libraries, older, lesser-used serials may even be weeded in order to provide later savings in terms of storage and binding. Whether such serials are readily available elsewhere must be considered. Acquiring them (setting up orders, approval and payment plans) may also be difficult, particularly those published outside the United States. Communicating with a wide variety of publishers whose publication schedules and billing procedures vary requires a skillful and knowledgeable staff. Receiving them regularly, along with the necessary record keeping, constitutes a continuing problem for library staffs. Staff can easily become immersed in intricate paper work as they "track" the thousands of titles received regularly by large libraries. Publishers of scholarly journals are particularly notorious for irregular or late publication schedules. Claiming missing issues is a continuing challenge for the best organized acquisitions department. Determining how and what to claim is in itself a problem. Claiming policies vary with each publisher. Some titles cannot be claimed at all; some must be claimed immediately to achieve results; some cannot be claimed for a year or for a similar specific period. Cataloguing serials with their title changes, numbering variations, obscure bibliographic information, etc., has long required catalogers with special expertise. Serials split and combine, stop and start, change publishers and place of publications, and add sub-series and supplements with abandon. If the library collects material in several languages, catalogers must have special language capabilities also. Updating serials records with accurate holdings is a continual burden. Each volume, as it is received, must be added in order to maintain current information.

Circulating serials, whether bound or unbound, is not without problems either, and special policies regarding loan periods, late charges, etc., are created especially for them. It may not even be clear to circulation staff that an item is a part of a serial, and not a volume of a monographic set or an edition of a monograph. Serials that are "analyzed" create additional confusion when accessed as a monograph but circulated as a volume of a serial. Some proliferate at an alarming (weekly or oftener) rate, and space must be left on the shelves for growth. Variations in size and shape in general are a problem for stacks managers. If they start out as "oversize" with subsequent changes in size, all sizes must be accommodated. Shelving journals newly received is a daily time-consuming task for staffs. Serials provide a continuing drain on binding budgets, for as subscription costs escalate, so do binding costs. Selection for binding, since all cannot be bound, is not only time-consuming but also difficult. Should the library bind the most heavily used? the most fragile? the most prolific? the most expensive? Should a volume be bound without missing issues, or placed on a "binding shelf" to wait for the claimed issue? Deteriorating monographs wait to be rebound so that journals can be bound for purposes of control and to facilitate use. While security and protection is a problem with all library materials, serials seem to suffer particularly from mutilation. Advertisements, illustrations and whole articles are ripped out despite the efforts of librarians to provide easy access to cheap photocopying. Replacement of back issues is virtually impossible except with microforms or photocopies since few out of print vendors can supply the variety of serials in a library's collection. The great mass of serial material received daily at large libraries is in itself intimidating, and gives staff the feeling of being on a "treadmill." Further problems in serials management may simply be maintaining a stable staff of persons trained and knowledgeable in the intricacies of serials control.

The tasks of managing a growing serials collection may be so overwhelming that there is little time or energy left over to view the situation from the patron's point of view. In fact, some library policies, developed to maintain better control, may be contributing to the patron's problems.

Librarians may assume that efficient serials control insures the availability of such materials for patrons without actually reviewing the situation from the patron's perspective.

What about the library patron having problems with serials? He or she may not even know that a desired item is a "serial," and may simply see it as a source of current information necessary to further research. Such perceptions are shared by faculty members and by undergraduates. The desired item may be in a journal, or an annual report, proceedings of a conference, or a volume of a monographic series, or even a newspaper. The user comes to the library with a citation from an index or bibliography or similar source, or is simply seeking current (periodical) information on a particular subject, as is the case with many undergraduates. Finding the specific title in the card catalogue, serial record or computer may be difficult since the cited or remembered title may differ from the title under which the library has catalogued and filed it. *AACR2,* while it has simplified the choice of entry by making title entry mandatory in many cases, has not solved the problem for patrons in cases of generic titles. The library may not fully catalogue and classify some serials (usually periodicals and newspapers), making subject searches virtually impossible. When the title is finally identified, it is necessary to determine if the specific issue is held by the library. Library record-keeping varies; and often only bound issues are added to public records, in which case the patron may not be able to tell if the current issue he or she needs has been received. There may simply be a time lag in the processing of pieces or maintenance of records that indicate up-to-date holdings. Perhaps there have been delays in publication of which the library may even be unaware. Whether the issue is bound or unbound may also determine where it is shelved in the library. There may be multiple copies in the library, each with different holdings. A subscription may have been cancelled (as is not uncommon in this time of budgetary problems). Possibly one subscription has been initiated at a later time. As frequently happens, the current or most recent issues, perhaps even the last 5 or 10 years, may be in one location, and all earlier issues in another location. As the search is narrowed, the patron must go to the shelf to look for the piece, or in those cases where current periodicals or a portion of the collection are in "secure" locations, have library staff do it. It may be alphabetically arranged in a segregated area, or it may be shelved with monographs with similar classification. If it is shelved by title, he or she may not be able to second-guess the librarians regarding the form of the title used for shelving (word by word? key word? corporate author?) "Unbound" issues (they may be less than current) may be in a box next to the bound issues, or simply shelved as if bound.

The patron searches through the issues but the desired issue is not there. If it is a bound volume, it may be charged out to another patron in cases where the library's policies allow such circulation. If it is unbound and (most probably) does not circulate outside the library, perhaps it has never been received, or has been lost since it arrived in the library. Perhaps it is a flimsy piece and has simply been mis-shelved. The patron may hear the library's classic explanation for the absence of a piece from the shelf—"it is at the Bindery." Actually, it may be in process, still in the library but being prepared for the Bindery. There is also the possibility that, if not charged out, it is being used "in-house" by staff for some reason. Library staff may have to be consulted to determine where it is "in process," or when it was sent to the Bindery, when it should be back, if it has been received, if it has been claimed, etc. When the piece is finally located for the patron, it is hoped that the article needed is intact, with no ripped out pages, etc. The patron may wish to look over other articles in that issue, or even other issues, or may just wish to photocopy the article. Let us hope that the photocopier works, or our poor patron's patience may have reached the breaking point.

However, if the patron is allowed to charge out the item, the problems may be just beginning. The loan period is very often shorter than for monographs, even though to the patron the item may be indistinguishable from a monograph. This is frequently the case with monographic series. Even a careful user who makes note of "dates due" to renew or return material will have to deal with exceptions. Serial volumes may not be renewable, and if kept past the due date, it is likely that the fine rate is higher than is the rate for monographs. If the serial issue is lost, the patron may be billed not only for the replacement cost (impossible to determine for serials) but also for binding or other charges.

Patrons obviously have problems with serials that library managers do not have. It is true that if a patron asks for help, those problems can frequently be easily solved. However, as use studies have repeatedly shown, asking for help is uncommon and is often viewed as a last resort, even by knowledgeable patrons.

Library literature reflects many of the serials management concerns of librarians, including budgets, selection, acquisitions, automation, cataloguing, binding, etc. Certainly the goal of such concerns is the accessibility of serials for users. Brown and Smith acknowledge in their text on serials that the "ultimate object of all serials work is to provide journals to the patron."[3] The direct process of making serials available involves such practical matters as circulation policies, loan periods, shelving arrangements, binding procedures, etc., which are also discussed in the literature, almost as an afterthought, however.

Osborn's work on serial publications is one of the general guides available, and it covers most of the topics relevant to serials work.[4] Other sources address various aspects of serials service. Melin suggests that ideally the same staff would be responsible for all aspects of serials work from "order and receipt to cataloging and finally to reference," and that this staff would be located close to the serials collection to answer questions regarding materials being received, bound, claimed, etc.[5] Potter espouses a different view and presents convincing arguments for integrating serials work with that of monographs.[6]

The literature discusses the choice of whether or not to classify, at the same time acknowledging that such a decision was probably made many years earlier and so the present staff can deal with the situation only partially.[7] It is generally agreed that while smaller libraries can avoid classifying and the costs involved, larger libraries will probably have to classify. In fact, recommended treatment of serials appears to vary according to the size and kind of library. Another subject that receives some attention in the literature is shelf arrangement. If classified, should serials or/and periodicals be interfiled with monographs? Should back issues that are bound be interfiled, and current issues segregated and shelved separately?[8] Arguments for improved security make a segregated collection desirable according to Taylor.[9] Another suggestion is to keep a set of frequently used indexes close to the periodicals section.[10] While unbound issues are more current, it is the bound issues that are more likely to be indexed and, therefore, more accessible bibliographically.

Davinson discusses the pros and cons of binding periodicals, including its high cost and the lack of availability for several weeks of items at the Bindery.[11] Dean reports on a study done at Johns Hopkins University Library that showed that 87% of a test group of bound periodicals were never used after binding.[12] Even if titles that are never used could be easily identified in advance, volume of use is irrelevant in large research libraries. Gore suggests an alternative to expensive binding procedures, or the other extreme of weeding, when he discusses "peg binding" as the "temporary binding that is permanent."[13]

Another issue frequently discussed is loan periods, with the general consensus being to keep these as short as possible.[14] Photocopy as a means to reduce mutilation is also frequently recommended.[15] Foster and Parker summarize the advice generally given when they say "bind in small units, reduce loan periods to a minimum, and provide cheap, fast photocopy service."[16]

Lancaster confirms the importance of such practical matters as loan periods, shelving arrangements, binding policies, etc., when he notes that "the more accessible that materials are made within a library, the more likely it is that they will be used."[17] He describes "ease of use" as resulting from a combination of "physical and intellectual accessibility." He discusses ways to analyze patron satisfaction, describing studies (including methodology), upon which rational decisions regarding loan periods, duplicate copies, etc., can be based. Lancaster emphasizes that "evaluation must occur at the level of the local institution," a conclusion with which many researchers agree.[18]

The Library at the University of Illinois at Urbana is also concerned with matters of serials management: careful selection within budget restrictions, efficient ordering procedures, prompt cataloguing, current records, easy availability, etc., and is continually attempting to deal specifically with patrons' concerns. A number of changes have occurred recently at UIUC as the Library attempts to make its treatment of serials more effective.

First, a general reorganization of staff, which began in 1978, resulted in the integration of the tasks being performed by the Serials Department (which included acquisitions and cataloguing, as well as claiming and receiving) with the same kinds of tasks being performed for monographs.[19] The Acquisitions Department is now responsible for ordering and claiming serials as well as monographs. The UIUC serial collection is estimated at well over 90,000 live titles. The responsibility for cataloguing serials is divided between the original cataloguers (many of whom are now in departmental libraries) and Automated Systems, the copy cataloguing unit. Serials are classified and fully catalogued at UIUC, and may be located in one of the 37 departmental libraries, the Undergraduate Library, or Central Bookstacks. This reorganization, including the use of support staff wherever possible, is believed to be responsible for the faster processing of serials.

A second factor that has contributed to the improved efficiency and productivity in serials work at UIUC has been the development of automation. In the Acquisitions Department, the installation of Faxon's LINX system to monitor the subscriptions to titles being received from Faxon is expected to simplify tedious record keeping, speed up claiming, improve accuracy, and free up staff time for more complicated tasks. Also, a component of the Library's automated circulation system, LCS (Library Computer System), has been developed to maintain information on-line regarding number and location of copies, issues received, etc., for all subscription and gift/exchange titles. Called "Check-Man," the system enables the staff to monitor the status of titles more easily and to initiate action, when needed. Some orders still must be controlled manually. While in the past all materials were centrally processed, many serial titles are now being received and checked in "directly" in departmental libraries, which also have the responsibility for selection. Materials considered inappropriate for the specialized collections of departmental libraries are ordered for Central Bookstacks, and are checked in and processed by the Acquisitions Department.

One of the earliest uses of automation at UIUC was for cataloguing. An increasing number of serial titles are being catalogued on OCLC by support staff.[20] An archival tape of the cataloguing records is created, which is added to the LCS database weekly, providing bibliographic access to newly received titles in less than two weeks. Complete holdings and circulation information, including call number, author and/or title, location, multiple copies, loan period, holdings, and marking instructions, etc., are added at the same time as the bibliographic record.[21] Patrons can access this information at any of the 90 public terminals on campus, as well as at terminals located at cooperating institutions throughout the state of Illinois.

Automation has been used for circulation at UIUC since 1978, when LCS was developed from a system that operates at the Ohio State University Library. Materials, including serials, are charged, discharged, recalled and renewed on-line. Missing or withdrawn status is noted in those cases where the Library has that information. Although a patron cannot tell to whom a piece is charged, he or she can tell if it is charged out, when it is due back, and the home campus of the patron to whom it is charged.

Serials can be searched on the database by title, author or author and title. Individual volumes of monographic series that are analyzed can also be searched by title or/and author, even though they are circulated as a volume of a serial. A recent enhancement to LCS, the addition of full bibliographic records for all monographs catalogued since 1974, and serials since 1977, through the use of WLN (Washington Library Network) software, has not only added subject searches to the search strategy but has also introduced some other capabilities useful in locating serial titles. Keyword as well as truncated searches have proved especially useful in searching serial titles, particularly proceedings of conferences, which can be successfully searched by place and date. If the item is bound, faculty with campus addresses can charge it out with a "mail option." It will be retrieved by staff and mailed. Since the LCS database includes not only UIUC's collection but also the collection of 23 other Illinois academic institutions, the item may be charged and sent to a faculty member of a neighboring institution.

Even the Library's binding unit is reaping the benefits of automation. Through the use of a microcomputer, supplied by the Hertzberg Bindery, information regarding serials to be bound is input and transmitted daily directly to a computer located at the Bindery, eliminating cumbersome paper order forms. Binding instructions for as many as 2,000 volumes per week have been transmitted quickly and accurately to the Bindery.

AACR2 has also been a factor in making serial titles more accessible, by limiting corporate authorship, and making title entries more realistic, straightforward and predictable from a patron's point of view. Consistency with regard to choice and form of entry by libraries throughout the country is also likely to be insured through the use of *AACR2*, making citations less troublesome. Generic titles may still be a problem, but

UIUC's circulation system automatically provides an author from an added entry, enabling author as well as title searches.

Another factor in providing easier serials access for patrons, at least indirectly, is the standardized format required by OCLC. OCLC makes serial identification mandatory as well as designating whether the serial is a periodical, newspaper, a monographic series or "other" by default according to the OCLC definition.[22] The category for each serial, then, is determined in a uniform way by the cataloguer, and consistency is insured in the circulation, binding and shelving of those titles. Other units can divide serials in any way they wish for convenient processing, but it is the cataloguing unit that will determine the category of each piece according to clearly defined and accepted criteria.

Physical accessibility to serial titles is another important factor for patrons, involving both shelving practices and binding capability. The Central Bookstacks, which receives the bulk of all serial titles received at UIUC, has recently developed a plan that is expected to increase physical accessibility through a change in shelving practice, cheaper (and, therefore, more) "binding," faster claiming, and generally better control.

For the most part, the departmental libraries shelve periodicals separately from monographs, which are shelved according to their Dewey classification. Current issues may be on display in a special "reading" area, while bound volumes are arranged in alphabetical order nearby. On a narrow subject, materials are selected specifically for scholars specializing in the subject, and are on open stacks. The Central Bookstacks, with its collection of approximately four million volumes covering all subject areas in all languages, is open only to faculty, graduate students, and special permit holders. All serials are interfiled, whether bound or unbound, with monographs in call number order. Pieces are received and shelved daily throughout the stacks, a time-consuming and costly process. They are difficult to monitor and are often misshelved. Claims are made for missing issues when a piece is bound, frequently too late to achieve results. Selection for binding, while based on use, is somewhat haphazard, and, since everything cannot be bound, many titles are neglected. While binding serials regularly cannot be overemphasized as a means of control and preservation, it is particularly important at UIUC since only bound volumes circulate.

The completion of an addition to the Central Bookstacks (the "Sixth Stack") in early 1984 which, through the use of compact shelving, has dramatically increased the capacity of the stacks area, has provided the impetus for a different system for shelving periodicals. Beginning January 1, 1985, current unbound issues of periodicals are being shelved in a segregated centrally located area. The project began with a small collection of general periodicals, formerly held in a "closed" stack area for protection and control. The materials are shelved in call number order and will eventually cover all subject areas (Dewey classifications 000-999). A specific staff person is in charge, with responsibility for servicing the material and helping patrons. Shelves are being labeled with special labels that include the call number and are color coded with claiming and binding instructions for each title. As soon as a complete "bindable" volume is received, missing issues are claimed and the piece is bound. At the same time, the shelves are searched for earlier unbound issues, which are then also bound. Most volumes receive on-site "peg-binding," a cheap and fast method to keep pieces together, provide some protection, and allow for circulation.[23] Not all titles will be peg-bound. Those that appear to be more heavily used, or for some physical reason (e.g., narrow margins) do not lend themselves to peg-binding, will receive class A binding. In the event that a peg-bound title becomes heavily used, it may be rebound with traditional binding or microfilmed. Adjacent study carrels are being renovated for periodical users, and a photocopy machine placed nearby. The area selected for the project is next to the Acquisitions Department, where journals for Central Bookstacks are received and checked in.

The project has the dual goals of better control and better access. The Library can methodically claim and bind every periodical title received in Central Bookstacks promptly, as well as identify and bind neglected back issues. Since the titles are concentrated on one deck, daily shelving tasks are less time-consuming than previously and more accurate. "Peg-binding," while recognized as a substitute for regular binding, nevertheless provides cheap, fast protection and control. The patron is able to find "current" issues in one place, with staff nearby to consult. Pieces are circulatable sooner, in smaller units, making them available to more users. Since the stack is "closed," and the titles are not "popular," it is not anticipated that patrons will interfere with one another's use, even though the issues are concentrated in one area. While it is viewed as a drawback to divide bound and unbound pieces, such is the policy in the rest of the library system. Use of "current" information may be different from use of "historical" information.

Signs are being placed throughout the Bookstacks, an explanatory flyer is being distributed to users (with an opportunity for comments), notices are being placed in departmental newsletters, etc., in an effort to inform patrons of the changes. Evaluative studies are being planned to determine patron satisfaction, binding success, losses, claiming efficiency, etc. There is still much to be done to improve user access at UIUC. The lengths of loan periods for serials needs analysis; billing policies need to be reviewed; withdrawal policies need consideration; and preservation and replacement plans need development, each with the ultimate goal of present and future service.

Making serials more accessible to users must be a primary goal of librarians. Better management and tighter control will certainly benefit the user in most cases but will not solve all problems. Local research to determine the most desirable shelving arrangement, the most appropriate binding priorities, the most practical retention plan, etc., may be the only way to make the library's serials collection accessible to its users. Until the electronic journal becomes a reality (probably with its own set of problems), most librarians must continue to deal with serials as they now exist.

REFERENCES

1. *Anglo-American Cataloguing Rules,* 2nd ed. (Chicago: American Library Association, 1978). p. 570.
2. *The ALA Glossary of Library and Information Science.* Heartsill Young, Editor. (Chicago: American Library Association, 1983). p. 166.
3. Brown, Clara D. and Smith, Lynn S. *Serials: Past Present and Future.* 2nd (revised) edition. (Birmingham, Alabama: Ebsco Industries, Inc., 1980). p. 353.
4. Osborn, Andrew D. *Serial Publications: Their Place and Treatment in Libraries.* (Chicago: American Library Association, 1980). 486 p.
5. Melin, Nancy. "Public Service Function of Serials." *Serials Review.* 6 (1) (Jan/Mar. 1980):39-44.
6. Potter, William Gary. "Form or Function? An Analysis of the Serials Department in the Modern Academic Library." *The Serials Librarian.* 6 (1) (Fall 1981): 85-94.
7. Borden, Joseph C. "The Advantages and Disadvantages of a Classified Periodicals Collection." *Library Resources and Technical Services.* 9 (1) (Winter 1965): 122-6.
8. Hubbard, William J. *Stacks Management, a Practical Guide to Shelving and Maintaining Library Collections.* (Chicago: American Library Association, 1981). p. 9-11.
9. Taylor, David C. *Managing the Serials Explosion, the Issues for Publishers and Libraries.* (White Plains, N.Y.: Knowledge Industry Publications, Inc., 1982). p. 53.
10. Kuhn, Warren B. "Service." In *Serial Publications in Large Libraries.* Walter Allen, Editor. Allerton Park Institute, no. 16. (Urbana, Ill: University of Illinois, Graduate School of Library Science, 1970). p. 175-90.
11. Davinson, Donald. *The Periodicals Collection.* (Boulder, Colo.: Westview Press, 1978). p. 207.
12. Dean, John. "The Binding and Preparation of Periodicals: Alternative Structures and Procedures." *Serials Review.* 6 (3) (July/Sept. 1980): 87-90.
13. Gore, Daniel. "The Temporary Journal Binding That is Permanent." *Technicalities.* 1 (2) (Jan. 1981): 11-12, 14.
14. Brown, *Serials,* p. 350. Osborn, *Serial Publications,* p. 341.
15. Taylor, *Managing the Serials Explosion,* p. 67-68.
16. Foster, Allan and Parker, Lynn. "Physical Forms and Storage." In *Periodicals Administration in Libraries.* Paul Mayes, Editor. (London: Clive Bingley; Hamden, Conn.: Linnet Books, 1978). p. 78-115.
17. Lancaster, F.W. *Measurement and Evaluation of Library Services.* (Washington, D.C.: Information Resources Press, 1977). p. 316.
18. Ibid., p. 386.
19. Gorman, Michael. "Reorganization at the University of Illinois-Urbana/Champaign: A Case Study." *Journal of Academic Librarianship.* 9 (4) (Sept. 1983): 223-5.
20. McBride, Ruth B. "Copy Cataloguing of Serials According to AACR2 using OCLC: the University of Illinois Experience." In *The Management of Serials Automation: Current Technology and Strategies for Future Planning.* Peter Gellatly, Editor. (New York: The Haworth Press, 1982). p. 135-49.
21. Golden, Sue. "Online Serials Circulation in a Library Network." *Wilson Library Bulletin.* 56 (7) (March 1982): 511-15.
22. *Serials Format,* Second Edition. (Dublin, Ohio: OCLC, 1983). SL FF p. 30.
23. Gore. "Temporary Journal Binding." p. 12.

Out of the Shoebox and Into the Computer: Serials Indexing 1975-1985

Martha Cornog

ABSTRACT. Over the last ten years, serials indexing has greatly changed in terms of production, formats and products, coverage, and producers and users. Computers and the growth of science have led to these changes. Serials librarians will have much influence on the evolution of serials indexing because they are part of the user environments in which serials indexes must survive.

Indexing is moving out of the shoebox and into the computer terminal in dramatic spurts . . .
The first problem—when is an indexer an indexer, an author, or a data base constructor, and how should the identification be made?
The second problem—when is an index an index, and when is it a data base, and is there a difference?

Dorothy Thomas[1]

In the early 1960s, we all knew what serials indexes were. Some were produced by the serials publishers themselves, appeared at the end of each volume, and were sometimes cumulated. Often they were included in the serial subscription price—no extra charge. Other indexes covering *many* serials were produced by abstracting and indexing (A&I) services. These often included abstracts, were usually cumulated periodically, and cost a small fortune.

Today in 1985, we have in the information marketplace a large and confusing variety of indexes, microforms, current awareness services, bibliographies, databases, and magnetic storage media—all designed to provide access to the contents of serials. How did this happen?

Two factors have propelled the evolution of today's serials indexes: scientific research and the computer. The enormous growth of science since the 1700s has brought about an exponential increase in the number of serials.[2] Scientists must publish their results, and journals have sprung

---

Martha Cornog is Special Projects Coordinator, National Federation of Abstracting and Information Services (NFAIS), 112 South Sixteenth Street, Philadelphia, PA 19102.

© 1986 by The Haworth Press, Inc. All rights reserved.

up in all fields to oblige them. Thus more serials to be indexed. Over the past 20 years, however, the development of more powerful and cheaper computer technologies has made it possible for publishers and A&I services to keep up with the growth of serials, to design new types of index products, and to appeal to new groups of customers. Coincidentally, 1975—just before the founding year of *The Serials Librarian*—marked an acceleration of changes that have continued with little let-up over the past ten years. And everything about serials indexes has been affected: production, formats and products, coverage, and "the players," the producers and users.

PRODUCTION TECHNIQUES

The indexer's shoebox is no mere metaphor. For several centuries past and well into the twentieth century, index entries for both books and serials were written on cards or slips of paper and interfiled alphabetically in shoeboxes or the equivalent. Cross references were added, also on cards or slips. Corrections and changes were made. Finally, the entire corpus was typeset—sometimes directly from the cards or slips, sometimes from an intermediate manuscript typed from the cards. Until the 1960s, "typeset" usually meant "hot type," where the words are cast as molten lead slugs and reproduced by means of a Linotype machine.

The first changes to index production came in the printing method. By the 1960s, computer technology had developed to the point where computer-driven photocomposition devices were beginning to edge out the old Linotypes. Now the index entries were keyed from cards or slips to produce a magnetic tape, the input to the photocomposition programs. The large A&I services such as Chemical Abstracts Service (CAS) were the first to adopt the new technology, which was much faster, cleaner, quieter, and more versatile. It also permitted computer-formatting of indexes, such as KWIC (keyword in context), and the rapid compilation of cumulative indexes. ABC-Clio (*Historical Abstracts*) and CAS (*Chemical Abstracts*) were the first to use KWIC and similar methods to produce indexes in the early 1960s.

By about 1975, most A&I services and journal publishers had switched to computerized photocomposition. As a result, citations, abstracts, and index terms became machine-readable. (And this led to the birth and growth of online, as discussed below.) Computer *formatting* as well as computer *printing* became more common. Index terms chosen either by indexers or by computer (as in the KWIC index) could be permuted, rotated, hierarchialized, sorted, and cross-referenced by computer.

The second set of changes pertained to how the indexers worked. Originally a two-step process—first cards, slips, or sheets of paper, then keying—indexing gradually became a one-step, online operation accomplished with the aid of text-editing. In many A&I services, the indexer now sits at a terminal, led by a "menu" through the indexing procedure. When index terms are typed in, the system automatically checks for correct spelling. Such items as authors' names, affiliations, and journal titles may also be verified. The American Petroleum Institute (API) and CAS were among the first A&I services to install text-editing systems in the late 1970s.

The H.W. Wilson Company, one of the oldest and largest U.S. indexing firms, continued with cards, hot type, and Linotype right up to the early 1980s; then over a three-year period, they installed a modern production system incorporating both text-editing and computerized photocomposition. However, the two-step approach is still widely used for serials indexing by publishers and smaller A&I services.

Some free-lance indexers preparing serials indexes have also come out of their shoeboxes. Text editing systems with special indexing programs have become available for microcomputers. The freelance indexer can now sit at home at a terminal, key in index terms, and watch the computer verify, sort, merge, and format the index. The floppy disc with the finished index may then be processed by the publisher as input to computerized photocomposition, without rekeying.

The third change pertains to machine-aided indexing (MAI). Text editing systems can help the indexer select terms—for example, by displaying sections of the indexing vocabulary, or by "suggesting" additional terms related somehow to a term already selected. Newer systems are currently under development that attempt to mimic the decision processes of the indexer. API's MAI programs currently yield about 60% of the terms an indexer would have selected for a particular abstract; the other 40% are provided by the index editor, who reviews all production output of indexer and computer alike. API's system commenced actual use in 1985, for one subject segment of the database.

FORMATS AND PRODUCTS

The switch to computerized photocomposition made possible magnetic tapes and online formats for serials indexes in the mid 1960s. The government A&I services such as those of the National Aeronautics and Space Administration (NASA) and the National Library of Medicine (NLM) funded the research and development for the first online systems. Meanwhile, the scientific professional societies with indexing services—API, CAS, the American Society for Metals—began experimenting with batch searches on their magnetic tapes, the tapes originally meant for computerized photocomposition. By 1975, most large government-produced serials indexes were online, and many of the non-profit-produced serials indexes as well. By the late 1970s, for-profit firms also began to produce serials indexes and to produce them in machine-readable formats.[3]

A series of directories published between 1976 and 1984 documents the rise in bibliographic and textual databases, chiefly produced by A&I services. A 1976 directory lists 301 databases, the 1979 edition 528, and the 1984 edition 1800 (includes numeric databases).[4] The number of print indexes has also increased over the same time period: a 1963 directory[5] lists 650 English-language print A&I services, which can be compared with another directory's coverage of 1760 in 1983, including some available only online.[6]

The availability of magnetic tapes for A&I information has also made possible customized spin-offs of indexes for individual users and user groups. *CA Selects,* a current awareness services from CAS, began in 1976. By 1979, 110 topics in chemistry were available and, by 1984, nearly 150. In 1983, BioSciences Information Service (BIOSIS), began B-I-T-S, a current awareness service of subtopic segments from the BIOSIS database, delivered to the customer on floppy disc instead of printout.

Faster computer processing and cheaper electronic storage also led to the growth of online full-text formats for serials. These of course, could not exactly be called "indexes"—yet searching the full-text online permits an index-like access to the serials' contents. In 1980, Mead Data Central introduced NEXIS, online access to the full text of magazines and newspapers. Starting with 6 in March, 1985, NEXIS now covers 130 titles. Other full text files have been introduced since 1980. In 1984, Information Access Company (IAC), introduced ASAP, two online full-text magazine databases. Interestingly, the service also offers access through controlled vocabulary as well as free text searching, combining the benefits of index databases with online document delivery.

The interrelationships of print and online formats for serials indexes have caused considerable concern within the industry over the last five or six years. A seeming "migration" of customers from the (initially very expensive) print to the (pay-as-you-go) online formats led to much experimental pricing as well as online price increases. Some online products, such as the American Psychological Association's PsycINFO, have begun to diverge from their print equivalents. Other index databases have been initiated without print index equivalents. Two of these, however (Engineering Information's Engineering Meetings Database and Management Contents' Management Contents Database), have since acquired corresponding print indexes, reversing the usual progression of print to online. (The print equivalent of Engineering Meetings Database is *Ei Engineering Conference Index* and of Management Contents is *Business Publications Index and Abstracts.*)

Other formats are also in use or under experimentation for serials indexes. The BIOSIS B-I-T-S service uses floppy discs. Microforms were much hailed in the 1960s and 1970s as the solution to bulky storage problems, and many A&I services are still available on microfilm or microfiche. In 1985, the storage buzzword is optical disc. The Library of Congress is currently carrying out a pilot project to store and access heavily used and archival materials, including periodicals, on optical disc. IAC has just announced the Infotrac Search System, an index to 60,000 journal articles per month, to be delivered on optical videodisc. These discs require expensive players, however, An even newer technology, compact disc read-only-memory (CD-ROM), may prove promising for personal computer storage, holding much more information than either floppy disc or hard disc and readable via a moderately priced special disc drive. International Standard Information Systems (a CLSI subsidiary) is planning to launch some serials index databases on CD-ROM.[7]

COVERAGE

As the scientific and other scholarly literature has increased over the past ten to twenty years and become both more specialized and interdisciplinary, serials indexes have expanded their coverage, both in numbers of items and topics. BIOSIS, for example, covered 125,000 items in 1967, 250,100 in 1977, and expects to cover 440,000 in 1985. American Theological Library Association indexes sustained an even greater increase, proportionately: 3,200 items in 1967, 8,000 in 1977, and 33,800 projected for 1984.[8] And while A&I services have, traditionally, most commonly covered the "hard sciences," in the last ten years new services have sprung up and expanded to cover business, law, more social sciences and humanities, and more interdisciplinary topics. For example, of the 34 members of the National Federation of Abstracting and Information Services (NFAIS) in 1975, 8 could be classed as social sciences members and only 1 as a humanities member; the remainder covered science, technology, or medicine. In 1984, however, 13 of the 46 NFAIS members covered social sciences, 4 the humanities, and 1 business/law. Many of the newer A&I services are founded on such interdisciplinary topics as sports and recreation, the environment, noise, deafness. A comparison of the subject indexes of a database directory issued both in 1979 and 1982 reveals many headings in the latter that did not appear in the former, e.g., asbestos, ergonomy, veterinary science.[9]

Online serials indexes have also expanded in retrospective coverage. Some A&I services and publishers have recently launched projects to index older serials, or to put back years of the print indexes online. Among such services and publishers are CAS, the American Geological Institute,

IAC for *Magazine Index,* and *The Times* of London. Putting older citations on magnetic tape will, of course, make possible the creation of retrospective subject bibliographies as new products.

Since the late 1970s in particular, many A&I services have taken considerable pains to increase their foreign coverage, particularly of Soviet, Japanese, and Mainland Chinese (People's Republic of China) documents. Such arrangements have often taken the form of exchanges or agreements for mutual benefit.

With increased coverage has also come an increased concern on the part of A&I services to provide access to serials covered in their indexes. Many provide document delivery for items in their indexes through online vendors (such as via Dialog's DIALORDER online ordering system) or directly.

THE PLAYERS

Who produces serials indexes and who uses them? In 1975, the majority of producers still consisted of non-profit professional societies, government agencies, and serials publishers. With the increasing popularity of online, however, many more for-profit organizations have begun producing serials indexes, both print and online. An analysis of entries in an A&I services directory[10] shows that new A&I products initiated by non-profit and government organizations far outstripped those initiated by for-profits until 1971. From 1971 until 1980, new A&I products were initiated about equally by non-profits and for-profits. From 1981 to 1983, nearly twice as many for-profit A&I products were initiated as non-profit.

The old firm classes of "who does what" have also changed. Some producers of serials indexes, such as CAS, have become online vendors for their own databases. Conversely, BRS, an online vendor, has begun producing the PRE-MED and PRE-PSYCH databases.

Users of serials indexes have changed as well. No longer just scientists or PhD candidates researching prospective projects, the serials index users in 1985 include managers, lawyers, physicians, and laypeople with many interests. While the print *Readers' Guide to Periodical Literature* and the *New York Times Index* have always been used by public library patrons, the new users are searching serials indexes online, and often without the assistance of a trained online intermediary. Here, the growth of computer technology has influenced serials indexes in a different way: through the personal computer. Anyone with a terminal and a modem at home can search online serials indexes through such end-user-oriented online systems as BRS After Dark and Dialog's Knowledge Index. And special user-friendly front-end systems such as Telebase System's EASYNET have recently been developed to make online searching easier and more convenient for end users by eliminating the need for passwords and search languages.

So what conclusions are we to draw from the last ten years of serials indexing and indexes? Where is this diversity and growth going? Is a database different from an index, and does it matter? What can the serials librarian expect in the near future?

> If we look at the whole of information dissemination as analogous to a biological genus, we can see many species—among them, printed publications, microforms, computer-readable services, online services, depositories of all types, and videodisks. We also see many environments into which these species may be selected for use: academic institutions, government agencies, industrial organizations, individual researchers, and a host of others. Such information environments change just as natural environments change. Thus, both environments demand different, changed species for ultimate survival. . . . [And] the information species that survive will be those best suited to service the user environments. . . . Like nature, the information dissemination markets of the future will include many environments. User selection will determine those species which best adapt to that environment as it also changes.[11]

So perhaps we can expect *more* diversity in serials indexes—more different "species," together with an "extinction" of those species that have not adapted to the ongoing user environments. And perhaps it is a matter of more theoretical than practical importance whether or not a "database" is an "index"; what is important is the overall *function* of access to information in a particular user environment, not the label used. And it is the selection decisions of serials librarians that help determine many of these user environments. Through user selection, serials librarians can expect to become deeply involved in shaping the *next* ten years of serials indexing.

REFERENCES

1. Dorothy Thomas, "Indexers and Indexing: New Bridges to Cross," *The Indexer* 14, no. 2 (Oct. 1984):81-83.
2. Derek de Solla Price, *Little Science, Big Science* (New York: Columbia University Press, 1963), p. 8.
3. Alex Tomberg, "The Development of Commercially Available Databases in Europe," *Online Review* 3, no. 4 (1979):343-352.
4. Martha E. Williams, Laurence Lannom, Carolyn G. Robins, comps. and eds., *Computer-Readable Databases: A Directory and Data Sourcebook* (White Plains, New York: Knowledge Industry Publications, Inc., 1982), p. viii; *Data Base Directory* (White Plains, New York: Knowledge Industry Publications, Inc., 1984).

5. National Federation of Science Abstracting and Indexing Services, *A Guide to the World's Abstracting and Indexing Services in Science and Technology* (Boston, Massachusetts: Gregg Press, 1972).

6. John Schmittroth, Jr., ed., *Abstracting and Indexing Services Directory* (Detroit, Michigan: Gale Research Co., 1983), p. 327.

7. "Brush Up Your Buzzwords," *Monitor* no. 49 (March 1985):4-6.

8. National Federation of Abstracting and Information Services. *Member Service Statistics* (Philadelphia, Pennsylvania: NFAIS, February, 1985).

9. Cuadra Associates, *Directory of Online Databases* 1, no. 1 (Fall, 1979); 4, no. 1 (Fall, 1982).

10. Schmittroth.

11. Russell J. Rowlett, Jr., "Information Dissemination: Evolution or Creationism?" in *Abstracting and Indexing Services in Perspective: Miles Conrad Memorial Lectures 1969-1983,* eds. M. Lynne Neufeld, Martha Cornog, and Inez L. Sperr (Arlington, Virginia: Information Resources Press, 1983), pp. 68-69.

Article Access—Too Easy?

Martin Gordon, MLS

ABSTRACT. The proliferation of online searching as well as its relative decline in cost has been both a boon and a bane for undergraduate use of journal literature. Preliminary working bibliographies for brief research papers can be constructed in a shorter period of time allowing more time for the creative, cognitive process which is the reason for the exercise in the first place. Dispersion of citations indicates a higher percent of the relative literature searched. However, the stationary level of the student's familiarity with the subject at hand counteracts these benefits to a far greater degree than most might wish to admit. Lack of analytic selection from the citations produced by the search as well as initial errors in qualifying limitations placed on the search (such as period of publication, for example) further exacerbate this problem.

Late in 1984, just as most of us were winding down our operations and preparing for a much deserved interlude of holiday festivities, an announcement that will be looked back upon as a milestone in electronic bibliographic access was made without fanfare. The cornerstone of the academic reference room collection, a tool that can be found in every college library, is to be made available online. The H. W. Wilson Company released a third class mailer that heralded the option of utilizing the database *Wilsonline* instead of placing sole reliance as theretofore on printed copies of the *Reader's Guide to Periodical Literature* and a host of other Wilson indices. From the inception of electronic citation retrieval in the late 50s, through the birth of such giants as *Dialog Information Service* and *Bibliographic Retrieval Service,* online literature searching has been the single most significant advance in access to periodical literature. Both the continuing increase in the number of such services as well as the rapid economic growth of the telecommunications industry as a whole insure that this capability is here to stay.[1]

And well it should.

Since they have to balance a diverse curriculum load, most undergraduates delay the initial step in research until a week or so before they must begin writing their paper. This is natural and not necessarily a result of some built-in procrastination syndrome, but rather a realization that *all*

Martin Gordon is the Periodicals Librarian at Franklin and Marshall College, Lancaster, PA 17604 steps in the research process should be fresh in one's mind at the time the actual writing is undertaken, and not least the first step—the selection of the sources to be used. Therefore, any saving of time directly lengthens the period in which they can prepare their draft.

Furthermore, with budget and housing constraints limiting the size of each individual collection, many articles may have to be obtained for the student from other libraries. Since online transmission of inter-library loan requests is fast becoming the primary vehicle for such communications, this off-site utilization of journal literature is even more feasible if the requests are submitted by the students before the eleventh hour is upon them. In fact, studies have recommended dependence on inter-library loan as an alternative to expensive, esoteric on-site collections that are apt to have only marginal direct benefit for student use.[2] Online literature searching has additional advantages for the student besides simply the saving of time. It presupposes a *mechanical* (if not qualitative) thoroughness in literature review that may (if properly utilized) increase the comprehensiveness of the student's bibliographies. Sources that would hitherto have been ignored will at least appear on the printout received as the result of a search request.

A potential danger lies, however, in a wholesale reliance on the online search as a substitute for the index table. Undergraduates by and large lack the in-depth subject knowledge and associative terminology to rely solely on Boolean matches as the basis for the construction of initial bibliographies. Preparing their papers is, indeed, a learning experience, and as such should involve a gradual familiarization with what has been published on the level appropriate for their assignment. It should not be an exercise in seeing how many citations they can append to their essay in the hope that quantity will either add to its substance or hide the lack thereof. The librarian is responsible for at least a cursory review of the student's request, but such a review generally lacks the personal contact and the question and answer dialog that hallmarks the sound reference encounter. In fact, requests are often outlined on a form and left for an entirely different librarian to execute. Undergraduates are often encouraged by such forms and verbal instructions to *limit* their search with qualifiers such as date of publication, known authors, language as well as subject descriptors under dire admonitions of being buried in a mass of printout pages if they do not exercise care in the choices they make.

I in no way mean by the above statements to decry the presence of alternative search methods at our disposal today. However, as most of you have done, I have had ample opportunity of working one on one with undergraduates and realize that their frenetic willingness to accept *any* group of possible support materials for their papers indicates that even those who can be characterized as having academic potential tend to downplay the need for *selective* review of sources once they have located them. In addition, students today place a great deal of trust in online generated data because they have been more fortunate than we to have had early exposure to the many marvels of the high tech world in which we all now live. This trust blinds them to various degrees as to the need to be in control of their research throughout all stages. Unlike monographic sources that tend at the undergraduate level to provide overall views of a topic, periodical articles are apt to be as pieces in a landscape of possible sources that require careful selection and placement in order to be of value. They ought not to be cited by virtue of their convenience or because they happen to be the first five or ten that appear on a printout. How well they mesh with one another as well as their ability to update or expand the monographic choices are of primary importance in selecting them.

Manual literature searching by means of printed indices, albeit laborious and time-consuming, forces the student into a cognitive stance at the onset of the project. It does not (as can ill applied online search products) weaken the resolve, perhaps not yet nurtured sufficiently in the student, to question and (dare I say it) even doublecheck the contents, scope or depth of the paper, as its preparation is laid out.

Let me submit, then, that while online literature searching has clearly been the distinguishing achievement as far as ease of access to periodicals has gone in the last decade or so, it has also been a potential pitfall, especially in the case of undergraduate use.

It remains the responsibility of the librarian to see to it that important steps are not excluded in the assembling of the bibliography. Only through such care can the power of online searching be constructively harnessed to achieve its primary goal—the realization of both expediency and comprehensiveness without the sacrifice of the true exercise in research that the library has always advocated—the careful, conscious discrimination in the student's selection of primary source material.

REFERENCES

1. Steven Sieck. "Information Storage and Retrieval," *Publishers Weekly* 226:36 (Nov. 23, 1984).

2. R.R. Flynn. "The University of Pittsburgh Study of Journal Usage: A Summary Report," *The Serials Librarian* 4:26 (Fall 1979).

Budgeting and Planning: A Tandem Approach

Bertha R. Almagro

ABSTRACT. The literature is saturated with articles in which all kinds of statistical data are available, pointing to the various rates of increase visited on books and journals over a lengthy period of time. The intention in this paper is not to regurgitate these figures, but rather to present a personal view on what are considered to be helpful approaches to planning and budgeting.

BUDGETS: WHAT THEY ARE, WHAT THEY REPRESENT, WHAT THEY ACHIEVE

Budgeting is by no means a mere accounting for the receipt and expenditure of funds, or a plan allowing one to live within available resources, but rather a process through which goals are identified and implemented. It is also in the present context the fiscal framework on which library programs and services rest. Budgets, and how they are allocated, provide a clear reflection of our priorities. Since the staff of each library is aware of its unique problems and/or circumstances, no specific plan can be designed as a universal panacea. Each institution must act according to its own needs and internal structure, tailoring the solutions to its problems in a way that conforms to these. A well-planned budget requires more than just the correct allocation of dollars; it must also include a well-developed plan of action that can be quickly implemented, should unexpected events occur.

To know what and where to cut without impairing the quality of the collection is comparable to the art of surgery; the wrong cut, and the damage is irreparable. A well-planned, well-implemented budget guarantees continued stability in the acquisition patterns of the library and the balanced growth of the collection.

Bertha R. Almagro, Assistant Librarian for Processing Services, University of Arizona Health Sciences Center Library, Tucson, AZ 85724.

HISTORICAL OVERVIEW:
THE EASY-GOING SIXTIES AND THE FRANTIC SEVENTIES

In the halcyon days of the sixties, administrators defined budgets as inadequate when they were not able to acquire *all* the material they wanted. This is a far cry from the current critical decisions faced by administrators caught between what *not to buy* and what *to cancel.* Toward the end of the decade, prices for books and journals began a steady and steep climb. The average rate of increase was cited at 9.3% per year, but for medical libraries it was more like 14%. The uniqueness of the material collected and the fact that many scientific books and journals were published outside of the U.S. accounted for this difference. Compounding the situation were increased charges imposed by subscription agencies. Studies conducted during that time provided clear evidence to the effect that this last situation had resulted from higher operating costs to agents and from drastic cuts in the discounts offered by publishers.

By the middle of the seventies, the dollar was facing one of its darkest hours in the international marketplace. The unholy alliance formed by inflation, rising prices, and devaluation was to be blamed for this critical period. Studies based on actual volumes purchased by research libraries supported an inflation rate of 80%. Scientific-technical categories reached the 100% mark, and even surpassed it in some instances. Contrary to all reason, the number of new books and journals also rose (1969—29,579 new books; 1974—40,846 new books), and the cost of these new publications reflected of course the average price increases which had become the trademark of the decade. Since library budgets never came close to matching the amount represented by the rate of inflation, a number of alternatives had to be chosen to respond to the limitations imposed.

With the zeal of true crusaders, librarians banded together to take advantage of cooperative acquisition programs and collection sharing—arrangements that incidentally have never been able to clearly prove their true efficacy. Concurrently, visions of automation were conjured up as an area offering the greatest potential for cost reduction. Unfortunately, as we all know, automation offers many benefits, but saving money is not one of them.

Running for Cover

A frantic race began, and a number of varied solutions to the problems confronting libraries were tried, most of which were based on hastily developed plans, and these for the most part proved to be nothing more than stopgap measures. Even worse, some of the solutions conjured up tended to do permanent damage over the long run to the quality and strength of many collections.

Substantial funds were transferred from book acquisition to cover the journal budget, and massive cancellations of foreign journal titles were pursued. The pernicious effect of these two actions are still felt, and the gaps that were created then persist today. The inability to acquire foreign titles retrospectively has diminished the value of many research collections. This is particularly acute in relation to journals, since continuity was disrupted, and in consequence access to knowledge about scientific efforts carried out in other countries was made more difficult than ever. One can wonder if this situation has helped increase the already limited interest in foreign titles, or if American interests were placed all along solely in American research?

In the midst of this maelstrom, established mechanisms to provide the orderly cancellation of journal titles were often overlooked. As a result, many libraries ended up cancelling the same titles, and so made their availability through interlibrary loan impossible.

Most of the panic could have been avoided had libraries been operating under well-developed, up-to-date plans that provided for alternative measures in the event of unforeseen events.

A good feeling for the economic market at the international, national, and state levels, knowledge of the financial standing of the institution served, and information obtained through articles published in library literature on administrative, fiscal, and collection development matters can help libraries operate with a maximum of efficiency. The messages received from such sources provide a solid framework on which to build a realistic and safe budget plan.

PREPARING THE BUDGET: TOOLS AND SOURCES OF INFORMATION

In preparing a budget, a varied amount of *primary* and *secondary* data must be assembled and examined. *Primary* data consists of payment records for materials acquired in previous years (preferably records of the last five years) that are used to assess the pattern followed by price increases in each category. From this data, a kind of "law of probable increase" can be mapped, allowing for the projection of the rise, fall, or stability of book and journal prices in the future. The fiscal reports provided by vendors, for example, can be of great assistance in observing the vast and changeable panorama offered by medical and scientific publications. To maximize this resource, Arizona Health Sciences Center Library approached its three main journal vendors (FAXON, EBSCO, and HARRASSOWITZ) and requested that the three-digit codes representing subject categories the library had assigned to each one of the titles in the renewal invoices be incorporated into the records kept in the vendor's

P.O. BOX 92901 EBSCO SUBSCRIPTION SERVICES
LOS ANGELES CA 90009   /213/ 772-2381

H I S T O R I C A L   P R I C E   A N A L Y S I S   B Y   H E G I S

02/24/84   PAGE   5

LA 77103-00

HEGIS	TITLE	FREQ	SUB	PRICE 1980 FEB	PRICE 1981 FEB	% INCR	PRICE 1982 FEB	% INCR	PRICE 1983 FEB	% INCR	PRICE 1984 FEB	% INCR	TOTAL	INCREASE %
000028	ANESTHESIA & ANALGESIA /SURFACE MAIL/	MO	AA	30.00	30.00	00.0	35.00	16.7	85.00	142.9	85.00	00.0	55.00	183.3
	ANESTHESIOLOGY /MD/ /FOR ALL COUNTRIES EXCEPT JAPAN/ /SURFACE MAIL/	MO	AA	20.00	20.00	00.0	20.00	00.0	20.00	00.0	20.00	00.0	.00	00.0
	INTERNATIONAL ANESTHESIOLOGY CLINICS/ALL EXCEPT JAPAN UK & IRELAND/	QR	AA	45.00	45.00	00.0	45.00	00.0	58.00	28.9	65.00	12.1	20.00	44.4
	SURVEY OF ANESTHESIOLOGY /ALL COUNTRIES EXCEPT JAPAN	BM	AA	35.00	40.00	14.3	45.00	12.5	45.00	00.0	50.00	11.1	15.00	42.8
** TOTAL FOR 000028		**		130.00*	135.00		145.00**		208.00**		220.00**		90.00	69.2
** 4 TITLES AVERAGE PRICE				32.50	33.75	03.8	36.25	07.4	52.00	43.4	55.00 05.8			

DEAR CUSTOMER:
BASED ON THE TOTALS THE AVG. YEARLY INCREASE IS EQUAL TO 17.3%

FIGURE 1

computers.[1] Since it was possible through use of these codes to produce a list arranged by subject category, the object was to obtain a printout of records fashioned in this format (Figure 1) as a means of identifying increases in *total expenditure, per title,* and *within each category.* The printouts usually cover a three or four year period. While providing invaluable financial information, they can also be used to monitor the growth of the collection in each subject area and to simplify the deselection process. The section corresponding to a specific subject can be sent to a department whose interest resides in that area, with a request that the listed journals be evaluated and recommendations made as to which titles might be safely considered for future cancellation. Even if no budget hardships are foreseen, this is a helpful way to assess the quality and needs of the collection through the eyes of those who use it.

Control over books is more difficult to obtain, as prices cannot be compared, except in the case of editions. Nevertheless, the total amount spent can be used as a predictor when the number of titles acquired yearly remains stable or fairly much so. Two specific areas are more sensitive to analysis: namely, standing orders (STOs) and approval plan items. Volumes received in the STO category are part of a large number of different series consisting of titles within a related area. Thus changes can be more easily identified.

A good example of an item in the STO category is offered by the series *Progress in Clinical and Biological Research,* published by Alan R. Liss, Inc. The pattern of publication of this title has been traced back to its first volume in 1975 and followed through 1983. An analysis of the date collected is given below:

No of v. Published		Average Price	Total Price
1975	4	$40.38	$ 161.50
1976	7	46.29	324.00
1977	7	55.29	387.00
1978	8	50.25	402.00
1979	10	51.90	519.00
1980	12	54.33	652.00
1981	39	47.64	1,858.00
1982	40	56.43	2,257.00
1983	31	55.97	1,735.00

The prices range from a modest $22.00 per volume to a high of $176.00. A tremendous increase is noted in volume output during the last few years' time.

Volumes received as part of an approval plan can also be closely monitored for price changes and used as predictors of future increases. The

AHSC Library has developed a control plan[2] that allows for the identification of titles received from each publisher according to specific subject category, and this has greatly facilitated the task of budget preparation. The tools just described are of course valuable for both budget preparation and collection development analysis.

Secondary data is available from a wide repertoire of sources such as: the *Wall Street Journal;* local newspapers; reports concerning the growth and industrial potential of the state; activities of the state legislature, and finally, the reports emanating from the parent institution addressing future plans and programs. Of great importance is frequent communication with faculty and administration, and any other source that can serve as a "pipeline" from which first-hand information can be obtained to formulate a realistic plan of action.

The Right Cut in the Right Place

Concurrent with the actions described above, plans must be developed to insure the application of appropriate measures, should a crisis occur. The previous approaches outlined can be helpful in minimizing problems, and journal cancellations could be enforced without (almost!) running the risk of cutting titles vital for studies, research and programs. The influx of books can be controlled by reducing the number of titles received through STOs and approval plans, based on the practice of ongoing review applied by a control plan. If drastic measures become necessary, either the STOs or approval plans can be placed on hold until the situation improves. Finally, direct purchases can be spaced or dropped to a minimum, acknowledging only requests made by faculty, students, or those coming from the reference section of the library.

The Unexpected Bonanza

It is as important to be prepared to adequately distribute any last minute funds as it is to be prepared for cuts. Dashing out on a mad spending spree can create hardships for the acquisitions department (preparation of orders, invoices, fiscal control, etc.) as well as spoiling the balance and quality of the collection. To avoid this situation, two possible plans of action are recommended. One requires that specific titles have previously been identified as potential selections for purchase. This action can deal with a large number of volumes or a few high priced titles (even one, usually a Reference tool). Cumulative abstracts or indexes, encyclopaedias, etc., are good targets for quick expenditure of funds, and usually worth the investment. The second plan favors prepayment for some expensive tool, whose subscription must be renewed periodically. We are all acutely aware of quite a few titles that would fit this category. By following this path, protection is provided against the untoward surprises that the following year's budget may bring.

Caveat Bibliothecarius

A few warnings seem appropriate at this time. Temporary measures have a way of evolving into permanent solutions; therefore, make sure that any measure applied has been carefully thought out. Emphasis has always been placed on meeting immediate needs. Avoid this trap, since support for ongoing teaching and research must be continued. Local needs must be the number one guideline from which collection development programs must evolve; likewise, cuts must be made keeping in mind these needs. Therefore, it is hardly ever advisable to follow measures taken by other libraries as a model. Contrary to the song that goes . . . "my land is your land" . . . , "their library is not one's own library." Each situation is unique and demands individual attention.

CONCLUSION

Through formalization of procedures, the drawing up of collection development policies, long-range plans and formulas for budget allocation, and increased coordination with other libraries, one's administration, faculty, and library staff, a clear and healthy plan of action should emerge. Frequent revision to identify new priorities and to adjust variances must be an integral part of any plan that is called upon. Success depends mostly on making sure that all mechanisms supporting the budget are finely tuned.

REFERENCES

1. Almagro, Bertha R. The qualitative/quantitative control of collection development. *Technicalities* 2(2):10-12 (Feb. 1982)
2. Almagro, Bertha R. Approval plan: The vendor influence. Paper presented at the Joint Meeting of the Medical Library Group of Southern California and Arizona and North California and Nevada, held in Tucson, Arizona, at the Holiday Inn Broadway, Feb. 20-22, 1985.

A Lesson Learned the Hard Way, or, The Cost of Relinquishing Acquisitions Control

Donna M. Goehner, PhD

ABSTRACT. This paper describes an approach to fund distribution for serials acquisitions that has proven less than satisfactory. A change in collection development policies giving primary responsibility for selection decisions to teaching faculty has resulted in a skewing of the balance in library holdings. The primary reason for the current imbalance is the tendency of academic departments to maintain periodical subscriptions at the expense of monographic publications.

During the past decade librarians have been faced with a plethora of challenges. Some of the more frustrating ones were the direct result of a situation facing most, if not all, professionals responsible for collection development—a continuous decline in funds available for new acquisitions. The pages of *The Serials Librarian* have documented some of the causes for the decrease in library materials budgets as well as the approaches taken within the library community to deal with the resultant problems, e.g., double-digit inflation in the prices of scientific journals;[1] the subscription agent's reaction to lower serials budgets;[2] serials reduction activities at the University of Massachusetts[3] and at Western Washington State College.[4] As recently as 1984 Paul indicated that "prohibitive costs of serial publications may well be regarded as the most serious problem of librarianship in the 1980s."[5] Granted that costs exceed financial resources in most libraries today, it is nonetheless necessary for librarians to respond to their users and attempt to provide resources that meet their informational needs. How to acquire materials that meet ever increasing demands with fewer financial resources is indeed a challenge demanding our best intellectual and managerial responses.

This challenge is being met by librarians daily in a variety of ways, and it would be presumptuous to suggest that there is a single strategy that can be universally employed to deal with the situation. However, it is some-

---

Donna M. Goehner is Acquisitions and Collection Development Librarian, University Library, Western Illinois University, Macomb, IL 61455.

times helpful to know which attempts were effective and which were not. The following discussion describes one approach to fund distribution for serials acquisitions that has proven less than satisfactory.

When reviewing the periodical acquisitions process at Western Illinois University from 1975 to 1985, the degree of change in our approach to the development of this portion of our collection is striking. Ten years ago the Library held virtually all responsibility for the distribution of funds for periodicals. Furthermore, all selection decisions were made by librarians; therefore, the size, strength, balance and coverage of the periodical collection was a reflection of their choices. There was, of course, consultation with the teaching faculty regarding materials selection, but the ultimate responsibility for what was acquired remained with the Library. So long as there were sufficient funds to permit acquisition of the majority of periodical titles judged to be essential for curricular support, few criticisms or complaints came from the faculty. By the late seventies, however, the increases to the library materials budget were declining, and to compound the problem, periodical subscription costs were increasing to the point at which drastic cuts became necessary. Western Illinois University's Library was not the only academic library experiencing the frustration of trying to maintain periodical runs under such conditions, and like many other institutions, Western had to make hard choices. In our case this meant the loss of several hundred periodical titles.

As expected, when the teaching faculty were informed of the cuts, they expressed concern and frustration. As the economic situation worsened and the Library continued to make further cuts in the periodical collection, the faculty became extremely vocal and insisted on having a larger role in the selection, or more appropriately, the deselection processes in the Library. They took their case to the Faculty Senate and the central administration, and their arguments were convincing. In 1980 an ad hoc Committee was formed to develop a new approach to library materials allocations; and that Committee forwarded a proposal to the Library Director which, once approved, resulted in a major shift in collection development policies. Since 1981 we have been operating under a system where more than 60% of the funds available for library materials are allocated to the academic departments. The departmental faculty members serving as representatives make all selection decisions and can purchase whatever materials they deem most important for the collection. Having been given the responsibility for collection development, many of the academic departments decided to reinstate periodical subscriptions previously cancelled by the Library. This action, in several cases, led to further expenditures of departmental funds for the acquisition of missing back issues, leaving even fewer dollars available for book purchases. Today, with funds still limited and costs continuing to escalate, the teaching faculty are finding it hard to make their dollars stretch as far as their needs extend.

As in the case of most radical changes in policy, results have been mixed. In some subject areas there has been improvement in the quality of the collection. But in many more areas there are greater imbalances and less quality in library holdings than under the previous system. One explanation for this situation stems from the reluctance of the teaching faculty to reduce their periodical subscriptions. There is a tendency for them not only to maintain all subscriptions on their current lists but to acquire additional periodicals. Each new subscription is a continuing commitment against their departmental allocation. Because that money is unavailable for other discretionary purchases, there are fewer and fewer monographs added each year.

At the present time the academic departments are spending 77% of the money allocated to them for library materials on periodical subscriptions. Even though most of the departmental representatives realize the potential danger of using their funds for periodicals at the expense of new books, there is no concerted effort on their part to change the current pattern. This is especially true in the case of the sciences. For example, in three subject areas—biology, chemistry and physics—the average percentage spent on current periodical subscriptions exceeds 84%. Specifically, in biology 92% of the total departmental allocation goes to pay for continuations; in chemistry the figure is 83%; and in physics 77%. The argument has been made that periodical literature is more important to scientific research and study than are monographs; thus, the teaching faculty are unwilling to cut back in that part of the collection. They argue further that if they cancel essential periodical titles now and funds later permit reinstatement, back issue costs could prove higher than the cost of continuing the current subscriptions.

Because those of us working on collection development in the Library are concerned about monographic holdings, two steps have been taken to ensure continuing development of the book collection. First, approximately $115,000.00 has been set aside for an approval plan which enables the Library to acquire a portion of new monographs published each year. Second, a general fund, containing approximately $50,000.00, has been created for retrospective monographic purchases. Selection of materials charged to this fund is made by librarians, and it is their responsibility to identify and acquire titles not supplied by the approval plan or by the academic departments. Because these dollars are limited, many more titles are always identified for acquisition than can be accommodated from the general fund. It is not surprising that we are beginning to find serious gaps in our book collection.

When the teaching faculty proposed a more active role in the acquisitions program, we may have been too quick in acquiescing to all of their demands. It might have been possible to limit the extent of their control in acquisitions decisions by attaching conditions to their proposals rather than giving them *carte blanche*. At this point it would be extremely difficult to convince the teaching faculty to give up the control they currently enjoy. They are perfectly satisfied with the situation as it stands, and the burden of making a case for greater library involvement would fall to the librarians through the Director. It is unlikely that those teaching faculty who believe they are using sound judgment in their collection development efforts would willingly surrender what is now their jurisdiction. For the time being it appears that librarians must be prepared to adopt a more passive role in working with the academic departments. As the teaching faculty continue to struggle with purchasing decisions that will remain troublesome as long as budgets are tight, their approach toward collection development may become more pragmatic. They may even come to the point of voluntarily returning authority for collection development to the library as they become convinced that librarians are knowledgeable and discerning professionals who will make responsible selection decisions. We would then have come full circle in our approach to collection building at Western.

Once relinquished, control is hard to regain, however, and it may be some time before librarians at Western again cast the deciding votes in acquisitions policies and practices. We have learned a hard lesson from which others may benefit. Do not abdicate lightly any of the traditional and fitting roles of the professional librarian. Not only is there a risk of jeopardizing the librarians' status in the academic community but serious deficiencies in library holdings may also be created that our successors will find it impossible to rectify. More importantly, surrendering these roles can do a disservice to future patrons, who depend upon librarians to provide an integrated and balanced collection containing resources of the highest possible quality.

REFERENCES

1. F.F. Clasquin and Jackson B. Cohen, "Physics and Chemistry Journal Prices in 1977-1978," *The Serials Librarian* 3:4 (Summer, 1979): 381-386.

2. Frank F. Clasquin, "The Subscription Agency and Lower Serials Budgets," *The Serials Librarian* 1:1 (Fall, 1976): 39-43.

3. Siegfried Feller, "Library Serials Cancellectomies at the University of Massachusetts, Amherst," *The Serials Librarian* 1:2 (Winter 1976-77): 140-152.

4. Stephen Campbell, "Approaching Serial Cancellations at Western Washington State College," *The Serials Librarian* 1:2 (Winter 1976-77): 153-159.

5. Huibert Paul, "Serials: Higher Prices vs. Shrinking Budgets," *The Serials Librarian* 9:2 (Winter, 1984): 3-12.

Serials Claiming

Mary J. Bostic, BA, MLS, MS, CAS

ABSTRACT. Automated serials claiming is described, and the impact it has had on library operations during the past decade is examined. Also included are descriptions of selected automated serials control systems and automatic claiming techniques and a list of additional libraries with serials control systems that allow automatic claiming.

Although serials control has been a difficult operation to automate, serials systems have entered into the scheme of things and are "alive and kicking." According to William Mathew, "technology presents us with a maze of paths and possibilities that could be tried. Yet there is not time, not money, not people enough to follow even a fraction of these paths to the end . . . But until choices are made and paths selected, the abundance of possibilities cannot be turned into a wealth of realities . . . Progress is made by moving down the paths, not standing on the crossroads reading the signposts."[1]

Serials systems over the past ten years have been an obvious target for automation. Earlier than the 1970s, most libraries could not even fantasize about automation. It became possible for them to experiment with automation in a limited way in the 1970s. In the 1980s, it is impossible now to keep libraries away from automation; it improves operating efficiency and provides a means of redistributing needed information so as to enhance the delivery of library services.

In other words, technology is revitalizing libraries and expanding their capabilities. At the very time when libraries are struggling to maintain their traditional collections and services in the face of inflation and eroding support, they must computerize their manual operations and expand their capacity to deal with information in a variety of electronic forms.

Until this decade, collection building and growth were ranked by the size of collections, and bigger was always better and more prestigious. The emphasis over the past decade has shifted from collections to access. Providing access to information is the principal goal and activity of libraries, but these must now also cope with technology and change. Consequently, libraries—though coming to terms with the new economic and

---

Mary J. Bostic, Acquisitions Librarian, Long Island University, Brooklyn, NY 11201.

© 1986 by The Haworth Press, Inc. All rights reserved.

technological realities—still have a long way to go for the most part before all their problems disappear. They are having to invest in the new technology and in new ways of doing the library's business. Users are no longer limited to what a library has, but to what it can provide.

Mason said that "revolutions demand judgements and commitments and judgements from the persons and institutions affected . . . Those affected have three choices: fight against the revolution, and hope to hold it back; ignore it, and hope that the impact on them will be minimal; or join it, and hope to influence the outcome for their own goals."[2] He went ever further in quoting Norbett Wiener: "There is one thing more important than 'know how.' He calls it 'know what,' by which we determine not only how we are to accomplish our purposes, but what these purposes are to be."[3]

Librarians over the past ten years have been contributing the "know what" to the current revolution—the "know what" of services to be offered, the "know what" of equitable service to all categories of users, and the "know what" by which they determine what the purposes of the library are to be.

REVIEW OF THE LITERATURE

As far as functions are concerned, there are direct correlations (with some exceptions) between the automation of one function and that of an accompanying one. Automation of claiming, for example, practically always accompanies automation of check-in, and binding information and holdings information are consistently automated together. Frequently all four revolve around the check-in method.

According to the general wisdom, any automated system would be wasted on holdings of under 150 periodicals. Much of the success of any system has been dependent upon the initial planning, staff availability, and the conviction that a change was necessary to eliminate the problems being encountered with the manual system.[4] To date, serials systems have taken a back seat to circulation systems and others because of priorities set by library managers; but during the past few years, the utilities and some serials subscription agents have shown interest in the problems of serials control. From 1980 to 1985, online serials control has become more commonplace.

Successful automation of serials control offers immediate benefit by way of service offered the public. The improved service potential from a current claiming system serves as stimulus to proceed with other serials automation projects. By solving the problems of manual files, much greater control over the claiming function is realized. It is axiomatic that automation of any aspect of library operations can be justified only if it improves service to the end-user, the library patron. Since serials are valuable and lively, librarians are having to find ways to handle them more efficiently and to provide access to *all* of them.

DESCRIPTION OF SELECTED AUTOMATED SERIALS CONTROL SYSTEMS

According to Marcum and Boss, one of the largest functions *still* to be affected by automation is serials control. In 1982 there were no more than fifty libraries known to have automated serials control. In mid-1982, four systems had been installed by at least six general libraries: OCLC's Serials Control Subsystem, Faxon's LINX, Ebsco's EBSCONET, and CLASS' CHECKMATE.[5]

Although OCLC's Serials Control Subsystem is the least known of OCLC's subsystems, it has been operational since January 1975. The major function of the SCS is to provide on-line control of serials by offering seven basic capabilities—one of which is claiming.[6] OCLC has actually been working on its serials control program for almost ten years. In the fall of 1979 it was reported that OCLC was planning to install a publishers name and address file. Libraries participating in the OCLC Serials Control Subsystem would have access to data in this file and would be able to use the data for claiming from their check-in records. In 1980, a claiming subsystem, which was being completed and prepared for installation, was the latest of the serials control enhancements at OCLC. The serials local data record was being modified and expanded to include new requirements to enhance claiming capability. A definition field was expanded to allow users a great deal of control over predicted issues and their receipt. A user is able to receive and/or claim every issue if the title is at all regular. The addition of a purchase field allows the user to enter data about purchasing and invoicing; these elements are used to supply information that allows the user to specify a claim mode of automatic, semi-automatic, or manual. The number of claims cycle is user-selected. The OCLC name/address directory is used to find appropriate control numbers, which in turn will be combined with the claims field to direct where the claim forms are sent and where replies are also to be sent. Both check-in and claiming benefit from this user-defined periodical frequency capability.

With the installation of the claiming capability in the spring, 1981, phase I of the Serials Control Subsystem was completed. Libraries have the option of specifying that the SCS issue claims automatically, notifying them that there may be a need for a claim, or waiting until they initiate a claim. They are able to obtain on-line summaries of outstanding and potential claims as well as cumulated statistical reports. Statistical reports include the number of issues received, the number of claims filed, the number of issues missing but not claimed, the number of outstanding claims, and the number of outstanding potential claims. By 1982, 212 institutions were authorized to use the SCS, and sixty-six were actively checking in serial publications.[7]

In 1980 the F. W. Faxon Company, Inc., offered a serials control system to its customers. Its SC-10 service, a component of LINX, offers serials check-in and automatic claiming of Faxon-placed subscription orders. The basic record for each title in a library's check-in file consists of two screens. Screen one contains a status code which includes "C1" for first claims. Screen two includes detailed information on missing issues being claimed. One of the major features of Faxon's serials check-in service is its claims warning system. The claims warning system is designed to routinely scan a customer's check-in file to select and print out titles that possibly need claiming action because of lapses, gaps, or delinquent first, second, or third claims.

The gaps portion of the claims warning system covers gaps when the subscription is still arriving but specific issues not received. The selection of the title appearing on the list is triggered by CG or "claim a gap" status code input into the check-in matrix when a gap is discovered.

The lapses portion of the claims warning system covers subscriptions that totally stop coming or have never started arriving. Selection of titles for the lapses report is based on an arrival number factor, one of the fields contained on the check-in screen.

The delinquent first, second, and third claim portion of the claims warning system contains titles for which first, second, or third claims are older than fifty-six days. Claims warning system print-outs are issued in duplicate. Faxon's remote access check-in department keeps one copy and handles all claims work required for all titles placed through Faxon, with the exception of the delinquent third claims since these titles are no longer automatically monitored by the system.

Faxon claims activity on behalf of the client is immediately reflected in the customer's check-in file. The check-in library receives the other copy of the claims printout and processes claims as required for titles not placed through Faxon. The gaps report is issued weekly; the lapses and delinquent first, second, and third claims reports are issued biweekly. In addition, an "irregulars to be reviewed" report appears every six months. This contains titles with irregular frequencies that have not had any check-in activity during the previous six months. This report is mailed directly to the library, which is responsible for processing all claims for irregular titles regardless of the source.

Among the batch reports routinely issued are those containing monthly check-in statistics reflecting analysis of the number of titles on the check-in file and the number of issues received, claims entered, and claims outstanding.

Lastly, an electronic mailbox is available to remote access check-in users that provides online message switching capabilities between the library and Faxon. This electronic mailbox can be used for ordering, claiming, requests for adjustments, or for specific questions.

EBSCO has also come to the libraries' aid. EBSCO's serials system, EBSCONET, which was developed in cooperation with a medium-sized health sciences library in 1978-79, was based on an earlier version of the UCLA Biomedical Serials Program.[8] The EBSCO system was available for formal presentation and demonstration to interested parties by the second quarter of 1981 and was available for installation by the third quarter of 1981.[9]

The System is designed to keep track of any serially received information. It has six major functions, one of which is claiming. Claiming starts in the EBSCO system with check-in. The first job is to bring up the appropriate check-in screen. One of the top lines on the screen predicts when the next issue of the title being reviewed should be received. Not every issue can be predicted. The prediction will indicate the year, the volume number, the issue number, and the issue date. If the issue in hand is not the one that the system has predicted, then the issue in hand is keyed in and at that point there are two options: to go to a claim format or to generate a claim. Claims are printed and mailed to publishers two times per week. If an immediate claim is not desired, the choice is to let the existence of that gap go into a claim file to be reviewed.

Irregulars present one of the most challenging problems in claiming. This system also provides for the claiming of irregulars, often a missing feature of other automated serials control systems. Irregulars can be automatically put in the Claim File and exposed to review, if nothing is received during a specified period of time. If there is no receipt of a given title within six months, a record automatically goes into the claim file to be looked at and a decision made as to whether to claim or not.

The contents of the claim file are all outstanding claims. This file indicates whether a title has been claimed two or three times or what the status is. The claim file is a review file. Two records connected with claims are important, and these are displayed on most screens. One is made up of claim notes in which miscellaneous comments appear. The other is a claim history note, which contains a record of everything that has been done.

In summary, the two most important features are first, the automatic identification of a gap or of a title that simply ceases to come, and, second, the existence of a claim file that is constantly available for review. If the decision is not to review and to claim immediately, this can be done at the point of check-in. A manual claim can be made at any time.

The Cooperative Library Agency for Systems and Services (CLASS) announced in 1981 the availability of a microcomputer-based serials control system. The system is a "stand-alone" serials control system using a

TRS-80 Model II microcomputer with floppy disk drives. Known as CHECKMATE, it is designed for small and medium-sized collections and supports, among other activities, claiming.

CHECKMATE can check in issues and automatically indicate the expected date of the next issue. The user may define claim intervals that will trigger the program to scan the file automatically. If an expected issue has not been received, the CHECKMATE System will print claim forms.

NOTIS (Northwestern Online Total Integrated System) has been developed by Northwestern University in Evanston, Illinois. The serials module of NOTIS is outstanding in its ability to handle all functions related to serials in one record, including claims. The most impressive feature of NOTIS is its claiming capabilities. The entire claiming function has been taken over by the computer. (This is quite an accomplishment considering the fact that many of the larger automated systems have been able to automate check-in but not claiming.)

Claiming overdue items is accomplished by means of "action dates." The first action date is the date by which the first shipment on the order should be received. If the order is a standing order for a serial or set, as each volume or issue is checked in, a new action date is calculated, which is the date by which the next issue should normally be received. Action dates are calculated automatically, but may be overridden by the operator. If the statement containing the action date is not modified by that date, the record number appears in a daily list of expired action dates. The operator displays the record and then decides if a claim is appropriate and what type of claim, if any, is needed.

Claiming is accomplished by means of a customized correspondence operator. A "memo statement" is created, which contains one or more short mnemonic codes, augmented, if appropriate, by the identification of the volume or issue being claimed. A batch program is run the next morning, which produces a window-envelope-ready letter to the vendor. In this letter each of the codes has been "exploded" into a full text paragraph and the variable volume/issue identification data have been inserted in their proper place. Hence a letter that is complete with bibliographic data and vendor name and address is produced.

PHILSOM (Periodical Holdings of Libraries of Schools of Medicine) is a network generally intended for medical school libraries. PHILSOM accepts libraries either as batch mode libraries or as online libraries. There are two types of claims in PHILSOM. The first type asks for any issue that has been skipped in checkin. The second type is a late issue warning, and it is for any title that has not come in after a specified length of time. In the batch mode system, claims are produced on the basis of a generalized algorithm that takes into account the frequency of a journal and when it was last received. The date the publisher expects to publish any individual issue is also noted. In the online system, notification of a claim is immediate if an issue is skipped, and this notification goes into the print queue to be printed later. The library sets a number of days that are allowed to elapse after the last receipt of a journal before a warning is produced. These claims and warnings are produced as a separate function, which prints out a list in order of vendor and alphabetically within vendor as a part of the claim and warning function.

BASIS, developed by Battelle's Software Products Centre, has a new serials module that allows claiming of serials to be done online. BASIS provides a turnkey approach to library automation, and can be used by both librarians and library patrons. The design for BASIS came from suggestions offered by the BASIS Technical Library Advisory Group.[10]

DESCRIPTION OF AUTOMATIC CLAIMING TECHNIQUES AMONG SELECTED LIBRARIES

Brigham Young University's on-line serials system has been in use since July 1978.[11] The system has three main functions, one of which is claiming.

Claims are initiated automatically by the computer. The computer activates the claiming process when the issue in hand does not match the expected issue information, or when activity for an otherwise active title ceases for a predetermined number of weeks. The operator can key a claim into the system for an issue at any time, depending upon need.

Once entered into the system, all claims follow the same pattern. The claim appears on a list that is generated weekly for normative review by the claims clerk. If the claim is approved, claim letters are generated. The claim letter program is run twice a week.

The computer-generated claim letters are worded individually, depending upon the following criteria: (1) Is this claim for a paid subscription/ standing order? (2) Is it for a gift item? (3) Is it for an exchange item? (4) Is this a first, second, or third claim for the issue? (5) Is the publication pattern regular or irregular? (Irregular publications are queried rather than claimed.)

Studies have shown that fifty percent of the automated claims are successful, as compared to twenty-five percent of manual claims issued using a Kardex system.[12] This is attributed mostly to the greater timeliness of the computer-generated claims.

The serials collections at the library of the University of California Berkeley Campus are regarded as particularly outstanding. By the end of 1975, these contained over 200,000 titles.[13] It is believed that this is the largest existing computerized serials file used for daily processing of serials in any library. The system has an extremely flexible and powerful updating facility. It produces, as a by-product of its updating mechanism, letters to vendors instructing them to send issues that have not been received. The serials processing system controls the ordering, invoicing, checking in, claiming, and binding operations for over 60,000 live serial titles acquired by the UCLA libraries.[14]

The University of Denver's Serials Management System has been in operation since 1976. There are several short programs used for special applications. The SER/EXPER 2 program is capable of issuing claim notices.

The UCLA Biomedical Library System has been extensively reported upon in the literature. Its major feature is a MARC-like record which, in addition to standard bibliographic information, has several local processing fields that facilitate the check-in, claiming and bindery functions and provide associated products. Many of the check-in, claiming, and binding operations are preprogrammed to function automatically with minimum activity required on the part of the terminal operator.

The processing fields include fixed fields that contain data for claiming and binding action triggered by the check-in process, and various note fields such as those for claiming, binding, supplement issues, etc.

In addition to skipped issue claiming, there are several other kinds of claiming that can be done. Records may contain a "months to claim" code assigned on the basis of frequency and country of origin, which represents the number of months allowed to elapse before overdue claiming is initiated. Another code is used for issuing requests for renewal. If a vendor does not accept subscriptions for a serial, this code is the calendar month of the year in which a re-authorization letter is sent out requesting the next issue. There are also codes that indicate when it is especially important for a serial to be claimed or when it should not be claimed.

In the serials claiming module, online operations exist for various categories of claims. The actual generation of claim letters is initiated by a claiming assistant who systematically reviews the titles flagged for claiming and makes the decision as to whether or not a claim should be issued. An overnight batch run then produces claim letters for selected items. At the time the claim is produced by the program, a code in the claim processing field is changed automatically to show that a letter has actually been generated.

Since the check-in, claiming, and bindery modules are all interrelated in the system, the bound and unbound holdings always reflect current processing activity. Public lists generated from the system include complete holdings statements, including notes on the date of the last receipt of an issue and all outstanding claiming and binding activity.

Automated serials claiming has affected the life of many libraries, and is likely to affect that of many more. It has proven that the serials librarian and the machine can work together successfully both in improving the effectiveness of the serials operation and in enhancing the quality of library services in general.

REFERENCES

1. Mathew, William. "The Impact of Technology on the Governance of Library Networks." In Allen Kent and Thomas J. Galvin, eds. *The Structure and Governance of Library Networks* (New York: Marcel Dekker, 1979).
2. Mason, Robert M. "The Challenge of the Micro Revolution." *Library Journal,* Vol. 109, No. 11, p.1219-1220, June 15, 1984.
3. Ibid.
4. Harp, Vivian. "Automated Periodicals System at a Community College Library." *Journal of Library Automation,* Vol. 7-8, p.83-96, 1974-75.
5. Marcum, Deanna and Richard Boss. "Information Technology." *Wilson Library Bulletin* 57, p.154, October, 1982.
6. Micciche, Pauline F. "The OCLC Serials Control Subsystem." In Peter Gellatly, ed. *The Management of Serials Automation: Current Technology and Strategies for Future Planning* (New York: The Haworth Press, 1982), p.219.
7. Ibid.
8. Potter, William Gray. "Available Automated Check-in Systems: A Panel Discussion." In William G. Potter and Arlene F. Sirkin, eds. *Serials Automation for Acquisition and Inventory Control* (Chicago: American Library Association, 1981), p.77-78.
9. Ibid.
10. "Battelle Turnkey System Extended to Serials Handling." *Program 18,* p.94-95, January, 1984.
11. Memmott, H. Kirk, K. Paul Jordan, and John R. Taylor. "On-line Serials at Brigham Young University." In *The Management of Serials Automation: Current Technology and Strategies for Future Planning* (A Monographic Supplement to *The Serials Librarian,* Vol. 6, 1981/1982), ed. by Peter Gellatly (New York: The Haworth Press), p. 61-62.
12. Ibid., p.64-65.
13. Silberstein, Stephen M. "Computerized Serial Processing System at the University of California, Berkeley." *Journal of Library Automation* 7:8, p. 299, 1974-75.
14. Tonkery, Dan. "Descriptions of Automated Serials Control Systems." In William G. Potter and Arlene F. Sirkin, eds. *Serials Automation for Acquisition and Inventory Control* (Chicago: American Library Association, 1981), p. 147.

APPENDIX

LIST OF SELECTED LIBRARIES WITH AUTOMATED SERIALS CONTROL SYSTEMS UTILIZING "CLAIMING" COMPONENT

Central State University

Clemson University

Harvard University

Miami-Dade Junior College. South Campus Library

Minot State College. Memorial Library

Mount Sinai School of Medicine. Department of Library Science

National Library of Venezuela

New York State Library

Pennsylvania State University. Milton S. Hershey Medical Center Library

Rand Corporation

University of Alabama Medical Library

University of California. Davis

University of California. Los Angeles

University of California. Riverside

University of California. San Diego

University of California. Santa Barbara

University of Cincinnati

University of Florida

University of Minnesota Libraries

University of South Alabama

University of Washington Libraries

University of Wisconsin Library

Washington University

Wharton County Junior College

The Use of Microforms in Libraries: Concerns of the Last Ten Years

Jean Walter Farrington

ABSTRACT. The use of microforms in libraries has grown over the past ten years, and microform will continue to be an appropriate medium for preserving certain types of materials. The future use of microforms is clouded by the potential storage capabilities of the new disc technologies. Yet noteworthy advances have been made in the bibliographic control of microforms and in the quality of readers and printers available. A review of the recent literature traces the changes in microform use and technology and the increased emphasis on educating users to the benefits of microforms.

In the past ten years (1975-1984), the use of microforms in libraries has grown while at the same time microforms have been overshadowed by newer, more sophisticated technologies. For individuals who held the euphoric view that microforms were a panacea for all library preservation ills and collection shortcomings, this was a time of coming to terms with reality. For those who feared that microforms had met their demise, there was new excitement about the format with the introduction of COM (computer output microform), the availability of new reference tools on microfiche such as *Phonefiche* and college catalogs, the adoption of standards for archival quality film, and the beginnings of true bibliographic control of microforms. Microforms maintained a place in library collections and perhaps even strengthened their hold in the area of preservation of documents.

In the 1950s, 1960s and even early 1970s, there was great enthusiasm for entire library collections on microfiche and little appreciation of the shortcomings of microform as a medium. In a 1976 article, Allen Veaner put it this way:

> The literature of the 1950s and 1960s continued almost unbroken the halcyon expectations of earlier decades but with one new factor: there was growing awareness that not only were some users not enamored of microforms; many hated them passionately. . . . Un-

---

Jean Walter Farrington, Head, Serials Department, University of Pennsylvania, Philadelphia, PA 19104.

daunted and undiscouraged, no doubt because of their lack of contact with the realities of academic work, the proponents of replacing books with film continued their promotional activities unabated.[1]

Microforms have never been satisfactory for long periods of reading, and library patrons have always been more or less resistant to using them given the difficulties.

Now it seems we have entered the age of the disc: the video disc, the optical disc, and, of course, the floppy disc. Microforms, a static storage medium, have been surpassed and supplanted, at least in the media, by the more dynamic, jazzier, disc format. A variety of projects are currently underway to test the longterm usefulness of the disc as a permanent storage medium; most notable are those at the Library of Congress involving putting nonprint items on video disc and storing periodical issues on digital disc. It is too soon to predict the cost-effectiveness of these new disc technologies and there are, as yet, no standards, but they are, without a doubt, great space savers.[3]

In an article on the college library of the future, Evan Farber predicts that by the end of the century, microfilm will have been replaced by video discs except for archival storage.[3] He does not define archival storage for whom, but it is a defensible view that research library collections will continue to rely on microfilms and microfiche for permanent copies of newspapers and periodicals and out of print titles that would otherwise be unavailable to their users. At the present time, microforms are quite cheap to purchase; also readers and reader/printers have been refined to the point that they are much simpler to use than the early models and do provide copies comparable to what one gets from a photocopy machine. Thus, despite the overshadowing by newer, fancier technologies, microforms do still belong in libraries. In fact, in the past decade, there has been an increase in the use of microforms as well as other developments that have added to their attractiveness.

A review of the library literature of the past ten years, specifically the annual reviews of micrographics that have appeared in *Library Resources and Technical Services*,[4] provides evidence of the growth, changes, and eventual sidelining of microforms and microforms technology. In the 1974 essay, titled simply, "Micrographics," Spaulding and Fair cite five noteworthy issues or events for that year. These are: (1) the problem of reduced library budgets; (2) a growth in the use of microforms due to the development of COM; (3) advances in bibliographic control resulting from two new publications, *International Microforms in Print* (containing 6,000 titles), and *Microform Market Place, 1974/75,* a comprehensive list of microform publishers; (4) user resistance to the microform format, and (5) the original publication in microfiche of the *American Journal of Computational Linguistics*. (Incidentally, this journal is still being published in both fiche and paper.) The authors' points here are definitely more positive than negative; library budgets were out of their control, and user resistance to microforms was not a new problem. The suggestion was that this resistance might itself be a passing thing. "In fact it would be difficult to overestimate the potential of COM as a force for changing attitudes toward microforms."[5]

The next two years, 1975 and 1976, witnessed the beginnings of the silver halide versus the non-silver films controversy and the Library of Congress' publication of its subject headings in COM fiche. In 1977, copyright questions were on everyone's mind, but also, the U.S. Government Printing Office initiated the micropublishing of material for depository libraries. Given the size of the government's publishing operation, their use of microfiche was not a small matter. In addition, more libraries were subscribing to periodicals in microfiche.

In 1978, the new technologies began to creep into the picture, and the title of the review article changed to include reprography and graphic communications. In 1980, it changed again, with the addition of video technology. Trends toward more interaction between computers and microforms were cited, with the most novel concept being the combining of computer terminals with microform readers. Also of paramount concern in 1980 was the long-standing matter of bibliographic control of and access to microform holdings. From 1979 on, the annual reviews devote more and more space and attention to computer-related and other technologies. Initially, this emphasis is on the emerging video technology as it relates to libraries; later, the focus of micrographics itself turns toward business and the data processing market. Clearly, the microforms technology did not itself evolve further. Of course, new readers and printers were introduced, but the basics remained the same. There was then and still remains the matter of a sometimes cumbersome interface between microform, machine, and user.

A sampling of articles published elsewhere in the literature during the same period reveals an overriding concern with user resistance to microforms and the need for patron education in the benefits of the micro format. Some examples of titles are: "Microform Attitudes and Frequency of Microform Use" (1975),[6] "User Environment and Attitudes in an Academic Microform Center" (1976),[7] and "Promoting Microform Collections in the Library" (1982).[8] More recently, there are these additions: "An Innovative Approach to User Acceptance of Microforms" (1983),[9] and "Microforms and Users' Feelings" (1984).[10] The differences between the early articles and the later ones generally have to do with who or what gets blamed for problems with microform. The earlier articles stress the need to spruce up microform reading areas to make them attractive and to have good equipment in working order. By and large, many libraries have put effort into making their microforms areas both appealing and functional. Certain libraries, such as those at Boston University and Princeton University, received a good deal of media attention when they did. More recent articles on patrons' approaches to microforms focus on educating librarians and patrons to the benefits, not the minuses, of microforms. This education is being conducted by persuasion as well as through formalized instruction or awareness programs. The promising note in all of this is that microforms are being allowed to be what they are: a preservation medium, the complete copy of an otherwise mutilated periodical volume, or a special resource the library would not otherwise own.

Probably the most laudable accomplishment of the decade was the bringing of bibliographic control to microforms. As every librarian knows, microforms have traditionally been given low priority for cataloging or any other special or even normal processing. Initially through the efforts of Grey Cole, the library community was made aware of the problems created by lack of access to the vast microform collections housed in large research libraries. A committee was formed to study the issue, consultants were hired, surveys taken, and the Association of Research Libraries was appointed to set up an office to deal with providing bibliographic control. Questions of handling of microforms in the context of AACR2 were raised and discussed, and sharing of the work of preparing analytics for large monographic series was formalized, with the records to be made available through the cataloging utilities. Since many individual libraries had already done analytics for certain series, sharing them meant that each library did not have to re-do the cataloging work over again. Today, through OCLC (and eventually RLIN), a library can add its symbol to one of these large series or sets and thereby, receive cards for all the individual titles in the series. This is a noteworthy accomplishment, for it serves to recognize microforms as a bona fide bibliographic format and to get them out of the backroom and into the mainstream of usable, accessible library materials.

With all that has happened in the last ten years to make microforms easier to access and easier to read, there are, indeed, legitimate reasons for libraries to retain and to continue to add to their microform collections. The argument for microforms is still a convincing one; they do take up less shelf space than bound volumes, and a library is more likely to have a complete (intact) run if it is in film or fiche, than if it is in hard copy. The cost of film is considerably less than the dollars that are spent for the replacement of hard copy issues. For special collections of material in specific subject areas, microfilm and fiche are ideal; they are affordable, and they enable a library to enrich its holdings immeasurably. For rare materials, out of print items, or impossible to bind materials such as newspapers and manuscripts, there is no currently available alternative to microfilm. These resources cannot be presented as superior to the printed page, but should be marketed to the library users for what they are; materials in a particular collection that would otherwise not be available.

The next ten years may be a quiet time for microforms as libraries deal with them in a realistic, no-nonsense way. During this period commercial video and digital discs may become available for purchase and use by libraries, but microforms will probably continue to be used for quite a long while. While personal computers and their attendant discs will continue to get the bulk of the attention and the glory (and for good reasons), microforms will be able to reside comfortably in the library world as full-fledged citizens, safe in the knowledge that their addresses and phone numbers are on file for all to find.

REFERENCES

1. Allen Veaner, "Micrographics: an Eventful Forty Years—What Next?" *The ALA Yearbook 1976:* 48.
2. Jean Walter Farrington, "Video Disc: A Versatile New Storage Medium," *The Serials Librarian,* 7: 35-40 (Winter 1982).
3. Evan Farber, "The College Library in the Year 2000," *Library Issues,* v.5 no.2 (1984) [1-2].
4. The annual reviews of "Micrographics . . ." for 1974-1982 appeared in the summer issue (no. 3) of *Library Resources and Technical Services.*
5. Carl M. Spaulding and Judy H. Fair, "Micrographics, 1974," *Library Resources and Technical Services,* 19: 207-225 (Summer 1975).
6. Robert J. Greene, "Microform Attitude and Frequency of Microform Use," *Journal of Micrographics,* 8: 131-134 (January 1975).
7. Arthur Tannenbaum and Eva Sidham, "User Environment and Attitudes in an Academic Microform Center," *Library Journal,* October 15, 1976, pp. 2139-2143.
8. Melinda McIntosh, "Promoting Microform Collections in the Library," *Microform Review,* 11: 172-175 (Summer 1982).
9. Marilyn P. Whitmore, "An Innovative Approach to User Acceptance of Microforms," *Journal of Academic Librarianship,* 9:75-79 (May 1983).
10. Arthur C. Tannenbaum, "Microforms and Users' Feelings," *Microform Review,* 13:180-182 (Summer 1984).

Store It, But Don't Ignore It

Valerie Jackson Feinman

ABSTRACT. Continually growing collections have mandated the use of storage arrangements in most libraries. Compact storage, storage buildings, weeding and conversion to microformat are all discussed. Reference is made to related topics in the recent literature. It is shown how application of various cost analyses and economic theory methods make available more meaningful and rational decision-making data.

Continued growth in library collections cannot be sustained indefinitely. Mechanisms for dealing with ever-increasing collections have been dated back to 1871, when then Harvard University President Charles William Eliot spoke publicly of his problems with an overcrowded library.[1] Harvard expanded its library in 1877 and again in 1895, placing a real strain on the University's funds. In 1902 Eliot in an address to the American Library Association made several suggestions that shocked the library world. The subject of his talk was: "The Division of a Library into Books in Use, and Books Not in Use, With Different Storage Methods for the Two Classes of Books." The proposals made included the following:

1. storage of little-used books in inexpensive buildings on cheap land
2. sharing of storage facilities with other institutions in the community
3. storage of no more than two duplicates of any one title
4. provision for compact shelving
5. storage of books by size, three deep on a shelf
6. building a storehouse with a flat roof to keep out summer heat
7. provision for the storehouse of double windows to keep out dust and cold

---

Valerie Jackson Feinman, Chief, Academic Technologies, and Assistant Professor (Libraries), Adelphi University, South Avenue, Garden City, NY 11530.

8. use of gratings for floors so that the entire building could be treated as one room for the purposes of heating and ventilating
9. allowing only stack attendants in the building.

These proposals created a sensation at that time, although many listeners to the talk were convinced that they had heard something worthwhile. Today of course all of these proposals are in use, or at least under consideration.

By the 1970s, national attention was being given to the problem of growth. As reported in the ARL/SPEC Kit #39, 1973,[2] two-thirds of the libraries queried were either storing volumes or facing the necessity of doing so. In 1975, ALA produced a pre-conference workshop on the topic: "Running out of space—What are the alternatives?" And by the 1980s even large, well-endowed universities were finding that building costs outweighed the advantages of the several storage options that were available. Expansion to allow for current acquisitions, including the ever-proliferating periodicals collections, became absolutely necessary.

Decisions made to cope with this expansion usually included deliberations on weeding, compact or remote storage, conversion to microformat, and the sharing of resources. The literature includes many articles hailing this or that technique as the best available. Decisions are usually based, however, on the situation of a library at a particular time. Or, to quote Alexander Pope: "Whatever is, is right."

If one follows Gore's[4] guidelines for use, one opts for weeding. If one is in the situation of the University of Illinois, Urbana-Champaign, one chooses compact storage, as chronicled by Gorman[5] and Collier.[6] Feinman[7] and Hubbard[8] chose remote storage. An historical setting for these decisions is provided by Montanaro.[9]

Storage, whether compact or remote or shared, has become mandatory. As defined by ARL, storage "signifies the removal of conventionally cataloged or processed units from their normal location in the stack sequence to a location in which accessibility for consultation or browsing is reduced in the interests of increasing stack space."[10] It allows the retention, in the original format, of materials that are little used, in a location with low cost for land and construction, and with minimal staff. Startup costs for a storage facility are relatively high, in terms of construction and staff planning, but upkeep costs are considerably lower. Minimum growth is expected, on the assumption of continual oversight accompanied by some weeding. Expansion, or a second storage building, when needed, is usually expected to bear a lower cost than that of providing infinite expansion at the beginning. Storage is no longer only a temporary solution, as described by Hubbard.[11] Steady acquisition of materials requires long-term planning for the storage of materials acquired. Expediency in decision-making is often governed by the existence of usable space. After all is said, and read, one maximizes what is available here and now for one's optimum use.

Most libraries reach a consensus to utilize several techniques:

— storage for must-keep items
— microform conversion for periodicals
— weeding for needn't-keep items

Quoting Pope, again: "Whatever is best administered, is best."

FACTORS IN THE STORAGE DECISION

Necessity demands storage of some materials. This should be accompanied by weeding and by conversion to microformat of, e.g., backfiles of periodicals.

The choice of type of storage building, whether compact or remote, depends upon conditions unique to each academic setting. Available building space on campus or off campus, costs, and logistical problems must be factored in in each case.

Choices made as to type of material to be stored are more universal. Until recently the prime consideration was use, and time was spent in developing selection criteria and selection policies. New models have been developed recently, based on cost analysis.

Obviously one wishes to keep only what will be used or needed, and to store what will be little used. Through an interesting set of calculations, Lawrence[12] developed a mathematical model to analyse the complex cost tradeoffs involved. Storage and weeding save space but impose their own costs, which offset potential savings. "There is some frequency of circulation at which it becomes cheaper *not* to house the publications in a conventional campus library."[13] He estimates the cost of circulation for three alternatives: campus housing, compact shelving, and interlibrary loan. From this data he suggests that for items circulated less than once in 21 years, it is less expensive to discard the volume and rely on ILL, unless there exists a storage building. In the latter case, items that circulate once or more in ten years should be retained on campus. Items with circulation rates varying between once in ten years and once in thirty-four years should be placed in storage, and the rest disposed of.

This data must be considered in terms of local factors such as transportation to and from storage, which vary from site to site. There is seldom local data re in-house browsing use. The sociological implications of the inability to browse cannot be assigned a monetary value. Demand for a title may be seasonal or cyclical or so short-termed that a traffic delay could hurt.

Brown,[14] a British economist, describes the factors in interlibrary loan costs, working out a cost per volume per year for both storage and ILL. Storage may prove cheap only if the cost of retrieval is cheap. He too points out the fact that cost analysis ignores browsing implications, in-house use, and the opportunity cost to the ILL user. His basic thesis in support of increased ILL is that it is difficult to justify the storage of volumes that are used less than once in twenty years and that weeding should be resorted to in such instances.

A further comparison of weeding and storage costs was made by Thompson.[15] He noted that weeding was expensive because it is both labor-intensive and irreversible. He estimated the cost per item per circulation to be $17.16 (in 1980), and suggested that high-density low-cost storage was a preferable alternative. Warehousing presents efficiency in floor space, and decisions are reversible. Moreover, selection costs may be simple: all items more than twenty years old *OR* that have not circulated in over ten years. This selection may be done at the clerical level. Retrieval costs may run about $3.16 per item. Opportunity costs are incalculable in terms of no possible browsing and the waiting time for delivery.

Extensive recent work has been done by Stayner,[16] who has characterized space problems as fundamentally economic in nature. Space problems "usually reduce to the allocation of materials to different storage regimes."[17] He also agrees with Fussler and Simon[18] on the long-term effects of continual weeding. Applying the conventional microeconomic model to the operations of a research library in order to understand the space problem, he develops complex equations that are well illustrated in the graphs provided. His results are fairly theoretical, yet shed light on the accuracy of past decision-making for storage materials. He stresses that access costs should be the focus of collection management.

Two components are seen as the cost of access to materials stored: the fixed storage cost per item and retrieval costs, which vary directly with the level of use of the item. These components are inversely related. Thus low-use items should be stored in low-cost storage. He acknowledges that last-use data is not always available, and does not take into account room-use. This study does provide a "rational basis for several collection management policies . . . which are usually only intuitively derived in practice."[19]

From these articles, specifically those by Lawrence and Stayner, which are highly recommended, it is seen that the application of cost analysis and economic theory techniques provide a strong and practical basis for decision-making regarding storage choices.

PERIODICALS STORAGE

If periodicals in one's library are in closed stacks or in circulation, then some use statistics exist for utilizing these techniques. Otherwise, one is dependent upon the subjective knowledge of the staff maintaining the periodicals collection. It would seem safe to relegate periodicals more than twenty years old to storage, subject to recall upon notice of heavy use. One library found it necessary to keep all psychology journals in the main library.

A parallel conversion to microformat can provide instant availability and should be considered for many titles. Or, after twenty years, or some other arbitrary length of time, all titles worth keeping could be considered for conversion. Prediction of use in periodicals is more complex than for monographs, as each issue may cover many topics. One finds that subject matter, illustrations, current events, medical breakthroughs, and fads all trigger interest in past issues of even esoteric titles. Guidelines should be set for relegation to storage, and flexibility must be maintained in their application. One must retain the ability to shift a complete title, or parts of it between the main collection and the storage location. If the library also uses microformat conversion, then it is fairly simple to convert titles when the time period is finished. All titles are not available in microform, and it is not desirable to have all titles in microform. Individual decisions must be made in terms of local need and preference. One's microform collection also grows unceasingly; it just isn't as noticeable. Some libraries are considering placing early runs of titles such as newspapers on fiche in an area that is not regarded as prime space.

Periodicals should then be treated as a subset of the general collection when storage decisions are being made, as special features may mark them as less amenable to guidelines developed using cost analysis and economic theory.

. . . BUT DON'T IGNORE IT

"The English never abolish anything.
They put it in cold storage."[20]

"To store" is defined as "to keep for future use." If a volume is put in storage and ignored, it will not of itself attract use. Patrons must be encouraged to use all the collection, not just that part on display. Retrieval must be efficient and cheerfully performed by carefully trained staff to keep the costs of retrieval as low as possible. This harks back to the theory of opportunity costs to the patron. Cumulative indexes to stored volumes should be kept with the part of the run on display to encourage "browsing" in the absent volumes.

Other techniques, borrowed from the marketing field, should also be used. A bulletin board could feature data about a long run or a unique collection. When one library acquired the complete run of a Black history title just prior to Black History Month, an exhibit and poster chronicled this. The run was exhibited briefly, before the first fifty volumes were sent into storage. The periodicals librarian and staff who know their collection well can feed information into a variety of sources when they see trends developing: departmental bulletin boards, library newsletters, campus newsletters, and faculty meetings. Liaison with departmental faculty will ensure that needed materials are taken out of storage for special projects. In concert with the New York Public Library's recent exhibit of banned books, many libraries ransacked their open and closed collections to mount a similar display. It is incumbent upon all librarians to keep their collections vital. Collection management and public service personnel must cooperate in this endeavor, or the stored collection will lose much of its value.

A SUMMERY SUMMARY OF COLD STORAGE

Decisions to consider storage options for growing collections may now be made with the help of several recent articles that have adapted techniques from other fields for use in collection management. Use remains the pivotal factor. And various cost analysis and economic theory methods cause the data used to be more meaningful and the results more rational than it would be otherwise. Librarians and administrators alike will applaud the possibility of more specific data for use in determining the type and amount of storage needed.

Storage is one of the new facts of life in libraries, along with higher costs and lower budgets. It can be a practical and popular adjunct to library life. One of the most important features not described in any of the articles in the bibliography is the need for positive thinking on the part of librarians involved in storage decisions and use. When you are proud of your storage arrangement, then your patrons will enjoy using its materials.

THE ADELPHI SITUATION TODAY

In an earlier paper[21] the planning and establishment of the Adelphi Annex as it existed in 1980 were described. In that location and at that time, browsing was impossible. Distance and staffing problems were numerous. Problems of retrieval became increasingly onerous at the same time, coincidentally, that the next-door public library offered to purchase the building being used for its expansion. Adelphi had already established an off-campus teaching site in Huntington, in a vacant public school building. This latter site included a newly established branch library. It was decided to move the Annex collection into the gymnasium of the public school, where library staff were conveniently located a few doors away, browsing would be possible, and intracampus delivery of materials had already been established. The greater distance from the main library was partially offset by these factors, and the move was planned for the summer of 1983.

Planning

The new site had less usable space than the Annex, and so a weeding program using nationally published guidelines was set in motion. For example, third and subsequent copies were discarded. Several titles known to have "gone missing" were returned to the main library. Backruns of periodicals were scrutinized, many were converted to microform, and many were designated for disposal, as their loss could be easily handled by interlibrary loan. The plan was to have almost full shelves.

Procedures

A moving company that specialized in library moves and had moved our collections into our expanded building, was hired to pack the remaining collection into carefully labeled, color-coded, numbered boxes. (Color codes were used to identify various categories within the collection: reference documents, circulation, periodicals, science branch.)

A diagram of the new area had been carefully prepared, color coded to assist in placement of the cartons, and copies were taped to the walls of the gymnasium.

The boxes were loaded into four moving vans, transported to the new site, and held in storage. The packing of materials occurred in mid August, when no classes were in session. Faculty had been warned well in advance that no retrieval would be possible during the moving period. The reason for this non-service becomes apparent now: the next step was to dismantle the shelving from the old annex, transport it, and erect it in the new annex location. Once it was in place, the unloading could begin. This method, although seemingly awkward, provided a real cost saving to the library.

The several thousand boxes were unloaded from the storage trucks and piled in the activities room adjacent to the gymnasium/annex. Local high school students were hired to unpack and move book trucks under the direction of library staff and faculty. One regular library member was assigned to each color coded area. The teams worked efficiently and quickly, reducing the carton-filled room to its original empty, lonely state in just short of the three weeks we had allowed.

When classes began in September, the Huntington Annex was open and operating, and regular shipments of annex requests began, handled by the Huntington Branch staff.

Problems

The unloading of the truck was rather undisciplined, so that the box needed next was always under several one didn't need at that point. Had the truck been loaded more systematically, unloading and reshelving time would have been shorter. When handling 8,000 cartons, of course, such inconveniences can be expected.

One of the storage trucks had a leak in its roof, and torrential rains that came at the time of the move caused damage to several cartons and their contents.

Several cartons designated to be returned to the main library and some cartons of discards were all delivered to the annex inadvertently.

Advantages

The forced move enabled a real evaluation to be made of the use of the Annex since its opening. Use statistics for this period, 1976-83, demonstrated clear patterns of use by subject area and type of material. It was found, for example, that the older volumes of psychology journals were the most heavily requested item. During the planning period these were all moved back into the main building, into a basement storage area vacated during the building expansion. These volumes are now available for on-demand retrieval within the building. Our systematic relegation has obviously been effective: the primary source of annex requests today is the interlibrary loan unit.

It should be noted that the expansion of the library building, completed in 1982, did not allow for any movement of materials back from the Annex. The increased stack space was designated for new collection growth, for expansion of nonprint facilities, including computer terminals and facilities, and for general student study space.

Recordkeeping

Decisions were recorded well in advance of the move, but many on-the-spot decisions were necessary, as when a soggy box was opened. Cleaning up the records continued long after the move was completed. Location designations for the Annex collection are shown on the screen of the Adelphi online catalog, ALICAT (Adelphi Libraries Catalog).

SUMMARY

After seven years in the "old" annex and one in the "new," Adelphi is firmly committed to the use of remote storage. The stored collections are in finite space and are under constant review. Good original decisions, followed by practical evaluation, keep the collection useful but not too well used. When a title is regularly requested, it is returned to the main library, for a semester or for permanent placement. In the case of periodicals, these may be converted to microformat or stored in the basement area.

The proximity of the Annex to the Branch library has effectively expanded the Branch collection, even though stored titles are usually old items. Online access to the Annex collection via ALICAT makes its use efficient for Branch personnel.

REFERENCES

1. Kimball Conro Elkins, "President Eliot and the Storage of 'Dead' Books," *Harvard Library Bulletin* 8, no.4 (Autumn, 1954):299-312.
2. Association of Research Libraries. Systems and Procedure Exchange Center. Kit 39. *Remote Storage.* (Washington, DC: Association of Research Libraries, 1977) (not paged).
3. Gloria Novak, "Running Out of Space—What Are the Alternatives?" *Proceedings of the ALA preconference,* San Francisco, June 1975 (Chicago: American Library Association, 1978).
4. Daniel Gore, "Curbing the Growth of Academic Libraries," *Library Journal* 106, no.20 (Nov. 15, 1981):2183-87.
5. Michael Gorman, "A Box Where Sweets Compacted Lie," *American Libraries* 15, no.4 (April 1984):210-11.
6. Martin H. Collier, "Sixth Stack Addition," *Library Journal* 108, no.21 (Dec.1,1982): 2235-37.
7. Valerie Jackson Feinman, "From Attic to Annex: the story of an off-campus storage facility," *The Serials Librarian* 5, no.4 (Summer 1981): 49-58.
8. William J. Hubbard, "Development and Administration of a Large Off-campus Shelving Facility," in *New Horizons for Academic Librarians: ACRL 1978.* Edited by Robert D. Stueart and Richard D. Johnson (New York: K.G. Saur, 1979):550-55.
9. Ann Montanaro, "Reaching a Storage Decision," *Collection Building* 4,no.3 (1982):24-33.
10. Association of Research Libraries (not paged).
11. Hubbard, p.550.
12. Gary S. Lawrence, "A Cost Model for Storage and Weeding Programs," *College and Research Libraries* 42, no.3 (March 1981):139-47.
13. Lawrence, p.140.
14. A.J. Brown, "Some Library costs and options," *Journal of Librarianship* 12, no.4 (October 1980):211-16.
15. Donald D. Thompson, "Comparing Costs; An examination of the real and hidden costs of different methods of storage," *ASIS Bulletin* 7 (October 1980):14-15.
16. Richard A. Stayner, "Economic Characteristics of the Library Storage Problem," *Library Quarterly* 53, no.3 (July 1983):313-27.
17. Stayner, p.313.
18. Herman Howe Fussler and Julian L. Simon, *Patterns in the Use of Books,* (Chicago:University of Chicago Press, 1969).
19. Stayner, p.326.
20. Alfred North Whitehead, *Dialogues.*
21. Feinman (op. cit.)

BIBLIOGRAPHY

— H. William Axford, "Collection Management," *Journal of Academic Librarianship* 6, no.6 (January 1981):324-29.

— "Compact shelving helps delay need for construction at CSU," *Library Journal* 108, no.14 (August 1983):1412.

— John G. Crane et al. "Dartmouth College Storage Library: a new and different kind of library," *Dartmouth College Library Bulletin* 22, no.1 (April 1982):40-46.
— Richard A. Desroches and Marie Rudd, "Shelf Space Management: A microcomputer application," *Information Technology and Libraries* 2, no.2 (June 1983):187-89.
— Robert D. Harvey, "The Two Collection Concept at Southwest Missouri State University Library," *Show-Me Libraries* 33 (September 1982):5-7.
— Paul B. Huenemann, "Solution for Too Many Books and Too Little Room [Mobile shelving system]," *Library Scene* 10 (December 1981):14+.
— David Abraham Kronick, "Goodbye to Farewells: Resource sharing and cost sharing," *Journal of Academic Librarianship* 8 (July 1982):132-36. Discussion, 8 (November 1982):300.
— Barbara P. Pinzelik, "Rearranging Occupied Space," *Collection Management* 5 (Spring/Summer 1983):89-103. Discussion.
— "Reducing Library Space Becoming a Priority," *Library Journal* 106, no.16 (September 15, 1981):1674+.

Introducing Serials Education

Thomas W. Leonhardt

ABSTRACT. A librarian new to serials work has much to learn. In addition to learning on the job, other aids are available. Self-help advice is offered and some American Library Association programs are described, with an emphasis on the Serials Section of the Resources and Technical Services Division.

What does someone fresh out of library school know about serials? It depends on where this person went to library school, to a large extent, but it is safe to say that no matter what was taught in library school, there is still a lot to learn and that in serials, as in other jobs, the opportunities and need to continue learning never cease.

Let's assume that the new graduate knows nothing about serials and has been hired by a small academic library to be in charge of acquiring new titles and maintaining serials records, including renewals. For budgetary reasons, there is no overlap between the tenure of the outgoing librarian and the newcomer.

As the administrator to whom this librarian reports, what advice can be given that will provide some help along the way. Let's assume that this administrator has done well and has hired someone who is intelligent, diligent, patient, curious and questioning, and who possesses a sense of humor. A person with good communications skills, too.

Learning the job won't be easy, even for such an outstanding prospect. Much will have to be learned by trial and error. A procedures manual, if one exists, will help, too, but our enlightened administrator knows that professional development will be necessary if this bright prospect is to become a first-rate librarian. What follows is some of the advice offered.

VADE MECUM

No matter what our line of work, it is reassuring to own a handbook that we can refer to for advice and help. For the serials librarian, that handbook is Marcia Tuttle's *Introduction to Serials Management* (Greenwich, CT: JAI Press, Inc., 1983). Tuttle's book contains chapters on serials in general, developing the serials collection, acquiring serials, cataloging serials, serving the public, preserving the serials collection, and data and resource sharing for serials. There is also an annotated bibliography.

Introduction to Serials Management was designed for use as a course book in library schools, but it is also suited for the practicing librarian and library administrators. It is thorough but not too long. You should read it cover to cover to get a broad perspective on serials before concentrating on specific areas of serials work.

OTHER READING

A handbook is not enough. You ought to read the current literature regularly, including at least these four journals: *Information Technology and Libraries, LRTS, Library Acquisitions: Practice & Theory,* and *The Serials Librarian.* These four titles are especially useful for the serials librarian in technical services. Those interested in collection development and public services for serials should consult Tuttle.

CONTINUING EDUCATION

Most bibliographic networks conduct workshops on serials cataloging. Even though you are not a serials cataloger and may have no intention of becoming one, these will help you immensely in your work as an acquisitions librarian. You will also help those further down the line and will endear yourself to the serials catalogers that have to work with you and use records that you are responsible for creating.

There are also regional serials workshops that are sponsored by the Serials Section of the Resources and Technical Services Division of the American Library Association. The *ALA Handbook of Organization,* on page 145 of the 1984/1985 edition, gives this charge to the Regional Serials Workshops Committee: "To encourage and facilitate regional serials workshops by developing materials which may be used in the planning for and presentation of such workshops; to serve as a clearinghouse for regional serials workshops through liaison with the Council of Regional Groups, state and sectional library associations, other local groups, and appropriate publications, and to assist the Serials Section and other library groups in designing and/or presenting workshops devoted entirely or in part to serials." Because the chair of this committee changes from year to year, you should consult the current *ALA Handbook of Organization* for the current chair. If you are not a member of ALA and RTSD, then write to the Executive Director of RTSD for more information.

If you are not a member of the American Library Association and the Resources and Technical Services Division, then you are missing the best opportunity of all for professional development. By belonging to RTSD you automatically receive the *RTSD Newsletter* and *LRTS*. The *RTSD Newsletter* will keep you informed about workshops, preconferences, and conference programs that should be of interest to you, and *LRTS* will provide you scholarly articles on various aspects of technical services and collection development, including articles on serials management.

The journals of RTSD offer participation from afar but to learn from your colleagues and contribute to the profession, attendance at the Annual Conference and the Midwinter Meeting of ALA provide opportunities that cannot be found in any other way.

The most obvious section offering involvement for a serials librarian is the Serials Section. It is an active section that works on practical problems, and it also helps develop standards for the profession. Those interested in really getting involved while they learn from their colleagues, should attend conferences and then pick out committees that strike them as interesting, important, and likely to be hard-working. Committee meetings are open to all conference registrants with the exception of closed meetings where personnel matters are being discussed by committee members. Show up at meetings that seem interesting, and then pick out a couple of groups that you want to get involved with. Speak up when you have a question or something to say. Volunteer to help out with something. Working committees seldom have enough help and will be grateful for your assistance. But once you volunteer to do something, be sure you follow through. Dependability is a most treasured characteristic.

Each year in the *RTSD Newsletter* an RTSD volunteer form is printed. Fill it out and state the kind of committee you'd like to work on. Mail it to the RTSD office in Chicago. If you have been attending conferences and committee meetings and have shown interest in the proceedings, your name will probably be recognized when executive committees make committee assignments.

For more sources and a broader approach to professional development you should write to the American Library Association's Office for Library Personnel Resources for a copy of "ALA Is Continuing Education," a list of workshops, training packages, and grants. It costs only a self-addressed, stamped (22-cent) number 10 envelope.

Local, state, and regional associations also offer chances to meet with colleagues, ask questions, and compare experiences and ideas. Even if you have to make personal sacrifices, you owe it to yourself to get involved with others doing similar work. If you have to, start your own local discussion group but make a commitment if you want professional growth, even if you never expect to change jobs.

THE UNIQUENESS OF SERIALS

As a parting word, I would advise against exploiting the uniqueness of serials. Each job in the library has a unique aspect as well as something in common with other library jobs. Recognize the uniqueness of serials work; recognize some of the incredibly complex problems that arise day after day; appreciate the uniqueness and the complexity and pat yourself on the back for being able to deal with it all. Never say: "But you don't understand serials."

It is probably true that others in the library do not understand serials work, certainly not to the degree that someone does who works with serials every day. If colleagues say things that tell you they don't understand what you're getting at, explain the problem to them. Make sure that you have been understood by asking for questions and continue to clarify until you are satisfied that they understand or that you have done your best. If they don't understand your work and problems, it may be partly your fault; and it is certainly your responsibility to provide the basis for better understanding.

Serials work can be the most frustrating thing you'll ever do. But if you apply yourself and learn your trade well, serials work can also be the most rewarding thing you'll ever do.

Access to U.S. Government Periodicals in Health Sciences Libraries: An Overview

Valerie Florance

ABSTRACT. The paper discusses the state of access to government periodical information in health sciences libraries. A scan of titles listed in major medical periodical indexes indicates that few government titles are regularly covered. Analysis of 1974 and 1984 *Monthly Catalog* listings for periodicals produced by the Department of Health, Education and Welfare and its successor, the Health and Human Services Department, indicates a shift in the subject orientation and overall format of periodicals issued. Some special characteristics of medical libraries which exacerbate the problem of limited access are also briefly considered.

During the last decade, a radical transformation has occurred in access to government information. The *Monthly Catalog of U.S. Government Publications* has greatly expanded its coverage, and sharpened and standardized its indexing. Private publishers have produced specialized tools which rival the *Monthly Catalog* in usefulness. Vendors of online bibliographic search services now provide access to a variety of government databases. The Government Printing Office (GPO) has stepped up sales campaigns for government publications, and private publishers offer subscription services and microfiche collections. With the loading of *Monthly Catalog* tapes into OCLC, even small public libraries have easy access to bibliographic data on government documents.

The changes outlined above have not substantially improved access to government serials in medical libraries for several reasons. The discourse that follows elaborates upon those reasons in an attempt to assess the current state of access to government periodicals in health sciences libraries. Analysis of titles indexed by major health sciences reference tools like *Index Medicus* and *Hospital Literature Index* indicates that, generally speaking, coverage of government titles remains about the same in 1984

Valerie Florance is the head of Computer and Media Services at the Spencer S. Eccles Health Sciences Library, University of Utah, Salt Lake City, UT 84112. She was formerly the Documents Librarian there and Editor of *MEDOC: Index to U.S. Government Publications in the Medical and Health Sciences.*

as it was in 1974. However, a shift has occurred in the kind of government information published in periodical format, which has decreased access to government periodical information for some medical libraries.

A preliminary profile of medical libraries and the place of government publications in their collections will help provide a context for the reader. The Medical Library Association (MLA) claimed 1229 institutional members in its annual report for 1983. Seven hundred and seventy of those members (62.6%) reported current subscriptions at less than 200 titles per year. In fact, 86.6% of those members held less than 600 current subscriptions. About 11% of MLA's institutional members are academic health sciences libraries (AHSLs), attached to medical schools.[1] Presently, only eight AHSLs are depositories. About 7% of the AHSLs acquire more than 1,000 documents annually; fully 40% acquire 100 or fewer each year.[2]

A 1972 survey of MLA's 759 institutional members indicated that nearly half of the 427 respondents could not (or would not) even describe their handling of government publications. Most did not house their documents in separate collections: monographs were cataloged or placed in vertical files, and periodicals were incorporated into journal collections. Only 12.6% of the respondents used the *Monthly Catalog* as an index, and a scant 4.6% used Superintendent of Documents classification to arrange materials on the shelf.[3] The National Library of Medicine has been a depository since 1977, but its developing collection of government information has not been reflected substantially in its publications.

A factor of considerable interest is the importance of periodical literature in scientific settings. The belief that scientific information must be new to be useful has made serials the centerpiece of most medical library collections. In many libraries, periodicals are housed on the main floor, their proximity to the entrance enhancing the aura of immediacy that pertains to their use. One result of this phenomenon is the importance placed on reference materials that index periodical information. This leads to an obvious starting point: how much government information appears in periodical format?

Following the Defense Department, the Health and Human Services Department (HHS) is the most prolific government publisher.[4] Its mission to serve the needs of both scientists and laypersons results in a diverse array of publications. Analysis of HHS publications distributed to depository libraries in 1980 and 1983 indicates that 31.6% are periodical titles.[5] Given that the government does publish periodicals, the next question is whether those titles are well-covered in existing health sciences reference materials. And if not, why not?

The National Library of Medicine's *Index Medicus,* along with its on-line counterpart (MEDLINE), is probably the most frequently consulted periodical reference source in medical libraries. Although *Index Medicus* is not the only periodical index for health sciences libraries, its treatment of government publications is the most comprehensive.[6] Table 1 shows government titles listed in Index Medicus in 1974 and 1984. While some titles have died and some have been born, the number of titles covered is about the same in the two years presented.

Hospital Literature Index, which covers about 400 titles, included the government titles listed in Table 2.

Other health science periodical indexes fall far short of even this limited coverage. The 1974 volume of *Cumulated Index to Nursing Literature* contained 183 titles of journals and serials indexed, of which seven were government publications. Its September-October 1984 issue lists 300 titles but only two government periodicals: *Children Today* and

Table 1

Government Titles Listed in Index Medicus

Title	1974	1984
Archives of Environmental Health		X
Bulletin of Prosthetics Research		X
Cancer Chemotherapy Reports	X	X
Cancer Chemotherapy Reports Supplement	X	
Children Today	X	X
Consensus Development Conference Summaries		X
Environmental Health Perspectives	X	X
Health Services Reports/Public Health Reports	X	X
Journal of the National Cancer Institute	X	X
Journal, Water Pollution Control Federation	X	
Mental Health Statistical Note		X
National Cancer Institute Monographs	X	X
National Clearinghouse..Poison Control Bulletin	X	
NIDA Research Monographs		X
Pesticides Monitoring Journal	X	
Proceedings, VA Spinal Cord Injury Conference	X	
Psychopharmacology Bulletin	X	X
Public Health Monographs	X	
Radiation Data and Reports	X	
Recombinant DNA Technical Bulletin		X
Schizophrenia Bulletin		X
Social and Rehabilitation Record	X	
Social Security Bulletin		X
Vital and Health Statistics Series	X	X

Table 2

Government Titles Listed in Hospital Literature Index

Title	1975	1984
Administration in Mental Health	X	
AdvanceData		X
Aging	X	
Alcohol Health and Research World	X	
American Education	X	
American Rehabilitation	X	
Bulletin of Prosthetics Research	X	
Children Today	X	X
FDA Consumer	X	
Federal Register		X
Health Care Financing Review		X
Manpower	X	
MMWR Surveillance Summaries		X
Monthly Labor Review		X
Occupational Outlook Quarterly	X	X
Public Health Reports	X	X
Social Security Bulletin	X	
Vital and Health Statistics (2 series)		X

Public Health Reports. The *International Nursing Index,* whose 1974 volume covered around 250 titles contained those same two (*Children Today* and *Health Services Reports,* the earlier incarnation of *Public Health Reports*). Its 1984 listing has dropped even those two titles.

Lest the reader think that these tables accurately reflect the true extent of government involvement in periodical publishing at the time, a look at *Monthly Catalog* listings of the same vintage will disabuse her/him of that notion. The 1974 *Monthly Catalog Serials Supplement* listed 1204 titles, of which 58 were periodicals produced by the Department of Health, Education and Welfare (DHEW); the 1984 edition lists 170 titles from HHS.[7]

The gap between titles published and titles indexed does not necessarily derive from a lack of knowledge on the part of the indexers. The nature of the government periodicals in question is an important factor. Of the 58 DHEW titles listed in the 1974 *Serials Supplement,* about 38% were indexes and/or bibliographies; Table 3 displays those titles.

Simple inspection of HHS titles listed in the 1984 *Serials Supplement*

(Table 4) indicates a shift in the kinds of periodicals being published. Only 18 of the 1984 titles can be classified as bibliographies or indexes. This represents only about 10% of the HHS group, a substantial reduction from the 1974 figure. It is also interesting to note that the bibliographies and indexes that are being published in 1984 are generally public health and library oriented (like *Immunization Abstracts* and *Health Sciences Serials*), while the 1974 titles in this group were more specialized (*Gastroenterology Abstracts and Citations* and *Diabetes Literature Index*, for example).

A scan of the remaining DHEW/HHS titles in the two *Serials Supplement* volumes provides added insight into the changing nature of government health periodicals. Table 5 presents a rough classification of the titles by format.

About 11% of the 1984 titles are directories and administrative

Table 3

DHEW Indexes Listed in 1974 Monthly Catalog Serials Supplement

---

Abridged Index Medicus
Artificial Kidney Bibliography
Carcinogenesis Abstracts
Cerebrovascular Bibliography
Current Bibliography of Epidemiology
Current Literature on Venereal Disease
Diabetes Literature Index
Endocrinology Index
FDA Clinical Experience Abstracts
Fibrinolysis, Thrombolysis and Blood Clotting
Gastroenterology Abstracts and Citations
Index of Dermatology
Index Medicus
Mental Retardation Abstracts
Monthly Bibliography of Medical Reviews
NLM Current Catalog
Parkinson's Disease and Related Disorders
Psychopharmacology Abstracts
Rehabilitation Services Admin. Quarterly Indices
Selected References on Environmental Quality as it Relates to Health
Smoking and Health Bulletin
Toxicity Bibliography

Table 4

HHS Indexes in the 1984 Monthly Catalog Serials Supplement

Abridged Index Medicus
Bibliography on Health Indexes
Current Awareness in Health Education
Health Sciences Serials
ICRDB Cancergrams
Immunization Abstracts and Bibliography
Immunization: Survey of Recent Research
Index Medicus
Journal of Human Services Abstracts
NIMH Library Acquisition List
NLM Audiovisuals Catalog
NLM Current Catalog
Physical Fitness/Sports Medicine
Psychopharmacology Abstracts
Publications of NIMH
Quarterly Bibliography of Major Tropical Diseases
Sexually Transmitted Diseases Abstracts and Bibliography
Smoking and Health Bulletin

Table 5

Format Classification of HHS Periodicals, 1974 and 1984

Format	1974	1984	% Change
Directories/Manuals	4 (6.8%)	18 (10.6%)	+55.9
Newsletters	7 (12.1%)	33 (19.4%)	+60.3
Periodicals	15 (25.9%)	23 (13.5%)	-47.9
Index/Bibl.	22 (37.9%)	18 (10.6%)	-72.0
Statistical Reports	10 (17.2%)	13 (7.6%)	-55.8

manuals, like the *National Drug Code Directory* and the DHHS *Grants Administration Manual.* This represents a percent change of +55.9% from 1974 Agency newsletters, like *Research Resources Reporter, Newsletter of the President's Council on Physical Fitness and Sports Medicine,* and the *Head Start Newsletter,* also show an increase since 1974.

The other three categories show substantial reductions between the two periods. Statistical reports containing little descriptive text, like *National Monthly Medicaid Statistics* or *Congenital Malformations Surveillance,* show a decline, as do periodicals. The most visible change is in the index/bibliography area, where the percent change is a substantial 72% decrease.

Given the inclusion criteria established by indexes like *Hospital Literature Index* or *Index Medicus,* probably only the periodicals and statistical reports classes would even begin to qualify for coverage. This amounts to about 43% of the 1974 group, but only 21% of the 1984 titles.

An informal analysis of periodical contents undertaken by the staff of the Eccles Health Sciences Library in 1983 corroborates this finding. It was determined that the majority of 15 or 20 government periodicals not covered by medical periodical indexes contained very general articles aimed at the layperson. The unscientific quality of the content rendered these periodicals ineligible under current indexing policies of the medical reference tools discussed here.

This is not to say that all medical library users require scientific materials; indeed, a look back at the figures cited earlier for medical library collection sizes reminds one that most medical libraries are not academic/research libraries. Most are hospital libraries or other small collections that include materials for use in patient education and health promotion programs.

For these popular or lay-oriented materials, the general reference tools familiar to depository librarians *might* offer a solution but for several important barriers. The first stumbling block is certainly lack of awareness. Although the Medical Library Association teaches a special continuing education class on government publications and accredits library school courses in health sciences librarianship, many librarians come to the workplace without much advance training about government information.

A related problem for small libraries is the virtual absence of government publications in existing collections. Many medical libraries developed their collections by reference to a core list commonly known as the "Brandon-Hill List." The 1975 edition of this list suggested 137 journal titles for small or medium hospital or small medical libraries; the only government titles included were: *Abridged Index Medicus, Journal of the National Cancer Institute,* and *Public Health Reports.* Of those three titles, only the first and third were recommended for first purchase. The 1983/84 edition of the Brandon-Hill list presents 135 journal titles. The same three government titles are included, but only *Abridged Index Medicus* is targetted for first purchase.[8]

Beyond this problem, perhaps the two most common barriers to the use of non-medical sources to government information are cost and usability. Table 6 indicates subscription rates for two important indexes to government periodicals last year and in 1974[9] For small non-depository collec-

Table 6

Subscription Costs for Non-Medical Periodical Indexes, 1974 and 1984

Title	1974 Cost	1984 Cost
American Statistics Index	790.00	1865.00
Index to U.S. Govt Periodicals	150.00	325.00

tions with few government publications on hand, such expenditures might be difficult to justify.

A final barrier to the use of these general indexes in medical libraries is their lack of specialized terminology. The National Library of Medicine has taken a strong leadership role in acquiring and indexing biomedical publications. Its thesaurus of subject terms, known as MeSH (Medical Subject Headings), is the accepted standard for medical catalogers and is used in *Index Medicus,* MEDLINE, and other important medical reference sources. The Library of Congress Subject Headings used in the *Monthly Catalog,* and proprietary indexing languages like those used in the *American Statistics Index* and *Index to U.S. Government Periodicals* are often too general to meet the specialized information needs of health sciences library users.

In conclusion, it is clear that access to government periodical information is, and will continue to be, problematic for health sciences librarians. The sources that form the backbone of medical library reference areas provide access to periodical literature. The increasingly limited involvement of HHS in the production of periodicals suitable for inclusion in these publications ensures the continuation of an indexing gap. The small size and limited resources of most medical libraries presently impede their ability to purchase more general non-medical sources that might help resolve the problem. The continuing challenge for librarians and agency publishers who appreciate the value of government information lies in discovering creative, inexpensive ways to bridge the gap.

NOTES AND REFERENCES

1. Medical Library Association. "Proceedings, 83rd Annual Meeting of the Medical Library Association," *Bulletin of the Medical Library Association* 72 No. 1 (January 1984):110; Richard Lyders, ed. *Annual Statistics of Medical School Libraries in the United States and Canada,* 6th Ed. (Houston: Association of Academic Health Science Library Directors, 1983), pp. i-ii.

2. Unpublished data derived from a 1983 survey of 112 academic health sciences libraries. Survey was performed by a task force of the Medical Library Association's Governmental Relations Committee. The Task force was originally headed by Priscilla M. Mayden, later by the author.

3. Unpublished data from a 1972 survey undertaken by the Eccles Health Sciences Library, preparatory to the original production of *MEDOC: a Computerized Index to U.S. Government Documents in the Medical and Health Sciences.*

4. U.S. Office of Management and Budget. *Report on Eliminations, Consolidations and Cost Reductions of Government Publications.* (Washington, D.C.: Office of Management and Budget, 1983?) Distributed by GPO as PrEx 2.2:G 74.

5. Part of the results of this analysis were published in Valerie Florance, "Presidential Policy and Information Dissemination: an Analysis of the Reagan Moratorium on Government Publishing," *Government Information Quarterly* 1 No. 3, (August 1984): 273-284.

6. The only health sciences source devoted exclusively to government publications is *MEDOC: Index to U.S. Government Publications in the Medical and Health Sciences.* However, since *MEDOC* (like the *Monthly Catalog*). only contains general annual entries for periodicals, its listings were not analyzed for this report.

7. Titles produced by the Education Department and those which report exclusively on welfare-related activities (e.g., AFDC statistics or child support enforcement) were excluded from both counts.

8. Alfred N. Brandon and Dorothy R. Hill, "Selected List of Books and Journals for the Small Medical Library," *Bulletin of the Medical Library Association* 63 (April 1975): 149-72 and 71 (April 1983): 147-75.

9. Figures for *American Statistics Index* and *Index to U.S. Government Periodicals* provided by Julianne P. Hinz, Head, Government Documents Division, Marriott Library, University of Utah. Because they provide only general annual entries rather than article-by-article coverage, both *MEDOC* and the *Monthly Catalog* were excluded from this table.

1975-1985: Formulative Years for the Subscription Agency

Rebecca T. Lenzini
Judith Horn

ABSTRACT. This paper discusses developments that have taken place over the past decade in the agency/library/publisher relationship, and indicates, with reference to Faxon's Linx, DataLinx and Publinx, how this relationship has been strengthened and how it will proceed in the future.

The Serials Librarian celebrates its tenth year of publication, offering those who have contributed to this issue an opportunity to reflect upon the changes these years have witnessed in the area of serials and their handling. The period has been a formulative one, not only for the publisher and the library, but also for the subscription agency, which has established its position firmly between the two.

In charting the evolution of the subscription agent over the past ten years, it is especially important to analyze the economic environment in which the publisher, the library, and the agency have operated. This article examines the trends that have affected serial publications as background to a discussion of the changing role of the agency in its relationship to both library and publisher.

RESPONSES TO A CHANGING MARKETPLACE

The Publisher: The period 1975-1985 was marked by a rapid rate of increase in the number of journals published, as illustrated in both Table 1 and Figure 1 which show a 174.1% increase in journal titles recorded in Faxon's bibliographic database.[1] This increase can be clearly explained by the trend toward specialization that became prevalent during these years not only in the sciences and technology but also in the social sciences and humanities. This increased specialization fostered a profusion

---

Rebecca T. Lenzini is Vice President and Director, Academic Information Services, and Judith Horn is Assistant Manager, Customer Service Support/MIS, F. W. Faxon Company, Inc., 15 Southwest Park, Westwood, MA 02090.

TABLE 1

GROWTH IN THE FAXON TITLE DATABASE 1974-1985

STATISTICAL BREAKDOWN EXCLUDING LOCAL USE

	1974 (% of Total)	1985 (% of Total)	% Increase 1985 over 1974
Fulfillable			
Prepaid Subscriptions	29,810 (47.9%)	56,059 (32.9%)	88.1%
Bill Later	8,269 (13.3%)	33,076 (19.4%)	300.0%
Total Fulfillable	38,079 (61.2%)	89,135 (52.3%)	134.1%
Inactive			
Discontinued	9,557 (15.4%)	21,849 (12.8%)	128.6%
Previous, Variant, Split, Merged, etc.	8,373 (13.5%)	36,813 (21.6%)	339.7%
Order Direct	5,171 (8.3%)	13,864 (8.1%)	168.1%
Additional Information Required (Undeliverable, etc.)	807 (1.3%)	7,675 (4.5%)	851.1%
Temp. Suspended/ Status in Question	224 (0.4%)	1,173 (0.7%)	423.7%
Total Inactive	24,132 (38.8%)	81,374 (47.7%)	237.2%
GRAND TOTAL (Excluding Local Use)	62,211 (100.0%)	170,509 (100.0%)	174.1%

of journals aimed at narrow fields of knowledge and, therefore, at narrow audiences.

Along with this profusion of journals came higher and higher prices. Since the target audiences for these specialized publications were limited and often small, publishers were forced to assess prices that would allow cost recovery and profits from a smaller reader base. Figure 2 and Table 2 compare the rise in the prices of journals to the rise in the Consumer Price Index (CPI). This comparison shows an overall increase in CPI of 90.8% from 1975-1984, as compared to 175.7% for U.S. periodicals and 138.7% for combined average price of foreign and domestic periodicals in those same years.

In reacting to the demands of this differentiation of knowledge, the publisher took and continues to take risks in establishing new journals. A close look at Figure 1 reveals that the number of title cessations and suspensions has also increased dramatically. In addition, the number of

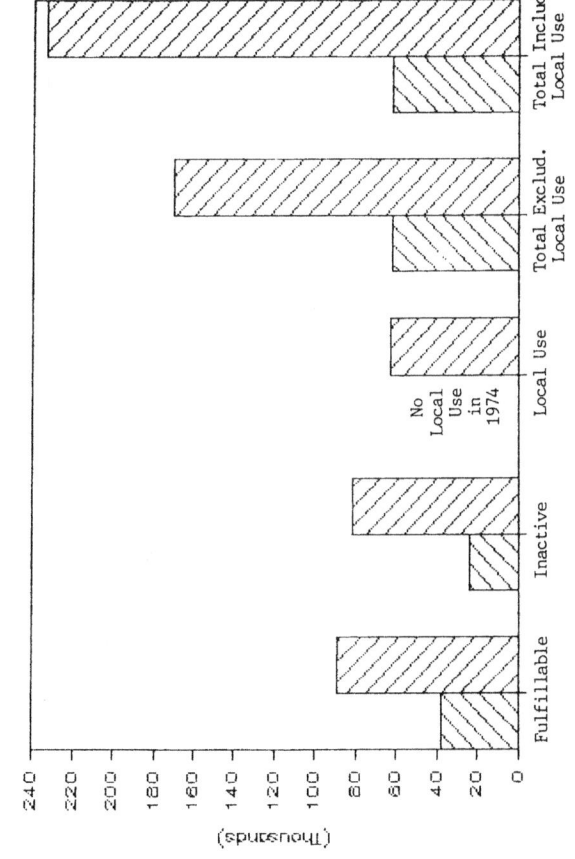

Figure 1
GROWTH IN THE FAXON TITLE DATABASE 1974-1985

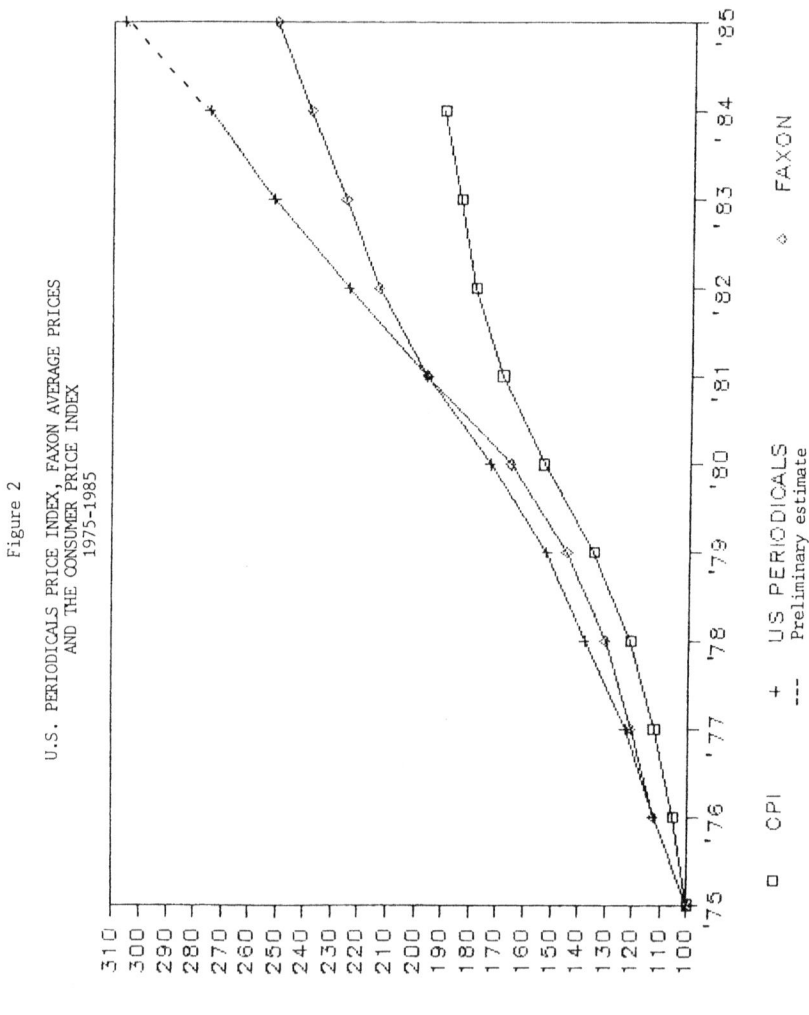

Figure 2
U.S. PERIODICALS PRICE INDEX, FAXON AVERAGE PRICES
AND THE CONSUMER PRICE INDEX
1975-1985

TABLE 2

U.S. PERIODICALS PRICE INDEX[1]
FAXON AVERAGE PRICES[2]
AND
THE CONSUMER PRICE INDEX (CPI):[3]
A COMPARISON 1975-1985

	Average Price		Index			% Increase Over Previous Year		
	U.S. Periodicals	Faxon	CPI	U.S. Periodicals	Faxon	CPI	U.S. Periodicals	Faxon
1975	$ 19.94	$ 34.55	100.0	100.0	100.0	-	-	-
1976	22.52	38.94	105.7	112.9	112.7	5.7%	13.0%	13.0%
1977	24.59	41.85	112.6	123.3	121.1	6.5	9.2	7.2
1978	27.58	45.14	121.2	138.3	130.7	7.6	12.2	7.9
1979	30.37	50.11	135.1	152.3	145.0	11.5	10.1	10.9
1980	34.54	57.23	153.2	173.2	165.6	13.4	13.7	14.2
1981	39.13	67.81	168.9	196.2	196.3	10.3	13.3	18.3
1982	44.80	73.89	179.0	224.7	213.9	6.0	14.5	9.1
1983	50.23	78.04	184.5	251.9	225.9	3.1	12.1	5.6
1984	54.97	82.47	190.8	275.7	238.7	3.4	9.5	5.7
1985	61.07*	86.79	N/A	306.3*	251.2	N/A	11.1*	5.2

1 Source: "U.S. Periodicals: Average Prices and Price Indexes" compiled by Norman B. Brown and Jane Phillips in *The Bowker Annual of Library and Book Trade Information*, 1977-1984 editions. For this comparison, the base year of the U.S. Periodicals Price Index has been shifted from 1977 to 1975.

2 Source: "Periodical Prices Update" published by The Faxon Company in *Library Journal* 1975-1979 and in *The Serials Librarian* 1980- . These are average prices paid per title by Faxon college and university clients for U.S. and foreign titles ordered through Faxon. For this comparison, an index of these prices has been created with a base year of 1975.

3 Source: U.S. Bureau of Labor Statistics, *Business Statistics*, 1982 and *Survey of Current Business*, December 1982. The CPI for 1984 obtained by telephone call to the U.S. Bureau of Labor Statistics, CPI Office. For this comparison the base year of the Consumer Price Index has been shifted from 1967 to 1975.

*Preliminary estimates.

journals changing to a "bill later" or irregular status has increased by 237% over the ten year period, illustrating the insecurity of selling these specialized publications and the problems in maintaining a continuing supply of materials to publish in them. We should note here, though, that some increase in the number of bill later titles in Faxon's database can be attributed to the acquisition and merger of Stechert MacMillan, a topic discussed later in this article.

The Library: The impact of both trends noted above was felt deeply by libraries, which were faced with expanding numbers of journals and rapidly escalating prices. The luckiest libraries were working with budget increases matched to general inflation rates, but Table 1 has already shown that periodical prices outstripped CPI. Other libraries were faced with static budgets or slashed allocations, as colleges and universities faced the reality of recession and low enrollments.

The library has long recognized that continuity in its journal holdings is of paramount importance and also that the cost of acquiring back issues to fill in a lapsed subscription is significant. It is not surprising to note that, faced with the serials acquisitions dilemma, the library began to reallocate funding away from books and toward serials. Table 3 presents an analysis of data provided by the *Bowker Annual* from 1975 to 1985 that clearly illustrates the increasing percentage of library budgets used to ac-

TABLE 3

ACADEMIC LIBRARY ACQUISITION EXPENDITURES:
Percent of Total Categorized Expenditures
for Books and Periodicals
1975/76 through 1983/84

	% of Total Categorized Expenditures[1]		% Change From Previous Year	
	Books	Periodicals	Books	Periodicals
1975/76	47.8	28.2	-	-
1976/77	46.5	30.1	- 2.7	+ 6.7
1078/79	43.5	34.6	- 6.5	+ 15.0
1981/82	41.8	37.0	- 3.9	+ 6.9
1982/83	51.7*	37.7	+ 23.7*	+ 1.9
1983/84	49.0	39.0	- 5.2	+ 3.5

[1]Source: *The Bowker Annual of Library and Book Trade Information*, 1977-84 editions. The percentages for 1983/84 obtained by telephone call to Julia Moore, editor of *The Bowker Annual*.

*In 1983 the R. R. Bowker Company refined its computer program for compilation of academic library acquisition expenditures. This refinement resulted in a reduction in the proportion of expenditures categorized as unspecified, and a corresponding increase in the percentages of other categories, particularly Books. Had the figures for 1982/83 been compiled on the same basis as in previous years, the trend of decreasing expenditures for books and corresponding increasing expenditures for periodicals in all likelihood would have continued without a break. Note that this trend reappears in the percentages for 1983/84.

quire serials. Note that the percentage of total expenditure allocated to monographs has also increased from 47.8 in 1975 to 49.0 in 1983/84. However, the perent change as compared to previous years' expenditure has decreased for monographs each year while the percent change for serials has been consistently positive. Nineteen seventy-eight/seventy-nine shows a particularly graphic change, as the monograph budget decreased by 6.5% while the serials budget increased by 15.0%.

The effect that the foreign exchange rate has played in the pricing of journals and library acquisitions cannot be ignored, especially when analyzing the years 1975-1985. Already faced with rising prices imposed by domestic publishers, libraries were hard hit by the high price of foreign journals brought on by a weak dollar. Figures 3 and 4 illustrate the dollar's decline and rise over the years 1975-1984 against five foreign currencies representing the highest journal producing foreign countries: The Netherlands, Germany, the U.K., France, and Switzerland. The dollar's strength, particularly in the last three years, is obvious. Figure 5 shows that foreign journals as measured in Faxon's database showed an increase in price of 86.8% in the years of the weak dollar (1977-1982) but a decrease of 3.8% as the dollar has strengthened (1982-1984).

However, some publishers, accustomed to the heavy inflow of weak dollars, have maintained artificially high dollar prices even today. The problem of the dual price, particularly among British publishers, has been well analyzed and documented in two recent articles by Hamaker and Astle,[2] and by Ruschin,[3] and is currently under discussion within the formal structure of the American Library Association.

The library experienced other changes as a result of this tight economic period, particularly in the area of technical services. Confronted by the need to maintain current levels of public services and materials acquisitions, the library looked to increased automation and to the technical services area for savings in staff and labor during 1975-1985. Technical services, in turn, has looked to the vendor for increased services and/or automation to offset these same losses.

The Subscription Agency: Caught between the library and the publisher during this period of economic stress, many agents went out of business. There has been in fact a dramatic reduction in the number of agencies serving libraries. This reduction was the subject of an editorial by Nancy Melin[4] and several letters and articles.[5] In retrospect, one can see that the failure of many small agents was directly attributable to economic stress.

The fact is that those agencies that have survived to 1985 are highly automated, and it is this automation that has allowed the economies of scale necessary to provide subscription services their profitability. Automation has also enabled the subscription agent to respond to the library's need for more management information and online systems, making up for the losses in staff and labor noted above. In fact, the entire rela-

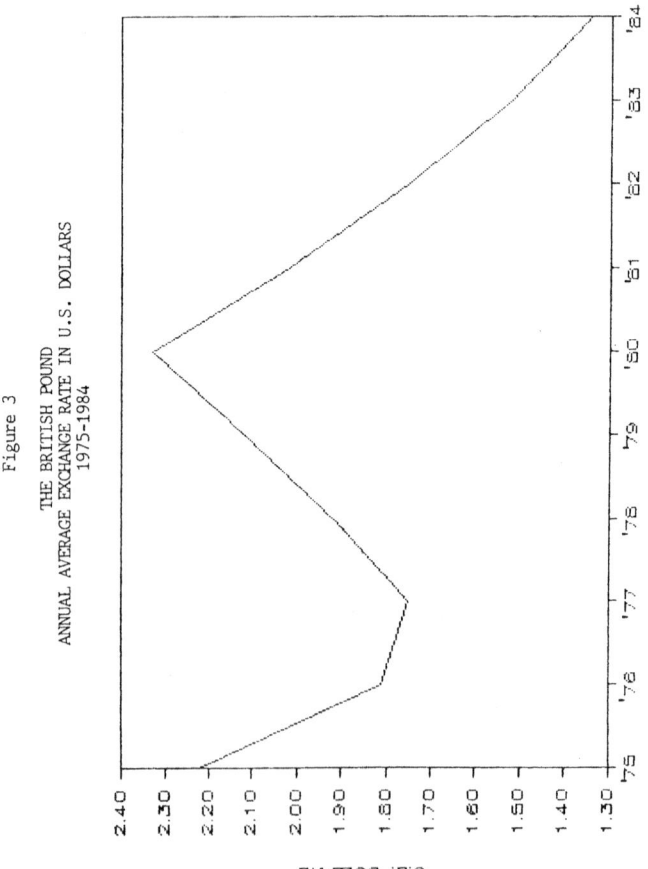

Figure 3
THE BRITISH POUND
ANNUAL AVERAGE EXCHANGE RATE IN U.S. DOLLARS
1975-1984

Source: Statistical Abstract of the United States, 100th edition, 1979 and 104th edition, 1984. Average exchange rates for 1983 and 1984 obtained by telephone call to the Federal Reserve Bank of Boston.

Figure 4

REPRESENTATIVE EUROPEAN CURRENCIES
ANNUAL AVERAGE EXCHANGE RATES IN U.S. DOLLARS
1975-1984

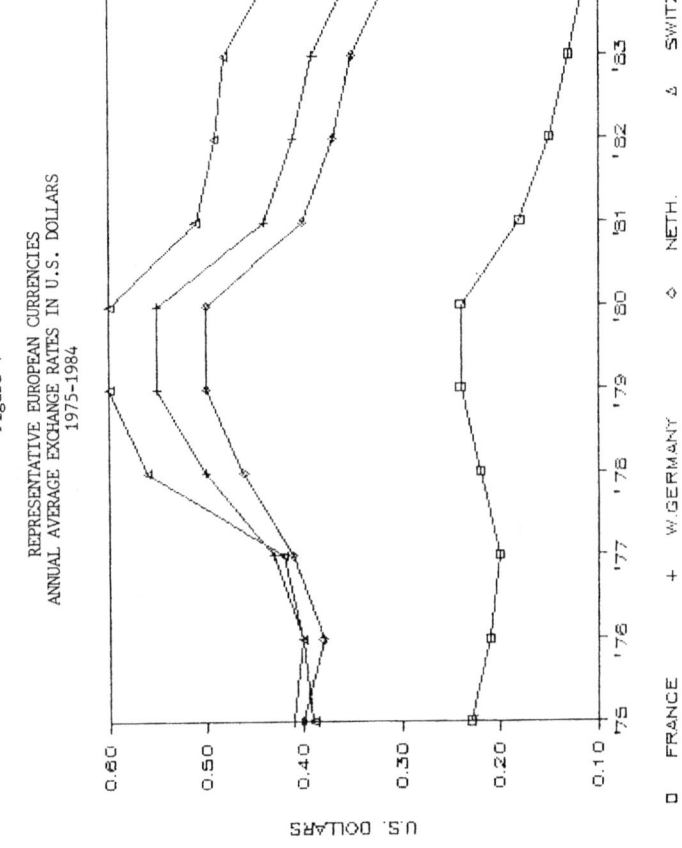

□ FRANCE + W. GERMANY ◇ NETH. △ SWITZ.

Source: Statistical Abstract of the United States, 100th edition, 1979 and 104th edition, 1984. Average exchange rates for 1983 and 1984 obtained by telephone call to the Federal Reserve Bank of Boston.

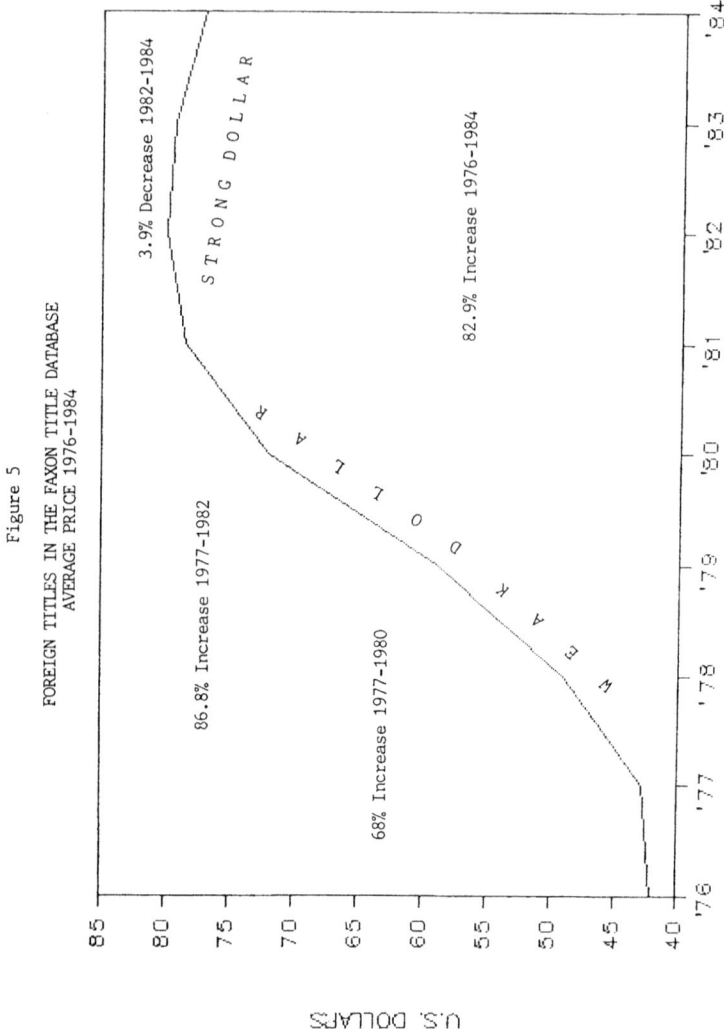

Figure 5
FOREIGN TITLES IN THE FAXON TITLE DATABASE
AVERAGE PRICE 1976-1984

tionship between library and agent has altered significantly in the years 1975-1985.

THE EVOLUTION OF THE SUBSCRIPTION AGENCY

In order to provide the basic serial services of ordering, claiming and renewing in a cost-effective manner, forward-thinking agencies like Faxon had already invested considerable effort and funds in automation by 1975. It is automation and the databases created in the process that have revolutionized the services agencies now provide to libraries and those provided publishers.

Chart 1 illustrates the progression of Faxon's services, which were based on the online data routinely compiled for subscription processing. Interestingly, 1975 marks the publication of the first periodical prices update article, which analyzed inflation in journal prices in various subject categories. This analysis has continued on an annual basis since 1977, and presently appears each year in *The Serials Librarian.*

Beginning in 1976, computer generated serials management reports appeared, offering to libraries the convenience of a vendor-produced record of payment information, price increases and additional serials information concerning the specific list of titles held by the library. These lists continue to be heavily used today; indeed, most libraries consider the availability of such lists as a fundamental requirement for the selection of any subscription agency. Clasquin offered a persuasive argument for the utilization of agency capabilities of this nature in his 1980 article entitled "The Subscription Agency: A Vested Maturity."[6]

Until 1980, the additional services provided by the subscription agency to the library were largely informational and based on the agent's own files. Although punched cards and magnetic tapes of invoicing information were available, these services were used by only a small percentage of libraries. Nineteen-eighty witnessed a significant redirection of agency efforts as online remote access serials systems begin to appear.

These systems, such as Faxon's Linx, connect the library to the agency's mainframe computer through telephone lines, using either dedicated or dial-up access. The library's specific issue receipt is recorded in the vendor's database, and this allows immediate claiming and computerized tracking of missed issues. Linx readily addressed the library's need to shift labor away from technical services to the vendor; at the same time, it improved serials control, thanks to automation.

DataLinx, access to Faxon's files of bibliographic, financial and publisher data, became available in 1981; in order to facilitate the online transmission of orders, claims and queries, an online message switching service was added as well. This electronic mail component has proven to

CHART 1

**DEVELOPMENTS IN THE AUTOMATION OF SERIALS MANAGEMENT
AT THE FAXON COMPANY 1975-1985**

AUTOMATED SERVICES		DATA PROCESSING HARDWARE & CAPACITIES
First Faxon Periodical Prices Update published (Library Journal, Oct. 1, 1974)	1975	IBM 370/158 2.54 Gigabytes storage capacity 1.0 Million Instructions per Second (MIPS)
Development of a variety of computer-generated serial management reports using bibliographic and financial data from Faxon's Title File and client specific information from our client History File (1976-78)	1976	IBM 3350 DASD 2.6 Gigabytes 60,000 transactions processed 8AM-4PM
	1977	
Implementation of a prototype online serials check-in system for use in Faxon's In-House Check-In Department	1978	
First Faxon computer-generated union list produced for the Special Libraries Association, Boston Chapter	1979	IBM 3032 5 Gigabytes 2.5 MIPS
Development of LINX, an online remote access serials management system, begins	1980	
Implementation of SC-10, the online serials check-in and claiming module of LINX Implementation of DataLinx, offering online access to various Faxon databases and electronic mail Non-Faxon Service, allowing clients to create a consolidated listing of titles ordered through other sources as well as Faxon, becomes available	1981 1982	 IBM 3081D 10 MIPS
PubLinx, an online remote access system for communication with publishers begins pilot phase Automated transfer of orders to publishers on magnetic tape is initiated INFOSERV, an online remote access database of new, revised and forthcoming titles, becomes available PubLinx establishes online transatlantic link with Pergamon Press, England Implementation of UNION LIST, an online union listing module of LINX *Faxon Librarians' Guide* becomes available online through INFOSERV Development begins on MICROLINX, an IBM Personal Computer-based serials control system, with online connections to the LINX Network	1983 1984 1985	IBM 3380 DASD 12.6 Gigabytes IBM 3081K 20.16 Gigabytes 15 MIPS IBM 3081Q (Oct. '85) 37.5 Gigabytes (June '85) 28 MIPS (Oct. '85) 180,000 transactions processed 8AM-4PM 350,000 transactions processed 2AM-10PM

be the cornerstone of the service because it connects the library not only to Faxon but also to other libraries.

In 1983, Faxon began to connect the "other side": the publisher. Through PubLinx, the publisher is able to view his own title information as it is maintained on the Faxon database, ensuring that the bibliographic and pricing information is as current as possible. Online communication via electronic mail makes short work of obtaining information that previously might have been delayed in the mail or misinterpreted over the phone. Claims are transmitted online to the PubLinx publisher who inputs claim responses directly into the Faxon system for reporting to the library. Those libraries that are online can then access such responses immediately, while others receive the information in computer-produced reports.[7]

Both Linx and PubLinx are examples of the use of automation by the agent to improve the quality and speed of basic subscription services. Another means for improving these services is the use of magnetic tapes for order processing. Faxon now provides orders on tape to more than 47 publishers throughout the world, enabling more accurate and speedier entry of orders, and, thus, better service to libraries. In the coming years, increased use of microcomputers by publishers, vendors, and libraries will alter our ways of dealing with one another in the areas of data-sharing and communications, and this will lead inevitably to even further improvements.

The relationship of the subscription agency to the library has expanded beyond online connections in the last ten years. In particular, the agent has assumed something of a consultative role, changing the traditional buyer/seller relationship to one of partnership. As noted in an earlier article:

> The vendor will assume a role as member on the library's technical services team and will provide vital operational support, which will enable the library to better serve the end user with reduced library staff.[8]

An even more fundamental shift is the growing role for the agent as library advocate in cases such as that of the dual pricing of British titles noted earlier in this article. What is the agent's responsibility in this case? Consider that the agent has a vantage point that the library lacks. The agent sees the full range of publisher pricing and, by using the automated support that is readily available, can in fact perform analyses that the library would be hard pressed to duplicate.

During the past ten years, the subscription agent has continued to perform in the role of middleman, showing no preference for one side above the other but enhancing services provided to both sides by taking full advantage of automation and serials databases maintained for subscription servicing. It is not clear whether this position will alter in upcoming years. What is clear is that the role of the subscription agency will evolve, as will that of the library and the publisher, as electronic full text emerges from fiction to fact.

NOTES

1. The total number of titles added is even larger if we include titles that have been added for "local use" only; that is to say, to support library local control functions such as check-in or union list (as shown in the final bar in Figure 1).

2. Hamaker, Charles and Deanna Astle, "Recent Pricing Patterns in British Journal Publishing," *Library Acquisitions Practice and Theory,* 8(1984): 007-014.

3. Ruschin, Siegfried, "Why are Foreign Subscription Rates Higher for American Libraries Than They Are for Subscriptions Elsewhere?," *The Serials Librarian,* 9, no. 3 (Spring 1985): 7-17.

On the topic of agency size and existence, see:

4. Melin, Nancy, "New Subscription Agency Giants: Lower or Higher Costs?," *Serials Review* (Summer 1982):7.

5. Rowe, Richard R. Letter to Editor, *Serials Review* (Fall 1982): 3-4.

5. Thyden, Wayne, "Subscription Agency Size: Threat or Benefit?," *The Serials Librarian,* 7, no. 3 (Spring 1983): 29-34.

5. Gellatly, Peter, "The Agency Question," an editorial appearing *The Serials Librarian,* 7, No. 1 (Fall 1982):5-7.

6. Clasquin, F.F., "The Subscription Agency: A Vested Maturity," *The Serials Librarian,* 4, no. 3 (Spring 1980):301-305.

7. Current PubLinx publishers include: American Mathematical Society, Cambridge University Press, Elsevier Science Publishers (Netherlands) Elsevier Science Publishing Company (NY), Alan R. Liss, MIT Press, Pergamon Press.

8. Lenzini, Rebecca T., "Vendor Services in the Information Age," *Technical Services Quarterly,* 1, no. 1/2 (Fall/Winter 1983):253.

Serials at the British Library Lending Division

Stella Pilling
David Wood

ABSTRACT. The British Library Lending Division has one of the largest collections of serials in the world. This paper outlines the history of serials at Boston Spa and describes various aspects of policy and procedures relating to serials, including selection, acquisition, record creation, automation, usage and binding. It concludes by considering the future role of the Lending Division in the light of continuing developments in electronic publishing and telecommunications.

A small village in West Yorkshire, 200 miles north of London, is an unlikely setting for one of the world's largest collections of serials, but at Boston Spa, not far from the town of Wetherby, is to be found the British Library Lending Division.

Serials have been important at Boston Spa ever since 1962, when the National Lending Library for Science and Technology (NLLST), the predecessor of the Lending Division, was established as a central collection for the supply of scientific and technical literature to UK libraries and industrial organizations. Its collection was founded on back runs of journals inherited principally from the Science Museum Library, but also from many other libraries too short of space to house them. With Dr D J Urquhart as its leader, the NLLST was developed as a major collection of scientific and technical literature dedicated to providing interlibrary loan and photocopy services.[1,2]

In 1973, as a result of recommendations made by the National Libraries Committee and the subsequent British Library Act, the British Library was formed. The Lending Division was created by merging the NLLST with the National Central Library—an organization formerly based in London and concerned largely with the humanities and social sciences. The serials collection at Boston Spa, by this time, had been expanded to cover the social sciences and the humanities as well as science and technology.[3]

Stella Pilling is Head of Serials Acquisitions and David Wood is Head of Collections at the British Library Lending Division, Boston Spa, Wetherby, West Yorkshire LS23 7BQ, United Kingdom.

The Lending Division is one of the three main Divisions of the British Library. The other two, namely the Reference Division and the Bibliographic Services Division, are both in London.

The British Library Lending Division is planned on the principle that the vast majority of interlibrary loan requests should be met from a central lending collection. The whole system is therefore organized specifically to provide a fast national and international loan/photocopy service. The Lending Division's statutory function is to support the library system of the United Kingdom by providing local libraries with items they do not hold, and to fulfill this objective, it acquires the material needed, or likely to be needed, to satisfy the requests received.

As is to be expected, the size of the budget for serials acquisition reflects the scale of the current serials collection. The Lending Division's acquisitions budget for 1984/85 was £ 3,293,000, of which £ 2,151,600 was for serials, £ 833,100 for monographs, and the remaining £ 308,300 for special categories of material such as music, conferences, reports, etc. It is clear from these figures that serials are an extremely important element in the Lending Division's expenditure, representing 65% of its acquisitions budget.

The scale of operations at Boston Spa sometimes comes as a surprise to visitors. The following statistics may provide some insight into and a general background to the serials operations at the Lending Division.

In 1983/84 the Lending Division received 2,772,000 requests, 576,000 of which came from abroad. Of these, 72% were for serials. Most of the serial requests sent to the Division are for serials in the English language (88%) with only 12% being for serials in foreign languages. Almost 80% of all requests received, (for both serials and monographs) are for items in science and technology. Of the 1,995,840 serial requests received in 1983/84, 89% were satisfied from stock, a fact that reflects the strength of the serials collection. The comprehensive nature of the collection, which includes esoteric as well as mainstream serial titles inevitably leads to a concentration of demand on a relatively small number of titles. Indeed, 90% of the demand for serials falls on fewer than 8,000 titles. Approximately 60% of all items are supplied as photocopies for retention by the end-user.

The users of the services provided by the Lending Division fall into four main categories. Special libraries, comprising industrial, commercial and government libraries, account for 37% of demand; academic libraries, i.e., university, polytechnic and college libraries, account for 30%; public libraries for 9%; and overseas organizations for 24%.

The size of the Lending Division's collection, and the demand made upon it bring their own problems, making it a unique institution among libraries. The number of staff employed is at present 728 (full-time equivalent) and the gross expenditure for 1983/84 was £ 12,247,000.

ACQUISITION POLICY

Since the Lending Division's aim is to meet most of the demand made on it from its stock, and since the major part of this demand is for serials, every endeavour is made to acquire and maintain as comprehensive a collection of "worthwhile" serials as possible, irrespective of subject, language or country of origin. The general acquisition policy is based on a number of criteria, including academic level, demand, availability and speed of supply from elsewhere, and country of publication.[4]

The term "worthwhile" in relation to serials, although difficult to define precisely, implies material of research level, and is broadly synonymous with the type of item required for higher educational, research or industrial purposes. In addition, a certain number of more popular, recreational serials are taken because of demand.

The number of currently received serials at the Lending Division is 55,000. They come from all parts of the world, and Figures 1 and 2 give some indication of the breakdown by country of origin. In total, the number of serial titles held, both current and non-current, is approximately 178,000, and the number of individual issues or parts recorded annually approaches 380,000. Although the serials collection is not classified by subject in any way, it has been estimated that of the 55,000 current titles, over 40,000 are in science and technology subjects.

DEFINITION OF A SERIAL

The Lending Division has its own definition of a serial, one which is, in fact, very similar to ISO 3297:

> A publication which is issued in successive parts, mainly at regular intervals, with a view to indefinite continuation.

Serial material at the Lending Division is usually identified by a number or date, and includes annuals, report series, yearbooks, memoirs, transactions and proceedings of societies, and monographs-in-series, as well as straightforward journals. Serials that the Lending does *not* take include annual reports and statements of account, newsletters of trade associations, local societies or pressure groups, school or church magazines, statistical compilations other than major national and international annual compilations, and newspapers. Bibliographic details and examples of serial titles not selected for addition to current stock, perhaps because they are on the borderline of selection criteria, are kept on file for future reference, in case of subsequent evidence of demand.

Normal practice is for the Lending Division to acquire only one copy

FIGURE 1

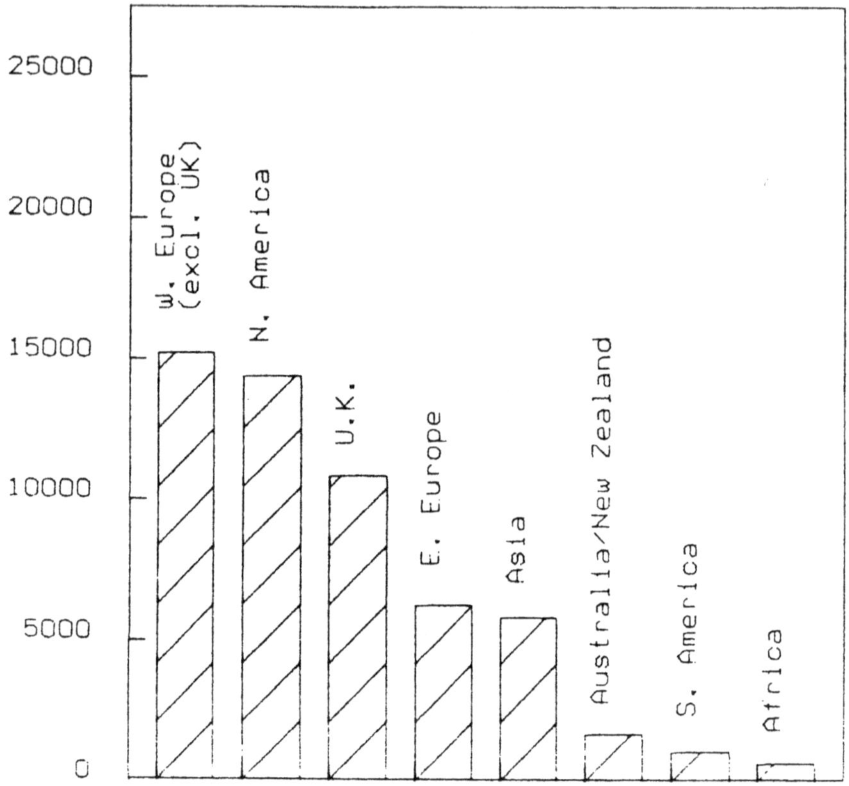

Currently received serials by broad geographical area.

of each serial title, but for those c1000 titles which are most heavily used, 2 or even 3 copies are taken. Use studies carried out from time to time enable staff to review the situation and to adjust the number of subscriptions for an individual title in the light of changing demand.

RESOURCE-SHARING AND RATIONALIZATION

Partly due to the need to economise, the last few years have seen slow but steady progress towards a more cooperative approach to collection development within the British Library. A reduction in the amount of overlap between the Reference and Lending Divisions has been achieved on a number of fronts without significantly affecting the services offered

FIGURE 2

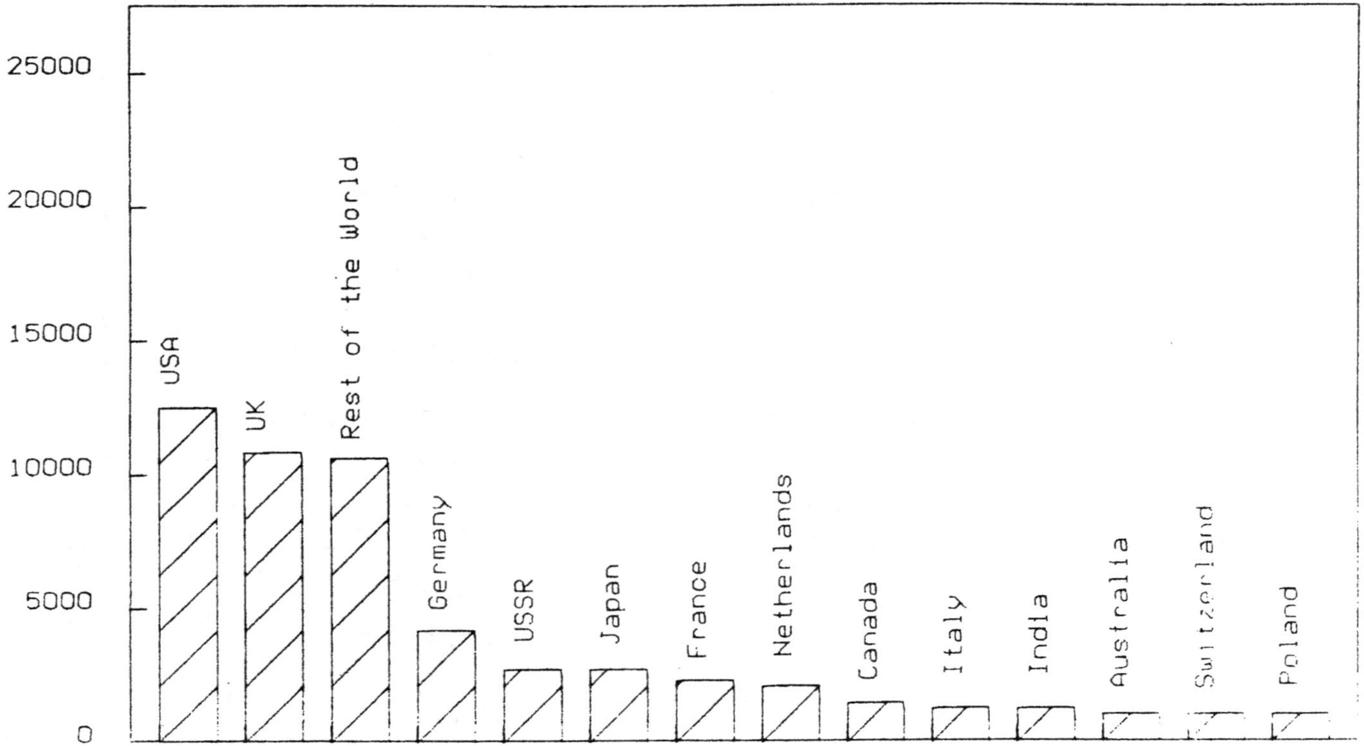

Currently received serials by country of origin.

by either. Further rationalization seems likely as the Reference Division embarks on a policy of making more of its non-British material available for loan through the Lending Division's services. Serial holdings in particular are strong candidates for rationalization since they are costly to acquire, many titles are used very little, and many requests can be dealt with by providing copies. As a result considerable progress has been made towards rationalizing the serial holdings of the Lending Division and the Science Reference Library. Cancellations of subscriptions are taking place at both locations and there is a regular exchange of information at the order stage.

SELECTION

New serial titles for addition to stock are selected from a wide variety of information sources such as failed requests (i.e., requests for serial titles not currently held at the Lending Division); publishers' announcements; catalogues; solicited and unsolicited sample copies; periodical directories; bibliographies and update information from indexing and abstracting services; and details provided by serial subscription agents.

As aids to selection, extensive use is made of a wide range of bibliographical tools, including online databases. Between 3-4,000 new serial titles are selected and put on order each year.

ACQUISITION

Since the Lending Division is not a copyright deposit library, all its material has to be purchased, or otherwise acquired, from its own resources. Whenever possible, the Lending Division prefers to buy its serials through commercial supply channels. Over 60% of its serials are bought through serial subscription agents, and at present 13 different agents around the world are used. Each agent it responsible for the provision of serials from one or more countries. Because of the scale of the business it can place with serial agents, the Lending Division is able to negotiate favourable terms for the provision and servicing of its serials, and advantage is taken, when appropriate, of prepayment discounts and one-line invoice arrangements.

Some publishers, however, will not supply libraries with their publications through an agent, and in these instances the Lending Division orders the items directly from the publisher concerned. More than 3,500 serial titles are obtained in this way.

For many countries, such as the Soviet Union, and others in Eastern Europe, exchange is a major means of obtaining Western journals because of the lack of hard currency. In consequence their own output is frequently not available to the book trade and can only be acquired on exchange. As a result, 12% of the Lending Division's current serials are the subject of exchange arrangements, and the Library has over 1200 different exchange partners around the world that supply almost 7,000 titles.[5] In the case of titles from the Eastern bloc, 53% are obtained on exchange, and for South America and Asia also the Lending Division relies heavily on this method of acquisition. (See Figure 3.) The Lending Division regards exchange arrangements as necessary—because it is the only way to

FIGURE 3

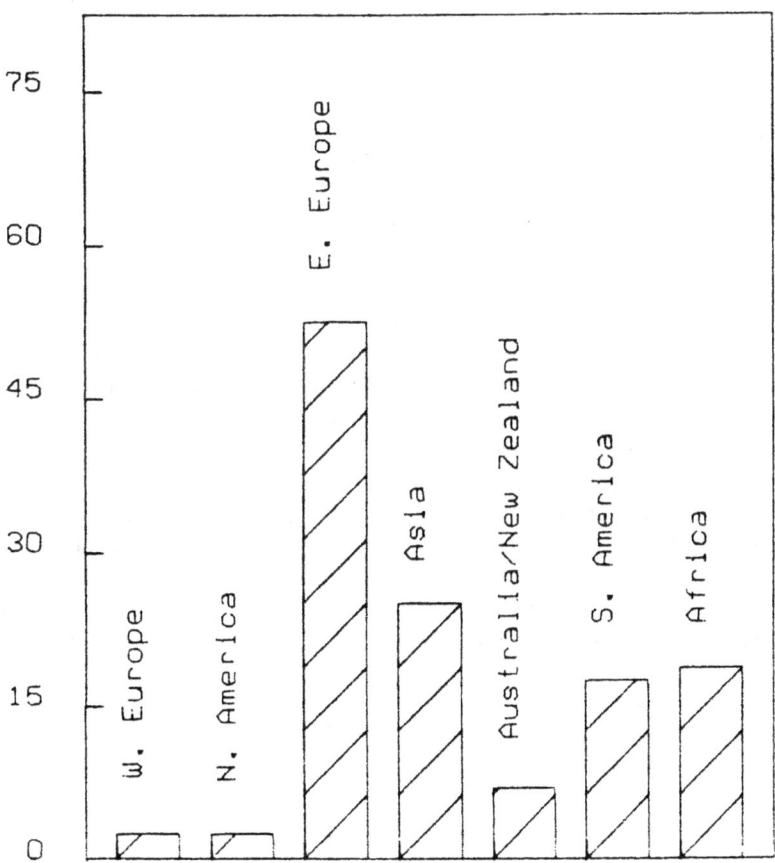

Percentage of current serials obtained on exchange by broad geographical area.

build up a really comprehensive collection of the world's serial literature—but undesirable, since the servicing of such arrangements entails a large amount of correspondence and a significant need for linguistic expertise. Material obtained on exchange tends to receive very little use—of the 50 most-used foreign language serial titles at the Lending Division, none is obtained on exchange.

British Library Lending Division publications are offered to the exchange clients in the first instance, but should these not be acceptable, suitable British serial publications are purchased through a subscription agent for direct transmission abroad. Many problems can arise in this area, and there is a need to revise arrangements at regular intervals to ensure a balance between what is received and what is sent.

DESELECTION

Over recent years, the declining value in real terms of the Lending Division's acquisitions budget has resulted in steps being taken to reduce expenditure on serials in line with the reduced spending power. More rigorous selection criteria were formulated, and in the summer of 1984 a substantial stock review was initiated with a view to taking rational cancellation decisions. Those titles that earlier sample surveys had indicated were never used, were checked at the shelf and reassessed according to current selection criteria. Four thousand titles were identified for cancellation, with an estimated saving of £ 110,000 in a full financial year. No detrimental effect on the quality of services provided is envisaged, but a system for reinstatement of cancelled titles exists, should subsequent demand necessitate such a step.

The Lending Division is very aware of its responsibilities in a national context, knowing that the selection and deselection policies of other libraries are based on the availability of material from the Division. In the last two years, for instance, British universities have notified the Division of more than 8,000 different serial title cancellations. Those titles (fortunately few) not already held have been placed on order. Confidence in the ability of the Division to provide a comprehensive back-up service is all important if local libraries are to pursue acquisition policies based on the availability of the national ILL service. Care must be taken not to destroy this confidence.

RECORDS

The master record of all serial titles held at the Lending Division is the "Main List" of serial titles, access to which is now available online within the Division itself. This master record consists of the following elements: shelfmark; title; comments including "formerly" or "continued as" information, cross-references, "ceased publication" details, etc; Lending Division's holdings; status, i.e., whether current, non-current, on-order, etc; details of the storage area where held; ISSN, if available; and the external holdings of libraries such as the Science Reference Library or Cambridge University Library. This "Main List" contains details of all serial titles on the shelves, current and dead, as well as numerous cross-references to previous, subsequent or alternative titles. Together with a wide range of bibliographic tools such as abstracts, indexes and periodical lists, it is used for checking requests received and for the identification of serial titles. All document supply centres can expect to receive some requests with inadequate or inaccurate bibliographic details, and has to cope with the problems posed by abbreviated serial titles.

To help staff in this area, the Keyword Index to Serial Titles (KIST) was developed in 1979 as a keyword approach to the Lending Division's serial collection. The index consists of an alphabetical list of all significant words in the titles of serials, both current and dead, held at the Lending Division, together with those of the Science Reference Library and the Science Museum Library. Under each keyword are listed all titles containing that word. KIST is issued quarterly on over 150 48x microfiche, and the basic records within the master file are continually being amended to reflect changes in titles or holdings. As a tool it has been used internally at the Lending Division for six years, and it has proved invaluable to the staff in the storage areas in their attempts to locate serials for which the precise title is not known.

There is also an annual publication entitled *Current Serials Received*, which lists all the serials currently received by the Lending Division. The 1984 edition contained over 56,000 current titles, covering all subject fields.

AUTOMATION

The Lending Division's serials system has been automated to some extent for more than 20 years.[6] At the beginning of the 1960s, when the National Lending Library for Science and Technology was founded, details of the 10,000 current periodical titles which had been inherited from the Science Museum Library were entered onto a punched card system, and the beginnings of the current shelfmark system were developed. These punched cards were used to generate lists of one sort and another, shelf tags, serial accession recording sheets and other printed records used in the administration of the serials collection. Over the years, much has changed. The in-house online serials system at the Lending Division is now supported by a Systime 8780 computer (equivalent to a VAX 780) and there are over 60 terminals linked to it around the Library.

The serials acquisitions functions mainly concerned with purchase control, invoicing details and the recording of on-order and chasing data, were automated in 1979. The most recent internal development is an online keyword checking system based on KIST and linked to the Main List of all serial titles, that is searchable under every significant word used in the title. The Lending Division has come a long way from the punched card system of the 1960s. Plans for the future include the automation of the serials check-in function, which is still performed manually, and to this end a number of commercially available serials packages are currently under consideration.

GIFT AND EXCHANGE SERVICE— THE NATIONAL REPOSITORY ROLE

One of the responsibilities of the Lending Division closely related to its main role of interlending is that of an exchange centre and national repository for material no longer required by other libraries.[7] The Gift and Exchange Service (GES) at the Lending Division arose from the amalgamation in 1973 of the activities of the British National Book Centre, which had been organized at the National Central Library in London, and the Donations Section of the NLLST, which dealt mainly with periodicals. Today, the GES section co-ordinates the donation of library material to the Lending Division, and the subsequent distribution to other libraries of items it does not itself require. Approximately 15,000 serial titles, including single issues, are offered to the Lending Division each year. Periodicals are accepted only as offers on cards. The cards are then checked selectively against Lending Division's stock to identify gaps in holdings and items required for stock are requested from the offering library.

The remaining titles offered, supplemented by duplicate items weeded from Lending Division's own stock once their high-use period has passed, are used to produce GES periodical lists, which are available to UK libraries on a subscription basis. On average, each monthly periodical list contains over 1,000 serial titles. In 1983/84 1.85 miles of donated material, both books and serials, were handled by the GES Section, and of this, 0.95 miles were added to stock. More donated books are absorbed into Lending Division's stock than periodicals, partly because the impact of photocopying reduces the need for duplicates, and partly because, as the years go by, the strength of the serials collection continues to grow, with a subsequent reduction in the number of gaps to be filled.

SERIAL USE SURVEYS

Surveys of serial usage have been carried out on three occasions at the Lending Division in recent years, with the purpose of identifying those titles in the collection with high, medium or low use.[8,9,10] These surveys provide valuable management information for the Lending Division itself, by giving an indication of the need for more or fewer copies of particular titles. Because of the nature and use of the Lending Division's collections, information of a more general nature can be derived from the surveys concerning the concentration of demand among serial titles, the size and possible content of core collections capable of satisfying a high proportion of the demand, and whether there are appreciable changes in the ranking of serials that might affect the value of core lists.

Rank lists of titles in order of demand have been produced as a result of these usage surveys in 1975, 1980 and 1983. The most significant fact emerging is that there is a very high concentration of demand on a relatively small number of titles. In 1975, 1,350 titles satisfied 50% of the demand on the Division during the survey period and 5,250 titles satisfied 80% of the demand. In 1980, 2,000 titles satisfied 45% of the demand, 7,500 titles 80% of demand and 18,975 titles (i.e., 14% of all titles held in 1980) satisfied 100% of demand. By 1983, 2,158 titles accounted for 50% of demand, 7,581 for 80% of demand, and 18,465 titles (i.e., 11% of all titles held) for 100% of demand. All three surveys show a similar concentration of demand on a relatively stable number of titles. Other data collected by these surveys include broad subject content, and date of material requested. Results are being followed up by continuous monitoring of some of the more heavily used titles and by comparisons with similar data from other countries.

Other surveys are conducted regularly within the Lending Division to monitor internal procedures and demand from users. As a by-product these surveys often produce data relating to serials, e.g., speed of service, types of user, broad subject breakdown and age of material, etc.

PRESERVATION

Use surveys provide valuable information for the Preservation Section at the Lending Division, since it is Library policy to spend a large proportion of its preservation budget on the stock receiving most use. Items that are seldom used receive a negligible proportion of binding expenditure. The main binding effort is applied in two directions (1) the protection by binding, either on receipt, or at an early stage, of those items likely to be most heavily used, and (2) the repair, at a later stage of those items showing signs of wear.[11]

Of the £ 500,000 spent on binding and preservation at the Lending Division in 1984/85, approximately two-thirds was spent on serials. The annual binding expenditure figure includes the cost of an on-site Binding Repair Unit, which has been in existence since 1979, and currently employs six people.

Three types of binding are used: plastic-fronted part-binding, cloth and buckram binding. Part-binding is used for approximately 6,000 of the most heavily-used serial titles, and was designed as a result of research carried out in 1961 by the Printing Packaging and Allied Trades Research Association (PATRA). Serial issues are intercepted at the check-in stage and sent in weekly batches for binding. Items return the following week, and the issues are therefore away from the shelves for not more than two weeks. The spines of the part-bound issues are colour-coded by year, making the task of finding a particular issue in a long run much easier. Issues that are too large or heavy for part-binding are bound in cloth using the same colour-code system. The part binding rather than volume binding policy stems from the nature of the Division's activities. Requests from remote users are for single issues and have to be satisfied in many cases by sending the item through the post. Single issue transactions reduce costs and minimize waiting lists.

STORAGE

Forty-nine of the 113 miles of shelving at the Lending Division are occupied by serials. Material dated 1975 onwards is housed in a "current" store (25.7 miles) and the rest in a "non-current" store (41.8 miles). Both are 72% full, i.e., 13% short of being operationally full.

Plans for expanding the storage space are in abeyance owing to funding shortages, and weeding plans are therefore in hand using as a guide the use data derived from the serial usage surveys mentioned above.

Material is stored at the Lending Division in such a way as to make retrieval quick and simple. As a general rule no reference to a catalogue is needed before the shelves are approached. Serial publications are arranged alphabetically in three sequences.

1. Serials dated up to the end of 1974

    all languages other than Cyrillic
2. Serials dated 1975 onwards
3. Serial titles in the Cyrillic alphabet together with their cover-to-cover translations into English.

The date split reflects the fact that serial use diminishes rapidly with the age of the material.

The Division has no traditional serials catalogue and the on-line system does not, on the whole, include details of holdings. In fact the shelves themselves represent the only full record of what is held. Through the use of slip boxes the shelves also provide cross-references to earlier or later versions of a particular title.

THE FUTURE

Although the Lending Division does not foresee any dramatic short term changes in the range of serial material it collects or the services it provides, it recognizes the need to be aware of developments that are likely to have an impact on its activities. It must be prepared to adopt new technologies in order to cope with new forms of publication and to provide the more efficient and faster services demanded by its national and international clientele.

The Division has always sought to respond to requests as quickly as possible, and a variety of automated systems have been introduced that allow users to transmit their requests rapidly to Boston Spa. However, there is a small proportion of users—particularly in the biomedical and pharmaceutical field—who want an ever faster service. As a result, the Urgent Action Service was established, whereby the requesting library telephones the Lending Division with its request rather than using standard requesting methods. The shelves are checked immediately for the item and the library is 'phoned back within three hours. If the item is available, it is either despatched at once using first-class post, or, for an additional charge, it is transmitted by telefacsimile. By this means, requests (particularly requests for serial articles) can be satisfied within a few hours.

The Lending Division has been involved with the ADONIS project since its conception. This project was set up by a consortium of scientific, technical and medical publishers, which proposed the creation of a central agency to capture document images of published journals on to optical discs. These discs would be made available to selected libraries, such as the Lending Division, which would use them in response to requests to produce copies of articles by fast, high-quality laser printer.[12] Although the project has been shelved for the moment, partly because of the high cost of creating the electronic store, it is quite likely that a similar project could be developed in the future, when the technology is more advanced and the equipment less expensive.

The APOLLO project, with which the Lending Division has also been involved, was conceived by the European Commission (EC) and the European Space Agency (ESA) in 1981. Its purpose is to explore the technical feasibility of electronic delivery of documents using high speed digital satellite channels, and the Lending Division is looking at the system with a view to using it for high speed transmission of facsimile document images within Europe.

These developments illustrate the way in which the British Library's document supply service is planning ahead and preparing to adapt for an electronic future. In the meantime it continues to occupy an important central role both nationally and internationally in the library world. Many libraries are very dependent on its services, and collections and serials in their traditional form are at the centre of its activities.

REFERENCES

1. D J Urquhart, "Plain man's guide to the National Lending Library for Science and Technology," *Library Association Record* 64(9) (1962): pp. 319-322.
2. R M Bunn, "How it all began," *BLL Review* 2(3) (July 1974): pp. 75-78.
3. M B Line, "The British Library Lending Division," *Journal of Information Science* 2(3/4) (1980): pp. 173-182.
4. D N Wood, "Acquisition policy and practices at the British Library Lending Division," *Interlending Review* 7(4) (October 1979): pp. 111-118.
5. D N Wood, "Current exchange of serials at the BLLD," *Library Acquisitions: Practice and Theory* 3 (1979): pp. 107-113.
6. A J Harley, "Automated serials control at the British Library Lending Division," *Program* 15(4) (1981): pp. 200-208.
7. A Allardyce and M B Line, "The repository role of the British Library Lending Division," in J W Blackwood (ed.), *The future of library collections: proceedings of a seminar held by the Library Management Research Unit, University of Technology, Loughborough, 21-23 March, 1977.* (LMRU Report no. 7, June 1977: pp. 64-69).
8. C A Bower, "Patterns of use of the serial literature at the BLLD," *BLL Review* 4(2) (April 1976): pp. 31-36.
9. A Clarke, "The use of serials at the British Library Lending Division in 1980," *Interlending Review* 9(4) (1981): pp. 111-117.
10. K Merry and T Palmer, "Use of serials at the British Library Lending Division in 1983," *Interlending and Document Supply* 12(2) (April 1984): pp. 56-60.
11. P A Haigh, "Binding at Boston Spa," *Interlending Review* 7(4) (October 1979): pp. 139-140.
12. Line, Maurice, "On-demand and online publishing and the bookseller: life-line, death knell, or irrelevant?" *The Bookseller* (4149) (June 29, 1985): pp. 2629-2631.

A Decade of Serials Librarianship in Australia: An Overview

Jean A. Conochie

ABSTRACT. The events that have caused change in the work of serials librarians in Australia in the last ten years are: (1) the extensive use of computers in libraries, (2) the introduction of AACR2, (3) the establishment of the International Serials Data System, (4) the rise and fall of budgets with consequent effects on serial subscriptions and binding, (5) the increasing unpredictability of arrival of serials from overseas and (6) the establishment of the Australian Bibliographic Network. The effects of these events are discussed, and the prediction made that the advent of on-line total library management systems will be the challenge of the next decade.

In the past ten years the two events that stand out as having profoundly affected the work of the serials librarian have been the extensive use of computers in libraries and the appearance of AACR2. The work of a serials librarian can be seen to cover the whole gamut of library activities from selection, acquisition, cataloguing, accessioning, routing, binding, accessing, lending and, finally, discarding. Although Pong[1] has established that, in a survey of twenty-three academic libraries in Australia in 1981, only four had the serials cataloguer as part of the Serials Department, this vital function is basic to the work of a serials librarian. Ralli,[2] however, argues for serials cataloguing to be left with, or transferred to, the Cataloguing Department.

To identify the effects of computer usage in libraries in Australia one must, in fact, go back twenty years in the literature where, in 1967, a survey sponsored by the Australian Advisory Council on Bibliographical Services (AACOBS)[3] listed in its forty pages, seven projects that related to serials. An update of this in 1969[4] produced another four, while in 1976[5] seventeen such projects appear. Most of these relate either to

---

Jean A. Conochie, CSIRO, Central Information, Library and Editorial Section, 314 Albert Street, P.O. Box 89, East Melbourne, Victoria 3002 Australia. Ms. Conochie holds the position of Principal Librarian, Bibliographical Services in the Commonwealth Scientific and Industrial Research Organization (Australia). From 1960-1984 she was also Editor, *Scientific Serials in Australian Libraries.*

computer-produced lists of serials which, in some cases, constitute the only form of serials catalogue for the particular library, or to subscription lists for supply to subscription agents. More detailed information about some of these lists appears throughout the literature.[6-13]

The notable exception to these rather unsophisticated approaches was that undertaken in the library now known as the State Library of New South Wales, where a complete serials automation project was first outlined in the *Australian Library Journal* in May 1969.[14] In 1973, a very frank account of the development of this system and the problems encountered[15] was sufficient to plant a seed of caution in other large libraries that might have attempted such a project. It should be noted that this system is still operational, but, as was found to the library's cost, it does not actually effect a saving in staff time. The benefits are in the extra facilities that it makes available.

Only one other mention about this time of a complete systems undertaking appears in the literature[16] and, although a further article mentioning holdings statements[17] appeared later in the year, there is no evidence of any outcome from these studies. Although most of us are dissatisfied with our manual systems, we note the caution of Paul[18] that "The breakdown of manual procedures is not in itself sufficient reason for introducing automation."

Two small systems used in periodical circulation in special libraries appear in the literature,[19,20] and no doubt many more are in use throughout the country.

Another computer application that vastly affects the work of the serials librarian was the advent of abstracting journal tape services. As early as 1967 the Commonwealth Scientific and Industrial Research Organization (CSIRO) took part in an SDI trial based on the *Chemical Abstracts* tapes. SDI services using these and some other databases began in 1971,[21] with coverage gradually growing to seven databases run by CSIRO, plus a number run by the National Library of Australia, (NLA). However, the advent of MIDAS (Multi-mode International Data Acquisition Service),[22] by which the Australian Overseas Telecommunication Commission offered a direct telecommunication link to the United States in 1978 and, later, to Europe, at a very reasonable cost, removed the necessity of running the tapes in Australia. Consequently, the CSIRO SDI services caused in 1980.

The initial impact of the SDI services was the production of extensive lists of references that the inexperienced user felt compelled to see. When access had been by way of the hard copy abstracting journals it was possible to determine from the abstract whether the article was directly relevant. Obscure references were sought only if they were of profound interest. When confronted with the computer-produced lists, almost all of which lacked abstracts, the first reaction was that the references must all be obtained. This put an enormous strain on serials acquisition. However, with greater user sophistication and the displacement of SDI services by immediate on-line literature searches, this tendency has abated somewhat.

Since the cessation of its SDI services, CSIRO has concentrated on building up databases of Australia's own literature in a number of specialised fields. Unhappily, as a consequence of economic stringency, its production of *Australian Science Index,* described by Morrison and May,[23] ceased at the end of 1983.

Concerning the effects of AACR2, as a cataloguing survey carried out in 1972 showed,[24] Australia has always been heavily oriented towards the "American" in the Anglo-American tradition. This is partly because we have accepted cataloguing copy from the Library of Congress for many years. A cataloguing card service based on LC cards was established in 1969 by the NLA, but this did not include serials. Australia's use of copy for serials has been through manual checking of all the large union lists of the world, notably *New Serial Titles* and the *British Union Catalogue of Periodicals.* The smaller libraries used the two Australian national union lists of serials, *Serials in Australian Libraries—Social Sciences and Humanities* (SALSSAH) and *Scientific Serials in Australian Libraries* (SSAL), described by Morrison and May[23] as cataloguing aids. These lists, having been compiled over a long period of time, had had to adapt AACR1 to keep a format consistent with earlier entries. For this reason it is probable that many cataloguers who thought they were following the American version of AACR1 were, in fact, using the British version of Rule 6 because it was not possible to establish the content of a publication just from a title, as was frequently all the union lists were able to use as the basis of their cataloguing.

The advent of AACR2, however, put an entirely different complexion on the process because of the radical change to use of title entry in almost all cases. The computerised form of the two union lists, viz. *SALSSAH on COM,*[25,26] which began in September 1978 and the *SSAL Supplement,* which first appeared in September 1979,[27,28,29] had to anticipate the changes that AACR2 might bring about. SALSSAH remained with AACR1 until the official changeover in 1981, and the resultant *SALSSAH on COM* is a mixture of AACR1 and AACR2, with no title references for generic titles entered under corporate body according to AACR1, but the expected references under corporate body for those entered in AACR2 form. The form of entry for corporate bodies is AACR2. *SSAL Supplement* made the bold assumption that AACR2 would opt for title entry in all cases, and so produced the microfiche in two sequences: one of titles with added entries for alternative titles, and the other, of corporate bodies with title references, similar to the BUCOP arrangement. It also used the concept of ignoring articles, prepositions, and conjunctions in the filing.

This was done by computer control of a series of stop-words, which necessitated a code to indicate language in conjunction with the title. Occasional mis-coding did lead to some strange sequences, but these were minimal.

It had been proposed that, with *SALSSAH on COM* appearing in one format and *SSAL Supplement* in another, the library community would after a reasonable trial period be asked which format it preferred, and a conversion would be done to make the two lists compatible. However, as detailed later, events overtook us, and the survey was never carried out.

Within individual libraries the whole range of solutions to the problems caused by AACR2, as stated by Elrod,[30] Roberts[31] and Currie,[32] were adopted, depending on the situation in each particular catalogue.

One of the disadvantages to the library community brought about by the change to COM catalogues and computer-produced serials lists about 1977/78, was that some libraries ceased to contribute to the national union catalogues because of the insistence that entries be on cards. Those who have any experience of manually compiling union catalogues will be aware that, to accept any format other than cards, increases the workload enormously. Despite the fact that it was pointed out at a conference in 1980[33] that the average library was being asked to spend only one and a quarter hours per month of a clerical assistant's or typist's time to send the necessary entries, many libraries set their faces against this as being a retrograde step. Significantly, it was not the large libraries that refused but the smaller college and some special libraries. Some libraries expected that the national union lists should be able to accept tapes. At that stage of development, this was not possible because the formats used lacked compatibility. Although work on the Australian MARC specification for serials began in 1978, it did not appear until 1983.[34]

One of the significant events for serials cataloguers, in 1975, was the appearance of *Cataloguing Australia,* the journal of the Cataloguers' Section of the Library Association of Australia (LAA). As the references attached to this article attest, this provides a forum in which the problems of serials cataloguers can be aired. The Section is also now conducting workshops and seminars in the various States, at which common problems can be discussed and appropriate time given to serials.[26,29,31,35] The problems are, of course, the same as those of our American colleagues, as detailed by Carter[36] and Edgar.[37]

The setting up of the Australian Committee on Cataloguing with representatives from the NLA, and LAA, and AACOBS also reassures us that our voice will be heard, and our complaints, where justified, transmitted to the Association of Bibliographic Agencies of Australia, Britain, Canada and the United States (ABACUS). As Fullerton[38] explains, although Australia did have input to AACR1, we had no direct representation in the drawing up of AACR2.

In the exchange of machine-readable data at the international level, Australia has been an active contributor. With the establishment of the International Serials Data System, Australia was one of the first to set up a National Centre. This occurred in October 1973.[39]

As for the subject of collection building and, unfortunately, in some cases, collection destroying, that have taken place over the last ten years, there is much to say. We find that, up until 1974, the accession of bound volumes of periodicals in university libraries, the group for which we have the best statistics,[40] showed a steady increase up to 1974, but since then has been falling rather dramatically. The NLA also collects extensively in serials, and reported in its annual report for 1970/80 that its serial collection had more than doubled in the ten preceding years. The NLA and the CSIRO have led for many years cooperative arrangements, by which they advise one another when they are cancelling significant serials not held elsewhere. But in the 1980 report of AACOBS,[41] the Working Party on Information Resources, notes that in a limited survey of serials cancelled by a selected group of libraries, the total number of current serial subscriptions fell by 7.6% from the high point of over 220,000 in 1978. Again, in the 1981/82 report "the library community was dismayed at the massive serial cancellation program which the National Library was forced to undertake." In this, again, we mirror the fortunes of our American colleagues.

In the field of acquisition, Australia suffers a peculiar disadvantage in our remoteness from the major centres of serials production, and is one aspect in which "technology" has had a most detrimental effect upon us. The demise of sea travel as the norm and the advent of the container ship has reduced the art of predicting the probable arrival of serial pieces from the realm of the mere gambler to that of the crystal-ball gazer. The time of surface transport can vary from a few weeks to six months. Most libraries have taken measures to ensure that their most urgently required journals are delivered by such methods as that known variously as Accelerated Surface Post (ASP) or Surface Air Lifted (SAL). However, the expense is such that not all periodicals can be acquired in this way. Some libraries utilise the services of the subscription agents who undertake to collect the material and send it in bulk but, once again, this is a matter of economics. With straitened economic circumstances, the whole concept of acquiring, binding, and retaining forever all the material that an individual library might require, has undergone drastic reappraisal. As noted in the 1980 AACOBS report,[41] "commercial binders must find it difficult to manage in the stop-go environment. When one considers how small the number of binders is who undertake library binding throughout Australia, the difficulty caused by the unpredictability of business may be readily realised."

Attempts to rationalise collections and ensure that one copy of each relevant journal is kept in each state are coordinated by the various State Committees of AACOBS. The methods used to ensure that cancellations are widely promulgated vary from state to state, but the objective of cooperation is the same. In 1978 the Library Council of Victoria funded a pilot study for a Serials Rationalization Scheme, based on the concept that particular libraries would take responsibility for keeping back runs of particular titles, and other libraries not designated for that title could discard it after five years, making sure first of course that the designated library had all issues. This was a very small study, which was based on one hundred journals and which ran for a year. The conclusion reached was that the sample was, in fact, too small for the results to be extrapolated. It had been intended that, if this experiment were a success, it might spread to other states. However, there are numbers of consortia in states and regions that do have cooperative storage arrangements and, to a certain extent, cooperative acquisitions programs that are working.

In 1981 the Australian library community moved into a new era with the establishment of the Australian Bibliographic Network (ABN).[42] This is based on the software of the Washington Library Network (WLN), which is gradually being adapted for Australian conditions. ABN began with 6 participating libraries, and now has almost 90. As with all such projects, monographs were the first to be dealt with, and it is only now that a reasonable body of serial entries is beginning to appear.

At the first ABN Conference held in July 1983, a whole session was devoted to serials on ABN and the difficulties that those few who had attempted to use this arrangement encountered.[43] The problems are not insurmountable but, because of the workload that faces the systems staff in programming all the changes that have been requested, the problems of serials have not yet been given a high priority. This is because not many libraries are yet inputting serials. The network operates on a democratic basis in determining priorities.

It was announced at the Conference that the two national union lists, *SALSSAH on COM* and the *SSAL Supplement* would be incorporated into the ABN database.[44,45] The former ceased at the end of 1983, and the entries from it are gradually being entered into the database, as changes in holdings or the bibliographical record become necessary. The *SSAL Supplement* continued in its separate form for another year, to the end of 1984, because there was a backlog to be overcome. It is anticipated that the tape of these 10,000 records will be added to the ABN database before the next issue, in March 1985, of the combined *National Union Catalogue of Serials* (NUCOS). The integration of these lists and the production of NUCOS marks the culmination of years of planning to try to bring the two union lists together.

The failure of AACR2, as originally issued, to accommodate the need for uniqueness in serial titles will dog us for years to come. As Turner[46] has stated "It is interesting to note how closely the unique title resembles the uniform title, in structure, placement within the catalogue record, and in MARC tagging. But the two are diametrically opposed in purpose. The uniform title was developed to bring together various manifestations of a single work that would otherwise be dispersed by their individual titles; the unique title is intended to differentiate titles which would otherwise be the same." The problem in ABN is that the unique title, being treated as a uniform title, is entered under a main entry tag. This means that, in searching, one needs to be aware of whether the title has its generic words grammatically linked to the corporate author, in which case it must be searched under title, or not so linked, in which case it is searched under main entry uniform title. This puts us right back to pre-*SSAL Supplement* days.

One of the great problems with the database is the duplication of records, since tapes are accepted from the Library of Congress, USGPO, the *British National Bibliography* and *Canadiana,* as well as our own *Australian National Bibliography* and records input by individual participants. There have been a number of "retrospective loads" of participants' tapes, and this also has resulted in duplication. Dealing with this duplication represents of course a considerable workload burden for the ABN Office.

In common with WLN, ABN operates an authority control module which, at this stage in the participants' expertise is causing some problems.[47] There is to be another Conference in 1985, at which it is to be hoped that the matter of authority control will be addressed. As serials librarians are well aware, the control of corporate body names is a vital ingredient in the control of a serial collection.

In an effort to build up the pool of serials records and minimise duplication of work, the Network Committee of ABN set up a Serials Subcommittee to look at ways of ensuring that retrospective material would be entered in AACR2 format relatively quickly. This Subcommittee proposed that each participating library be asked to enter 5% of its current serial titles for each of the next two years. This has been accepted in principle, but has not yet been promulgated because neither the incentive nor the mechanism for doing the work has been developed. The Subcommittee has been replaced by a project planning team that is working on this concept. The prospect of a database of high quality serials records opens up an exciting prospect for serials librarians in the future.

The final development affecting serials librarians in Australia stems from the realisation that there are now total library management systems available as turnkey packages. The argument as to which department should catalogue serials now disappears, since the physical location of the operator will cease to be relevant. Numbers of libraries in Australia have purchased, or are about to purchase, such systems.[48] However, as always, serials control is the most difficult problem to deal with. The systems now in operation have not yet had time to prove themselves in the Australian environment. I leave it to my successor in ten years' time to report on the outcome of this advance.

REFERENCES

1. Alfred Pong: "The Serials Department," *Australian Academic & Research Libraries* 12(3), Sept. 1981, pp.191-198.
2. Tony Ralli: "Serials, Series and AACR2," *Cataloguing Australia* 7[i.e., 6](4), Oct./Dec. 1980, pp.23-30.
3. *Current Projects in Library Automation: an Australian Directory* (Canberra: AACOBS, 1967) 40 p.
4. *Computers and Libraries: an Australian Directory* (Canberra: AACOBS, 1969) 67 p.
5. Mary Ellen Jacob: "LASIE Survey of Australian Automated Library Systems" *Lasie* 6(5), Mar./Apr.1976, pp.2-42 *and* 7(4), Jan./Feb.1977, pp.9-12.
6. Dorothy Peake and Marea Terry: "Computer Printed Union List of Serials in Branch and Department Libraries in the University of Sydney Library," *The Australian Library Journal* 19(4), May 1970, pp.149-153.
7. "A Computerized Periodicals System for Small and Medium-Sized Special Libraries," *Lasie* 1(4), Nov./Dec.1970, pp.11-[27].
8. "University of New South Wales Serial List," *Lasie* 3(5), Mar./Apr.1973, p.27.
9. G. Stecher: "Development of Computer Based Systems at La Trobe University Library," *Australian Academic & Research Libraries* 5(4), Dec.1974, pp.158-162.
10. Charles M. Baxter: "The University of New England Catalogue System," *Lasie* 8(1), July/Aug.1977, pp.8-19.
11. James Emmett: "METCAT—Automated Library Cataloguing for North Brisbane College of Advanced Education," *Lasie* 8(2), Sept./Oct.1977, pp.37-[54].
12. G. Stecher: "Systems Development at La Trobe University: Going it Alone with Mini-computers," *Lasie* 8(5/6), Mar./June 1978, pp.29-43.
13. Wendy May: "Computer Applications in a Small Regional College Library," *Lasie* 9(4), Jan./Feb.1979, pp.22-33.
14. R. Rothwell: "The Serials Automation Project at the Public Library of New South Wales," *The Australian Library Journal* 18(4), May 1969, pp.136-145.
15. J.D. Fernon. *The Automated System for Serials in the Library of New South Wales* (Sydney: Library of New South Wales, 1973) 43 p.
16. Ray Walsh: "A Total Systems Approach to the Control of Serials," *Australian Academic & Research Libraries* 4(1), Mar.1973, pp.30-32.
17. Ray Walsh: "Computerised Serials Control: Holdings Statements," *Lasie* 4(3), Nov./Dec.1973, pp.25-33.
18. Huibert Paul: "Serials Processing: Manual Control vs. Automation," *Library Resources & Technical Services* 21(4), Fall 1977, pp.345-353.
19. Stuart R. Flavell: "Your Journal, Sir/Madam. . ." *The Australian Library Journal* 25(6), June 1976, pp.190-191.
20. Robin Jenkins and Jane Wheeler: "Periodical Circulation in the Department of Main Roads Library," *Lasie* 10(3), Nov./Dec.1979, pp.9-[14].
21. John Shortridge: "Bibliographic Database Activities in CSIRO's Central Information, Library and Editorial Section," *Lasie* 13(5/6), Mar./June 1983, pp.23-33.
22. "Midas," *Lasie* 8(4), Jan./Feb.1978, pp.3-5.
23. Perry D. Morrison and Douglas R. May: "Cooperative Use of Serials in Australian Libraries," *The Serials Librarian*, 1(3), Spring 1977, pp.231-241.
24. Janet D. Hine: "A Cataloguing Survey," *The Australian Library Journal* 22(1), Feb. 1973, pp.24-27.
25. Glenn Sanders: "Fear and Loathing in the Union Catalogue, or Electric SALSSAH Rides Again," *Lasie* 7(5), Mar./Apr. 1977, pp.28-40.

26. Pam Dunlop: "The Impact of Serials Cataloguing in the National Library," *Cataloguing Australia* 6(3), July/Sept.1980, pp.71-74.

27. B.J. Cheney, J.A. Conochie and H.J. Kidd: "The Computerisation of the Union Catalogue in CSIRO," *Lasie* 8(5/6), Mar./June 1978, pp.13-19.

28. Jean A. Conochie: "MARC Format for Serials—Particularly as it Relates to SSAL," *Cataloguing Australia* 4(3/4), July/Dec.1978, pp.28-39.

29. Jean A. Conochie: "The Effect of AACR2 on SSAL," *Cataloguing Australia* 6(3), July/Sept.1980, pp.75-76.

30. J. McRee Elrod: "Desuperimposition, AACR II, and the Smaller Library Catalogue," *Cataloguing Australia* 5(3), July/Sept.1979, pp.29-32.

31. Enid Roberts: "Methods of Dealing with the Problems Caused in Serials Catalogues by the Adoption of AACR2," *Cataloguing Australia* 6(3), July/Sept.1980, pp.77-78.

32. Gillian Currie: "Serial Cataloguing using AACR2 and the Implications for Machine Readable Files," *Cataloguing Australia* 8(2), June 1982, pp.12-19.

33. P.H. Dawe: Commentary on paper by Noel Stockdale "National Union Catalogues," *Bibliographical Services for the Nation: The Next Decade, Proceedings of a Conference held in Sydney, 26-27 Aug. 1980*. (Canberra: National Library of Australia, 1981) (Development of Resource Sharing Networks: Networks Study no.16) pp.151-154.

34. *Australian MARC Specification: Serials* (Canberra: National Library of Australia, 1983) 190 p.

35. Enid Roberts: "AACR2 and Serials," *Cataloguing Australia* 6(3), July/Sept. 1980, pp.65-70.

36. Ruth C. Carter: "Playing by the Rules—AACR2 and Serials," *Serials Management in an Automated Age: Proceedings of the First Annual Serials Conference, October 30-31, 1981, Arlington, Va.* (Westport, Conn: Meckler, 1981) pp.11-29.

37. Neal L. Edgar: "Serials Cataloguing Up to and Including AACR2," *The Serials Librarian* 7(4), Summer 1983, pp.25-46.

38. Jan Fullerton: "Implication of AACR2 in National Bibliographic Services," *Cataloguing Australia* 5(4), Oct./Dec. 1979, pp.13-25.

39. Janet Braithwaite: "Survey of National Library of Australia's Cataloguing Projects in 1974," *The Australian Library Journal* 24(3), April 1975, pp.115-119.

40. *Library Statistics* 1972—(Melbourne: Library Association of Australia, University and College Library Section). Supplement to: *Australian Academic & Research Libraries*.

41. *Library Services for Australia: the Work of AACOBS.* 1956/1970—(Canberra: AACOBS)

42. *The Network and the Nation: the Work of ABN 1981-84* (Canberra: National Library of Australia, 1984) 52 p. (Development of Resource Sharing Networks: Networks Study no.25)

43. Janet Robinson: "Serials and Serial Retrieval on ABN," *First ABN Conference, 12-14 July, Melbourne: Papers and Proceedings.* (Canberra, National Library of Australia, 1983) (Development of Resource Sharing Networks: Networks Study no.22) pp.45-51.

44. Averill M. B. Edwards: "The SALSSAH Experience," *Ibid.* pp.57-65.

45. Jean Conochie: "The SSAL Experience," *Ibid.* pp.52-56.

46. Ann Turner: "AACR2 and Serials," *The Serials Librarian* 6(1), Fall 1981, pp.27-39.

47. Toby Burrows: "The Future of Authority Control in ABN," *Cataloguing Australia* 10(4), Dec.1984, pp.9-17.

48. Richard J. Goodram: "University of Tasmania Library Plants Tulips: the AWA/URICA System Implemented," *Lasie* 11(4), Jan./Feb.1981, pp.14-20.

Serials Librarianship in India

K. C. Garg, BSc, MA, Associateship in Information Science
S. P. Gupta, BSc, MA, MLib, ISc

ABSTRACT. This paper presents in brief a discussion of problems and practices in serial librarianship in India.

India is a vast country with a network of libraries spread all over the nation. During the last ten years the number of libraries has increased considerably, and during this period also there has been here, as elsewhere, a tremendous growth in the number of serials published. At the same time, the cost of these publications has increased to the point at which acquiring all needed items is sometimes difficult. India depends very much on foreign publications for study and research in almost all subject fields. Serials have of course been an indispensable item in the stock of most Indian libraries by virtue of their informational and research potential. Although, India has made laudable progress in the field of science and technology, it does not produce enough serials itself to get rid of its dependence on foreign serials.

Although the term "serials" includes periodicals, newspapers, annual publications, reports, conference proceedings, etc., this paper focuses attention on periodicals only. The librarianship concerned with periodicals includes a consideration of their selection and acquisition, recording, cataloguing, maintenance, circulation and documentation services. This paper gives a brief review of the problems and practices of periodicals librarianship in various libraries in India. First it should be said that serial librarian's job in India is full of problems and challenges. The primary concern of the periodicals' librarian is to ensure that the periodicals selected for subscription meet the demands of the users. Then of course they must be ordered, renewed and paid well on time so that they are received regularly and punctually, routed/displayed, brought to the notice of the library's clientele and finally bound and stored properly so that they can be made available at call when needed.

Selection: The selection of periodicals is generally based on what is

---

K. C. Garg is Scientist "B" (Information Group), National Institute of Science Technology and Development Studies (NISTADS), Hillside Road, New Delhi-110 012, India. S. P. Gupta is Scientist "B" (Information Group), Central Road Research Institute, New Delhi-110 020, India.

© 1986 by The Haworth Press, Inc. All rights reserved.

found in publishers' catalogues, union lists, lists of titles covered by various indexing and abstracting services, references in the literature, announcements and reviews of new titles. Another particularly valuable source are the requests received from the library users. The selected periodicals are generally reviewed by a library committee, which consists of a team of members drawn from the various disciplines of the institutes or universities. This committee also invites suggestions from other working faculty members regarding the continuance or deletion of periodicals that are subscribed to or the addition of new ones. The final decision is made by the committee on the basis of the cost of the periodical and its utility to the faculty/department concerned. However, if the committee finds that a periodical is costly and at the same time useful, an attempt is made to share it with some other library, if it is subscribed to.

Acquisition: Periodicals are acquired by different libraries by subscription, exchange, gift or membership in learned societies. Most periodicals are acquired by subscription. The periodicals librarian faces many problems in their acquisition by reason of far flung markets, foreign exchange problems, unorganised periodicals trade, bogged down official procedures, erratic postal services, etc. Different kinds of libraries follow differing methods of periodicals subscription. The most common methods used in India to obtain their periodicals are either directly from the publishers or through subscription agents, which may be local or foreign. In the case of direct subscription, all correspondence regarding orders, payments, supply and follow-up action for missing issues is seen to by the subscriber in writing directly to the publisher. This of course results in much correspondence work for the librarian. Furthermore, the work involved in the processing of invoices to obtain bank drafts for foreign exchange is considerable as each invoice has to be processed separately. In the case of subscriptions obtained through agents, all necessary correspondence with the publisher is taken care of by the agent on behalf of the subscriber. The subscription agent who handles the subscription collects the total amount of subscription in rupees in advance and transmits it to the respective publishers. The periodicals are directly received by the concerned library at its address. Although, in this method the workload for the librarian is reduced; the method has its own limitations. For example; payment for the subscription is not remitted to the publishers in a timely way, the result can be disruption of the supply of the periodical. Sometimes, as it turns out, payment is not remitted at all to the publishers, and this may only be traced when direct correspondence is made with the publisher. Another difficulty is that reminders for missing issues may not be sent on time to the publishers. Again the result is disruption of the supply. Sometimes, it happens too that the foreign exchange is misused by private agents.

When such cases of misuse of foreign exchange came to the notice of the Government of India, the State Trading Corporation of India (STC) was asked by the Government to enter the book trade field. STC did this in 1974 presumably for the benefit of the Government organisations/institutions that were experiencing various problems with private vendors. Yet many libraries that placed their orders with STC together found that STC's own services were far from satisfactory.

Later on the Indian National Scientific Documentation Centre (INSDOC) launched the Centralised Acquisition Project (CAP) to handle subscriptions to foreign periodicals required by various laboratories of the Council of Scientific and Industrial Research (CSIR). The project is doing reasonably well. But still there are some problems regarding late payment, non-receipt of periodicals, etc.

Problems of Missing Issues and Non-receipt of Journals: Since most periodicals in India are acquired from foreign countries, it takes 4-6 months to receive them by surface mail. Not a readily acceptable situation. Non-receipt and missing issues not only cause disappointment among our research scholars but seriously hamper their work. Wrong delivery by the Posts and Telegraph Department has also been a cause of concern to the librarian. And poor packaging sometimes leads to undue wear and tear to items. Moreover, auditors frown at financial losses caused by non-receipt of items. Every year the librarian has to face the auditors. These invariably demand a list of missing issues along with their costs for the period under review. The librarian is put in a very embarrassing and awkward position in having to furnish such information. However, some criteria have been laid down by professional associations like the Indian Library Association (ILA) according to which a certain amount of loss is regarded as reasonable. The problem of missing issues continues, however, as it results in incomplete sets that remain unbound in the hope that missing issues will be received later on. Keeping loose issues on the shelves has brought further problem. The publishers are sometimes kind enough to replace missing issues, but in other cases they reply with the remark "Issues were mailed when published." Librarians attempt to complete their sets of missing issues by exchanging lists of duplicates and missing issues among themselves. This procedure to some extent helps to complete the gaps in their holdings, but is in the end not enough.

Impact of Exponential Rate of Growth of Periodicals and their Cost: The steady rise in the cost of periodicals and increase in their number has forced the librarians to cut subscriptions. Because of limited funds and shrinking space, some libraries have started acquiring microforms of periodicals to save space. Microforms of course require a costly expenditure for reading machines, and users in India, as elsewhere, are not fond of them as they are not so convenient to use as are print items. Resource sharing has been thought of by some librarians; and in some big cities like Bombay, Delhi, Calcutta, Madras, etc., resource-sharing practices, including cooperative coverage by various libraries, inter-library loan, etc., are being followed.

Recording and Maintenance: As soon as periodicals are received in the library, they are recorded in a register or ledger or on cards arranged alphabetically. Bigger libraries are using the Kardex system. A few libraries are using the three card system devised by Dr. S. R. Ranganathan. A record of receipt of periodicals is essential for audit purpose, and of course in sending reminders for non-receipt of periodicals.

In smaller libraries where the number of periodical titles received is small, say a dozen or so, these are displayed on reading tables or book racks. In bigger libraries, those receiving a few hundred or thousand periodicals, special display racks are used. In most of the libraries broad subject grouping is used in displaying the periodicals, and an alphabetical index is maintained.

Current issues are displayed and back issues are stored till the volume is completed, and then sent for binding for their long-term preservation. Bound volumes are generally maintained in alphabetical sequence. In some big scientific and research libraries, old volumes, which are considered to be little used, are stacked separately, and current volumes, say for ten years or so, are kept separately for the convenience of the users. Repository centres for withdrawn publications exist in some cities like Delhi and Bombay.

Circulation: In small libraries the circulation of periodicals is not a problem. Generally the latest issues are kept on display for a few days and then allowed to be borrowed by users. In big libraries the number of periodicals received is quite large and their subject content varied. Some libraries duplicate the contents pages of periodicals immediately on their receipt and send them to various groups. In others the periodicals are routed to interested parties. In most scientific and research libraries, the practice is to keep the latest issues of periodicals on display for some fixed time, say three months, to provide equal opportunity to all users for access to them. Afterwards the users are allowed to borrow them.

Cataloguing: Printed catalogues of bound volumes of periodicals are brought out by some big libraries, while the small libraries maintain a record in card form only. Efforts have been made by the Indian National Scientific Documentation Centre (INSDOC), New Delhi, and the Social Science Documentation Centre of the Indian Council of Social Science Research (ICSSR), New Delhi, to compile union catalogues of scientific periodicals and social science periodicals in India. A union list of current scientific serials has also been compiled by INSDOC.

Automation: Some organisations with computer facilities have tried to computerise their periodicals, acquisitions routines, such as ordering, the sending out of reminders, circulation, and compilation of periodicals holdings lists, etc. INSDOC has made efforts to computerise the union catalogue of scientific periodicals in India.

Conclusion: The problems faced by Indian librarians could be reduced, if the periodicals trade in the country were organised properly and government organisations, like STC and INSDOC were to take more interest in the trade. Publishers agents need to be appointed in India. The problem of missing issues could be reduced if more care were taken by the Post and Telegraph Department in the handling of periodicals. Periodicals will continue to create problems for Indian librarians until such time as electronic on-line processing becomes a reality.

Serials Librarianship in Nigeria, 1975-1985

Briggs C. Nzotta, PhD

ABSTRACT. A study is made of developments in serials librarianship in Nigeria during the past decade. Evidence shows that serials collections in Nigerian academic and special libraries are generally small. However there was considerable growth in the collections during the period. Efforts are made through current awareness services to assist users to exploit the collections.

There is adequate arrangement for bibliographic control of serials though this is impaired by the ignorance of publishers. Various efforts at interlibrary cooperation, production of union lists of serials and automation have not yielded very fruitful results.

INTRODUCTION

Serials play an important role in virtually all libraries. Because serials are published at intervals, they are vehicles for the dissemination of the most current information in any field. Therefore, so long as every library aims at giving the most up to date information to its clientele, it of necessity must acquire serials and organize and exploit them for library service.

As in many other spheres of activity, the developing countries have not advanced to the same high level in serials librarianship as have their developed counterparts. Thus, in Nigeria, for example, little literature has been generated on the subject. In *Nigerian Libraries,* the official journal of the Nigerian Library Association, which started publication in 1964, only one article on an aspect of this subject, an article published in 1971 by Lawani, was identified.[1] And Ibrahim had an article published elsewhere in 1984.[2] Otherwise the few other Nigerian writings available, like those of Aguolu,[3] Ehikhamenor[4] and Shoyinka,[5] simply mention periodicals in discussing broader subjects.

Little writing on serials librarianship may reflect low regard for em-

---

Briggs C. Nzotta, Senior Lecturer, Department of Library Studies, University of Ibadan, Ibadan, Nigeria.

I am very grateful to Mrs. C. F. Adedeji and Mr. J. E. Ikem, both of Ibadan University Library for their assistance in various ways while writing this article.

pirical study of the problems associated with serials in libraries. Nevertheless, in professional practice Nigerian librarians have been providing serials for their clienteles. This article examines the state of serials librarianship in Nigeria during the decade 1975-1985.

Here "periodicals" and "journals" will be used synonymously to indicate publications issued at intervals by learned and professional societies and organizations. The term "serials," on the other hand, is used as an all-embracing term. It includes not only journals, but also newspapers, yearbooks and the like. The present study focuses attention mainly on scholarly journals and newspapers.

METHODOLOGY

Most of the data and information for this article were collected by means of a mail questionnaire. The study was limited to university and special libraries, libraries very closely connected with research and advanced studies. Therefore, the libraries dealt with are those most likely to acquire serials (specifically scholarly journals) in considerable quantity.

Whereas today there are twenty-four well-established universities in Nigeria, in 1975 there were only ten. Similarly the number of research institutes owned by the Federal Government of Nigeria has grown considerably—from twenty in 1975 to thirty at present. The questionnaire was sent to the ten university libraries and twenty research institute libraries that were in existence by 1975. To show the variety of the research interests of the research institutes, the special libraries to which the questionnaire was sent include those of the Central Bank of Nigeria, the Centre for Management Development, the Nigerian Industrial Development Bank, the Cocoa Research Institute of Nigeria, the Nigerian Institute of Medical Research and the National Cereals Research Institute. Included also was an international organization that is only partially supported by the Federal Government, the International Institute of Tropical Agriculture.

Responses were received from six of the university libraries and nine of the special libraries. Recipients were strongly requested to complete and return the questionnaire within two weeks. This short response period accounts for the low response rate.

ACQUISITION

Between 1975 and 1985 a general increase has occurred in the serials collections of Nigerian academic and special libraries. In the university libraries a growth rate of 21-25% was experienced in current journal subscriptions during the decade. The increase was usually either from about 4,000 to 5,000 journals or from some 5,000 to 6,000 journals. Thus, typically, the University of Ife Library raised its journal subscriptions from 4,383 in 1975 to 5,373 in 1984 (a 22.6% increase); while Ibadan University Library's journal subscriptions rose from 5,165 in 1975 to 6,382 in 1984 (23.6%).

The journal collections of the special libraries are much smaller than those of the university libraries. The collections of the two groups cannot be compared at all. Current journal subscriptions in the research libraries varied from as low as 50 at the National Horticultural Research Institute Library to 1,145 at the Institute of Agricultural Research. A mode of 100-200 journal titles is currently received in the majority of the libraries. The growth rate of the journal collections in these libraries during the past decade has been much more varied than in the university libraries. Thus, journal subscriptions at the International Institute of Tropical Agriculture rose from 500 to 650 titles (a 30% growth), while that of the Forestry Research Institute climbed from 115 to 363 (216%).

Most of the libraries subscribe to a variety of Nigerian newspapers. The number of such subscriptions has grown over the decade in line with the increasing number of Nigerian newspapers. Of newspapers acquired, the lowest number is five, while the maximum is twenty. Before the present, rather oppressive economic situation of the country, some of the large university libraries subscribed to notable foreign newspapers like *The Times* (of London) and its supplements, *The Guardian* (of Manchester) and *The New York Times.* However, as the financial position of the universities worsened and it became difficult for institutions to get governmental approval for foreign exchange transactions, such subscriptions were discontinued in the 1980s.

A remarkable fact one studying library collection development and management in Nigeria soon learns is that Nigerian libraries are rather poor at keeping library records or statistics. It is difficult to get accurate details of expenditures on the acquisition of different types of material, allocation of funds to various subjects, etc. Part of the reason for this is that librarians often do not have full control over library budgets (where such separate budgets are even available), and this is especially so in special libraries which are usually small units of their parent institutions.

In the present study only one library, that of the Forestry Research Institute of Nigeria, was able to give figures of its expenditures on journals in both 1975 and 1984 for comparative purposes. These show that while it spent 904 pounds sterling on journal subscription in 1975 (for 115 titles), in 1984 its outlay had risen to 10,250 pounds sterling (for 363 journal titles). Thus for an increase of 216% in journal subscriptions there was an increase of 1,034% in costs. This discrepancy shows clearly how the costs of journals have risen phenomenally during the decade.

Nigerian libraries are dependent almost entirely on imported materials for building their collections. Over 90% of library books are imported. The situation is even worse with journals. This is understandable because journals are much more complex than books to publish and sustain. Since scholarly journals are specialized and sometimes very limited in scope, the predominantly non-literate societies of developing countries cannot provide adequate markets to sustain most of these journals. Consequently, in none of the libraries surveyed are more than 5% of its journals published in Nigeria. For most the range is 1-2%, or even less.

Since most journals are imported, foreign subscription agents are used to the virtual exclusion of local ones. Famous international agents like Blackwell's in the United Kingdom, Faxon in the United States and Swets & Zeitlinger in Holland are the most popular with Nigerian libraries. The United Kingdom and the United States are also the major sources of the journals acquired by the libraries. A few libraries mentioned three lesser known agents, one of which is in France. Only three university libraries have tried to use local agents. Three local agents were used, two private companies and a university bookshop. In a number of the libraries some journals, especially local ones, are received through membership in learned societies. The newspapers are usually supplied each morning by local vendors.

Nigerian academic and special libraries acquire some journals, though usually an insignificant number, as gifts and exchanges. The total number of materials received each year is normally less than ten. The notable exceptions are Ibadan University Library, which received 323 items in 1975 and 26 in 1984; and the library of the International Institute of Tropical Agriculture, which received 300 and 700 items in the two years respectively. Many Nigerian institutions have few or no publications of their own, and their library collections are skeletal. Therefore the libraries have hardly anything to exchange or give away.

ORGANIZATION AND SERVICES

All the university libraries have separate serials departments. Each department is responsible for acquisition and processing of serials, checking invoices and passing on the bills to the university bursar for settlement, claims and all relations with subscription agents or publishers of journals, maintenance of serials records, preparation of periodicals for binding and care of the bound and unbound collections. The department is headed by a librarian. Other members of staff include one or two paraprofessionals and four or five library assistants.

Except at the libraries of the International Institute of Tropical Agriculture and the Nigerian Institute of International Affairs, special libraries do not have separate serials departments. At the two libraries that do, the staffing pattern is similar to that of university libraries. The departments also perform similar functions.

In Nigerian libraries, serials, except newspapers, are generally classified using the same classification scheme as for books. Unlike the case of many other libraries where serials are classified, in Nigeria serials are shelved separately, not together with the books.

Various types of shelves are used to display current issues of journals. Some have provision for keeping recent back issues of the journals as well. The current journals are also arranged in classified sequence, and then alphabetically by title in each class.

Most libraries provide current awareness services by preparing lists or indexes of the contents of the most recent periodicals received. The Nigerian Institute of International Affairs Library has gone further than the other libraries in preparing these current contents lists. Each article listed has a brief abstract or summary of its content.

The frequency of the contents lists varies from library to library. They are intended to be produced quarterly, monthly or fortnightly. Virtually every one of them is now produced irregularly. The lists are distributed to academic and/or research staff, but not to students.

There is usually free access to the current periodicals room and the stacks for the bound volumes. While current issues of journals are not lent out, bound volumes can be borrowed by some classes of users, as academic and research staff and graduate students.

Serials in microform are not popular in Nigeria. Only a handful of university libraries and the Nigerian Institute of International Affairs Library among the study group put some local newspapers on microfilm for preservation purposes. Some of these also acquire microfilm copies of back issues of The *Times of London.*

Because of easy access to photocopying machines in the libraries of the developed countries, theft and mutilation of journals have been considerably reduced. Kuhn testifies to this fact in the case of American libraries.[6] There are, however, few photocopying machines in Nigerian libraries. And of these, many break down frequently and are not promptly repaired. The cost of making photocopies is also high. Therefore, photocopying has not made significant impact on serials librarianship in Nigeria. The security of journals is particularly threatened in academic libraries. For instance, as Ibrahim reports:

> Titles in high demand are occasionally deliberately wrongly shelved by readers to monopolise the use of such journals. Where journals are not hidden, and where lazy students find it difficult to copy the required parts, such parts are mutilated.[7]

Certainly such malpractice would be reduced if there were adequate, cheap and reliable photocopying machines.

BIBLIOGRAPHIC CONTROL, INTERLIBRARY COOPERATION AND LIBRARY AUTOMATION

With regard to bibliographic control, interlibrary cooperation and library automation in Nigeria, the first half of the decade under consideration (1975-1980) was a period of hope, optimism, lofty ambitions and many proposals. Of course Nigeria was experiencing a period of economic boom. Petro-dollars were plentiful, and many people thought money did not constitute a problem in executing any project. However, as the recession started in 1980, funds for carrying out proposals began to diminish rapidly. Thus, the second half of the decade has been a period of little progress and of non-realization of most of the worthy proposals of the first half.

As Shoyinka reports,

> The National Library [of Nigeria] has been a leader in sub-Saharan Africa in adopting international standards, and is playing an ever increasing role on the international library scene.[8]

Thus, the National Library became a member of the International Serials Data System (ISDS) in December 1977. Subsequently it established the Nigerian National Serials Data Centre (NSDC), which issues the International Standard Serial Numbers for serials published in Nigeria. Soon afterwards it began to publish the *Nigerian File of International Standard Serial Numbers*. Nigerian serials are also listed in the *National Bibliography of Nigeria*.

The efforts at bibliographic control of Nigerian serials by the National Library have not been very successful for a number of reasons. Many publishers do not apply to the NSDC for ISSNs to be given to their serials. Consequently, the Centre does not have a comprehensive record of all current Nigerian serials. Furthermore, the National Library does not have the resources to publish the *Nigerian File* and the *National Bibliography* regularly and on time. These publications invariably appear many months after their due dates.

Usually interlibrary cooperation, union lists and catalogues, and library automation are interdependent. At present there is minimal cooperation among Nigerian libraries. Most of this cooperation is informal and among groups of libraries located very close together or in the same town. Part of the reason for such little cooperation is that the necessary facilities, especially easy means of communication, are not available. Interlibrary cooperation thrives best of course among libraries with large and varied special collections where the members of the group depend on one another for special materials that are not commonly available. In the case of Nigerian libraries, most have relatively small collections consisting mainly of essential texts and serials in their various subject fields. Moreover, libraries of the same type tend to have largely similar materials. The little collections of the separate libraries are hardly adequate to meet the needs of its own clientele, and there are few photocopying machines or other facilities for making copies for others. Finally, it is risky trusting original materials to the vagaries of a poorly developed communications system. Such conditions then do not provide much scope for interlibrary cooperation on a large scale. Nevertheless, Nigerian librarians have shown considerable interest in interlibrary cooperation, as is evidenced through their writings on the subject, and the emphasis given it at conferences and workshops, and the proposals made concerning it.

The publication of union lists and catalogues gives clear evidence of positive steps being taken in the direction of interlibrary cooperation. Their preparation often involves the use of computers. It might be said in passing that all major efforts at library automation in Nigeria have been aimed chiefly at computerizing circulation and serials processes.

With regard to serials librarianship specifically, the National Library of Nigeria has been trying for a long time to produce a union list of serials of some Nigerian academic and special libraries. These attempts have not yet been as successful as expected. They led to the publication of the *National Union List of Serials in Nigerian Libraries: A Record of Serial Titles Held by Libraries Participating in the Library Cooperation Programme.* The first edition of this union list of serials was produced in 1977; a projected second edition has not yet been published.

The first successful effort at producing a union list of serials in some Nigerian libraries was that master-minded by a single individual, Lawani. This work was first produced in 1970 and revised in 1973. It covered only the scientific and technical periodicals held in eighteen academic and special libraries, and was mimeographed.[9] The Nigerian Science and Technology Development Agency, when it was in existence in the 1970s, also produced a union catalogue of scientific and technical serials in its libraries.

Following the above projects, some university libraries, individually and collectively, have also tried with varying success to automate some of their processes, including serials. Ibadan University Library was the first to publish a list of its serials holdings using a computer.[10] Others include the libraries of Ahmadu Bello University, the University of Lagos, the University of Nigeria, the University of Port Harcourt and the University of Ilorin. These efforts have all been grounded owing to one problem or another.

The most elaborate project so far for producing a union list of serials in some Nigerian libraries is that currently being undertaken by the Committee of University Librarians of Nigerian Universities. The project was commissioned in 1977, and is still continuing. Its aim is to compile a

Union List of Serials in Nigerian Academic and Research Libraries. Ibadan University Library is executing the project on behalf of the Committee. An interim report on the project issued in February 1984 shows that eight academic and two special libraries are participating. The outputs expected are alphabetical lists of all journals in all participating libraries as well as separate lists for each library. It is anticipated that the various lists will also be arranged by subject. However, the project has experienced some problems. For instance, the holdings of one of the libraries could not be listed in the first printouts because its serials records were not available. About a third of the complete set of data cards could not be read because they had been poorly kept previously.[11] The enormous problems faced in executing this project and the many years it has taken without yielding any fruitful results underline the great difficulties in the application of automation to serials librarianship, as well as other aspects of the profession, in Nigeria.

PROBLEMS

Serials librarianship in Nigeria is beset with a number of problems. The most serious ones will be highlighted here.

Foremost among the problems is the question of funds. Most Nigerian libraries have very small serials collections not out of volition, but simply because the funds for collection development, and even library services generally, are just not available. Since the late 1970s the financial position of even the largest libraries has continued to worsen. Therefore, it has become extremely difficult to renew journal subscriptions, let alone the acquiring of new ones. A classic case is that of the oldest university library, Ibadan University Library, which also has the largest serials collection. As Ehikhamenor reports

> The vote for books and journals for the 1978/79 [session] slumped down to 62,000 Naira [One Naira = US $1.54 in 1979] representing 12.7 percent of the figure for the previous year and 9.4 percent of the budget estimates submitted for approval. Renewal of journal subscriptions alone was estimated at 180,000 Naira. In general, the financial situation was so bad that the continued existence of the Library was even beset with uncertainty. The survival measures adopted were far-reaching and in fact disastrous. . . they included:
>
> 1. Suspension of acquisition of new materials such as current books and journals, major works, as well as back files of journals.

2. Cancellation of outstanding foreign orders for books, which constituted as much as 90% of all orders.
3. Cancellation of foreign journal subscriptions, which comprised as much as 99% of all subscriptions.[12]

The gap created in the serials collection of Ibadan University Library during that period has not been filled until today. Yet even though the financial position of the library has improved considerably since that time, it remains unsatisfactory, especially when inflation is taken into consideration.

The fact that over 90% of serials in Nigerian libraries are imported creates other problems. In 1969 a Canadian librarian lamented the effects of delays in the shipment of library materials, which in the case of his library took between nine and 84 days.[13] The situation in Canada is surely considerably improved today, 15 years afterwards. On the other hand, the Nigerian situation is far worse today than even the Canadian of 15 years ago. Imported library materials take from 6 to 12 months or more to arrive in Nigeria. Air freight is very expensive, so that is not a practical alternative to surface shipment. It becomes an enormous uphill task to claim missing issues of periodicals or issues lost in transit. Yet this is a common occurrence.

Another problem associated with the importation of serials and monographs is the issue of securing foreign currency for the transaction. As many developing countries, including Nigeria, are getting economically poorer in the 1980s, their governments have introduced many stringent measures to restrict foreign exchange transactions. Appeals by librarians, intellectuals, publishers, booksellers and other groups that exchange of knowledge and ideas should not be fettered do not seem to impress the policy-makers. Thus, it is now becoming extremely difficult for Nigerian libraries to utilize the little votes they get for periodicals and other materials that have to be imported.

The education system has expanded rapidly during the period under consideration. Thus, whereas by 1975 there were about twelve universities, today the number has doubled to twenty-four. The old universities have also increased their annual intake of students; and as new programmes are being introduced in these universities, their teaching and research staffs have likewise grown. Similarly polytechnics, colleges of education and technology, have also increased greatly in number and size.

As the number of Nigerian academic and research staff of professional bodies grows, the need for providing avenues for them to publish and share ideas and experiences increases proportionately. The publish or perish syndrome exists among academics everywhere. This situation has led during the last decade to the proliferation of scholarly journals in various disciplines and professions. It has been difficult to keep track of such new journals. For instance, in library and information science, some of the 19 state divisions of the Nigerian Library Association, some of the library schools and some of the state public library services have begun to publish their own journals—whereas before 1980 there were altogether only a handful of library journals.

At the same time the mortality rate of these local journals is quite high. Many never go beyond the first two or three issues. This is not surprising because their publishers are usually amateur groups with no strong financial backing and virtually no experience in journal publishing. They only have their enthusiasm to see them through.

The proliferation of such short-lived journals constitutes a problem in serials librarianship. It is difficult to decide which of the journals are likely to survive and are therefore worth acquiring in the first place. Many of these journals have no formalized system of marketing, and so time and effort can be wasted in addressing correspondence to the wrong quarters.

Little attention has been paid to serials librarianship in the curricula of Nigerian library schools. Inadequate time is given to the subject, which is usually dealt with tangentially in the course of teaching other subjects like technical processes, cataloguing and classification, and acquisitions. Yet there is enough serials librarianship by its size and complexity to deserve to stand as an independent course. If this were to happen, a sufficient number of capable personnel would be produced to run the serials departments of libraries. This happy state of affairs proves elusive still, however.

Nigerian libraries and librarians are showing a lot of interest in automation. Normally the first areas they consider for automation, as stated earlier, are circulation and serials functions. Automating these functions is of course never easy, and in Nigerian libraries is fraught with special difficulties because of inadequate infrastructures. For instance, electricity supply is erratic and unreliable, there are no sufficient maintenance engineers to service the computers, and spare parts have to be imported at exorbitant prices through time-wasting processes.

CONCLUSION

In the past decade some advances have been made in serials librarianship in Nigeria. Though the serials collections of Nigerian libraries are relatively small, there is evidence of considerable growth. These collections are managed along professional lines and efforts are made to offer service of high quality to clienteles.

Nigerian librarians are fully aware of the importance of serials in library service. They are desirous of using modern techniques in executing their responsibilities. They, however, have to battles against many odds.

The present Nigerian government is making serious efforts to make the economy buoyant again. There is, therefore, good reason to believe that there will be improvements soon in the financial position of libraries. Prospects for further advances in serials librarianship in the next decade are for that reason bright.

REFERENCES

1. Lawani, S. M., "Towards Objective Methods of Selecting Periodical Titles," *Nigerian Libraries* 7, nos. 1 & 2 (Apr. & Aug. 1971): 21-26.
2. J. L. Ibrahim, "Serials Librarianship in Nigerian University Libraries: The Experience of a Serials Librarian," *The Library Scientist* 11 (1984): 80-85.
3. C. C. Aguolu, "Information Resources in Nigerian Higher Education: Problems of Development and Growth," *Libri* 28, no.1 (March 1978): 21-57.
4. Fabian A. Ehikhamenor, "Collection Development under Constraints," *Nigerian Library and Information Science Review* 1, no.1 (May 1983): 42-56.
5. Patricia H. Shoyinka, "Bibliographic Control in Nigeria," *Libri* 28, no. 4 (Dec. 1978): 294-308.
6. Warren B. Kuhn, "Service," In Walter C. Allen, ed. *Serial Publications in Large Libraries* (London: Clive Bingley, 1971), p.185.
7. Ibrahim, "Serials Librarianship," p.82.
8. Shoyinka, "Bibliographic Control in Nigeria," p. 299.
9. S. M. Lawani, ed. *Union List of Scientific and Technical Periodicals in Nigerian Libraries.* 2nd ed. (Ibadan: Library and Documentation Centre, International Institute of Tropical Agriculture, 1973). 532p. (Mimeographed).
10. Ibadan University Library, *Catalogue of Serials in the Library.* (Ibadan: Ibadan University Library, 1975). 558 p.
11. T. Olabisi Odeinde, *"Union List of Serials in Nigerian Academic and Research Libraries: Status Report."* (Ibadan: February, 1984). 6p. (Mimeographed).
12. Ehikhamenor, "Collection Development under Constraints," p.52.
13. Peter Gellatly, "The Serials Perplex: Acquiring Serials in Large Libraries," In Walter C. Allen, ed. *Serial Publications in Large Libraries* (London: Clive Bingley, 1971) p.45.

Ten Years of Living With Magazines

W. A. Katz, PhD

ABSTRACT. Describes recent happenings in magazine publishing, indicating why some magazines have failed, others have prospered and still others have remain unchanged. Points out the need for an understanding of magazine history and economics as a prerequisite in the setting of periodicals budgets. Discusses such matters as article refereeing, audience predilections and abstracting and indexing. Lists characteristics that have emerged in magazines over the past decade.

Looking back on the past ten years of magazine publishing, one is irresistibly drawn to two conclusions about their development and regression. First, an alliance with the past is necessary for an understanding of the future, and magazine history is no exception. Second, readers are unaware of the existence of such concerns.

Few people feel any attraction or repulsion about a particular magazine's past, present or future. The exception may be the occasional scandal or changing of the guard that takes place in some popular magazines, and there is no denying that the editors of *Cosmopolitan* and *Playboy* are almost folk heroes. On the whole, though, the history of magazines is not a popular subject whether it be Frank Luther Mott's gigantic study, or the present (and commendable) Greenwood Press series, "Historical Guides to the World's Periodicals and Newspapers."

Among scholarly journals there is possibly more interest, albeit that this interest tends to be highly parochial and lethal. The editor of some of these publications can literally determine who or who does not get tenure or promotion.

On balance, though, the anatomy of an editorial office is about as fascinating to the public as aerobics to creative slouches. It hardly requires a sociological, historical or, for that matter psychoanalytic theory to explain the lack of interest.

As a magazine is an impersonally conceived object, it can be rejected when the editor fails either to inform or entertain. One may materialize the spirit of acceptance and rejection in three magazines, *The New*

W. A. Katz is a professor in the School of Library and Information Science of the State University of New York at Albany, Albany, NY 12222.

Yorker, Playboy and *Harper's Monthly*. Scholarly, scientific and otherwise esoteric journals that pepper the pages of citation indexes, but not the newstands or coffee tables of America, fairly well follow *The New Yorker* procedure.

The New Yorker is an example of what has happened to most magazines over the past decade. Nothing.

Content to claim to be the world's best magazine (and who is to argue?), it drifts from excellence to excellence. It seems to go on interminably with a natural informality identified, at least by a few, with its 77-year-old editor, William Shawn. True, the financial pages reveal Samuel Newhouse plans to acquire 17 percent (read $25.5 million) of the privately held company, and Shawn has appointed two co-editors, but this is not the stuff of leading headlines, or reader interest.

If one examines the version of the "nothing" approach in library literature, it becomes apparent that this is a tradition. It takes more than a decade to move or draw library-oriented magazines from their patterns of rich fulfillment, or if you prefer, particular lack of content. So it has been, and so it remains. Ten years hence, it will be the same.

There are exceptions. Then exchange of owners and sometimes even the editorial policy of the magazine is the stuff of conversation among those who prefer *Folio* to *American Baby* or the *PLMA*. Consider, for example, *Harper's Monthly*. Pushed to the edge of financial disaster, it could no longer do nothing. Thanks to a drastic overhaul of the appearance and the content of the magazine, it moved back into the viable black. Although *Harper's* is no longer faithful to its long history of liberalism, it is at least making money.

The craftpersons at *Harper's* represent a second trend in magazine publishing. If most do nothing, some try a little harder. The result is usually the switch from soft to strong opinion, from few to at least more readers. Of course, just effort is not always enough, e.g., *The Saturday Review* and *Us,* as well as dozens of nameless computer magazines. It takes cranky, inspired editorial leadership, and no small smattering of luck to succeed.

Where the *New Yorker* remains steady on course and *Harper's* takes up therapy, *Playboy* is representative of another group. Here the triumph of bad taste continually brings in the dollars. Well, almost. Sometimes there is slippage. In the case of *Playboy,* the teen-age audience grew up. The magazine, despite a changeover to a woman director, is still out-of-tune with the times. Circulation isn't exactly off, but then it isn't going anywhere either. It's a marvelous example of failure to accommodate readers. Another may be *The Reader's Digest,* where with the owners dead, another sheriff and local priest no longer seem to be able to hold the flock's attention.

Of course not all of this motion, or lack of motion, is due to editorial decisions. The past ten years proved a near disaster to many magazines in terms of advertising revenues, although this is now improving. Wedded to increased postal costs and inflation, which hit paper and personnel as well as printing, publishers saved themselves by raising the cover and subscription costs.

Using 1977 as a base year, the 1984 periodical index is now at 223.5. If one goes back to 1974, the price increase is closer to 250 percent. A lesson learned by commercial magazines is that the close to 100-year dependence on advertising for survival no longer applies. The subscriber can carry much of the cost of the magazine. Gone are the days when the publisher virtually gave away the magazine in order to insure a large audience for the advertiser.

Although the general magazine pretty well died out years ago with the failure of *Life, Saturday Evening Post, Colliers* and company, the notion of mass advertising took longer to kill off. Along with its demise has developed the specialized magazine that now dominates the industry. Here one immediately thinks of the ultimate attraction of computers to publishers. From only four or five computer magazines a few years ago, there are now well over 600, and speculation over their fate is similar to the talk heard about boom or bust in the stock market. Robotics is considered the next "go for readers" area, but meanwhile popular scientific titles, as well as those devoted to hobbies, crafts and the out-of-doors continue to engage everyone from the rustic to the intellectual.

Founded in 1972, *Money* is typical of a renewed interest in the horse race called the stock market, and this is matched only by dashing out to get the latest copy of a health magazine such as *The Runner,* one of scores of new entries guaranteed to insure youth and well-being. If video and racquetball are American finds, one can be assured there are magazines immediately in the wings to meet and encourage the needs of other fads and developments.

Not all Americans demand only entertainment and inspiration. Witness the encouraging growth of magazines (from *Lilith* to *Issues in Health Care of Women*) for women who no longer will settle for *Good Housekeeping*. There are more titles, too, for gays and civil activists such as Hispanics, Blacks and the disabled. If commercial hysteria seems to be the rule at the drugstore news racks, the same kind of dedicated, but more distinguished, value system is operational in the founding of at least a few thoroughly commendable new magazines.

Speculation on the number of new titles introduced each year varies, depending on the definition of magazine, journal, periodical, etc. A conservative estimate, including scholarly titles as well as popular ones, would be in the neighborhood of 400 a year in the United States alone. This does not count newsletters, throwaways, or, for that matter the ubiquitous little magazine. The rate of failure will be at least 60 percent. The residue becomes part of *Ulrich's International Periodicals Directory* and its 65,000-plus world-wide titles, not to mention what else one can locate in the *Standard Periodical Directory* as well as in Len Fulton's *International Directory of Little Magazines and Small Presses.*

There is nothing in the past decade that indicates either a slowing or a faster flow of new magazines, or, for that matter, a higher or lower death rate. They all seem quite constant. One is faced with the engaging task of trying to maximize library budgets to meet this economic and social condition. If it is true that most magazines do nothing, while a few improve, and a few decline, the amount of latitude for trimming already-existing periodicals budgets is limited. Hardly news, but one must be committed to an understanding of magazine history and economics to appreciate why it is increasingly more difficult to make choices.

Looking at the scholarly and scientific area of journals, much the same situation exists. Most do nothing new over the years. A few improve, if only out of necessity. Their numbers increase at the same pace as commercial titles, although it is true they tend to follow more set patterns. For example, scholarly journals concerned with computers and information science are self-appointed breeders and pursue multiplication. In less glamorous areas, such as plain, unadulerated bibliography or genealogy the growth rate is considerably more consistent with the reality of the number of readers.

One particular concern that seems to excite administrators is the matter of a journal's being refereed. Some 10 years ago when an edition of *Magazines for Libraries* was in preparation, publishers were asked if they issued refereed journals. Few understood the term. It means that papers submitted are read by experts who then, usually without knowing the name of the author, accept, reject or otherwise ask for revisions. While an established principal among equally well established scientific, and some literature journals, it is foreign to others. The usual reply is that the process is not necessary, particularly among those where there is a strong editor. The mystique of the refereed title seems to be winning over hesitant faculty who long for someone else to make decisions about the good and the bad, who, indeed, have the mistaken notion that "refereed" is a magic insurance policy of quality. While the process has its points, particularly as a method of screening material that is not well known to the editor, it is no guarantee of quality. No matter what one thinks of the process, the past decade has seen an ever increasing number of refereed journals. Their number is likely to increase in the decade ahead.

Judgments of better or worse, good or bad differ from discipline to discipline. A lawyer finds the *Review of Metaphysics* somewhat less useful than the *American Bar Association Journal*, but *Magazines for Libraries* takes into account their individual merits and, concerned as much with utility as with conceptions of utility, hails them both as useful additions in libraries—at least those with lawyers and philosophers about.

Over the past decade, strong efforts have been made to calculate scientific, objective ways of judgment. These range from new equations for citation studies to qualitative varieties of discrimination that depend as much on insight as on archaic selection patterns. Each tends to bring to light a new process of deliberation that may help the librarian navigate out of darkness into light. Then again, too many such navigators become so involved with sections and subsections that what is technically a brilliant achievement ends in total darkness.

Faced with the patterns in magazine publishing, it is understandable that the librarian should develop a longing for the ultimate theory of selection. Unfortunately, there is no central theory. There is not likely to be one.

Turning to some of the revolutionary gestures and events of the past ten years, one finds no insatiable desire or theory of development that is central. Still, some of the essential features of magazines during the mid 1970s and early 1980s can be summarized.

1. Indexing and abstracting services now transcend the rationalization that this or that title can't be purchased because it is not indexed. Virtually every periodical is indexed or otherwise noted in some service.

The problem that has rapidly developed over the past ten years is one of quantitative and unrealizable fantasies about library budgets. There is a limit to just how many indexes and related services, particularly when they overlap, the library can purchase. One solution is the online version.

2. More and more magazines are available online in full text. These can be printed out in part or searched word by word. Vendors such as NEXIS and the Information Access Corporation, not to mention BRS and Dialog bring everything from *Time* and *People* to the *Harvard Business Review* to the screen. This may be the most important development of the past decade. The confusion over trying to find a magazine article in *Readers' Guide to Periodical Literature* will be solved at a terminal.

While the online popular and scholarly title are and will be available in this form, few publishers are likely to give up the traditional print edition. The two do and will flourish side by side. The next step, growing out of this, will be delivery of years of magazines on disks that can be searched by the individual library. This is not the beginning of the electronic magazine, nor the end of the paper age. If anything, the online journal will encourage even more reading of the paper version.

3. The wedding of the media became increasingly evident in the past decade. Television has not driven out magazines, it has married the form. Several magazines, including *Playboy,* now offer their

magazines on cable television. The term "magazine" is the central theme of several television shows that borrow liberally from the columns of fashion and home focused titles. Experience indicates that once someone becomes involved with the television version, there will be a demand for the printed magazine. Viewdata and teletex have been a failure. The vision of the person sitting at home calling up selected pages of a magazine or a journal has not worked out.

4. Censorship gained ground over the past ten years, and the U.S. Supreme Court ruled that local juries may decide what is obscene for their own communities. An immediate target for many local juries was the ubiquitous *Hustler* and its capricious editor Larry Flynt. While few tears were lost for Flynt, the Supreme Court decision has had a chilling effect on some large commercial ventures, helped no little by the current drive against pornography by everyone from members of the women's movement to born again Christians.

5. The phenomenon of the little magazine continues, and there are more and more basement efforts to compete with the commercial press. Some 3,500 now exist in the United States and Canada, and in the past decade the estimate is that littles grew in numbers by at least 150 to 200 a year. Surprisingly, the rate of attrition is quite small, and most continue to publish for three to ten years or more.

6. The popular magazine as never before is depending more and more on good design and snappy graphics to win readers. A case in point: *Harper's Monthly.* And, for that matter, *Atlantic,* which not only changed editorial direction, but dropped the drab dress of almost a century for a new look. Appearance does not make a good magazine, but it helps to sell individual copies.

7. In terms of just being available, more magazines can be found in more places than ever before. The past ten years have taught publishers the value of supermarkets as well as airports and drug stores for individual sales. This, in turn, means a continued disposition of the public to look to magazines for information and relaxation. Figures indicate that while only 20 percent of the people enter a library in a year, at least 80 percent read one or more magazines.

Once this is understood by librarians, there should be an ever increased effort to make at least the better known magazines and journals readily available and to put them on prominent display in the library. One can't help but wonder how many more people might use a library if they realized they could sit to read instead of standing in a supermarket line or shifting from one foot to another in a drugstore.

8. Finally, in reviewing magazines over the past ten years—both in *Library Journal* and for various editions of *Magazines for*

Libraries—it seems to me the content is no better or worse than in the past. Given that, the same basic rules of evaluation apply. There is the good and the bad, at least as I and consultants who help to put together *Magazines for Libraries* are able to calculate. Whether it be a subject expert or a casual browser who determines the purely qualitative aspects of editorial content, it ultimately comes down to what Stuart Mill observed, i.e., that which is good can be defined as that which promises the greatest pleasure.

Pleasure may progress from the pure utilitarian to the pure craving to become lost in a dream. One should not try to reconcile the irreconcilable by confusing the two. A balance is needed, and if any sin has been committed in the past ten years, it is the librarian's rapture over utility, the too quick dismissal of the other dimension of the pleasure equation. Reading the literature one sometimes has the distinct impression that libraries are to be run for the one or two percent of the population wed to a computer who have an insatiable thirst for information and more information. They are a lively, fast moving group who deserve attention, but they are not the only emigrants from reality. Magazine publishers realize this, and they offer something for everyone. Librarians, of course, must continue to do the same.

Magazines in the past decade have continued to exert an influence on the lives of almost everyone, and there is no reason to think that this will not continue. It follows that librarians have to be aware of the power of magazines, not only as weapons of utility, but as posts of relaxation. Once it is understood that there are few great revolutionary gestures in magazine publishing, that there are few great illusions, it is possible to chart a steady course of appreciation and selection based upon salutary understanding of times past, present and future. This binding of the past and the future is the proper pursuit of any discriminating study of magazines.

The Journal, Scholarly Communication, and the Future

Kathy G. Tomajko
Miriam A. Drake

ABSTRACT. The purpose of this article is to relate how new technologies are affecting the way scientists and technologists communicate. The discussion includes the origins of the scientific journal, the problems and promise of the contemporary journal and an exploration of developing technologies, such as electronic bibliographic data retrieval, personalized information systems, electronic mail, text editing, teleconferencing, electronic publishing, telefacsimile, optical and laser disc storage with an emphasis on their effect upon scholarly communication in the future.

A. M. Turin, a British computer pioneer, said in 1950, "I believe that by the end of the century the use of words will have changed so much that one will speak of machines that think without expecting to be contradicted."[1] At the Online '84 conference in San Francisco, Allen T. Cobb remarked that "we live in an age where new ideas can reach maturity in just a few decades . . . Our current approaches to information and data management will look as primitive 20 years from now as Gutenberg's wooden type fonts look to us today."[2] Rapidly developing technologies are producing significant changes in the ways people communicate, acquire data, and produce, process and disseminate ideas and information. The purpose of this article is to relate how new technology is affecting the way that scientists and technologists communicate, especially in the publishing arena. Emphasis is placed on the journal literature.

The discussion includes a summary of how scientists and technologists have communicated in the past, how they presently communicate, and how they may communicate in the future. Particular attention is given to journal publication, computers, telecommunications and innovations, such as electronic mail, electronic publishing, teleconferencing, and expert systems.

Kathy Gillespie Tomajko is Assistant Department Head, Information Exchange Center, and Miriam A. Drake is Director of Libraries, Price Gilbert Memorial Library, Georgia Institute of Technology, Atlanta, GA 30332-0900.

© 1986 by The Haworth Press, Inc. All rights reserved.

THE PAST

"Journal publishing represents the heart of the scientific and technical communication. It is the most extensive mode found in the published literature and represents the greatest amount of resources."[3] It is generally agreed that formal scholarly communication began with the journal. Before the emergence of the journal, scientists communicated by means of personal contact and correspondence or letters. ". . . communication by letter was restricting in that the information could be disclosed to only one person at a time or to a very limited number if copyists were employed. Publication in conventional book form was cumbersome, time consuming, and uneconomic as the author was forced to delay until he had gathered enough matter to justify publication."[4] Two factors were instrumental in the emergence of the scientific journal—the newspaper and the development of scientific societies. Newspapers date back to the Roman *Acta Diurna,* which was posted daily to inform the public of government decrees, legislative proceedings, athletic events, etc. The *Journal des Scavans* is generally considered the first scientific journal; it began publication on January 5, 1665. The Royal Society of London's *Philosophical Transactions,* the first English scientific journal, emerged four months later on May 6, 1665. The purpose of the *Philosophical Transactions* was to record the experiments of society members and to publish selections from correspondence with their European counterparts, whereas the *Journal des Scavans* was more concerned with book reviewing than with the communication of original science.[5]

Many journals that appeared in the 17th and 18th centuries failed in one or two year's time, owing to lack of a sponsoring society, lack of significant scientific output, or problems of communication. Up to the year 1800, Fielding H. Garrison identified 701 scientific and medical periodicals that had been published worldwide.[6] The first learned periodical published in the United States was the *Medical Repository,* which appeared in the year 1797. Others that followed are the *American Journal of Science and Arts* in 1818 and the *Philadelphia Journal of Medical and Physical Sciences* in 1820.[7] By the middle of the 18th century, the journal had become the accepted medium of scientific communication, and in that century and the 19th scientific journals began to specialize according to scientific discipline. And with the industrial revolution of the mid-1800s came also the beginning of trade/technical journals. By the year 1900, there were an estimated 10,000 scientific journals worldwide.[8]

Journal publication during most of the 20th century has changed very little except for its continuing exponential growth and dissemination in differing formats. Andrew Garvin indicated in 1980 that "the increase has been so exponential that we have been able to generate more printed information in the past ten years than in mankind's complete history."[9] Some of the reasons given for the rapid growth of journal literature are increasing numbers of scholars working throughout the world, pressures to publish for professional advancement, increase in funding for scientific research as a result of Sputnik and other such technological advances as well as a trend toward specialization in science and engineering that has resulted in a proliferation of societies, each issuing its own journal and other publications.

TODAY'S JOURNAL

According to Bernard Houghton, there are three major groups of scientific and technical periodicals, and these can be subdivided by function:

1. learned society and professional institution journals
   (a) primary; (b) communications; (c) general purpose; (d) review
2. commercially published journals
   (a) primary; (b) technical and trade; and (c) controlled circulation
3. house journals
   (a) prestige; (b) information on products; (c) internal house organs[10]

Although, the scientific periodical has been a principal medium of communication for over 300 years, it has a number of inherent problems. Some of these are: (1) delays in publication; (2) restrictions by editors on the length of papers due to high costs of publication and demand for journal space; (3) dispersion of articles among a very large number of journals, making scanning difficult and individual subscriptions to numerous titles prohibitive; and (4) referee problems when the appropriate referee for a given article is not available.[11]

There have been numerous proposals to remedy these problems. Journals on microform, publication of separates, synopsis journals, and selective dissemination of information (SDI) are just a few that have been specifically mentioned in the literature.

In addition, access has been an inherent problem. As journals began to proliferate, the need to locate articles in scattered publications led to the development of abstracting and indexing services. There are now over 2,000 such services in the areas of science and technology. A & I services were first published in the mid-1800s. Currency is a problem with these services, but this has been alleviated by machine readable files that can be updated and made available online. Current contents publications have become a popular current awareness tool as have SDI online databases. "The emergence of new specializations and the development of interdisciplinary research resulted in the requirements of scientists and technologists being more selective and these could not be adequately satisfied by services which simply presented their abstracts in a conventionally published arrangement."[12] There is also a problem with overlap (two or more services indexing an article) and underlap (no coverage of some journals by such services).[13] One solution to this problem suggested by Kollin is "gatewaying"—complementary databases would be integrated in a way transparent to the user in order to prevent overlap and duplication.[14]

FUTURE COMMUNICATION

How will the new technologies affect scholarly communication in the future? F. W. Lancaster stated in 1978, "the scientist of the future will use his terminal to receive text, to compose text, to search for text, to seek answers to factual questions, to build information files, and to converse with colleagues."[15] Today, a scientist using a personal computer and modem can work and communicate as Lancaster predicted in 1978. Text creation, processing and publication no longer require paper and ink. Bibliographic, factual and numeric data are accessible through the researcher's own personal computer. Even implantable terminals or "electronic clothing" in which the terminal is embedded in one's clothing are feasible.[16] Online tables of contents, current contents, personalized information services, and full-text databases will facilitate the retrieval of information needed by the researcher.

MEDLARS, a database of the National Library of Medicine, is considered to be the first machine-readable database to be made available; the year was 1965. Since that time, the growth in such databases has been astronomical. There are presently 2,453 databases files available, according to Cuadra Associates' *Directory of Online Databases,* fall 1984. There has been more than a 600 percent increase since fall 1979, when this directory listed 400 such databases. There are now 1189 producers of databases worldwide as compared to 221 in 1979.[17] During the 1960s and early 1970s online database content was made up primarily of bibliographic information. Machine readable data files now include factual or numeric data, such as time series, survey data and data from chemistry and physics handbooks.[18] It is likely that by the year 2000 most handbooks and reference books will be available online or on optical discs.

In many cases, these databases are now being accessed by an intermediary, e.g., a librarian, but in the future it is likely that scientists will perform information retrieval processes themselves. Use of natural language is gradually being incorporated into user interfaces for easy retrieval from machine readable data files. Voice-actuated input or interaction is another option that may be available. The capability to translate search terms from one language to another, a desirable feature, is being tested at the present time.

Imagine "an immense SDI service through which a scientist is automatically notified of any new report, added to any accessible data base, that matches a stored profile of his interests."[19] This personalized information system will allow the scientist to view citations, abstracts, and finally retrieve the full-text of the articles or relevant portions of books.

Personalized information services will be an outgrowth of expert systems. These systems are "computer systems that embody a given body of knowledge in such a way that they imitate the methods used in the human mind, both for representing knowledge and processing it."[20] Expert systems are examples of innovation that results from the development of computer and information technologies. Applications of expert systems are many and varied, including use in diagnostic and preventive medicine, fault diagnosis, science, engineering, geology, etc. Information retrieval that uses expert systems presently being developed set up appropriate database connections and make necessary language translations so that the output from different databases has a uniform appearance to the end-user. In using an expert system, it would not be necessary for the user to know system protocols; natural language could be used; and appropriate databases would be selected by the computer based on information in the user's query or profile. The expert system also could engage in clarification dialogue with the user, if the query is nebulous or incomplete.[21] These systems are still in the developmental stage, but there is no doubt that they will significantly affect scholarly communication, including information retrieval and analysis in the not too distant future.

Another option available to scientists and engineers is the ability to download relevant citations and abstracts into private electronic files for future reference. The complete text of articles may also be downloaded if desirable. This could take the place of reprint files that are so typical among researchers today.

"Imagine another new product... a little flat box with a screen on the front that's as easy to read as a sheet of paper. By touching the box in certain spots, we can display one page of a 10,000 page book. A few deft touches, and we have searched the entire volume in less than a second, and now each hit is instantly retrievable. This box is certainly more costly than a book, but a medical reference manual in such a form would be an extremely valuable tool for doctors... And of course any reference book would become a thousand times more useful... Text Sciences Corporation, is already producing a floppy-disk version of the electronic book, or hand-held database...the 'BookBank(tm).' "[22]

When the text of articles, papers or reports is ready to be written, various word processing and text-editing software packages are available to facilitate writing and editing processes. Files created by these packages can be transmitted to other computers for review, editing and publication.

If feedback from one's colleagues (invisible college) is desirable, preliminary findings or reports can be submitted to them through an electronic mail system, computer bulletin boards or computer conferencing. Responses to the original researcher/author can be transmitted in the same way. BITNET is one such computer network presently available to academicians and researchers throughout the world. Presently, this international network is comprised of 270 computers at over 95 sites, including research centers and institutions of higher education such as Carnegie-Mellon University, Brookhaven National Laboratory, Haifa University, IBM Madrid Scientific Center, and many more. An additional feature of an electronic mail network is a directory that scientists can search online to find researchers and organizations with similar interests.

Often, a professional meeting or conference serves as a forum for the initial promulgation of research results. As the process of scientific communication has grown, the national meeting has developed an increasingly significant function in the overall communication process. Teleconferencing or an electronic meeting may take the place of the traditional in-person conference.

As Lancaster predicted, "it is possible that the need for professional conferences, in their present form, may be greatly reduced . . . because small groups of scientists will be able to arrange their own specialized 'teleconferences' using the facilities provided by the on-line communications networks."[23]

Three major types of teleconferencing are currently in use: (1) simple audioconferencing; (2) enhanced audioconferencing; and (3) videoconferencing. Enhanced audioconferencing includes audiographic teleconferencing, which allows images to be transmitted from one location to another and automatic identification of who is speaking. Two additional kinds of teleconferencing are the computer conference and narrowcast— "the transmission of live television one way from a central site to a number of other sites. It is usually complemented by two-way audio transmission so that the audience may enter into discussion with the speaker."[24]

The results of several studies reported by Martin Elton in his book, *Teleconferencing New Media for Business Meetings,* were that about 40 percent of meetings could be substituted by audioconferencing and 10 percent by videoconferencing, while 50 percent could not be effectively substituted. He also reported that "the audio-only medium is as good as an in-person meeting for cooperative tasks, such as information exchange and problem-solving."[25] Significant considerations in the use of teleconferencing are possibilities for increased communication and savings in travel. Studies have shown that teleconferencing does not necessarily decrease travel to conferences but provides an opportunity for an increased number of participants to attend the meeting or conference. While teleconferencing is one method by which more scholars will communicate in the future, there are situations that will clearly necessitate face to face communication.

Typically, the reading of a paper/report at a conference is followed by formal publication. Computer and telecommunication technologies have made it possible for creation, editing, transmission to publisher, refereeing and production to be carried out more rapidly and efficiently. Communication between authors, editors and referees is transacted electronically and can be carried out interactively. Appropriate referees can be assigned "through some profile matching algorithm which allocates each report to those available referees whose interests and experience coincide most closely with the scope of a particular article."[26] Ultimately, any editorial changes or comments can be transmitted to the author by electronic mail. This process should significantly accelerate the publication process and so prove advantageous to authors, publishers, and readers alike.

Once articles/papers are ready for publication, publishers will have the choice of making their publications available electronically, on paper or possibly in both formats. Various other formats, such as microforms, separates, optical discs, etc., will likewise be available to them.

ROLE OF LIBRARIANS

What will happen to libraries as a result of these new technologies? Donald W. King states, " . . . most major technological advances will come from outside the library and information science field for use by mass markets or high technology communities. But libraries are likely to be a beneficiary of such advances."[27]

The functions and tasks of the librarian or information specialist will change to conform to this new environment. For researchers unwilling or not able to adapt to computers and automation, the librarian will still serve as an intermediary. In most cases, however, the major functions of librarians will be the training of end-users and the synthesizing of information.

Storage of text and document delivery will become more diverse as a result of new technology. High speed, low cost telefacsimile is rapidly becoming a reality. Telefacsimile equipment currently being developed can convert text to digital form, store the text and deliver it to a remote location on demand. As the 1981 ARTEMIS study indicated "electronic delivery of the full text of a document, accomplished at the push of a button, has been an elusive dream of those who deal in information since computers first began to be applied to the publishing and printing process. This report shows that electronic delivery of scientific and technical literature is technically possible today. It tells how one converts a document into a digital form (either text or facsimile) which can be stored in a computer database and transmitted, via telecommunications, to a printer convenient to a user."[28] Facsimile transmission by means of microwave, satellites or cable TV with local printout capabilities are some other options available.

Full-text databases, such as NEXIS and Magazine ASAP already make full-text document retrieval readily available online. "Full-text is here to stay. Its usage will increase as conversion, storage and software technologies are refined and costs drop."[29]

Libraries will also need to evaluate the appropriate means to store the results of the continuing information explosion. There are numerous options, including storing master copies on magnetic tapes or on optical or laser discs, electronic storage in computers and even using traditional books and journals. Micrographics were originally thought to be the solution to the storage problem. In fact, one publisher, Comtex (or Scientific Datalink, Inc.) began to publish original journals in microform only, in 1982; few, if any, publishers have followed suit. Recently, the Society of Manufacturing Engineers offered a journal, *Manufacturing Insights,* on videocassette. With the new technology, a single optical digital disc can contain the text of the entire *Encyclopedia Brittanica.*

McGraw-Hill recently announced that it plans an electronic information bank of its publications for the purpose of personalized electronic delivery to their customers; McGraw-Hill president Joseph Dionne predicts that 50 percent of their revenues could result from this kind of electronic delivery by the year 1990.[30]

Librarians need to be prepared to face many new challenges in the area of information storage and retrieval. With the increase in interdisciplinary research, most scientists need to be aware of research in areas other than their own specialization and outside their immediate research community or invisible college. Libraries will be essential to the interdisciplinary research process. Making research results known to the public by means of formal publication will continue, but publication may not be on paper. "The right to know, the right to access to knowledge, is inherent in our system. It is basic to all scientific inquiry."[31] As F. W. Lancaster said "now is the time for responsible organizations to study the implications of the rapid technological changes that are occurring for the operations of publishers, primary and secondary, for the operations of libraries and information centers, and for the individual scientist as producer and user of information."[32]

CONCLUSION

The scholarly journal has come a long way in its 300-year history. Computer, telecommunications and optical disc technologies have stimulated significant innovation in data retrieval, data and information storage, scholarly communication and scholarly publishing. These innovations are just beginning to be integrated into the day-to-day work of scientists and engineers. Expert systems and personalized information systems are in the earliest stages of development.

Scholarly communication in the future will utilize diverse media and methods. "A thoughtful analysis suggests that most of the new technologies . . . should result in reduced cost, use of less energy-related resources, better information services and higher quality information.[33]

In addition, the new technologies will enable greater and more widespread information distribution than is now available and at lower cost.

REFERENCES

1. Marvin Cetron et al., *Encounters with the Future: A Forecast of Life into the 21st Century* (New York: McGraw Hill, 1982), p.209.

2. Allen T. Cobb, "Hand-Held Information Systems: Present and Future," *Online '84 Conference Proceedings* (Weston: Online, 1984), p.60.

3. Donald W. King et al., *Scientific Journals in the United States: Their Production, Use, and Economics* (Stroudsburg: Hutchinson Ross Publishing Co., 1981), p.7.

4. Bernard Houghton, *Scientific Periodicals: Their Historical Development, Characteristics and Control* (Hamden: Linnet Books, 1975), p.12.

5. Ibid., p.14.

6. Ibid., p.18-19.

7. David C. Taylor, *Managing the Serials Explosion: The Issues for Publishers and Libraries* (White Plains: Knowledge Industry Publications, 1982), p.11.

8. Houghton, *Scientific Periodicals*, p.21.

9. Andrew P. Garvin et al., *How to Win With Information or Lose Without It* (Washington: Bermont Books, 1980), p.60.

10. Houghton, *Scientific Periodicals*, p.32.

11. Ibid., p.42-43.

12. Ibid., p.93.

13. Ibid., p.86.

14. Richard P. Kollin et al., "New Trends in Information Delivery," *Information Services and Use* 4, No. 4 (August 1984), p.227.

15. F. W. Lancaster, *Toward Paperless Information Systems* (New York: Academic Press, 1978), p.106.

16. Craig Fields, "Terminal Access Technology of the 1990's", *IEEE Transactions on Professional Communications* 20, no. 1 (June 1977), p.6.

17. *Directory of Online Databases* 6 (Santa Monica: Cuadra Associates, Fall 1984), p.5.

18. Peter Hernon, "Numeric Databases and Their Relevance to Library Collections and Services: A Summary Analysis," *Numeric Databases* (Norwood: Ablex Publishing Co., 1984), p.297.

19. Lancaster, *Toward Paperless Information Systems*, p.109-110.

20. Ann Clarke et al., "Expert Systems and Library/Information Work," *Journal of Librarianship* 15 (October 1983), p.280.

21. Ibid., p.286-288.

22. Cobb, *Online '84 Conference Proceedings*, p.63-64.

23. Lancaster, *Toward Paperless Information Systems,* p.113.
24. Martin C. J. Elton, *Teleconferencing: New Media for Business Meetings* (New York: American Management Association, 1982), p.9-10.
25. Ibid., p.42.
26. Lancaster, *Toward Paperless Information Systems,* p.108.
27. Donald W. King et al., *Telecommunications and Libraries: A Primer for Librarians and Information Managers* (White Plains: Knowledge Industry Publications, 1981), p.163.
28. Adrian R. D. Norman, *Electronic Document Delivery: The ARTEMIS Concept for Document Digitalisation and Teletransmission* (White Plains: Knowledge Industry Publications, 1982), p.vii.
29. Debbie Hull, "Marketing and Pricing of Full-Text End-User Services," *Information Services and Use* 4, No. 3 (June 1984), p.170.
30. "An Electronic McGraw-Hill," *Newsweek* 104 (December 10, 1984), p.69.
31. Ben Russak, "Publishing Primary Scientific Journals During the Next Decade," *IEEE Transactions on Professional Communication* 20, no. 2 (September 1977), p.53.
32. Lancaster, *Toward Paperless Information Systems,* p.166.
33. King, *Telecommunications and Libraries,* p.163.

Index

AACR. *See Anglo-American Cataloging Rules*
AACR2. *See Anglo-American Cataloging Rules,* 2d ed.
Abridged Index Medicus, 219,220,221
Abstracting and Indexing Coverage Project, 70
abstracting and indexing services, 113. *See also* indexes/indexing
  automated, 161-168,254-255
  coverage, 285,291-292
  currency, 291
academic libraries
  acquisition policy, faculty involvement, 182-184
  administration, 13
  claiming systems, 191-194
  economic factors, 13-14
  online searching, 169-171
  serials department organization, 15-18
accessibility, 149-160,291
  bibliographic, 156-158
  management policies, 149-160
  to patrons, 151,152-156,157-160
  physical, 158-159
acquisitions
  in Australian libraries, 257-258
  automated systems, 99,156
  British Library Lending Division policy, 241-242,244-246
  control, 97,98-99
  department organization, 11
  by exchange, 245-246
  faculty involvement, 182-184
  fund distribution for, 181-184
  in Indian libraries, 264-265
  of monographs, 183
  networking and, 98-99
  in Nigerian libraries, 270-272
Acta Diurna, 290
administration, 7-8. *See also* management; organization; planning
ADONIS Project, 79,251
American Library Association (ALA)
  serials librarianship workshops, 212-213
  Serials Section, 6,7,212,213
    continuing education activities, 213
    union list guidelines, 146,147
American Statistics Index, 222
Anglo-American Cataloging Rules, 106-107
  ISBD discrepancies, 118
  need for revision, 117-119
Anglo-American Cataloging Rules, 2d ed.
  advantages, 122-123
  Australian use, 255-257,258-259
  disadvantages, 123-124
  implementation, 119,120,121-122
  online catalog and, 124
  planning, 119-121
  proposed revision, 125
  serials cataloging rules, 98,107-109, 134-135
  serials definition, 150
Atlantic, 286
Australia, serials librarianship in, 253-261
Australian Bibliographic Network (ABN), 258,259
authority control, 130
authorship, 133,134
automation, 14,65-89,91-95
  acquisitions applications, 99,156
  advantages, 186
  annotated bibliography, 29-63
    bibliographies, 30,35-36
    budgeting, 34,61
    cataloging, 31-32, 36-41
    collections, 31-32,41-45
    organization, 34, 61-63
    reviews, 30-31,36-41
    serials control, 32,45-50
    standards, 33-34,58-60
    subscription agencies, 32-33,51-55
    union lists, 33,55-58
  in Australian libraries, 253-257,258-260
  binding record-keeping applications, 157
  of British Library Lending Division, 247-248
  cataloging applications, 93, 130-131, 156-157
  circulation applications, 100
  claiming system applications, 185-194
  costs, 75

decentralized development, 65
electronic mail, 77-78,294
full text services, 78-81,285,295-296
future effects, 95
indexing applications, 161-165,166-167
in Indian libraries, 266-267
in Nigerian libraries, 274-276
organizational pattern effects, 7,8-9
personalized systems, 293
pre-1976 developments, 66-67
quality control, 93
staffing effects, 8,94
stand-alone systems, 75-77
turnkey systems, 75,259
subscription agencies' use, 32-33,51-55,
   75-76,231,235-238
union list applications, 143-146
user friendly systems, 93,94

back issues. *See also* missing issues
   replacement, 152
   shelving, 155
BALLOTS system, 66
BASIS claiming system, 191
bibliographic description, *See* cataloging
bibliographic networks, 71-72
   definition, 97
   record authentication procedures, 69,71-72
   serials control and, 97-101
Bibliographic Retrieval Service, 68
bibliography, 7
binding procedures, 99-100
   alternatives, 155
   in Australian libraries, 257
   automated records, 157
   British Library Lending Division
      procedures, 249-250
   costs, 152
   microform cataloging and, 137
   policies, 152
BIOSIS, 165
BITNET, 294
Blackwell's, 272
Brandon-Hill List, 221
British Library Lending division, 239-252
   acquisition policy, 241-242,244-246
   automation, 247-248
   deselection policy, 246
   development, 239
   Gift and Exchange Service, 248
   national repository role, 248
   optical disc program, 251
   preservation activities, 249-250
   records, 246-247
   resource-sharing, 242,244
   satellite-transmission project, 251
   selection policy, 244
   serial use surveys, 248-249
   storage procedures, 250

Urgent Action Service, 251
users, 240
volume of operations, 240
British National Book Center, 248
browsing, 203,205
budgeting, 173-179
   in academic libraries, 13-14
   for acquisitions, 181-184
   annotated bibliography, 34,61
   inflationary effects, 174
   information for, 175-179
   in Nigerian libraries, 276-277
   serial price increases and, 230-231
   union lists and, 142

Canada, union lists, 73-74
catalog
   card, closing of, 120,121
   online, 94,124,130-131
cataloging, 97,98. *See also* Anglo-American
      Cataloging Rules; Anglo-American
      Cataloging Rules,* 2d ed.
   annotated bibliography, 31-32,41-45
   in Australian libraries, 256
   authority control, 130
   authorship entry, 133,134
   automated, 93,130-131,156-157
   changes, 103-106
   cooperative, 130
   corporate entry, 107,108-109,123,130,134
   department reorganization, 21
   developments, 133-140
   in Indian libraries, 266
   in integrated serials department, 9-10
   ISBD and, 104-106
   ISDS and, 103-106
   of microforms, 108,136-137,198
   minimal level, 138
   monographic vs. serials, 23,24
   networking and, 98
   retrospective, 130
   separate vs. integrated, 9-10,23
   standardized, 130
   successive entry, 70,138
   title entry, 104
      changes, 104,136
      distinctive, 105
      problems, 135-136
   uniform, 109,135
   union lists and, 143
   workshops, 212
censorship, 286
check-in, 22,23,99
   OCLC capability, 67-71
CHECKMATE system, 77,187,189-190

Chemical Abstracts Service, 162,163,164
circulation
  automated, 100,157
  in Indian libraries, 266
  problems, 152
  storage vs., 203
claiming
  automated systems, 185-194
    techniques, 191-193
  policies, 151-152
classification, 155,158,159
collection development. *See also* acquisitions
  in Australian libraries, 257
  faculty involvement, 182-184
  union lists in, 142
COM. *See* computer output microform
Commonwealth Scientific and Industrial
    Research Organization (CSIRO), 254,
    255,257
computer output microform, 195,196,197
computer terminals, user friendly, 93
CONSER Project, 68-71,109-114
  Abstracting and Indexing Coverage
    Project, 70
  authentication process, 69,72
  data base, 68-71,88n,111,112,113,137-138
  description, 98
  initiation, 66
  objectives, 68
  OCLC and, 69,71,74,111,113
  purpose, 110-111
  serials format revision, 130
  union lists and, 144-145
continuing education, 212-214,221
Conversion of Serials. *See* CONSER Project
Cooperative Library Agency for Systems
    and Services (CLASS), 77,189-190
copyright, 81-83
Copyright Act of 1976, 67,81-82
corporate entry, 107,108-109,123,130,134
culture, 13-14,15,17
Cumulated Index to Nursing Literature,
  217-218

data bases
  copyrighted, 82-83
  number, 292
Department of Health and Human Services,
  publications, 216,218-219,220
Department of Health, Education and
  Welfare, publications, 218,219
deselection, 151,182,246
Dialog, 68,78-79
digital disc, 196

Directory of Online Databases, 292
disc format, 196
DOBIS data base, 73-74
document delivery services, 78-81
  full text, 78-81,285,295-296
  national systems
    United Kingdom, 239-252
    United States, 83-84,85
  regional systems, 84-86

Ebsco
  serials control system, 99,187,189
  serials price increases, 176
EBSCONET, 187,189
education
  continuing, 212-214,221
  for health sciences librarianship, 221
  for serials librarianship, 211-214,278
electronic mail, 77-78,294
Eliot, Charles William, 201-202

facsimile transmission, 80,81,295-296
Faxon
  automated services, 235-237
  bibliographic databases, 6,225,226,227,
    235-237
  international use, 272
  LINX system, 73,76,145,156,187,188-189
  serials acquisition functions, 99
  union list capability, 73,76,100,145,156,
    187,188-189
full text services, 78-81,285,295-296

Geac, 76
Genuine Article, The, 80-81
government documents
  in health sciences libraries, 215-223
  microform, 197

Harper's Monthly, 282,286
Harvard University Library, 201
health sciences libraries, government
    periodicals use, 215-223
health sciences literature, indexes, 215-223
holdings statement, 75

Hospital Literature Index, 215-216,217,
  218,221
H. W. Wilson Company, 163,169

Index Medicus, 215-217,221,222
Index to Government Periodicals, 222
indexes/indexing, 161-168
  coverage, 165-166

formats, 163-165
freelance, 163
to health sciences periodicals, 215-223
location in library, 155
machine-aided, 163
producers, 166
production techniques, 162-163
users, 166-167
India, serials librarianship in, 263-267
Information Access Corporation, 78,79
INNOVACQ, 75-76
INSPEC, 103
interlibrary loan. *See also* resource sharing
British Library Lending Division
system, 240
by online transmission, 77,170
storage vs., 203-204
International Directory of Little Magazines and Small Presses, 284
International Federation of Library Associations and Institutions (IFLA), 146-147
International Nursing Index, 218
International Serials Data System (ISDS), 103-104,257
International Standard Bibliographic Description (ISBD), 104-106,118,130
International Standard Serials Number (ISSN), 66,98,104,138,274
Introduction to Serials Management (Tuttle), 211-212
inventory control, 97,99-100
"invisible college", 294

Journal des Scavans, 290
journals
library, 3
refereed, 284-285,291,295
scholarly, 289-291

LEXIS/NEXIS, 78,79
librarians
generic, 8,21
scientific communication role, 295-296
library journals, 3
Library of Congress
AACR2 use, 123
Name Authority Cooperative Project, 69
Optical Disk Pilot Project, 79-80
subject headings, on COM, 197
Linked Systems Project, 71
LINX system, 73,76,145,156,187,188-189
literature searching

manual, 171
online, 66-67,78-81,169-171
little magazines, 284,286
loan policies, 154

magazine publishing, 281-287
Magazines for Libraries, 284-285,286-287
management, 149-160
case study, 156-159
MARC format
CONSER and, 66,111-112
union lists and, 143-144
MARC serials Editing Guide, 98
McGraw-Hill, 296
Medical Library Association, 216,221
MEDLARS, 292
MEDLINE, 68,216,222
MEDOC, 223n
microcomputers, 68,86,87
Microform, 195-199
advantages, 198-199
bibliographic control, 197,198
cataloging, 108,136-137,198
patron resistance to, 196,197-198
printers, 196,197
serials back runs on, 137
Minnesota Union List of Serials (MULS), 66
missing issues
claiming
automated systems, 185-194
policies, 151-152
in Indian libraries, 265
monographs
acquisition, 183
price increases, 174
Monthly Catalog of U.S. Government Publications, 215,216,218,219-220, 222
Monthly Catalog Series Supplement, 218-221

Name Authority Cooperative Project (NACP), 69
National Information Standards Program, 75
National Lending Library for Science and Technology, 239
National Level Bibliographic Record-Serials, 98
National Library of Canada, DOBIS data base, 73-74
National Library of Medicine, 216,292
National Periodicals Center, 83-85
National Serials Data Program (NSDP), 20,66,104

Index 303

National Union Catalog, 74-75,118
networking. *See* bibliographic networks
New Serial Titles, 74,122
New Yorker, The, 281-282
newspapers, historical development, 290
NEXIS, 78,79,164,296
Nigeria, serials librarianship in, 269-274
Northwestern Online Total Integrated System (NOTIS), 76-77,190
OCLC. *See* Online Computer Library Center, Inc. (OCLC)
Ohio College Library Center. *See* Online Computer Library Center, Inc. (OCLC)
online catalog, 94,124,130-131
Online Computer Library Center, Inc. (OCLC)
  acquisition subsystem, 66,71,99
  check-in capability, 67,71
  CONSER Project and, 69,71,74,111,113
  data base, 72
    copyright, 82-83
  Linked Systems Project, 71
  Local Data Record, 145
  offline products, 145
  security system, 94
  serials subsystem, 66,67,99,187-188
  standardized format, 158
  union list capability, 73
online searching, 169-171
  full text, 78-81
  on mainframe computers, 66-67
  student literature use effects, 169-171
optical disc storage, 79-80,148,296
organization, of serials work, 7-11,19-28
  in academic libraries, 15-18
  automation effects, 34,61-63
  developments, 21-22
  in Nigerian libraries, 272-273
  separate vs. integrated, 6,7,9-11,21-27

patrons
  microform use, 196,197-198
  serials access, 151,152-156,157-160
  stored materials access, 205-206
periodical, definition, 150
Philosophical Transactions, 290
PHILSOM claiming system, 190-191
Phonefiche, 195
photocopying, 67,80,152,155,273
planning, 173-179
Playboy, 281,282
preservation, 249-250

printers, microform, 196,197

quality control, of automated systems, 93

Reader's Guide to Periodical Literature, 169
records
  British Library Lending Division system, 246-247
  Indian libraries' system, 266
  manual systems, 91,93
  quality, 93
  updating, 152
  variability, 153
refereed journals, 284-285,291,295
Register of Additional Locations, 75
Research Libraries Group (RLG), 66
Research Libraries Information Network (RLIN), 66,70,71
resource sharing
  in India, 265-266
  in Nigeria, 274-275
  in United Kingdom, 242,244
routing procedures, 99-100
RTSD Newsletter, 213

satellite-transmitted documents, 251
SC 350 serials control system, 99
scholarly journals, 289-291
  categories, 291
  history, 290-291
  refereed, 284-285,291,295
scientific communication, 289-298
  current status, 291-292
  future developments, 292-295
  historical development, 290-291
  librarians' role, 295-297
Scientific Serials in Australian Libraries (SSAL), 255-256
selection
  in academic libraries, 151
  British Library Lending Division policy, 244
  in Indian libraries, 263-264
selective dissemination of information (SDI), 254-255,291
"serialism", 16-17
serials
  accessibility, 149-160
    bibliographic, 156-158
    management policies, 149-160
    to patrons, 151,152-156,157-160
    physical, 158
  cancellations, 142,175

cessations, 226,227
characteristics, 15
control. *See also* management; organization; planning
   acquisitions, 97,98-99
   annotated bibliography, 32,45-50
   bibliographic description, 97,98
   inventory, 97,99-100
   modes, 97-100
   networking and, 97-101
definition, 97,150,241
foreign, 174,175
increased number, 6,174,225-226
indexing, 161-168
missing issues, 151-152,185-194,265
mutilation, 152
price increases, 7,174,176-177,226-231, 232-235
   budget effects, 230-231
   Consumer Price Index and, 228,229,230
   foreign exchange rates and, 23,232,233
   in India, 265-266
   journal specialization and, 226
   in Nigeria, 271
   publishers' role, 225-230
   subscription agencies' role, 23,235
specialization, 225-226
use
   per article, 15
   storage and, 204-205
   survey, 248-249
Serials in Australian Libraries Social Sciences and Humanities (SALSSAH), 255,256,258
serials librarianship
   in Australia, 253-261
   education for, 211-214,221,278
   in India, 263-267
   library administration and, 7-8
   in Nigeria, 269-279
series, definition, 150
shelving, 152,155,158-159,273
Southeastern ARL Libraries Cooperative Project, 85-86
stack management, 152
staff
   attitudes towards department mergers, 22
   automation effects, 8,94
   decreasing size of, 14
   non-professional, 14,17
   responsibilities, 8,9,154-155
   users services reassignment, 8
stand-alone systems, 75-77

Standard Periodical Directory, 284
standards, annotated bibliography of, 33-34, 58-60
standing orders, 177,178
Stechert MacMillan, 230
storage, 201-210
   British Library Lending Division procedures, 250
   case study, 201-209
   circulation costs vs., 203
   compact, 202,203
   definition, 202
   disc format, 196
   facilities, 201-203
   future developments, 296
   guidelines, 204-205
   in Indian libraries, 266
   interlibrary loan vs., 203-204
   patron access and, 205-206
   remote, 202,203,204,206-209
   retrieval costs, 204
   weeding vs., 202,203,204,207
subscription agencies, 225-238
   automated systems, 75-76,231,235-238
   annotated bibliography, 32-33,51-55
   binding services, 99-100
   in budget planning, 175-177
   increased charges, 174
   in India, 264-265
   in Nigeria, 272
   serials' acquisition function, 99
   union lists and, 73
   in United Kingdom, 244
successive entry, 70,138
Swets and Zeitlinger, 272
System Development Corporation, 68

technical services
   abolition of, 20-21
   budgetary problems, 231
   decentralization, 6,7,9-11,21-27
   origin, 5
   specialization, 24,25
teleconferencing, 294-295
televised magazines, 286
title entry
   changes, 104,136
   distinctive, 105
   problems, 135-136
   uniform, 109,135

Ulrich's International Periodical Directory, 284

uniform titles, 109,135
Union List of Serials, 21,74
union list(s), 141-148
　activities, 146-148
　annotated bibliography, 33,55-58
　Australian, 255-256,258-259
　automated, 143-146
　bibliographic record availability, 72
　budgetary factors, 142
　Canadian, 73-74
　as collection development tool, 142
　CONSER Project and, 144-145
　development, 100
　directory, 146
　guidelines, 146-147
　Indian, 266
　manually compiled, 66
　MARC format, 143-144
　Nigerian, 275-276
　OCLC capability, 73
　revision, 143-144
　standardization, 142-144
　subscription agencies' capability, 73
unique serial identifier. *See* uniform title
UNISIST, 103
United Kingdom
　British Library Lending Division, 239-252
　journal prices, 23-233
United States Newspaper Project, 113
United States Postal Services identification code, 98,104,138
University of Toronto Library Automation System (UTLAS), 66,71
user friendly systems, 93,94
users services, technical staff reassignment to, 8

vendors. *See* subscription agencies
video disc storage, 79-80,196,296

Washington Library Network (WLN), 66, 71-72
weeding, 151
　storage vs., 202,203,204,207
Wilsonline, 169
workshops, 212-213

For Product Safety Concerns and Information please contact our EU
representative GPSR@taylorandfrancis.com
Taylor & Francis Verlag GmbH, Kaufingerstraße 24, 80331 München, Germany

www.ingramcontent.com/pod-product-compliance
Lightning Source LLC
Chambersburg PA
CBHW071803300426
44116CB00009B/1190